RENAISSANCE PARATEXTS

In his 1987 work *Paratexts*, the theorist Gérard Genette established physical form as crucial to the production of meaning. Here, experts in early modern book history, materiality, and rhetorical culture present a series of compelling explorations of the architecture of early modern books. The essays challenge and extend Genette's taxonomy, exploring the paratext as both a material and a conceptual category. *Renaissance Paratexts* takes a fresh look at neglected sites, from imprints to endings, and from running titles to printers' flowers. Contributors' accounts of the making and circulation of books open up questions of the marking of gender, the politics of translation, geographies of the text, and the interplay between reading and seeing. As much a history of misreading as of interpretation, the collection provides novel perspectives on the technologies of reading, and exposes the complexity of the playful, proliferating, and self-aware paratexts of English Renaissance books.

HELEN SMITH is Lecturer in Renaissance / Early Modern Literature at the University of York. She has published widely on early modern textual culture and is currently completing a monograph, *Grossly Material Things: Women and Textual Production in Early Modern England*. She is Co-Investigator on the AHRC-funded project, 'Conversion Narratives in Early Modern Europe'.

LOUISE WILSON is a Research Fellow at the University of St Andrews, where she works on the MHRA Tudor and Stuart Translations series. She was previously a post-doctoral researcher at the University of Geneva, working on Lukas Erne's forthcoming *Shakespeare and the Book Trade*. Louise has published on the paratexts and readerships of romance, and is currently completing a monograph entitled *Humanism and Chivalric Romance in Tudor England*.

RENAISSANCE PARATEXTS

EDITED BY
HELEN SMITH
AND
LOUISE WILSON

CAMBRIDGE UNIVERSITY PRESS
Cambridge, New York, Melbourne, Madrid, Cape Town,
Singapore, São Paulo, Delhi, Tokyo, Mexico City

Cambridge University Press
The Edinburgh Building, Cambridge CB2 8RU, UK

Published in the United States of America by Cambridge University Press, New York

www.cambridge.org
Information on this title: www.cambridge.org/9780521117395

© Cambridge University Press 2011

This publication is in copyright. Subject to statutory exception
and to the provisions of relevant collective licensing agreements,
no reproduction of any part may take place without the written
permission of Cambridge University Press.

First published 2011

Printed in the United Kingdom at the University Press, Cambridge

A catalogue record for this publication is available from the British Library

Library of Congress Cataloguing in Publication data
Renaissance paratexts / edited by Helen Smith, Louise Wilson.
p. cm.
Includes bibliographical references and index.
ISBN 978-0-521-11739-5 (hardback)
1. European literature – Renaissance, 1450–1600 – History and criticism.   2. Paratext.
I. Smith, Helen, 1977–   II. Wilson, Louise.
PN721.R448   2011
002.09′024–dc22
2011000383

ISBN 978-0-521-11739-5 Hardback

Cambridge University Press has no responsibility for the persistence or
accuracy of URLs for external or third-party internet websites referred to
in this publication, and does not guarantee that any content on such
websites is, or will remain, accurate or appropriate.

Contents

List of figures   *page* vii
Notes on contributors   xi
Acknowledgements   xiv

    Introduction
    Helen Smith and Louise Wilson   1

PART I   ORDERS OF THE BOOK   15

1   'Imprinted by Simeon such a signe': reading early modern imprints
    Helen Smith   17

2   'Intended to Offenders': the running titles of early modern books
    Matthew Day   34

3   Changed opinion as to flowers
    Juliet Fleming   48

4   The beginning of 'The End': terminal paratext and the birth of print culture
    William H. Sherman   65

PART II   MAKING READERS   89

5   Editorial pledges in early modern dramatic paratexts
    Sonia Massai   91

6	Status anxiety and English Renaissance translation *Neil Rhodes*	107
7	Playful paratexts: the front matter of Anthony Munday's Iberian romance translations *Louise Wilson*	121
8	'Signifying, but not sounding': gender and paratext in the complaint genre *Danielle Clarke*	133

PART III BOOKS AND USERS 151

9	Unannotating Spenser *Jason Scott-Warren*	153
10	Reading the home: the case of *The English Housewife* *Wendy Wall*	165
11	Pictures, places, and spaces: Sidney, Wroth, Wilton House, and the *Songe de Poliphile* *Hester Lees-Jeffries*	185
	Afterword *Peter Stallybrass*	204

Notes 220
Select bibliography 264
Index 268

Figures

1.1 Title-page to *Taylors Revenge* (London: Edward Allde, 1615). By permission of the Guildhall Library, City of London. *page* 19
1.2 Title-page to William Hawkins, *Corolla varia contexta* (Cambridge: Thomas Buck, 1634). By permission of the British Library, London. 26
1.3 Title-page to Anon., *The Owles almanacke* (London: Edward Griffin, 1618). By permission of the British Library, London. 30
3.1 John Conway, *The poesie of floured prayers* (London: T. Purfoot for Valentine Simmes, 1611), A6r. By permission of the British Library, London. 51
3.2 Richard Barnfield, *Greenes funeralls* (London: John Danter, 1594), B1v–B2r. By permission of the British Library, London. 54
3.3 Final opening of Edmund Spenser, *Amoretti and Epithalamion* (London: Peter Short for William Ponsonby, 1595). Reproduced by permission of The Huntington Library, San Marino, California. 57
3.4 The Countess of Pembroke's translation of Garnier's *Tragedie of Antonie* (London: Peter Short, 1595), B6v–B7r. Reproduced by permission of The Huntington Library, San Marino, California. 61
4.1 Final page of Geoffrey Chaucer, *The boke of Canterbury tales* (London: Richard Pynson, 1526). By permission of the British Library, London. 70
4.2 Final page of *The cronycles of Englonde* (London: Wynkyn de Worde, 1520). Reproduction from the original held by the Department of Special Collections of the University Libraries of Notre Dame. 72

4.3 Final page of William Langland, *The vision of Piers Plowman* (London: Robert Crowley, 1550). Reproduced by permission of The Huntington Library, San Marino, California. 74

4.4 James VI of Scotland, *The essayes of a prentise, in the divine art of poesie* (Edinburgh: Thomas Vautrollier, 1584), P4r. Reproduced by permission of The Huntington Library, San Marino, California. 77

4.5 Final page of Geoffrey Chaucer, *The book of fame* (Westminster: William Caxton, 1483). By permission of the British Library, London. 80

4.6 Final page of Geoffrey Chaucer, *The workes of Geffray Chaucer* (London, 1550). Reproduced by permission of The Huntington Library, San Marino, California. 82

4.7 Final page of John Taylor, *Great Britaine, all in blacke* (London: Edward Allde for John Wright, 1612). Reproduced by permission of The Huntington Library, San Marino, California. 83

4.8 Final page of John Taylor, *Taylors motto* (London: Edward Allde for John Trundle and Henry Gosson, 1621). Reproduced by permission of The Huntington Library, San Marino, California. 84

4.9 Sir John Davies, *Nosce teipsum* (London: Augustine Mathewes for Richard Hawkins, 1622), L3r. 86

8.1a Title-page to Michael Drayton, *Endimion and Phoebe* (London: James Roberts for John Busbie, 1595). By permission of the British Library, London. 137

8.1b Title-page to Thomas Lodge, *Phillis* (London: James Roberts for John Busbie, 1593). By permission of the British Library, London. 138

8.2 Edmund Spenser, *Colin Clouts come home againe* (London: Thomas Creede for William Ponsonbie, 1595), F4v–G1r. By permission of the British Library, London. 140

8.3 Samuel Daniel, *Delia. Contayning certayne sonnets: vvith the complaint of Rosamond* (London: John Charlewood for Simon Waterson, 1592), H2v–H3r. Reproduced by permission of the Huntington Library, San Marino, California. 141

8.4 Edmund Spenser, *Colin Clouts come home againe* (London: Humphrey Lownes for Mathew Lownes, 1611), B2v.

Reproduced by permission of the Huntington Library, San Marino, California. 144

9.1 Trinity College, Cambridge, shelfmark VI 2 63, f. Q3r. Reproduced by permission of the Master and Fellows of Trinity College Cambridge. 161

9.2 Cambridge University Library, SSS 22 27, f. 2C4r. Reproduced by permission of Cambridge University Library. 162

10.1 Title-page to Gervase Markham, *The English Hus-wife* (London: John Beale for Roger Jackson, 1615). Reproduced by permission of the Huntington Library, San Marino, California. 166

10.2 Frontispiece to John Partridge, *The treasurie of commodious conceits* (London: Richard Jones, 1573). Reproduced by permission of the Huntington Library, San Marino, California. 169

10.3 Gervase Markham, *Country contentments, in two books* (London: John Beale for R. Jackson, 1615), Q2r, Q3r. Reproduced by permission of the Huntington Library, San Marino, California. 174

10.4 Gervase Markham, *Countrey contentments, or The English husvvife* (London: John Beale for R. Jackson, 1623), A3r–A4r. Reproduced by permission of the Huntington Library, San Marino, California. 176

11.1 The statue of Venus and Cupid on the Fountain of Adonis. *Songe de Poliphile* (1561), f. 131. By permission of Cambridge University Library. 190

11.2 The Fountain of Adonis. *Songe de Poliphile* (1561), f. 130. By permission of Cambridge University Library. 192

11.3 The 'theatre' of the Fountain of Venus. *Songe de Poliphile* (1561), f. 123. By permission of Cambridge University Library. 194

11.4 Poliphilus and Polia bound with chains of roses and led in the Triumph of Cupid. *Songe de Poliphile* (1561), f. 121v. By permission of Cambridge University Library. 195

11.5 Polia's vision of Venus and Diana. *Songe de Poliphile* (1561), f. 146v. By permission of Cambridge University Library. 196
11.6 The 'Trinitarian' arbour. *Songe de Poliphile* (1561), f. 44. By permission of Cambridge University Library. 199
11.7 The 'water labyrinth'. *Songe de Poliphile* (1561), f. 43. By permission of Cambridge University Library. 200

Contributors

DANIELLE CLARKE is Professor of English Literature at University College Dublin. She has published widely on early modern women, gender and sexuality, and the politics of editing. Her books include *'This Double Voice': Gendered Writing in Early Modern England*, co-edited with Elizabeth Clarke (2000), and *The Politics of Early Modern Women's Writing, 1558–1640* (2001). Clarke is currently at work on a book-length project examining the evolving relationships of language, gender, and power in the early modern period.

MATTHEW DAY is Head of English and Creative Writing at Newman University College, Birmingham. His main research interests are the literature of travel, and print culture in the early modern period, and he has published a series of articles and chapters on these topics. Day is co-editor of the Print Networks series.

JULIET FLEMING is Associate Professor of English at New York University. Her research interests include Renaissance literature, material texts and literary theory. Her book on *Graffiti and the Writing Arts in the Early Modern Period*, which won the Choice Outstanding Academic Title Award, was published in 2001.

HESTER LEES-JEFFRIES is Fellow of St Catharine's College, Cambridge. She has published a number of articles on space and landscape in early modern literature, and her monograph *England's Helicon: Fountains in Early Modern Literature and Culture* was published in 2007.

SONIA MASSAI is Reader in Shakespeare Studies at King's College London. She has published numerous articles on Shakespeare and Shakespearean appropriations, early modern and Restoration drama, editing and textual studies. She has edited *World Wide Shakespeares: Local Appropriations in Film and Performance* (2006) and *William Shakespeare's Twelfth Night: A Sourcebook* (2007). Her monograph *Shakespeare and the Rise of the Editor* was published in 2007.

NEIL RHODES is Professor of English Literature and Cultural History at the University of St Andrews. His publications include *Shakespeare and Elizabethan Popular Culture* (edited with Stuart Gillespie, 2006), *Shakespeare and the Origins of English* (2004) and *The Renaissance Computer: Knowledge Technology in the First Age of Print* (edited with Jonathan Sawday, 2000). He is co-General Editor, with Andrew Hadfield, of the MHRA Tudor and Stuart Translations series, for which he is currently preparing a companion volume, *English Renaissance Translation Theory*.

JASON SCOTT-WARREN is Senior Lecturer in the Faculty of English at Cambridge University, and Fellow of Gonville and Caius College. He has published widely on cultural history and material textuality in early modern England, and is author of *Sir John Harington and the Book as Gift* (2001) and *Early Modern English Literature* (2005).

WILLIAM H. SHERMAN is Professor of Renaissance / Early Modern Studies at the University of York. He is the author of *John Dee: The Politics of Reading and Writing in the English Renaissance* (1995); of *Used Books: Marking Readers in Renaissance England* (2007); and of articles on Renaissance drama, travel writing, and the history of the book. He is currently working on a book-length project on Renaissance libraries.

HELEN SMITH is Lecturer in Renaissance / Early Modern Literature at the University of York. She has published widely on early modern textual culture and is currently completing a monograph, *Grossly Material Things: Women and Textual Production in Early Modern England*. Helen is Co-Investigator on the AHRC-funded project, 'Conversion Narratives in Early Modern Europe'.

PETER STALLYBRASS is Walter H. and Leonore C. Annenberg Professor in the Humanities and Professor of English and Comparative Literature and Literary Theory at the University of Pennsylvania. His numerous publications include *Subject and Object in Renaissance Culture* (edited with Margreta de Grazia and Maureen Quilligan, 1996) and *Renaissance Clothing and the Materials of Memory* (with Ann Rosalind Jones, 2001).

WENDY WALL is Professor of English Literature at Northwestern University. A specialist in Renaissance literature and culture, she is author of *The Imprint of Gender: Authorship and Publication in the English Renaissance* (1993) and *Staging Domesticity: Household Work and English Identity in Early Modern Drama* (2002), which was a finalist for the James Russell Lowell prize awarded by the MLA and a 2002 Choice Outstanding Academic Title Award Winner. Professor Wall has published on topics as wide-ranging as editorial theory, gender, national identity, the history of authorship, Renaissance husbandry, food studies, domesticity, theatrical practice, and Jell-O. She is currently at work on a book tentatively entitled *Strange Kitchens: Knowledge and Taste in English Recipe Books, 1550–1750*.

LOUISE WILSON is a Research Fellow at the University of St Andrews, where she works on the MHRA Tudor and Stuart Translations series. She was previously a post-doctoral researcher at the University of Geneva, working on Lukas Erne's forthcoming *Shakespeare and the Book Trade*. Louise has published on the paratexts and readerships of romance, and is currently completing a monograph provisionally entitled *Humanism and Chivalric Romance in Tudor England*.

Acknowledgements

Above all, the editors would like to thank our contributors. It has been both a pleasure and an inspiration to work with them. Many of the authors delivered earlier versions of their chapters at the Renaissance Paratexts conference held at the University of York in July 2006. We would like to thank the Modern Humanities Research Association for their generous sponsorship of that event, and Henry Woudhuysen for helping us to secure the necessary funding. The participation of a number of additional speakers, chairs, and attendees helped to shape both the volume as a whole and many of its component parts. Particular thanks are due to Christy Anderson, Guyda Armstrong, Tom Berger, Pete Langman, Peter Lindenbaum, Mike Jones, Laurie Maguire, Marcus Nevitt, Mary Partridge, Helen Pierce, Fred Schurink, Cathy Shrank, Emma Smith, and Randy McLeod, who has also shared with us much of his ongoing work on early modern paratexts.

Our colleagues at both York and Geneva have been a constant source of support, information, and knowledge, and we would especially like to thank Lukas Erne, Mark Jenner, Richard Rowland, and Bill Sherman for their wit and wisdom throughout the past several years. At Cambridge University Press, Sarah Stanton and Becky Taylor have been unstinting in their patient and generous guidance. We would also like to thank the anonymous readers whose comments were invaluable in shaping the collection. In a book so concerned with questions of presentation and material meaning it seems appropriate too to reveal the temporal disruptions of the paratext, and to thank the typesetters, designers, and production staff who will/have made this book what it is.

Introduction

Helen Smith and Louise Wilson

This introduction is a paratext. It is not the first paratext you have encountered in your approach to this book. You will have noticed its title, and registered its scholarly cover, either on the bookshelf or in a digital reproduction by an internet seller like Amazon or Abebooks. You may have found this volume through a series of epitexts: a review, a publisher's flyer, or a search of a library catalogue or online database. Perhaps you followed a footnote in someone else's work or a reference in a bibliography, or one of the contributors was shameless in promoting his or her chapter to you over coffee at a conference. A passage or pithy sentence may have been quoted in another text, persuading you this volume might be worth consulting. Some readers may never even reach this point, merely checking the copyright information on the flyleaf to create a catalogue entry or fill out a meretricious bibliographical note.

Even now that you hold the book in your hands (or are scrolling through it on a computer screen), it is unlikely that you came straight to page one, particularly given the number of pages that come before it. You may have checked the table of contents, or leafed through the index, to find out which chapters are relevant to your work. It is possible that you went straight to the list of contributors to find out who the authors are, and what pretensions they hold to expertise in their field. Or perhaps you read the acknowledgements to see what networks the editors are part of, and what academic circles we are trying to move into through flattery and thanks. Even the physical body of the book is paratextual, shaping your reading. Did you open this volume at a random page to check the font size and shape, the cleanness of the typeface, the size of the margins and the quality of the pages: how pleasurable this book would be as a thing to read? Or did you perhaps consult a few leaves out of sequence, seeing what grabbed your attention, and where your fancy led? Maybe one of the images we have included caught your eye and drew you in.

However you have responded to the paratexts of this book, you are one of a long line of readers, all of whom have paid attention, wittingly or unwittingly, to the physical presentation of the text, and to the various additional or supplementary texts, information, and addresses which surround it. Perhaps the best-known reader of these apparently marginal spaces is Gérard Genette, the scholar whose work brought the term 'paratexts' into critical use. Genette's influential 1987 book *Seuils* was translated into English in 1997 under the title *Paratexts: Thresholds of Interpretation*.[1] The book proclaims itself to be an 'inventory' (3) of the 'verbal or other productions' (1) that affect a reader's approach to the text, and it examines and tabulates an array of liminal forms. In his analysis, Genette distinguishes between features like titles, dedications, and footnotes which are situated within the same volume as the text, which he calls peritexts, and epitexts: 'those messages that, at least originally, are located outside the book' (5) and include author interviews, letters, and diaries. Where previous generations of scholars have seen paratexts as primarily informational, providing concrete detail about the text and its origins, Genette argues that they should be read as transactional. He describes the paratext as 'a privileged place of pragmatics and a strategy of an influence on the public, an influence that – whether well or poorly understood and achieved – is at the service of a better reception of the text and a more pertinent reading' (2). The purpose of the paratext is, according to Genette, to guide the reader into the riches of the book, and to structure his or her approach to what s/he is about to read.

The present volume is at once a response to, and an extension of, Genette's wide-ranging taxonomy. It has become a critical commonplace to suggest that Genette's survey of paratextual possibilities is insufficiently attentive to historical difference and change. Genette raises this objection himself, explaining 'that it is appropriate to define objects before one studies their evolution' (13). The synchronic approach of *Paratexts* is in part a result of Genette's structuralist background; *Paratexts* is the final volume of Genette's trilogy on transtextual poetics, coming after *The Architext* (1979) and *Palimpsests* (1982). It is thus a late stage in Genette's project to generate a 'general poetics of transtextuality' which accounts for intertextuality in a transcendent way, incorporating all relations within and between texts and between texts and their readers.[2] This emphasis on poetics exposes Genette's focus on the linguistic elements of the book, an attention that Jerome McGann argues is too limited, since, he points out, 'texts ... are embodied phenomena, and the body of the text is not exclusively linguistic'.[3] A number of the chapters in this volume engage with early modern books as objects which are visible as well as legible. All are aware of the book as an object which is handled by particular readers, and whose physicality is constructed through the processes and operations of the printing house.

Renaissance Paratexts reveals the importance of investigating the particular paratextual conventions in play in different historical periods. As Genette makes clear, some paratexts 'are as old as literature; others came into being – or acquired their official status, after centuries of "secret life" that constitute their prehistory – with the invention of the book; others, with the birth of journalism and the modern media' (14). A number of the paratexts we listed at the beginning of this introduction are strikingly modern, particularly those made possible by computer technologies. Others, including the author interview and the review, developed alongside the periodical industry from the eighteenth century onwards.[4] A few are much older than the printed codex. Most, however, came into being in the period with which this volume is concerned, following the invention of printing in around 1436, and the corresponding development of the book into the forms which are familiar to us today.

The early modern book differed from modern volumes in a number of important ways, not least in its construction. Working from manuscript copy, a compositor would pick letters from the upper and lower cases before him, and arrange them in a composing stick, from which they were transferred to a wooden forme. Another worker used leather-covered balls to coat the finished forme with ink. It was then placed in the bed of the press, and the paper was pulled on to it to create an impression. The completed sheets were dried in the printer's warehouse, and stacked. They were then folded: once to make a large-format folio, twice to make a smaller quarto, and three times to produce an octavo. Some books were even smaller: in 1614 John Taylor, the 'Water Poet', issued the first edition of his one-and-a-quarter by one-and-an-eighth inch 64mo thumb bible.[5]

Some paratexts, like printers' flowers (small type ornaments) and running titles, were an essential part of the printing process, locked into a skeleton forme to frame the text they accompanied. Composing sticks had moveable 'cheeks' which could be adjusted to create space for printed marginal annotations. Others, including dedications, addresses to the reader, indices, and errata notices, were generally printed separately and added to the work at the end. This physical and temporal separation allows many early modern paratexts to be highly self-reflexive, commenting on the quality of printing contained in the book they accompany, or on the processes and accidents of production. George Chapman, for example, closed an elegant address 'To the vnderstander' (or, according to its running title, 'the reader') by boasting of his pride in the quality of his translation of Homer, and disarming potential criticism by shifting the blame for any flaws on to the printer, confessing, 'Onely the extreame false printing troubles my conscience, for feare of your deserued discouragement in the empaire of our Poets sweetnes'.[6]

Printers sometimes employed their own binders, while on other occasions books were sold unbound, and the purchaser took the loose sheets to a binder. The binder relied heavily on paratexts, particularly the signatures and catchwords that appear at the foot of early modern pages, to guide him or her in constructing the book. Thus early modern paratexts had a variety of functions, and prompted very different readings, some literary or hermeneutic, some practical and physical. Book purchasers could choose to have their books bound individually or to have a number of texts collected into one volume, along topical, generic, or material lines, meaning that each text became a new peritext to its companions. Many early modern paratextual authors seem to have been alert to the fact that it is a volume's margins and framing devices which, as Genette asserts, both make it a book, rather than a text or fragment, and allow it to present or announce itself as such (1). As the Puritan divine and botanist William Turner admitted as he prepared his 1568 *Herbal* for the press:

The Printer had geuen me warning / there wanted nothing to the setting oute of my hole Herbal / saving only a Preface / wherein I might require some both mighty and learned Patron to defend my laboures against spitefull & enuious enemies to al mennis doynges sauing their owne / and declare my good minde to him that I am most bound unto by dedicating and geuing these my poore laboures unto him.[7]

The dedication which follows, in which Dr Turner expends many words in praise of the 'great man' Queen Elizabeth's linguistic ability and 'Princelye liberalitie', risks being undermined at its very beginning by the author's admission that it is a last-minute addition, included at the insistence of his printer.

The proliferation and movement of paratextual features during the early modern period established many of the conventions of the physical book that we still experience today. The range of features which did not survive (including the printer's or author's address to the reader), or which appeared in a multiplicity of forms, however, also suggests, as Jason Scott-Warren argues in this volume, that the journey of the book towards its current conventional presentation was not an inevitable progress, teleologically driven to create an ever more streamlined reading experience. The books of the early modern period offer the reader a range of paratexts, many not listed by Genette, which make it clear that the history of the paratext is as

Introduction

much one of obstacles and communicative failures as it is one of clarity and reader-management. In *Reading Material in Early Modern England*, Heidi Brayman Hackel reproduces a moment from a dialogue between two model students who occupy the pages of Edmund Coote's *The English schoolemaister* (1596). One declares: 'by your leaue we shall first reade ouer againe all that we haue learned, with the preface, titles of the chapters, and notes in the margent of our bookes, which we omitted before, because they were too hard'.[8] For Hackel, this is evidence that readers did pay attention to the paratextual furniture of the book; it also suggests that paratextual reading could be seen as a more difficult, and more advanced, skill than the ability to read the text itself.

It is not only its primary resources that make the early modern period particularly relevant to a study of paratexts. In recent years, Renaissance scholars have increasingly turned their attention to the material make-up of the text, driven, to varying degrees, by a re-engagement with questions of editorial practice; by the bibliographical demands of the burgeoning field of book history; and by a more general attention to material culture and 'thing theory'.[9] Following in the footsteps of Jerome McGann, who insists on the need to interpret bibliographic as well as linguistic codes, researchers have shown themselves to be increasingly sensitive to the physicality of the printed word and its manuscript counterpart, and to the structures and meanings conveyed by the book as object, rather than the book as text. Notably, Seth Lerer has examined the hermeneutic practices encouraged by the inclusion of errata lists in early modern printed books; William Slights and Evelyn Tribble have surveyed printed marginalia; Thomas Corns and Peter Stallybrass have interrogated technologies of marking place; Ann Blair has focused on the politics of the index; and Anthony Grafton has offered a magisterial history of the footnote.[10]

In *The Commodification of Textual Engagements in the English Renaissance*, Michael Saenger argues that we should read front matter as inherently commercial in its engagements, while Hackel suggests that prefatory letters should be read as texts which 'define and shape' the reading experience.[11] Perhaps the most sustained engagement with 'the envelope or packaging' of a particular early modern text has emerged from the recent project, led by Terence Cave, to chart 'the paratexts, those ephemeral materials that carry [More's] *Utopia* over the threshold into new cultural contexts and which therefore provide a rich repertory of signs indicating what was at stake in that act of *translatio*'.[12] The *Utopia* project, which catalogues and describes the various paratexts of More's book as it moved across early modern Europe and between languages, allows us to grasp the extent to which paratextual materials work both outwards, altering the contexts and possibilities of the book's reception, and inwards, transforming not only the appearance but the priorities and tone of the text.

Genette and his successors have, as William Sherman points out in this volume, tended to focus their attention on those peritexts that open the book, collapsing the paratextual into the prefatory. Genette's account, though it does include some median details, including running heads and footnotes, overwhelmingly privileges front matter over the other spaces and surrounds of the printed book. This concentration is perhaps a result of his insistence that the paratext is above all functional, designed to 'ensure for the text a destiny consistent with the author's purpose' (407). We discuss the question of authorial intention below, but it seems clear that it is easier to extract an author's apparent design from the explicit instructions of the preface or dedication, or even from the title or epigraph, than from, for example, a terse envoi.

One result of Genette's emphasis on the paratext's preparatory function, however, is that the liminal space which should be a two-way zone of passage takes on a one-way function, becoming 'an instrument of adaptation' that 'helps the reader pass without too much respiratory difficulty from one world to the other' (408). This reading is reinforced by Genette's endlessly inventive metaphors for a book's paratext, which is variously described as an airlock, a canal lock (408), or, most famously, a threshold (2), all spaces which can be traversed in two directions, but which, in Genette's formulations, are seen to have a purely acclimatising, one-way function. In contrast, Genette's alternative metaphor of the paratext as a 'fringe' (2) better suggests its presence at each moment of reading: like the fringe of a rug, paratexts are the visible ends of constitutive structures that run throughout the length of the work, but that can also be perceived as distinct elements.[13] As several of the chapters in the present volume show, paratextual elements are in operation all the way through the reader's experience of the text, not merely at the start, and they continuously inform the process of reading, offering multiple points of entry, interpretation, and contestation.

If Genette's threshold is 'a "vestibule" that offers the world at large the possibility of either stepping inside or turning back' (2), the Renaissance paratext is an ever-expanding labyrinth, as likely to lead to a frustrating dead-end as to a carefully built pathway, or to deposit the reader back outside the building rather than guide him or her into the text. Even properly liminal paratexts, including indices and addresses to the reader, operate in multiple directions, structuring the reader's approach not only to the text in question but to the experience of reading, and of interpreting the world beyond the book. In its situation as a space which both frames and inhabits the text, the paratext occupies the position of Derrida's *parergon*: 'neither work (*ergon*) nor outside the work [*hors d'œuvre*], neither inside nor outside, neither above nor below, it disconcerts any opposition but does not remain indeterminate and it *gives rise* to the work. It is no longer merely around the work.'[14]

In a variety of ways, the chapters which follow reach out to the world beyond the book, in line with Genette's inclusive assertion that 'in principle, every context [including historical period] serves as a paratext' (8). Neil Rhodes and Hester Lees-Jeffries investigate the ways in which spatial, geographic, patronage and kinship connections function as a series of interconnecting interpretative sites. In a rather different move, Wendy Wall and Jason Scott-Warren examine the ways in which paratexts structured the mental worlds of their readers, creating particular ways of responding not only to other printed books but to the contexts and social structures within which they were read. Paratexts do, as Genette suggests, shape our approach to the books we are reading. They also work upon our imagination, structuring our ways of thinking about the world.

Writing three years apart, both John Earle and Francis Lenton drew on paratextual metaphors to describe shopkeepers. Earle explained: 'His Shop is his well-stuft Booke, and himselfe the Title-page of it, or Index. Hee vtters much to all men, though he sels but to a few, and intreats for his owne necessities by asking others what they lacke.'[15] Two modes of accessing the contents of a book – the index and the title-page – are here presented as fundamentally interchangeable, serving both to catalogue and advertise the contents of the volume they accompany. Lenton (who may well have been influenced by Earle's earlier publication) engaged in similar terms with the figure of the woman sempster, suggesting: 'Shee is very neatly spruc'd vp and placed in the frontispiece of her shop, of purpose, (by her curious habit) to allure some Custome, which still encreaseth and decreaseth as her beauty is in the full, or the wane'.[16] These examples suggest the extent to which the paratextual architecture of the printed codex became an available metaphor for social and commercial life. In her chapter below, Wendy Wall goes further, allowing us to suggest that this metaphor may in fact be a submerged structure of thought, creating, in her terms, an 'indexical ... imagination': a way of approaching the world which is structured by the physical forms in which it is described.

The chapters in this volume are united by their challenge to Genette's repeated assertion that the meaning and function of the paratext are determined by 'the author and his allies' (2), and that paratexts operate as a way of establishing and securing authorial intention. 'By definition', Genette argues, 'something is not a paratext unless the author or one of his associates accepts responsibility for it' (9). Features such as reviews, as well as some of the elements discussed in this volume, including bindings and collections, and manuscript annotations (a common, and often illuminating, feature of early printed books), are thus, for Genette, excluded from 'the paratext, which is characterized by an authorial intention and assumption of responsibility' (3).[17] Recently, however, scholars of the early modern period have questioned the historical authority of the author, arguing that textual production was a substantially more collaborative process than is assumed by post-Romantic notions of the solitary genius.[18] The identification of an authorial presence, critics argue, is an ideological product of the impulse to establish intellectual property, and authorial rights in, as well as responsibilities for, particular texts.[19]

Genette himself recognises that 'the invention of the printed book did not impose this particular paratextual element (the name of the author) as quickly and firmly as it imposed certain others' (37), and the lack of an authorial name, or its subordination to the name of a patron or playing company, on many early modern title-pages should alert us to the dispersed and fragmentary nature of authorial control in the period. Arthur Marotti suggests that paratexts are zones where multiple, and sometimes competing, authorities and sources are the norm, describing each piece of prefatory matter as 'a site of contestation and negotiation among authors, publishers / printers, and readership(s)'.[20] Recent scholarship, particularly on early modern dramatic publication, tends to place paratextual and other decisions firmly in the domain of the printer. Zachary Lesser, for example, reads prefatory material as a revelation of printerly, rather than authorial, intentions and political, religious, or literary affiliations.[21] The relative autonomy of many early modern printers allows us to contest Genette's assumption that the publisher (a term which does not strictly apply to members of the early modern book trade; the equivalent figure would most often be the bookseller)[22] is necessarily one of the author's 'allies', equally committed to the clear explication of the singular meaning which informs the text. An 'advertisement to the Reader' at the end of Henry Burton's 1636 *A divine tragedie lately acted* illustrates the possible discrepancy between authorial desire and printed reality, asking the 'covrteovs reader':

Be pleased to understand, that thorow some oversight at the presse, the foregoing Examples are not orderly placed. Indeed it was the authors minde that they should have beene otherwise to wit, 1. 2. 3. and so all the rest, in order one after another, as they are numbred in the booke, and to this end gave direction, but the same was not considered of these who were imployed for the printing, untill it was to [*sic*] late. Now this we thought good to certifie thee of, that so the mistake may be imputed, to the parties deserving it, and not to the Author, who is blamelesse herein.[23]

The physical appearance of the page is, in this instance, revealed to be explicitly opposed to the author's intentions and to the clearer explication of his meaning.

Several of the chapters in this volume engage, explicitly or implicitly, with the question of authorial engagement in paratextual decisions, and the detailed unpicking of particular peritextual moments by Sonia Massai, Matthew Day, and Juliet Fleming reveals a more complex picture either than Genette's assumption of authorial intention, or than Lesser's attribution of these features to the productive matrix of the printing house. A number of the essays which follow investigate paratexts often assumed to be printerly (imprints, printers' flowers, running titles, corrections) and argue that they may, at times, be determined by the author or by a collaborative impulse, while elements we might assume to be authorial, particularly prefatory addresses, are revealed to be the product of printing-house agents or practice. Moreover, many of these chapters further illuminate Stephen Orgel's insight that the early modern book was unfinished even in its printed form. He insists that 'the purchasers of early modern books were much more actively involved in their materialisation', choosing a particular binding, ordering the contents, and, perhaps most importantly, writing in their pages.[24]

Some marginal annotations were enactments of authorial desire: Henry Burton begged the reader to 'correct' 'the mistakes and omissions of the Printers' 'with thy pen'.[25] Other readers created less obviously sanctioned paratexts for their books: paratexts which cannot be assumed to be in any straightforward sense authorial, but which often contribute decisively to interpretation, or offer a new context for our understanding of the social life and significance of the text. The title-page of the Huntington Library copy of William Turner's *Herbal*, for example, bears the inscription: 'A sincer testimonie off Cap Wil: Shay his reall affection too his approued frind Maistre Tailzoure appothecarie in Yorrk. 1643.'[26] Where Turner had used his printed dedication to emphasise the general benefit of his *Herbal*, as well as the intellectual skills necessary to appreciate it, Shay's inscription highlights the practical utility of the book to a member of the medical profession, as well as its symbolic value as a gift expressive of the friendship between a soldier and an apothecary within the northern Royalist stronghold of York. The sense of early modern paratexts as an expanding and ongoing category of engagement is central to this volume, and poses a vigorous challenge to Genette's restrictive definitions.

What John Jowett describes as 'the innovative fluidity of a stage of emergence'[27] that characterises the overlapping functions of authors, editors, printers, and readers in the early modern period also disrupts Marie Maclean's distinction between the fictive world of the text and the 'real' world of the paratext. For Maclean, drawing on speech-act theory:

> The paratexts involve a series of first order illocutionary acts in which the author, the editor, or the prefacer are frequently using direct performatives. They are informing, persuading, advising, or indeed exhorting and commanding the reader. On the other hand the world of the fictional text is one of second order speech acts where even the most personal of narrators belongs not to the real world but to the represented world.[28]

The chapters collected here suggest that this division is untenable; both text and paratext operate at the level of representation, and even the most direct of exhortations to the reader is in some sense second order, engaged in the construction of one represented world even as it promises to interpret another. Seth Lerer gives an example of the fictional status of the most apparently directional of paratexts when, speaking of errata sheets, he suggests that 'the need to narrativize the story of . . . errors – to offer up a personal history of detection and correction – makes the true subject of the early humanist book not so much its content but the complex relationships among textual and political fealty that write the history of its own production'.[29]

In the first chapter of this collection, Helen Smith constructs a similar argument, turning her attention to the apparently straightforward space of the imprint: the details of publisher and place that appear at the front of nearly every early modern printed book. By engaging with a series of fake and fictionalised imprints, Smith unspools the range of meanings and different versions of authority contained within this seemingly informational space, and suggests that a careful reading of the early modern imprint can inform our sense not only of the mechanics of print production, or the negotiations between author, printer, and reader, but of the ways in which book agents and their readers constructed their own place within the world of the book, and within the early modern city. Matthew Day examines another neglected, and informational, paratext – the running title – and discovers that running titles are often discursive, polemical, and refreshingly witty. He contests our assumption that running titles are the abbreviated product of the printing house, and shows that they were, at least on occasion, the results of authorial direction. Moreover, Day provides evidence that some early modern readers and writers cared about the content of running titles, and responded to them in a variety of ways. His work suggests that we must be wary of looking at early modern pages through modern eyes which privilege the central text block and relegate the margins, particularly the upper and lower edges, to a category of supplementary furniture which the reader can safely ignore. At least some early modern readers, Day's chapter indicates, read the whole space of the page.

Remaining within the spatial dynamics of the printed sheet, Juliet Fleming continues her exploration of printers' flowers: small type ornaments used to decorate and demarcate the text. Like Danielle Clarke, Fleming suggests that non-verbal cues – in this case typographical arabesques – can signify genre, and may even mark particular literary groupings, or be used to establish an authorial canon. Her work on this tool of the trade returns us to the practicalities and literary commitments of the early modern printing house, even as it challenges our broader notions of the ways in which paratexts function in relation to texts. Where we see a frame as a decorative enclosure, argues Fleming, the early modern reader saw the frame as the basic architectural structure onto or into which other materials may be placed. The book, Fleming's chapter dares us to suggest, is constituted by its paratexts; the text must fit its paratextual frame.

In drawing to a close this section of the volume, which elaborates a series of neglected paratexts, William Sherman notes Genette's and other critics' emphasis on front matter. Sherman turns instead to the back of the book, investigating the almost endless variety of ways in which the reader is ushered out of the printed text and the book itself is, more or less successfully, brought to a close. Not only does Sherman expose the variety of closing elements and conventions that marked the early modern book, he tests the extent to which these terminal gestures actually mark themselves, or the book they back onto, as either final or complete. It is fitting then that Sherman's 'The End' is not the end of our volume. Where the first section of this collection pays attention to the physical and semiotic detail of previously unexamined paratexts, the second investigates the ways in which paratextual authors negotiated their prospective readerships. Sonia Massai examines a series of title-page pledges that assure the reader that the text which follows has been 'newly corrected and amended'. Arguing against a recent critical tendency to read these statements as hollow marketing strategies, Massai investigates the variety of ways in which dramatic texts were indeed amended, corrected, and 'perfected'. This enterprise once again returns us to the early modern printing house, but further complicates the distinctions we may be tempted to make between authorial, editorial, compositorial, and, importantly, readerly interventions. As Massai concludes, 'it is simply impossible to disentangle the individual contributions of the multiple agents involved in the transmission and retransmission of these texts in print' (103). Rather than dissuading us from paying careful attention to paratextual clues, however, Massai's chapter demonstrates persuasively how important it is to take peritextual claims seriously, and to test them against the full range of available evidence.

Neil Rhodes balances the projects of reading particular paratexts and of extending Genette's taxonomy in his reading of the prefaces to a series of Renaissance translations, particularly Florio's *Montaigne*. Rhodes reads the content of these prefaces as evidence for the status anxiety felt by the medial figure of the translator. At the same time, he suggests two new categories of paratexts, arguing first that translation itself should be understood as a second- or third-order metatext, distinguished from its associated paratexts by its vertical rather than horizontal relationship to the text: it is a paratext of transmission rather than mediation. Rhodes also hints at the possibility of reading relations of lineage and kinship as social paratexts, an insight developed further in Hester Lees-Jeffries's account of the *Songe de Poliphile*. Louise Wilson examines the prefatory practices of Anthony Munday, an energetic translator of Iberian romances, to shed light on the playful peritextual conventions of the genre in its English incarnations. By drawing attention to Munday's subversive appropriation of humanist constructions of pragmatic reading, and of humanist and religious attacks on romances, Wilson demonstrates the sophisticated intertextuality of apparently straightforward dedications and addresses to the reader. She also illuminates some of the printing-house networks and friendships that shaped the content of, and supplied another readership for, these texts.

Danielle Clarke investigates a different constellation of relationships, and asks us to consider the extent to which early modern paratexts contribute to the construction of one or more gendered textual identities. Turning to the complaint genre as perhaps the prime example of female-voiced textuality, Clarke examines a variety of paratexts to argue that these material markers also signify in ways that modern readers tend to associate with the linguistic structures of the written texts. Certain paratextual features or combinations, Clarke argues, offer the reader subtle clues about genre, structure, connections between the part and whole of the text, and about hierarchies of voices and subject positions. Clarke is careful to emphasise the rhetorical heritage of the complaint genre; in doing so, she reminds us that certain typographic features may have had as much an oral and aural as a visual function.

In the final section of this volume, the question of readership is extended in a series of detailed case studies. Jason Scott-Warren offers an example of peritextual breakdown in Spenser's 1590 *Faerie Queene*, and contests the teleological assumptions of many current accounts of the material text which argue that the gradual accretion of paratexts allowed the early modern book to become ever more navigable. Instead, Scott-Warren argues, some paratexts are baffling and resistant to negotiation, and the proliferation of early modern paratexts – including Sir John Harington's instructions to the reader on how to use the paratexts that accompanied his translation of Ariosto's *Orlando Furioso* – marked an ongoing recognition of the vagaries of interpretation. Scott-Warren does, however, suggest the extent to which paratexts might shape readerly expectations: *The Faerie Queene*, he argues, though it is missing many of the peritextual features we might expect, contains a series of unwritten paratexts which coax particular, and predictable, responses from its readers. Wendy Wall offers another illuminating case study in her account of the different incarnations of Gervase Markham's influential how-to book, *The English Housewife*. Like Scott-Warren she finds that early modern technologies of reading are often baffling and resistant to ready interpretation. Wall's argument is provocative: in charting the ways in which Markham's perennially popular text was altered for, and presented to, succeeding generations of readers, she suggests not only that the text gradually adapted itself to a changing readership, but that that readership was itself constructed by the demands and facilities of the text. *The English Housewife*, Wall concludes, was instrumental in developing the 'indexical domestic imagination' – and the corresponding moral skills – of the early modern English housewife.

Hester Lees-Jeffries also tackles issues of domestic space, asking 'what might it mean to read, or write, a particular text in a particular place?' Her chapter invites us to compare the garden at Wilton House, a frequent retreat for both Philip Sidney and his niece Mary Wroth, to the places not only of their related romance texts but of a possible source for both authors: the *Songe de Poliphile*. Though Genette does not include illustrations in his discussion of paratexts he does comment on the paratextual relevance of this 'immense continent' (406). Where a more sustained attempt to incorporate images into the category of the paratext might risk relegating pictures to a supplementary function, Lees-Jeffries's reading of illustrations as nodal points which draw in and direct the reader, shaping their approach to the surrounding text, indicates that illustrations do have a number of paratextual functions. It is, however, families, places, and fountains, that Lees-Jeffries most suggestively argues function as paratexts and intertexts. These – like the many other paratexts discussed by our contributors – are not immutable instructions to the reader: early modern paratexts are revealed throughout this volume to be a series of flexible and mutable relationships, as well as spaces which offer themselves for imaginative engagement.

In his Afterword, Peter Stallybrass returns to two themes which surface throughout this volume: visual paratexts and the paratextual construction of the author. Arguing that we have not yet developed ways to properly conceptualise the inter-relations of illustration and text, Stallybrass draws our attention to visual paratexts which are not strictly illustrations – the decorated capitals that mark many early modern printed books – and argues that far from being, on the one hand, merely furniture or, on the other, seamlessly integrated into the textual or visual unit, these are examples of 'a reading that doesn't see and a seeing that doesn't read, of a visual paratext that moves in and out of focus' (210). Stallybrass goes on to draw the traces of authorship into sharp focus, arguing that the numerous paratexts of both early print and manuscript reveal authorship as 'a form of ascription': something that is written rather than a figure who writes. Such a conclusion makes a fitting end to this volume, concerned as it is with the ways in which books present themselves and the circumstances of their creation to the reader, mediating the relationship between the book and the world in numerous inventive, complex, and unexpected ways.

PART I

Orders of the book

CHAPTER I

'Imprinted by Simeon such a signe': reading early modern imprints

Helen Smith

In his 1594 'discourse of apparitions', *The terrors of the night*, Thomas Nashe declared: 'Gentlemen (according to the laudable custom), I am to court you with a few premisses considered: but a number of you there bee, who consider neither premisses nor conclusions, but piteouslie torment Title Pages on euerie poast, neuer reading farther of anie Booke, than Imprinted by Simeon such a signe'.[1] In this chapter, I want to declare myself as one of the 'bad' readers Nashe decries, progressing no further than 'Simeon such a signe', and asking what challenges of reading and interpretation reside in the limited space of the early modern imprint: the text at the bottom of the title-page which gives details of a book's printer, bookseller, and sometimes place of sale. These paratexts, I argue, operate within generic conventions, which, read carefully, reveal imprints to be fictive engagements with a surprising range of literary and cultural concerns. As Lotte Hellinga observes of the colophon from which it evolved, the imprint, which may seem to be merely 'a statement appended to a text giving particulars about its genesis or production, is a text in its own right, and is therefore open to interpretation according to the time, place and circumstances of its origin'.[2]

The factual nature of imprints is well established. Gérard Genette notes, in passing, that the title-page 'generally includes ... the name and address of the publisher'.[3] W. W. Greg concluded, 'the object of imprints ... is to impart certain information respecting the circumstances in which the material book has been produced and is being distributed'.[4] Where other title-page elements, including the title, authorial presence, and the beauties of frontispiece decoration have all been explored, the imprint has been assigned to the realm of dull fact and abbreviated informativeness.[5] I want to turn first, therefore, to an example that challenges Greg's assertion of the imprint's transparently informational status. John Taylor's *Taylor's Revenge* declares itself to have been printed 'At *Rotterdam*, at the signe of the blew

Bitch in *Dog*-Lane, and are to be sold, almost anywhere. *AND* Transported ouer sea in *A Cods belly*, and cast vp at *Cuckolds Hauen* the last Spring-tide. 1615' (Figure 1.1).

The literary, rather than literal, nature of this imprint is clearly signalled. The book's journey 'ouer sea in *A Cods belly*' draws on the biblical story of Jonah's sojourn in the belly of the whale, and has parallels with a number of quasi-mythical narratives popular in the period, including the stories of the tyrant Policrates of Samos and the pauper Florentius of Hippo, both of whom discovered valuable rings in fish intended for the table. In a similar vein, the imprisoned St Machaldus of Man and St Egwine of Evesham were purported to have discovered the keys to their fetters inside the fish that constituted their prison diet. Taylor's imprint thus draws on a long providential heritage, as well as an alternative tradition of singing or speaking fish in popular ballads and monstrosity literature.[6] There may also be a cruder, embedded pun: 'cod' was a term for the testicles, so that Taylor's book is doubly enclosed in the lower regions of the sexualised body, marking its provocative and witty status.

The reference to Cuckold's Haven is more explicitly intertextual. Taylor's pamphlet was written as an attack upon William Fennor, who he claimed had failed to meet him for a public contest of wit.[7] In his accusatory *Revenge*, Taylor draws upon the language of Fennor's *Cornu-copiae, Pasquils night-cap* (1612), which describes the erection of a horned post at 'Cuckolds hauen' by a fictionalised London citizenry.[8] Fennor, like Taylor, was drawing on a topographical referent that, as well as being a known point in the extended London cityscape, enjoyed a brief literary vogue in the early part of the seventeenth century.[9] Following its 1605 appearances in the anonymous play *The London prodigall*, and in Chapman, Jonson, and Marston's *Eastward ho*, the term appeared in six works by Thomas Dekker between 1606 and 1618, as well as in a number of texts by other writers.[10] Taylor's imprint, like Fennor's invocation of Cuckold's Haven, signals his text's participation in a comic, satirical mode that is deeply rooted in its London context.

I will return to Taylor's exuberant fantasy, and to some of its fictional cousins, but first I want to detour through a handful of imprints that are, at least on the surface, examples of those 'normal cases' Greg describes as being 'capable of strict interpretation [and which] generally mean what they say'.[11] It is not my contention that one of the less intrusive elements of the early modern paratext, sometimes as little as a single word in length and rarely exceeding four short lines, can spin the kind of detailed yarn of cause and effect, action and retaliation, that we associate with narrative fiction.

TAYLORS REVENGE

OR

THE RYMER WILLIAM FEN-
NOR *Firkt, Feritted, and finely fetcht*
ouer the Coales.

WHEREIN

His Riming Raggamuffin Rafcallity, without
Partiallity, or feare of Principallity, is *Anagra-*
matized, Anotomized, & Stigmatized.

The occafion of which Inuectiue, is breifly fet downe in the
Preface to the Reader.

Reuenge doth Gallop when it seemes to creepe,
For though my wrong did winke, it did not sleepe.

PRINTED
At *Rotterdam*, at the figne of the blew *Bitch* in *Dog*
Lane, and are to be fold, almoft any where.
AND
Tranfported ouer fea in *A Cods belly*, and caft vp
at *Cuckolds Hauen* the laft Spring-tide. 1615.

1.1 Title-page to *Taylors Revenge*, 1615.

Nonetheless, where Greg draws a line between factual imprints and their suspect and ill-meaning 'fictitious' counterparts, we may instead discover that both 'factual' and 'fictitious' imprints participate in a different category: the fictional, understood not simply as their 'feigned' or 'false' elements, but as the narrative possibilities these brief statements describe or evoke. Imprints, like other paratexts, signify in sometimes unexpected ways. To borrow Genette's formulation, which he uses to describe the choice of cover photographs, 'interpretation ... is generated, or reinforced, surreptitiously by a paratextual arrangement that in theory is wholly innocent and secondary'.[12]

It is possible to identify a number of formal properties belonging to the imprint, from its standard position at the foot of the title-page (and in the earlier part of the period its occasional repetition as a colophon at the end of a work) to its internal logic. Greg offers a brief taxonomy of the three possible forms an imprint might take: 'Corresponding to the earliest practice is the simplest type of imprint, "Printed by A" ... The employment by the printer of a distributing agent gives rise to imprints of the type, "Printed (by A) for B". Full differentiation finally is manifested in the rare type, "Printed (by A) for B to be sold by C"'.[13] It is worth noting that Greg's description of the second type of imprint, 'Printed (by A) for B', misrepresents what we now understand to be the relationship between the bookseller who commissioned publication and the printer s/he employed. In the imprint to Nashe's *Terrors of the Night* – 'LONDON, Printed by *Iohn Danter* for *William Jones*, and are to be sold at the signe of the Gunne nere Holburne Conduit. 1594.' – it is clear that William Jones sponsored the publishing operation, and John Danter undertook the work of printing at his behest.[14] Imprints like this contain the three key indicators of name, place, and – missing from Greg's description – date, which are essential to the production of what Roland Barthes terms 'the reality effect', in which particular details are revealed to possess no function other than to establish, in the reader's mind, the verisimilitude of the narrative. As Barthes points out, 'at the very moment when these details are supposed to denote reality directly, all that they do, tacitly, is signify it'.[15] When the story, like the story of most imprints, consists only of name, date and place, the effect is one of absolute verisimilitude: a reality effect that renders its rhetorical or narrative impact invisible. This 'reality' is neatly captured in David McKitterick's description of 'the conclusive finality of the date of publication set at the foot of the title-page of a printed book', despite the evidence of false, mistaken, and altered dates in numerous imprints.

One of the most compelling fictions of the early modern imprint is that of possession. In 1616, Hester Ogden applied to King James for a patent to print her father William Fulke's *Confutation of the Romish Testament*. In a petition to the Bishop of London she explained:

one Adams a Stacioner in London hath printed divers of the said bookes, hauing by sinister meanes, gotten a Copie of them from yor Supp^{tes} father in law (who had no right in them, they being giuen by will as aforesaid) to the preiudice of his Matie for the moytie of the benefit of the said license; and to the vtter vndoing of your poore Suppt^e, and her 8. small children; 2 of wch haue perished even through famine (as God and her neighbo^{rs} can witnesse) to the vnspeakable troble & torment of her heart.[16]

This unfortunate story belies the tenuous nature of Ogden's legal claim. While she insisted that her father had bequeathed the book to her, the stationers Thomas Adams, John Bill and Bonham Norton asserted that, as successors to Fulke's original publisher, George Bishop, and as printers of a number of the theologian's other works, the copy actually belonged to them. In 1618, after a protracted battle, Ogden was awarded the patent in the names of two assigns, although the stationers had a long established right to print translations of the Bible. Ogden sued Bill, Adams and Norton for existing stocks of the book, and then lobbied James for a royal proclamation 'for the furnishing of every Parish Church with one of the said Bookes'.[17]

The imprint of Ogden's 1633 edition of Fulke's text explains that it has been 'Printed by Augustine Matthewes *on* [sic] *of the assignes of* Hester Ogden. *Cum privilegio Regis.*' It offers an immediately compelling assertion of ownership and well-established proprietary rights, supported by the authority of a royal privilege. Above the imprint appears the brief statement: 'THE 4th Edition, wherein are many grosse absurdities Corrected'. This can be read as a continuation of the narrative of editorial care and amplification that marked Bill and company's 1601 and 1617 editions, each of which claimed to contain 'THE WHOLE WORKE, PERVSED and enlarged in diuers places by the Authors owne hand before his death, with sundrie Quotations, and Authorities out of Holy Scriptures, Counsels, Fathers, and Historie, more amply then in *the former Editions*'.[18] It may also be read as an allegation of poor practices and slipshod quality control among the text's original printers, particularly damaging in a period when concerns about the inferiority of Bible printing were widespread.[19] When this imprint is compared to those of earlier editions the reader begins to understand the extent to which apparently factual statements participate in competing narratives of ownership.

Read as stories that cross a range of texts, imprints can reveal much of the social and historical context behind their production, exposing issues of finance, trade networks, familial alliances, and inheritance. Ogden's story is told within the bounds of a paratextual genre that is concerned with the production of authenticity and the certification of provenance and availability. Each early modern imprint that appeared both drew on and helped to accumulate a steady stock of verisimilitude, which could then be exploited by false imprints that imitated the standard form for a variety of purposes. That verisimilitude, however, was decisively disrupted by the publication of the Martin Marprelate pamphlets in the late 1580s. The first of the tracts, *Oh read ouer D. Iohn Bridges* (1588), claimed to be 'printed oversea in Europe within two furlongs of a bouncing priest at the cost and charges of m marprelate gentleman'.[20] The text flaunts its illicit printing, while pre-empting the strategy of some later fake imprints used by English secret presses which imaginatively relocated themselves to the relative safety of the Continent.[21] Different editions of Thomas Doughty's *The practise how to finde ease, rest, repose, content, and happines* in 1618 and 1619, for example, declared themselves to have been printed in, respectively, Douai and Rouen, though both were published secretly in England.[22] Both texts signal their Jesuit purpose by the inclusion of the phrase 'with permission of Superiors'.

Marprelate's tract encourages an imaginative remapping: it fictionalises, while preserving, its London geography. The text was, as Patrick Collinson has pointed out, printed at Mrs Crane's house in East Molesey, a two-furlong journey across the Thames from Hampton Court Palace, where Whitgift and other 'archpriests' were in conference.[23] When the press moved to Northamptonshire, the imprint of the second edition (also 1588) recorded this shift, informing readers that it had been 'printed on the other hand of some of the priests', and revelling in the escape of print from the English capital. An ambiguous relationship to London life was signalled in the fourth tract, *Hay any worke for Cooper* (1589), on which the pseudonymous author flaunted his familiarity with the London landscape, describing himself as 'Martin the Metropolitaine' but boasting that his tract, printed in Coventry, was produced 'in Europe, not farre from some of the bounsing priests'.

An alternative fiction of place is spun in the false imprint to one of James VI and I's royal proclamations, translated into French for distribution in France. In the imprint of the *Apologie pour le sermon de fidelite* (1609), John Norton translates his name into the language of the printed text, informing the reader that it was printed 'Chez Iean Norton, Imprimeur ordinaire du

Roy, és langues etrangeres'. A further example of this popular mode of punning translation is provided by Richard Field, who published Spanish texts as 'Ricardo del campo' and Latin texts as 'Theophilum Pratum': Theophilum signalling his interest in religious controversy, and Pratum being Latin for Field.[24] In the case of the *Apologie*, however, the text was not printed *chez* Norton's London printshop, but was, according to the STC, produced in France by a French printer. The imprint claims the text as a cosmopolitan Londonite, obscuring the reality that books printed in England were generally of lower quality than those printed abroad, that good-quality paper was easier to come by in France, that foreign language composition was a skill possessed by few English pressmen, and that – a net importer rather than a net exporter – England's texts often had little hope of crossing the channel. The fiction of this imprint, endorsed by James, is that English printing was a sophisticated industry with a long reach. It is also, perhaps, a fiction of a text which comes directly from the king, and does not suffer the dislocations and alterations of displaced publication. The economics of print and dissemination are masked by a story of authority, regulation, and a thriving London publishing industry.

Rather different fictions of place feature in many imprints, even those, like Nashe's *Terrors of the night*, which appear most obsessively factual and were scrupulous in declaring their real place of origin and the location of their point of sale. Responding to Greg's assumption that the bookseller announced on the title-page was a text's sole retailer, Peter Blayney argues that: 'The primary purpose of an imprint was the same in early modern England as it is today: to inform *retailers* where a book could be purchased *wholesale*'.[25] However, as Nashe's complaint about the passing reader enraptured by 'Simeon such a signe' suggests, it seems likely that members of the book trade *and* the amorphous body of the reading public were the target audience.[26] One of the imprint's most compelling fictions, narrated in cleft sticks, on posts and stalls, and in peddler's packs, was the claim of absolute proprietary rights by a single stationer or small consortium. Imprints often identify booksellers more explicitly than printers, whose names are abbreviated or reduced to initials, suggesting that the identity of the printer was relevant primarily to other stationers, who could easily identify them by their initials and materials, while booksellers spelled out their identity for the benefit of a wider public.[27]

Both Blayney and, for a later period, Adrian Johns have shown just how detailed a map of parts of early modern London it is possible to construct from the evidence of imprints.[28] The geographical information given in many of these texts allows us not only to chart shop positions but to gain some insight into the ways in which members of the primarily London-based print trade imagined the city and their place within it. The London of early modern imprints is, however, a city that appears strange to modern eyes, populated as it is by conduits, alleys, great North doors, and shop signs, rather than by streets and numbers. In describing location as precisely as they do, early modern imprints participate in the 'fictions of settlement' described by Lawrence Manley, which are 'tied to the task of producing and reproducing the socio-economic relationships essential to urbanization. London's "fictions of settlement" were ... actions or practices, modes of ideological innovation that actually contributed to the process of sedentarism.'[29] Printers were not only informing readers or fellow stationers of their whereabouts, they were also producing a fiction of themselves as established settlers in a reliable, mappable, navigable city.[30]

It is, perhaps, this move towards urbanisation that informs John Stow's 1598 *Suruay of London*, in which he closes an extended description of recent shifts within the city with the observation that:

Powlters of late remoued out of the *Powltry* betwixt the Stockes and great Conduite in Cheape into *Grassestreete* and *S. Nicholas* Shambles: Bowyars, from *Bowyer* rowe by Ludgate, into diuers places, and almost worne out with the Fletchers: Pater noster Beade makers and Text Writers are gone out of Pater *Noster* Rowe into Stationers of *Paules* Church yard: *Patten* makers of S. *Margaret* Pattens lane, cleane worne out.[31]

The city is seen to have taken its shape, and the names of its streets, from the trade practices of those who work within it. Elsewhere in his *Suruay*, Stow makes clear the imbrication of mercantile elements in the fabric of the city, citing, for example, Wolfe's former master, the stationer John Day, as 'a late famous printer of many good bookes' who 'builded much vpon the wall of the cittie towards the parish Church of Saint *Anne*'.[32] The disruptions of mercantile and trade movement which Stow describes are, meanwhile, enacted in the imprint to his text. Where Stow records the emptying out of the Drapers from Lombard Street and Cornhill, his printer, John Wolfe, uses the imprint to record his own newly established presence in their old location, stating that the books 'are to be sold at his shop within the Popes head Alley in Lombard Street'. Like Stow, Wolfe makes clear his commitment to the fabric of the City, as well as its incarnation as a metropolitan authority, describing himself as 'Printer to the honorable Citie of London', a formula he used on four other occasions in the mid to late 1590s, printing articles sponsored by the City Corporation relating to poor relief, details of tithes, and trade regulation.[33]

In *Imagined Communities*, Benedict Anderson notes that print and the early modern interest in topography emerged at much at the same time.[34] Developing this observation, Brian Stock suggests that the particular constellation of landscape, printing, and silent reading – however open to question the chronology of any of those three 'revolutions' may be – provoked a new mode of 'reading' the landscape in which place and space began to be understood as interpretable texts.[35] Rather than seeing space, the observer began to read it. On a different note, Tiffany Stern has persuasively argued that a London plastered with playbills and title-pages, along with other textual phenomena such as libels, was 'inscribed with a huge variety of texts ... The city was textual, not in a new historical sense so much as in a literal one – it was covered in texts. Festooned with advertisements, plague bills, and proclamations, London's pleasures, their consequences, and their prevention were inscribed on almost every street.'[36]

These printed materials, however, were not securely legible. Woodcut and engraved pictures, lines and rules, and printers' devices and flowers all marked these texts as visual. Lengthy titles were broken up not according to verbal units, but according to the aesthetic and practical demands of pattern and space. Different fonts, altered from line to line or even word to word, produced compelling optical effects. As Juliet Fleming reminds us, such elements produce title-pages as sites that hover between the visible and the legible, making 'the visual proposition "this is what writing looks like" even as they continue to manifest their own isotropic beauty, encourag[ing] readers to think about writing under the aspect of appearance, and to engage in the production of their own perceptual and conceptual analogies between the two visual systems'.[37] What Joseph Loewenstein terms the 'volubility' of early modern semantic culture is enshrined in the overlapping modes of understanding presented by the printed page and the cityscape it decorated and described.[38]

Even within the most textual of publishers' identifying marks – the imprint – we find a reminder of the strong visual identity of early modern London: the sign. The diversity and occasional obscurity of shop signs is satirised by Subtle in Jonson's *The Alchemist* (1612):

> He first shal haue a Bell, That's *Abel*;
> And by it, standing one, whose name is *Dee*,
> In a rugg Gowne; There's *D.* and *Rug*, that's *Drug*:
> And, right anenst him, a dog snarling *Er*;
> There's *Drugger, Abel Drugger*. That's his signe.[39]

Early modern texts proclaim themselves to be sold at a multitude of signed locations, including the Angel, the Golden Anchor, the Half Moon, the

Harrow, the Cat and Parrot, and the Hedgehog.[40] Robert Milbourn, presumably in collaboration with Thomas Buck, even reproduced his sign – a greyhound – in pictorial rather than textual form on the title-page of William Hawkins's 1634 *Corolla varia contexta*, reproducing the visual marker of his trade identity (Figure 1.2).[41]

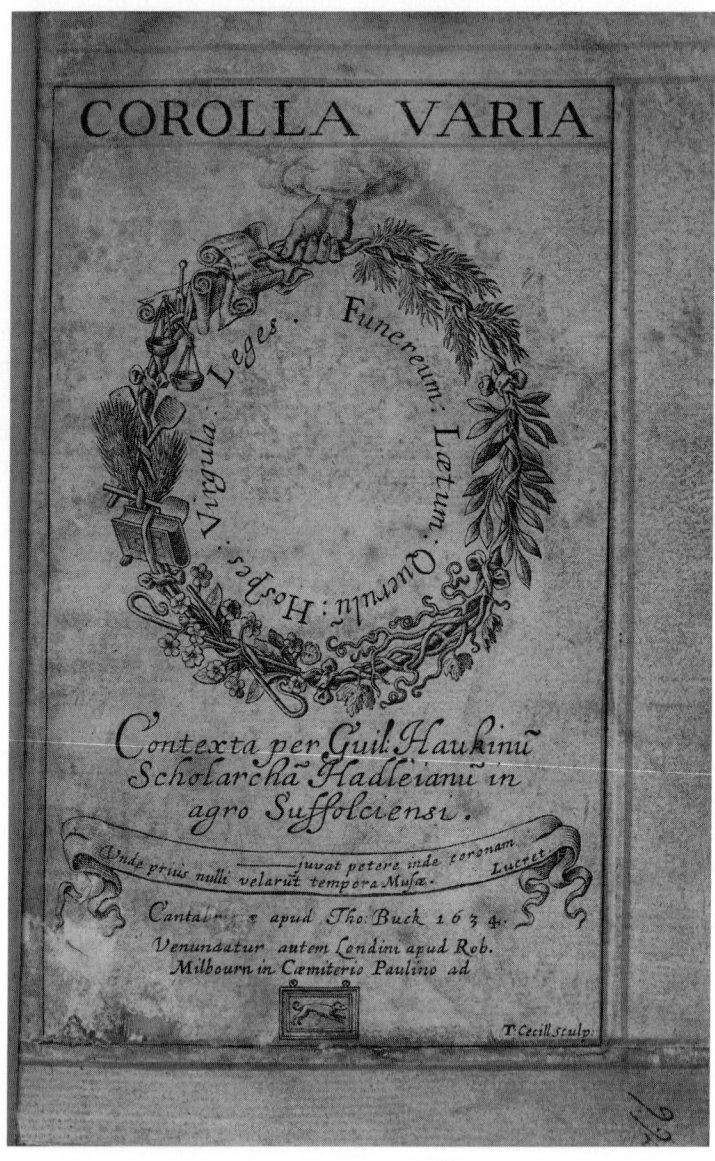

1.2 Title-page to William Hawkins, *Corolla varia contexta*, 1634.

In the imprint to Nashe's *Terrors of the night*, William Jones's corner of London is described not by street name, the textualised marker of its topographic identity, but by its sign: 'the Gunne'.[42] Jones's shop is also located by its proximity to a place of communal and civic significance, standing as it does 'nere Holburne Conduit', one of a number of conduits which provided water but which were also 'symbolic and moral centres of the City'.[43] Shop signs frequently became shorthand for the buildings they marked, as well as, on occasion, metonymically referring to the shop's occupant or owner. In his *Pennyles pilgrimage*, John Taylor described a convivial scene, in which the assembled company:

> [did] *Trundle* downe health, after health
> (Which oftentimes impaires both health and wealth.)
> Till euery one had fill'd his mortall Trunke,
> And onely *Nobody* was three parts drunke.[44]

The joke here is at the expense of Taylor's friend, the bookseller John Trundle, who operated at the sign of Nobody, and, in this instance, took on the identity that described both his premises and their signifier.

What is textualised in the early modern imprint is a social and semiotic mode of understanding urban habitation. The degree to which textual, civic, emblematic and social topographies overlapped in this period is made clear in many of Stow's descriptions of London in which street names and shop, house, or tavern signs intermingle as markers of place and direction, sitting comfortably alongside one another in a continuum of linguistic and iconographic ways of thinking about the city. In his description of Aldgate Ward, for example, Stow explains:

In the mid way on that South side, betwixt *Ealdgate* and *Lymestreete*, is Hart horne alley, a way that goeth through into Fenchurch streete ouer against Northumberlande house. Then haue yee the Bricklayers hall, and an other Alley called sprinckle alley, of an holy water Sprinkle sometime hanging there, now named Sugar loafe Alley of the like signe. Then is there a fayre house: with diuers Tenements neare adioyning, sometime belonging to a late dissoluted Priorie since possessed by Mistresse *Cornewallies*, widow and her heires, by the gift of king *Henry* the 8. in rewarde of fine puddings (as it was commonly said) by her made, where with she had presented him.[45]

Place is described through reference to buildings, civic legend and guild identity, as well as by street names, and streets derive their nominative markers from the material presence of communal and religious activity (a holy water sprinkle) and from trade signs.

The signs themselves, as materialised in the textual fictions of the imprint, allow a number of important stories to emerge. Perhaps the most significant change in printers' signs during this period is the disappearance of saints from the space of the imprint and the walls of the shop, reflecting the changes of religious affiliation brought about by the Reformation. References to saints are largely restricted to colophons rather than the slightly later space of the imprint, indicating their greater currency in the late fifteenth and early to mid-sixteenth century. One late example comes at the close of the anonymous medical text, *The treasure of pore men*, in a colophon explaining it has been 'Imprinted in London in fletestrete, beneth the Conduit at the Signe of Saynt John Euang-liste, by Thomas Colwell, 1575'. In a more local shift in signifying, Robert Bostock's sign of 'the King's head' must have taken on a very different significance when it appeared at the foot of a 1636 sermon delivered at the Northampton assizes than when it marked a covenanter pamphlet in 1648, shortly before Charles's execution.[46]

Another change, noted by David Garrioch, is the extent to which signs which were at first diverse, and spoke most often to the family histories or personal narratives of the shop owner, gradually lost their individuality and became generic signifiers for the trade, like the three golden balls which marked a pawn shop.[47] Richard Tottell's use of the 'Hand and Star' seems to stand on the cusp of these two impulses. While the trade association of Tottell's sign is by no means as explicit as that exemplified in William Blainchard's 'signe of the Printers Presse' or Peter Coles's adoption of 'the sign of the Printing-press', John Bidwell points out that it nonetheless stood as an emblematic statement of 'his dependence on imported paper, which he confessed every time he directed customers to his shop – with the sign of the Hand & Star, a common watermark in early English imprints, signalling paper imported from France or Italy'.[48]

The king's printer, Christopher Barker, invoked a different kind of dependency when he fronted his second shop with the sign of the Tiger's Head, borrowed from the crest of his patron, Sir Francis Walsingham. With this act of appropriation, Barker created a form of commercial heraldry, which reminds us, as it must have reminded potential purchasers, of the close links between the early modern book trade and noble patronage. William Seres's sign of the hedgehog adopted part of the Cecil insignia, reflecting William Cecil's interest in his press. Imprints, and the signs they enshrined, also acted as markers of continuity and professional association. What Garrioch calls 'a poor person's heraldry' is evident in the transfer of the sign of 'the Bell from Robert Toy to his apprentice George Bishop, then to Bishop's own apprentice Thomas Adams, and finally Adams' former apprentice Andrew Hebb'.[49] The complexity of this heraldry, continuing into the early eighteenth century, is mocked by Addison in *The Spectator* no. 28, in which a supposedly anonymous projector declares:

> It is usual for a young Tradesman, at his first setting up, to add to his own Sign that of the Master whom he served . . . This I take to have given Rise to many of those Absurdities which are committed over our Heads; and, as I am informed, first occasioned the three Nuns and a Hare, which we see so frequently joined together. I would therefore establish certain Rules, for the determining how far one Tradesman may *give* the Sign of another, and in what Cases he may be allowed to quarter it with his own.[50]

For those with a less rationalising turn of mind, however, tracing the adoption of signs and premises allowed Londoners to establish a genealogy of trade practice, particular values, and business concerns.

The generic conventions of place are repeated and distorted in the fictional imprints of early modern England, like that to William Goddard's *A mastif vvhelp* which claimed to be 'Imprinted amongst the Antipedes, and are to be sold where they are to be bought'. Goddard's imprint declares the satirical intent of the epigrams which follow, and which establish themselves as inversions of convention and even of personal relationships: as opposed to expected norms as if they were issued in the Antipodes. In his first satire, Goddard commands his '*Mastiff vvhelpe*': 'Not onelie barke, but make as yf thoudst bite / Grynn, snarle, and on thy best freind look soe grym / As yf thoudst at one snapp devoure him'.[51] As in the Martin Marprelate tracts, however, Goddard's imprint also puns on its real place of origin: it was printed in Dort, in the Low Countries, here reimagined as literally beneath the globe.

Like most false and fictional imprints, Goddard's obscures the identity of the stationers who produced it, undermining the claims to ownership and authority made in other texts. In this instance the motive seems clear: satire was subject to 'th'huge statute lawes' invoked by John Donne, and a stationer might not wish to be associated with a risky text, though the author happily identifies himself on the verso of the title-page.[52] The fictional imprint did not identify a readily identifiable point of sale, and therefore could not participate in the mode of advertisement which saw title-pages posted around London. This practical concern raises issues of finance: would the bookseller or printer accept the costs of a text which refused to affiliate itself to his or her premises, or were such books sponsored by patrons or the author? Such economic considerations may prompt us to re-evaluate the commitments not only of authors but of the printers, booksellers, and other publishing agents who produced texts like John Ainsworth's *The trying out of the truth*, 'Published for the good of others by E.P. in the yeare 1615'.[53]

Some imprints are revealed as sites which foreground the collaboration between the several figures involved in the book's production. One such negotiation appears on the title-page of *The Owles almanacke* (1618), attributed to Dekker, which illustrates how generic the anti- or fictional imprint had become (Figure 1.3).

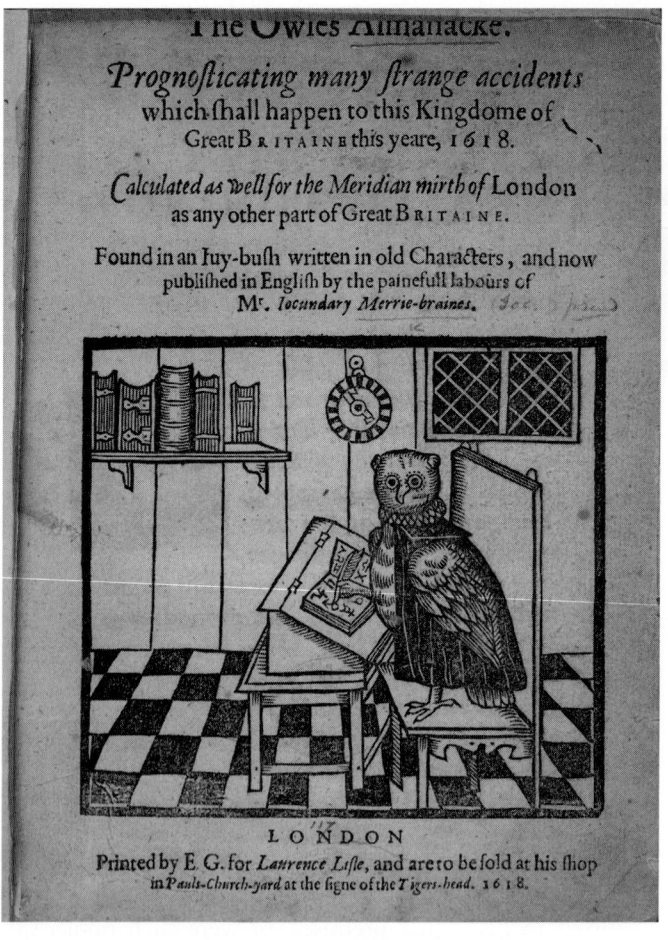

1.3 Title-page to Anon., *The Owles almanacke* (London: Edward Griffin, 1618).

This title-page features both a fictional imprint, elevated to the midpoint, and a factual identification of the printer, Lawrence Lisle, which lends him the proprietary authority to retail his own fictions of patronage and protection in a subsequent dedicatory address to Sir Timothy Thornhill.

The condition of most fictional imprints is anonymity. The Marprelate tracts drew their authority precisely from their refusal to specify either author or printer, laying claim to the popular authority of anonymous texts, which, as Natalie Zemon Davis points out, derived 'from their commonality, their seeming to belong to everyone'.[54] The first attempts to answer the Marprelate tracts were unsuccessful, as Martin consistently mocked his respondents' seriousness of purpose and the heavy-handedness of the traditional modes of refutation they employed. These attempts drew on all the weight of the state and episcopal authority, and their imprints declared the royal authority of their printer and the licence granted by the bishops: the prime targets of Martin's satire. The second generation of anti-Martinists, however, proved better able to play Martin at his own paratextual games, with Nashe's *Returne of the Renowned Caualiero* (1589) declaring 'If my breath be so hott that I burn my mouth, suppose I was printed by Pepper Allie'. As Mar-Martin explained in *Martins months minde* (1589), 'It is therefore thought the best way ... to answere the fooles, according to their foolishness ... wee will returne them the Cuffe, in stead of the gloue, and hisse the fooles from off the stage, as the readiest meanes to out-face them'.[55]

In the two stages of anti-Martinist response we are presented with two modes of reading Martin's fictional imprints: one which counters them with an accumulation of authority and specificity, another which engages in their own mode of vital play. In this example, the imprint becomes a crucial part of the reading experience, giving the lie, thanks to its exuberant fictionality, to R. B. McKerrow's insistence that title-page information is useful only as an advertisement, and has no relevance for the reader.[56] Some evidence also remains to suggest that real readers did pay attention to the space of the imprint, and that they were concerned with questions of status and authenticity. Early modern readers read imprints not as puzzles to be solved but as statements of fact to be tested and corrected. One reader of Francis Godwin's *Nuncius Inanimatus* (1629), a short tract on the utility of carrier pigeons, scored out 'Utopia' from the imprint, and replaced it with 'Londini, Anglia', rejecting the transparent fiction of its nowhere origins while accepting the convention that prefaced a Latin text with a Latinised imprint.[57] The Bodleian copy of Henry Bond's *A new boke of gauging* (1634) has the legend 'printed for W. Lugg' corrected to W. Lugger,[58] while George Thomason regularly annotated the tracts he collected, correcting publication dates or adding additional, more precise, information.

John Taylor's partner in argument, William Fennor, certainly read Taylor's imprint. In *Fennors defence* (1615), he insisted:

> I must hunt out your Bitch, of Azure hue:
> You that at Roterdam haue Spies to houer,
> And in Cods bellies transport Slanders ouer,
> And without Licence belcheth them abroad.[59]

Riffing on the unlicensed anonymity of Taylor's text, Fennor literalises Taylor's playful imprint, implicating his enemy in the world of overseas printing and illicit dissemination that also marked Goddard's mastiff whelp's journey from Dort. In his further response to Fennor, *A cast over the vvater* (1615), Taylor threatens 'Now Fennor once more Ile giue thee a twitch / For hunting hotly after my Blue *Bitch*', converting Fennor's literalised description back into his own dogged determination to hound his opponent (in an epilogue he threatens Fennor with his 'sharp fang'd Muse' and offers him a satirical bone to 'gnaw vpon').[60] Taylor's invocation of snarling dogs signals the satirical purpose of his pamphlet. As Kathryn Perry points out, aggressive or voluble animals, like bitches and mastiffs, or the almanac-producing owl, were common markers of satirical texts.[61] Furthermore, they were associated with a lowness of both style and content that may go some way to explain Taylor's reference to Rotterdam in the Low Countries, identifying it not just as a source of illicit print but as a metaphorically appropriate site for the production of 'low' texts.

The blue bitch may have collapsed into the figure of its satirical author, but Taylor's other animal, the book-smuggling fish, proved real. Cut open on a Cambridge market stall, a large cod was found to contain three books attributed to the Tudor divine, John Frith.[62] As Thomas Mall, one of many commentators on this providential catch, pointed out 'in some sort [the books] ran the Fortune of the Author, being held in the Sea, and kept in *Jonah's* Prison, the belly of a Fish, being in danger there to be consumed, as the Author was like to have perished in the Dungeon at *Oxford* by the noysome stinch of Fish'.[63] This brings us back to Taylor's cod's belly, and to what Ken Ruthven has described as an 'as yet untheorised aromatics of reading'.[64] Books printed at Rotterdam were sometimes smuggled into the country in barrels of salt fish, lending the act of illegitimate reading a particular aroma.[65] The conjured smell of fish may be read as an epitext, linking and shaping the readerly experience of two very different books.

Nonetheless, Taylor's cod is not to be read as a straightforward case of art imitating the unlikeliness of providential life. The fish that turned up on a Cambridge market stall did so eleven years *after* John Taylor published his attack on Fennor. It is possible that the Cambridge divines – for whom, as Alex Walsham points out, these books arrived at a suspiciously opportune moment – were struck by inspiration after reading Taylor's *Complete works*, published three years earlier.[66] Perhaps, though, this is the reality effect gone into overdrive, with Taylor producing a fiction so compelling that Nature herself, driven by the conventional imprimaturial story of verisimilitude, locatability and authority, was inspired to create a real piscine referent, taking the absurd fiction of an imprint which mocks and exposes the narrative implications of date, time, and place, and turning it into pungent, traceable fact.

CHAPTER 2

'Intended to Offenders': the running titles of early modern books

Matthew Day

Page 340 of the second volume of *A Short-Title Catalogue of Books Printed in England, Scotland, & Ireland and of English Books Printed Abroad, 1475–1640* contains an error. In such a complex and indispensable work it might seem churlish to highlight this minor weakness apart from the fact that, as David McKitterick has pointed out, this 'slip' is no mere act of carelessness.[1] At the head of the seventh out of nine columns for the works of the prolific and popular late Elizabethan/early Stuart minister, Henry Smith, Katherine Panzer (one of the work's main compilers) offered an insight into her view of this prolix pastor. Perhaps exasperated by the 161 separate and complicated STC entries required for his oft-reprinted, sometimes pirated and certainly prodigious output, Panzer replaced the normal 'running head', as McKitterick terms it, of '**Smith, Henry**, *Minister – Collections – cont.*' with the mischievous '**Smith, Henry**, *Monster – Collections – cont.*'[2] As well as disclosing her sense of humour, Panzer's amendment points towards the use of the paratext for interpretative purposes. It moves away from a means of categorising Smith by his profession ('minister': itself an interpretative action) and towards what might be understood as a comment ('monster') on the intricacies of his entry in STC. The switch exemplifies Gérard Genette's observation that the threshold of a text can mediate it to the reader.[3]

This chapter examines such moments in early modern books through a focus on running titles. In doing so, it seeks to establish a number of things. First that, despite the assumptions of scholars, the running title was sometimes the province of authors rather than printers. Second, that both those involved in book production and those who read texts were alive to the possibilities of running titles and attended to them. Third, that this awareness meant that early modern books deployed this paratextual feature not only for what might be termed 'practical' purposes such as restating the work's title, giving a chapter title or page number, but also for what might be called 'interpretative' acts. Finally, this chapter demonstrates four main ways in which those involved in textual production used running titles: for advertising purposes; for religious persuasion; to guide readers' reception of the text; and to engage in polemic, whether political, satirical, xenophobic, or religious.

It would be misleading to suggest that scholars of early modern print culture have entirely overlooked running titles. Their focus, however, has tended to be bibliographic. Ronald McKerrow's *Introduction to Bibliography*, with its useful distinction between headlines and running titles, makes no comment as to their usage, giving only four lines to the topic.[4] Philip Gaskell's *A New Introduction to Bibliography* is more expansive but argues that running titles merit little attention.[5] Neither McKerrow nor Gaskell draw attention to the role that the top of the page could play in guiding readers to interpret the text. McKerrow, for example, noted the common practice of using the work's title or a section title as a running title: 'A line of type at the top of a page, above the text, is called a "head-line"; or, if it consists of the title of the book (or of the section of the book) on every page or every "opening" (i.e. two pages facing one another), sometimes a "running-title" or "running head"'.[6] It has been left to Genette to observe that in some instances the use of this paratextual space arouses curiosity: 'in the original edition of the *Chartreuse* (a novel without intertitles) the running heads are distributed more or less capriciously; in the original edition of the *Rouge*, the running heads are unfaithful, or fairly liberated' (316). His work, however, focuses on nineteenth-century French literature. This study examines early modern print culture. In highlighting the diverse uses made of the running title in this period, this chapter ranges across genres, formats and time-frames in an effort to demonstrate, if not that this practice was universal, that it was, at least, well established.

The failure of scholars to investigate the early modern use of running titles has perhaps derived in part from confusion about terminology. The alternatives noted in McKerrow's definition are themselves indicative of this. Other work further complicates the issue. Michael Seidel uses the term for what might be better termed subtitles and even David McKitterick's allusion to a 'running head' might more accurately be called a column heading.[7] Rather confusingly, the *OED* offers: 'a short title or headline placed at the top of the page, sometimes restricted to one which is continued throughout the whole of a book' but it gives as its first usage a quotation which suggests a different interpretation: 'the running title on the several heads is easily added, being the same with that of each chapter'.[8] Perhaps the most helpful definitions of the various complex usages covered by the term 'running title' are those provided by Seán Jennett. He distinguishes between different types of running titles using the term 'running headline' when the text remains the same throughout a book; 'section headlines' which 'consist of the titles of whatever subdivisions (chapters, books, parts, etc.) the book may have'; and he invents the term 'page headline' which 'summarizes the contents of the page over which it appears'.[9] Combinations of these arrangements, in which, for example, a verso carries the running title and the recto a chapter heading, are possible.[10] Early modern commentators seem not to have troubled to differentiate between the possible alternatives, commonly using the term 'running title' as a catch-all phrase, or merely alluding to the 'top of the page'.

If this terminological confusion amongst scholars has contributed to scholarly neglect of running titles so has the general failure to recognise the term's early provenance. The *OED*'s first usage dates from 1668 but the term was already known in 1626 when John Cameron used it without explanation in his *An examination of those plausible appearances which seeme most to commend the Romish Church, and to preiudice the Reformed*. Cameron observed that: '*in many passages of this booke, beside the* running title *I have used the word* Prejudice'.[11] He did so with a rhetorical flourish, for the text's running title reads: '*Popish Preiudices against the*' (verso) '*Reformed Rel.*[igion] *examined and confuted*' (recto).

Cameron's *Examination* was one of a number of early modern texts that drew attention to the running title. Such references are useful because they reveal the close attention authors paid to this aspect of book production. John Wallis's letter to Collins that is the source of the *OED*'s 1668 definition laments the slow production of his *magnum opus, Mechanica, sive, de motu* (1670–1) and observes that:

> the running titles on the several heads is easily added; being the same with that of each chapter, which being found in the beginning of the chapter, serves all along till the next chapter. Only the number of the proposition handled in that page is to be changed.[12]

Wallis's letter demonstrates the involvement of the author in even the most routine use of running titles. The diverse set of relationships between authors and printers ranging from close partnership to unauthorised publication of texts means it would be foolhardy to assert that authors were solely or routinely responsible for running titles, but it is possible to show both that some authors exercised control over this aspect of book production, and that readers noticed them. Moreover, in some cases, adversaries exploited this expectation to criticise authors.

Samuel Purchas's comments in *Purchas his pilgrimes* (1625) reveal that the author might be deemed to bear responsibility for page headlines even if he did not himself devise them. In a standard apology for errata occasioned by his necessary absences from the press, Purchas lamented the mistakes 'in the Titles ouer each page; half of which I thinke, are mine owne, the other such as pleased the Corrector, needing correction enough, and sometimes not giuing sufficient direction to the Reader'.[13] The practice of using page headlines was also adopted in Joseph Mede's collected works in 1672. This scholarly edition of the divine's output sought to help readers through those works which 'could not be without great inconvenience divided into *Chapters* . . . by what is set in the top of every Page, which doth summarily import what is contain'd therein'.[14] It was the editor rather than the author who was responsible here. But in both instances, the purpose of the page headline was more than 'an amusing diversion for a bored reader, . . . a mannerism that costs . . . some time and trouble'.[15] Rather, it was intended to direct the reader and to shape his or her response to the text.

Whoever was responsible for running titles, be they running, section, or page headlines, there is evidence to show that early modern readers were attentive to them. In 1662, Dr John Gauden, Bishop of Exeter's, *A discourse concerning publick oaths, and the lawfulness of swearing in judicial proceedings* deployed this space quite conventionally. After the Dedicatory Epistle it used a single heading for the whole work which read: '*The lawfulness of Swearing*' (verso) '*in Judicial Proceedings.*' (recto).[16] Gauden's opponent, Samuel Fisher, exploiting what he deemed Gauden's prolix and rambling style, implied that the running title bore no resemblance to the text, marvelling:

he *entitles* his Book on the top of every *page*, from one end thereof to the other . . . the *Lawfulness of Swearing* in *Judicial Proceedings* and yet *wanders* so wide *off* from it . . . in his Disputation for it: For he comes not (whatever the matter is) so much as near any proof of the *warrantableness* of *such kind* of Swearing.[17]

By contrast, according to Anthony à Wood, Louis de Moulin's fear of disclosing his religious orientation appears to have shaped the publication of the nonconformist's *Patronus bonae fidei* (1672). This attack on the Church of England, observed Wood, 'hath five distinct running titles, all differently paged, to the end that the sheets so printed might the better by that means escape the Searchers to the Press'.[18] A year later, John Sergeant exploited a disparity between the running title and the contents of the main text in his dispute with Edward Stillingfleet. In *Errour non-plust, or Dr Stillingfleet shown to be the man of no principles* (1673) Sergeant attacked Stillingfleet's work,

A discourse concerning the idolatry practised in the Church of Rome (1671). In particular, Sergeant objected to the final chapter. It established six principles on which Catholics and Protestants were agreed. After that came a further thirty points which claimed to disclose '*the particular wayes that God hath made choice of for revealing his will to mankind*'.[19] For Sergeant, to whom the issue of religious principles was important, the running title was revelatory:

Notwithstanding that Dr *St.*[illingfleet] is thus shy to name these thirty Paragraphs, *Principles* ... yet 'tis manifest by his carriage he *meant* them for such, and would have them *thought* such too; for they immediately *follow* after the *six Principles voluntarily agreed on*, as if they were the *other* sort of Principles, *not voluntarily agreed to* ... Again, the Running Title superscrib'd to them is [*The Faith of Protestants reduc'd to Principles*:] All which manifests to us beyond Evasion that he makes use of and relies on them as Principles, though he be something bashful to call them so *directly*.[20]

In their specific references to running titles, these seventeenth-century examples articulate what is evident from earlier practice: that both producers and readers of books in early modern England paid close attention to what came to be termed 'running titles'. We can now examine *how* the producers of texts used this paratextual feature.

In 1625, George Wither complained in *The schollers purgatory* that unscrupulous printers published anything they thought would sell, giving books 'such names as in [their] opinion will make them saleable, when there is little or nothing in the whole volume suitable to such a Tytle'.[21] As the work of McKerrow makes clear, running titles often repeated the title-page of a work and if they did so it follows that they were part of this marketing exercise. Yet in their attempt to appeal to readers, running titles often differed from the title given on the title-page, frequently highlighting a different aspect of the text. As early as 1565 Richard Shacklock's translation of Osorius's letter to Queen Elizabeth used alliteration to declare itself 'A PEARLE FOR' (verso) 'A PRYNCE' (recto) in its running titles and half-title, though it was more prosaic on the title-page which described it as *An epistle of the Reverend Father in God Hieronimus Osorius Bishop of Arcoburge in Portugal, to the Most Excellent Princesse Elizabeth*.[22] If Shacklock's running title claimed to guide one particular reader, John Payne's *Royall exchange: to suche worshipfull citezins/marchants/gentlemen and other occupiers of the contrey as resorte therunto* (1597) sought to clarify the nature of its contents through the running title. Its title-page might indicate a tract about trade but its running title revealed it was a 'Christian Exhortation' encouraging all who worked and traded at the Royal Exchange to 'talke and co[n]ferr ... of the omnipotent a[n]d allseinge God, of religio[n] and good lyfe so necessarie at all seasons'.²³ In 1601, William Perkins penned a sermon-like explication of Philippians chapter 3, verse 7. The work was entitled *The true gaine: more in worth then all the goods in the world.* The running title made clear his position: '*Christ the true*' (verso) '*and perfect Gaine*' (recto).²⁴

Moving away from religious works, W. Shute's translation of Jan Orlers's and Henrik van Haestens's *The triumphs of Nassau* (1613) offered an interpretative title-page which emphasised the outcome of the battles in which Maurice, Prince of Orange, had been engaged: *A Description and Representation of all the Victories both by Land and Sea, Granted by God to the Noble, High and Mightie Lords, the Estates Generall of the United Netherland Provinces. Under the Conduct and Command of his Excellencie, Prince Maurice of Nassau.* The running title took a more personal approach reading, '*The heroicke acts of his Excellencie*' (verso) '*Prince Maurice of Nassau*' (recto), thereby elevating his victories to 'heroicke acts'.²⁵ By contrast, a 1640 pamphlet shows how a text's running title could cut to the chase of its contents. The title-page reads: *A certaine relation of the hog-faced gentlewoman called Mistris Tannakin Skinker, who was Borne at Wirkham a Neuter Towne betweene the Emperour and the Hollander, Scituate on the River Rhyne Who was Bewitched in her Mothers Wombe in the Yeare 1618. and hath Lived ever since Unknown in this Kind to any, but her Parents, and a few other Neighbours. And can Never Recover her True Shape, Tell [sic] she be Married, & c. Also Relating the Cause, as it is Conceived, how her Mother Came to be so Bewitched.* Its running title summarised the position succinctly: 'A relation of the woman monster'.²⁶ Even more disconcerting was the running title of William Burkitt's *The peoples zeal provok't to an holy emulation by the pious and instructive example of their dead minister* (1680). It read 'The Dead Speaking', and this eye-catching paratext was further enhanced by the use of a heavily printed gothic font which differed from the remainder of the text.²⁷ These examples demonstrate not only the inevitably condensed nature of running titles compared with the greater expanse of the title-page, but also that running titles departed from the title-page to use a different vocabulary and greater rhetorical flourish as in Shacklock's and Burkitt's texts and the 1640 pamphlet.

It was not only narrative, exegetical or rhetorical works that used the running title for marketing purposes. Different editions of Nicholas Culpeper's translation of the Royal College of Physicians' *London dispensatory* demonstrate a more complex use of the running-title space. This text was intended amongst other things to offer practical advice, and initially the running titles helped readers categorise the simples required for many of the medicines: 'Let [the reader] have a care he mistake not one thing for another, *viz*. Herbs for Roots, or either of them for Flowers: If he cast but his eye up to the top of the Page, he shall there see which it is'.[28] Culpeper's policy became more onerous as editions progressed and interpolations disrupted the neat categorisation of the first edition. By the time of the sixth edition, although the policy was retained, it was simplified. The recto of every leaf now read '*The sixt Edition, Much Enlarged*', thereby halving at a stroke the number of pages on which the running title needed to be varied. The change also highlighted one of ten attributes that this particular edition claimed to possess including not only, 'Three hundred useful Additions' but also adding, third on the list, that 'On the top of the pages of this Impression is printed *The sixt Edition, Much Enlarged*'.[29] The running title thus mutated from being a guide to interpretation of the text to becoming part of the work's advertising mechanism.

Culpeper's *London dispensatory* exemplified the second main purpose to which running titles were used in early modern texts: that of offering readers guidance or information about the text and how to interpret it. At times, this might be unrelated to the text itself. The Protestant apologist Robert Crowley was one of the most inventive users of running titles. In his 1586 tract entitled *Fryer John Frauncis of Nigeon in Fraunce* he conveyed a particular wish through the running title enjoining: 'Reade all: or Reade Nothing'.[30] Four years later in *A deliberat answere made to a rash offer, which a Popish Antichristian Catholique, made to a learned Protestant (as he saieth) and caused to be published in printe: Anno Do. 1575* (1588) Crowley noted that he had '*set ouer the heads of the pages ... this admonition*: First trie then trust.'[31] He had done so because he claimed the work to which his pamphlet was a reply – Edward Rishton's translation of Jean d'Albin de Valsergues's *A notable discourse plainlye and truly discussing who be the right ministers of the Catholique Churche* – concluded a number of sections with the phrase '*proove this & then I will relent and recant, & not before*'.[32] Crowley stated that, by contrast, he did not '*require any of you* [sc. Catholic readers] *to giue credit to that which I haue written: before you haue tried the same, and found it worthy of credit*' and he used the running title as a reminder of this injunction.[33] A different use for the running title was found by Calvin, according to John Evelyn who believed that '*Calvin* hath put the Name of *Jesus* at the top of every page of his Institution, to endeavour to sanctifie his books by that Holy Name, as the *Jesuites* make use of it to hallow their unholy actions and opinions'.[34] In a variety of ways, then, running titles were used by writers to encourage readers to interact with or receive the text in a particular way. This injunction might be unrelated to the specific contents of the main body of the text.

If some running titles were unrelated to the text itself, others sought to use a running head throughout a text to offer a generic interpretation of the whole piece. This could apply to religious or secular texts. Thomas Day's *Wonderfull straunge sightes seene in the element, over the Citie of London* (1583) is a case in point. Perhaps unnerved by what may have been the aurora borealis on 2 September 1583, Day used the running titles to encourage people to heed God. He repeated the half-title which stood at the head of the main text and read 'The Call of England' – the caller being God – because the 'flashes, much brightnesse, many streames, and straunge and unwonted collours of the rainebow. As also with the collour of the fire of Brimestone' were clearly intended to 'call all our disobedience, unto speedy obedience'.[35] In the same year, but in a different sphere, William Cecil, Lord Burleigh, used the running title to convey a political message. As part of the Government's response to the execution of Edmund Campion, *The execution of justice in England for maintenance of publique and Christian peace, against certaine stirrers of sedition* (1583) sought to justify the execution. Its running title positioned Campion in a particular way stating 'Execution for Treason' (verso), 'and not for Religion' (recto), driving home the Government's message.[36] The Dutch version of the tract repeated this paratext, but the Italian and French editions were more circumspect, perhaps because of the strength of Catholicism in those countries.[37] Whether religious or political, then, these texts used a generic running title, or running head, in an attempt to shape reader response. In all these examples, the running titles deployed vocabulary not found on the title-page, and in some instances they were unrelated to the contents of the specific text they headed.

A far more common practice was the use of the running title to clarify or reinforce an aspect of the text. This practice might be regarded as interpreting the title-page, as well as the contents of the book. In the mid-1560s, when participating in the apparel controversy which occupied the Church of England, Crowley's *A briefe discourse against the outwarde apparell and ministering garments of the Popishe Churche* deployed its running title to pun 'The unfolding of' (verso) 'the Popes Attyre' (recto).[38] Both Protestants and Catholics, at times, spoke of the other as heretics, and a tract of 1566 demonstrates how a running title could elucidate a title-page. John Barthlet's *The pedegrewe of heretiques wherein is truely and plainely set out, the first roote of heretiques begon in the Church*, suggests its orthodox nature by stating that it was '*Perused and alowed according to the order appoynted in the Queenes Maiesties Iniunctions*' but the running title makes the text's partisan nature clear: '*The Pedegrewe*' (verso) '*of Popish Heretiques.*' (recto).[39] Similarly, Rishton's translation of Valsergues's *Notable discourse* (1575) demonstrated what it thought of the Protestant position in its running title which read 'A notable discourse' (verso) 'Against heresies' (recto).[40] At the end of the seventeenth century, religious tracts were still using running titles to spell out what was opaque in the title-page. The anonymous *Our ancient testimony renewed concerning our Lord and Saviour Jesus Christ, the Holy Scriptures, and the Resurrection occasioned at this time by several unjust charges published against us, and our truly Christian profession* (1695) enlightened readers about the 'us' of the title-page, through its running title: '*The General History of the* Quakers'.[41]

Throughout the early modern period, then, religious tracts used running titles to try to shape the reader's response to a text, through a generic running headline which sought to interpret the work as a whole. Techniques ranged from using puns and alliteration to clarifying the religious position of a text or providing additional information. Yet those involved in religious dispute were not the only writers to use running titles to interact with the title-page in witty ways. Thomas Nashe's response to Gabriel Harvey's *Foure Letters and Certaine Sonnets* (1592) was entitled *Strange newes, of the intercepting certaine letters, and a conuoy of verses, as they were going priuilie to victual the Low Countries* (1592). Nashe's title-page appears to make no reference to Harvey's work, presenting itself instead as a news pamphlet. The running title, however, makes explicit the connection between the two books, reading 'Foure Letters' (verso) 'Confuted' (recto).[42] Once the link with Harvey's text is made, the title-page can be re-read. It intimates that Harvey's *Foure Letters and Certaine Sonnets* is on its way to the gutter ('the Low Countries') probably via a backside ('Priuilie'). Thus running title and title-page interact to best an opponent.

If religious controversy and personal flytings constituted the kinds of texts in which generic running titles (or 'running heads' as Jennett terms them) of an interpretative nature flourished, there was one more, perhaps predictable, focus for such a use of the paratext. In the xenophobic world of early modern England, running titles were used to target other countries. Not surprisingly, the object of scorn depended on international relations at the time of publication. In the late sixteenth century, anti-Spanish sentiment was high and the English translation of Bartolomé de las Casas's history of Spanish activities in the New World took the opportunity to pass judgement. While its title, *The Spanish colonie or briefe chronicle of the acts and gestes of the Spaniardes on the West Indies, called the newe world, for the space of xl. yeeres* was relatively neutral, it had a much more aggressive running title: 'The Spanish Cruelties'.⁴³ Nine years later, the printing of George Ker's confession likewise linked treachery with the Spanish. *A discoverie of the unnaturall and traiterous conspiracie of Scottish Papists* (1593) claimed on its title-page to be 'set downe, as it was confessed and subscrivit', and in its running title connected the traitors with Spain: '*A discoverie of the Spanized Scottisch traytors*'.⁴⁴ That the habit of glossing the title of a work continued even though the enemy changed is evident from an anonymous tract of 1673 concerning diplomatic tension between the English and French Governments. The already clearly anti-French, *A free conference touching the present state of England both at home and abroad in order to the designs of France* was yet more partisan in its running title declaring '*The interest of* England' (verso) '*in reference to the* French *Designs*' (recto).⁴⁵

Running titles, then, did far more than merely repeat the title of work: they interpreted it and did so in a variety of different ways. Yet the interaction of these running heads with the text on particular pages could only be generic. Section headlines, as Jennett calls them, offered greater flexibility. The repetition of chapter headings in the space at the top of the page could involve the use of a greater range of rhetorical devices than was permitted by deploying a generic running title. Moreover, this use of section headings is to be found relatively early in the sixteenth century. Texts involved in the 1530s dispute relating to John Frith used both section and page headlines in their attempts to undermine their opponents and make their own case. Frith faced the powerful opposition of Sir Thomas More, and was ultimately burned at the stake. William Tyndale's *The souper of the Lorde* and Frith's *A book made by John Frith while he was prisoner in the Tower* both opposed More and deployed section headlines for a range of purposes including asserting religious principles, confuting matters of religion, and making attacks on More and Catholics.⁴⁶ Frith's *A book made by John Frith*, for example, began with a section headline that asserted, 'It ys non article of oure fayth necessa' (verso) 'rie to be beleved under payne of da[m]pnacion' (recto). It proceeded to statements which helped readers understand their place in the book such as 'An answer to the preface' (verso) 'of master mores boke' (recto) and 'An answer to the treatsye [*sic*]' (verso) 'that master More made' (recto). It then progressed through some theological points summarised as 'The mynde of the faythfull fathers' (verso) 'uppon the wordes of Christes mandye' (recto) or 'The mynde of the olde doctours' (verso) 'uppon the wordes of Christes bodye' (recto) before moving to the section targeted at More himself, 'Master more' (verso) 'pleyeth the sophister' (recto).⁴⁷ A further tract against More, George Joye's *The subversio[n] of Moris false foundacion* (1534) also inveighed against what it deemed 'The false markis' (verso) 'Off [*sic*] moris False chirche' (recto) and alleged 'The spirit of trouth ledeth us not' (verso) 'Into Moris unwryten verites' (recto). It claimed (on both the verso and the recto of some pages) that 'Moris popyshe preisthed [*sic*] perissheth' and 'Moris false fastinge is fallen'.⁴⁸ Not yet guides to the contents of every page, but more specific than running titles, such section headlines seem intended to shape the reader's response. They provide, in effect, a guide to the structure of the work, serving to emphasise key sections. In doing so they act not only as indicators of ideological difference, guides to locations within the texts and examples of rhetoric, but they also deploy *ad hominem* attacks. Such a combination was also to be found in a later, more famous, religious pamphlet war but there the section headlines became page headlines.

The Martin Marprelate controversy has received much critical attention but the use of running titles in the epitome, as opposed to the earlier synonymous epistle, of Martin Marprelate's *Oh read ouer D. Iohn Bridges for it is worthy worke* (1588) has been little studied. There, page headlines are used to attack Marprelate's opponents and, in some instances, two are used on a single page. These paratextual comments serve a range of purposes from outlining key points – 'What offices and officers the Church is to be gouerned by'; to attacking the opponent's argument – 'Iohn of London against bishops, and so against himselfe'; and on to *ad hominem* attacks – 'Deane of Lincolne (sometimes unlearned Iohn Whitgift) his question', or 'Iohn of London, Iohn of Exeter, and Thomas Winchester, hypocrits'.⁴⁹ Marprelate was also keen to associate his Church of England opponents with Catholicism. We hear that 'Dean Iohn coseneth his brethren with popish reasons' that 'The bishops have no better warrant for themselves, then the Pope' and that 'L Bb. [are] in dignitie popes, in office proud prelates & c.'.⁵⁰ Less concerned than More, Frith and Tyndale with articles of faith, Marprelate nevertheless used similar methods in his page headlines. Attacks on the opponent's arguments were combined with personal insults, while Marprelate went a stage further in his use of page headlines by deploying them to clarify the general thrust of his argument: that the Church of England was too close to Roman Catholic traditions.

If Marprelate's tracts stood at one end of the publishing spectrum, being cheap pamphlets, roughly printed on an itinerant press, John Foxe's *Actes and Monuments* was at the other. An enormous and officially sanctioned folio, it emerged from one of the busiest and most significant early modern printing houses. Although they differed in many ways, Marprelate's and

Foxe's works had one feature in common: they both used page headlines to proclaim a religious position. Susan Felch has described the paratextual features of the second edition of the *Actes and Monuments* as 'a negotiation between a belief in self-authenticating texts [as part of the Protestant tradition] and the need to establish interpretative coherence'.⁵¹ She notes that the addition to the 1570 edition of 'descriptive running titles' (page headlines) directs the reader's perusal of the text. Such a practice differed from the 1563 edition which used a running title of 'Actes and Monuments' (verso) 'of the Church' (recto) throughout.⁵² However, the running titles, section and page headlines deserve closer attention than Felch awards them since they disclose a growing awareness of the possibilities presented by the running-title space.

The bibliographic history of the 1570 edition of *Actes and Monuments* is notoriously difficult to understand.⁵³ Although we cannot with confidence ascribe to any individual the change in practice relating to running titles in the 1570 edition, we can tentatively chart its development. After the preliminaries, the headlines on signatures E1*r* to M6*v* are the same as the running title for the first edition. They act almost as a section title. On signature N1*r*, at the start of the second book of volume one, however, a further element is added. 'Of the Church' is supplemented with '*King Lucius*' in italics. This pattern, of surrounding 'Actes and Monuments' and 'Of the Church' with at least one, and sometimes two, italicised sections is continued, and it is not long before anti-Catholic sentiment emerges. Signature P2*v* refers readers not only to '*Boniface letter to a k. of Engl*' but also to the '*Inco[n]venie[n]ce of Nu[n]ries & Mo[n]kery*'. This arrangement continues until 2L1*r*. After 2L1*r*, reference to the work's title as either 'Actes and Monuments' or 'of the Church' disappears altogether. The text now moves towards section headlines which are the same for a number of pages, before ultimately progressing to page headlines. A number of these headlines contain anti-Catholic, particularly anti-papal, comments, but the majority might be described as bearers of information. Interestingly, however, the headlines of many of the cancel pages, particularly those found early in the work, do emphasise anti-papal sentiment and are in contrast to the arrangements which precede them.

P. S. Dunkin noted that many of the cancels in the early signatures bore a different form of running title from those which had come earlier in the text, but he did not comment on their content.⁵⁴ Thus, signatures *11*r*–*13*v*, for example, share the same page headline of '*King Henry 3. The miserable thraldome and oppression of England under the Pope.*' This is followed in signature *14*r–v* by '*King Henry 3. Exactions and miserable extortions in*

England under the Pope.' Signatures s1*r*–s2*v*, comment '*K. Edgar. King Edgar a great maintainer of monkery. His concubines and bastards*'. These are in stark contrast to the more subdued running titles or section headlines of '*Acts and Monuments*' or '*of the Church*' which are to be found on the un-cancelled signatures which surround them. What is clear, then, is that the cancel pages not only adopt the format routinely deployed after signature 2LI*r* but that they are much more anti-Catholic in tone than the headlines of the earlier sections. When substituting cancel pages, those responsible took the opportunity to attack those who had offended the Protestant Church. Thus, it was not just pamphlets that exploited running titles, section and page headlines for polemical purposes; works which carried the weight of state authority did so too in their effort to promote a history of the English Church.[55]

As noted above, it was not only in religious disputes that the running-title space was used for polemical purposes. As a collection of travel narratives Samuel Purchas's multi-volume text, *Purchas his pilgrimes* (1625) inevitably dealt with encounters between nations. At the time of publication, Anglo-Dutch relations had been soured by the 'Amboyna massacre', despite the religious sympathies of the two countries and their alliance against the Spanish. The notorious (as far as the English were concerned) event, took place in 1624 when Dutch East India Company merchants had apprehended, tried and summarily executed ten members of the English East India Company who they believed were plotting to overthrow the Dutch fort at Amboyna. A diplomatic incident ensued and anti-Dutch sentiment on this matter continued for more than twenty-five years. It was against this background that Samuel Purchas shaped a manuscript he had received from Robert Hayes, an East India Company employee, outlining his experiences at the hands of the Dutch in 1622. Pamela Neville-Sington has revealed that in his capacity as editor Purchas added anti-Dutch comments in the page headlines. He complained of 'The Hollanders base vsage of the English', that 'Heathens [were] more kind then Hollanders, to the English', that the 'Dutch [used] force and fraud', and engaged in 'Inhumane and brutish crueltie'. He persisted in lamenting the 'Periurie, insolencie, and crueltie of the Dutch', and observed that 'the Hollanders will doe not right, nor take no wrong'.[56] Not surprisingly, Purchas had some misgivings. In a 'Note touching the Dutch' that followed the 'Address to the Reader' in volume one, he alluded to the 'Titles on the tops of pages, intended to Offenders, but in such unwarie termes as might by ill willers be extended to the whole Nation'.[57] He produced paste-overs and his misgivings were well-founded, for, as late as 1630, the Dutch Ambassador to England complained about the running titles, citing ten of the nineteen for which Purchas had issued cancel slips.⁵⁸ Despite being buried deep in a multi-volume work, therefore, page headlines could still attract attention.

Running titles, whether in the form of running, section or page headlines, comprised a part of the paratext of early modern books of which both those who produced and those who read them were acutely aware. They need to be studied not only for their bibliographic importance but also for what they tell us about the hermeneutics of the paratext. This space on the page was not deployed mindlessly to reproduce the title of a work or even the chapter headings, but was ingeniously, often wittily and sometimes scurrilously used in a variety of ways in an effort to shape the response of readers. Throughout the early modern period and across a diverse range of texts published in different formats, the producers of early modern books mediated them to readers through running titles. They used a complex set of varying hermeneutics at times endorsing, adapting or re-interpreting the title-page, volume or chapter heading, at others seeking to shape the reading of specific pages or groups of pages. Whether in authorised publications such as Burleigh's pamphlet or Foxe's martyrology, or in works written against those in power, these sections of the paratext could be used to make a point. Authors and those who worked with them asserted the validity of their own position, rhetorically endorsing it, restating it, or refining it, and they mocked their opponents, ridiculing their arguments, insulting them as individuals and belittling their texts. In doing so the use of running titles went far beyond a utilitarian functionality. Noticeably, the running title was often used by those involved in book production to release material which was 'intended to offenders'. Sometimes, as in the case of *Purchas his pilgrimes*, it succeeded a little too well.

CHAPTER 3

Changed opinion as to flowers

Juliet Fleming

> The flower is one of the typical passions of the human spirit. One of the wheels of its contrivance. One of its routine metaphors . . .
> To liberate ourselves, let's liberate the flower. Let's change our minds about it . . .
> By some devolative revolution, Let us return it, safe from all definition, to what it is. – But what, then? – Quite obviously, a conceptacle.
> (Francis Ponge, 'Changed Opinion as to Flowers').

Printers' flowers are the designs produced in printed books through the use of type-ornament. That is, they result from the pressure on paper of individual pieces of inked type that bear decorative designs rather than letter symbols. Used individually, printers' flowers, which are also called fleurons, are as old as moveable type itself, but, in the middle of the sixteenth century, designs were developed that were intended to be used not as single units, but as composed into serial patterns. So combined, printers' flowers could be used to make ornaments and borders of any size and shape: and within a few years of their first appearance, in Venice in 1552, they were being used by printers across Europe. Henry Denham may have been the first English printer to use flowers in combination, which he did for the first time in 1564; by 1566 their use in England was widespread. But there is, to date, no comprehensive index of English printers' flowers; and in this chapter I refer to individual designs using the numbers assigned to them by Francis Meynell and Stanley Morison in their foundational article of 1923, 'Printers' Flowers and Arabesques'.[1]

In two earlier essays I have described the allure, and some of the functions, of sixteenth-century printers' flowers. 'How to Look at a Printed Flower' aimed to specify the aesthetic being of English type-ornament, arguing that, when the 'arabesque' designs of printers' flowers were combined with the new technology of standardised reproduction that was moveable type, they produced patterns that could be supposed by Europeans to have no representative aim, and thus began to comprise an aesthetic order that, perhaps for the first time, was freed from the obligation to signify.[2] My second essay, 'How Not to Look at a Printed Flower', was concerned with some of the more overtly practical functions of flowers, demonstrating, for example, that one such function was to keep pages clean during printing, since the presence of type-ornament prevented the paper from bowing down during pressing, to pick up ink that might have strayed onto the furniture outside the text block.[3] In both essays my aim was to free sixteenth-century type-ornament from the associative burdens it carries as long as it is considered to represent flowers.[4] Beyond this, I tried to identify, as the special achievement of printers' flowers, an iconic neutrality that interrupts what might be called the semiotic drive of the printed page. I wanted to show that, although printers' flowers form part of a printed page, their purpose can be fully understood only if it is considered outside the pressures of a discursive logic – that is, if we can approach them, not only without asking what it is that they mean to say, but accepting, also, that there are visual orders that 'show' nothing.

My aim in this third essay is to re-engage the question of semiosis and, this time, to allow it some purchase within the subject of printers' flowers. But I do not intend to retreat to the position against which my first two essays were written, or to encourage the thought that, as one early historian of print put it, sixteenth-century printers' flowers are 'germane to the subject matter' (being 'frequently emblematical and monitory').[5] For if the term 'germane' is taken to mean that flowers spring from the same stock as the subject matter, and thus have an iconic relation to the content of the texts they help to present, the proposition is quickly disproved. Iconic connections could be quickly established, where they are not immediately obvious, in some texts printed after 1620, and particularly in those that were the work of jobbing printers (who might, for example, print a funeral sermon with a border of death's heads and hour-glasses). However, such indexing was rarely attempted in the sixteenth century, when printers chose their flowers, almost exclusively, from a limited repertory of non-representational arabesque designs.[6]

Against this, it may be said that there are sixteenth-century English books – John Conway's *The poesie of floured prayers* is one such – that, at least to modern eyes, apparently intend to engage the floral connotations of their own type-ornament. For Conway's title describes a florilegium, or gathering, of choicest prayers ('flower' was conventionally used to indicate an excellent rhetorical trope or figure), while also suggesting, what is indeed the case, that these chosen prayers are embellished with flower-like patterns:

in each of its four editions the text of Conway's book is set within a fixed or skeleton frame of type-ornament, such that every page is bordered, on all sides, with running fleuron designs (Figure 3.1).[7] But 'floured' also suggests that which is refined or bolted: flour is the best part, or 'flower', of the wheat (such, apparently, is the origin of the term), and floured prayers would also be the better part of a collection of prayers, selected through a process of sifting. Since the noun 'flour' came into being as a metaphor from 'flower' it is impossible, as well as unnecessary, to say which term Conway intended for his title: my point is only that the heavy presence of printers' flowers in these volumes will not help us decide, even if it could be established that they were there at his request. For if the flowers in printers' flowers could be positioned by Conway or his printer or compositor to connote anything at all, it is not flowers as they grow in the field, but flowers as these are used, in their turn, as metaphors, to evoke that which is embellished, ornamented, or otherwise marked as being at the height of excellence. Whichever term Conway intended in his title, botanical specimen or fine meal, it would clearly be a mistake to attempt to 'liberate' it from its metaphorical state by returning it to the field or mill.

In addressing the semiosis of sixteenth-century type-ornament, I will not, then, be attending to what can be said about flowers, either as the organs of plants, or as one of the 'routine metaphors' of our traditions. Instead, I want to address the fact that one of the most important functions of sixteenth-century printers' flowers, as described by the earliest historians of print, was to articulate the division of texts. For printers' flowers were concerned with the meaningful positioning of writing within the physical and cognitive spaces that comprise the interior architecture of early modern books, and my aim here is to demonstrate that, in late sixteenth-century England, this architecture began to exhibit, at certain local levels, some degree of conformity as to the design elements chosen, with the result that the specific disposition of flowers began to function, albeit in fleeting, unsystematic, and sometimes unintended ways, to mark books as being the products of particular printers or coteries, and, at least in one case, as belonging to a particular genre.

I

The first use of the English term 'flowers' to describe type-ornament occurs in Joseph Moxon's *Mechanick Exercises* (1684), which advises printers to provide themselves 'with Flowers to set over the Head of a Page at the beginning of a book'.[8] Seventy years later, in *The printer's grammar* (1755),

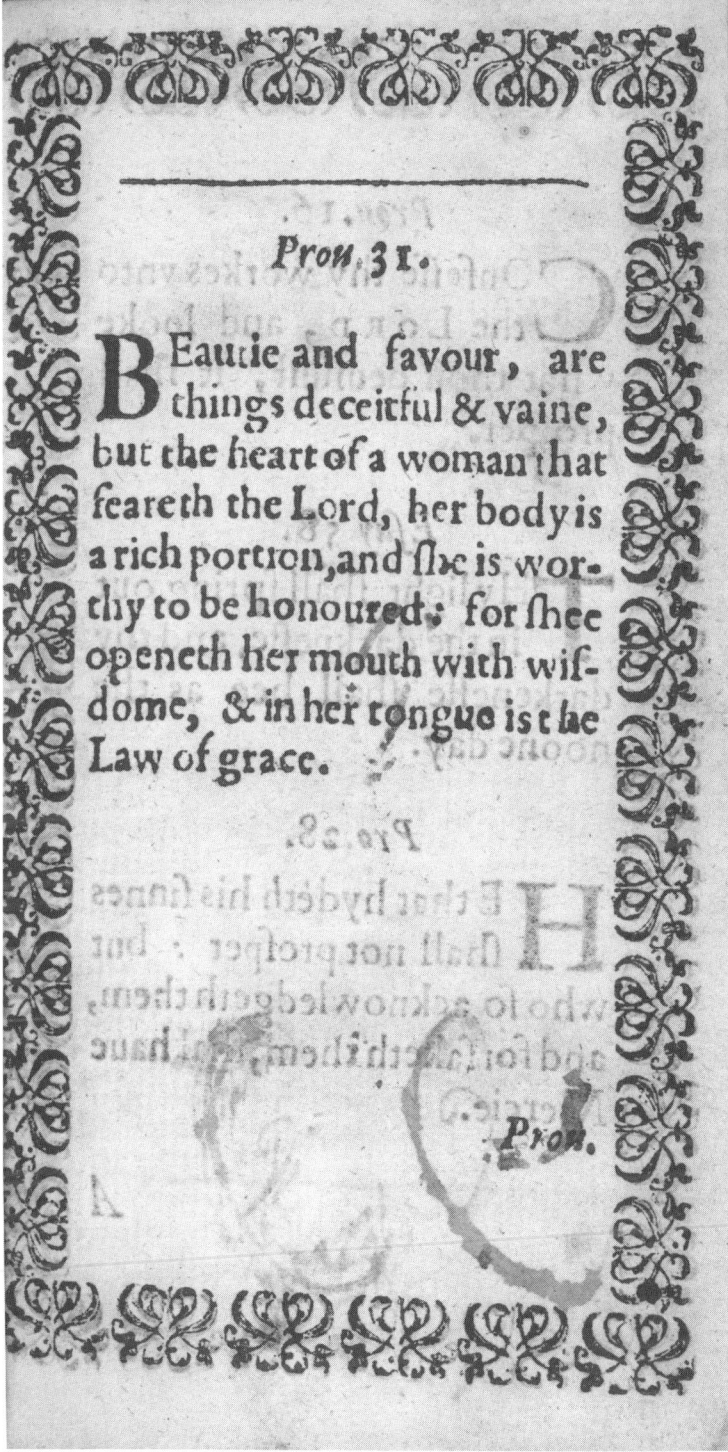

Prou. 31.

Beautie and favour, are things deceitful & vaine, but the heart of a woman that feareth the Lord, her body is a rich portion, and she is worthy to be honoured; for shee openeth her mouth with wisdome, & in her tongue is the Law of grace.

3.1 John Conway, *The poesie of floured prayers*, 1611, sig. A6r.

John Smith gave a more extended account of this practice, noting that flowers were used 'at the Head of such pages as either began the main Work, or else a separate part of it', as well as on 'several other occasions' (it should be noted that Smith's description amalgamates past and present practices, and when he says that flowers 'are' or 'were' used for particular purposes he speaks in an imperfect present tense that designates no particular period):

> Thus they are used in Miscellaneous work, where a single row of Flowers is put over the Head of each fresh subject, but not where two or more are comprehended under same title; which commonly have 'Another' – 'By the Same etc.' for their Head. As therefore flowers appertaineth to Heads, it ought to be a rule that a single row of them should be put over a Head that begins a Page, be it Part, Chapter, Article or any other Division, in work that has its divisions separated by flowers. But as the construction of flower head pieces entirely depends upon the fancy of the compositor, it would be presumption in us to direct him on this point; we therefore leave the displaying of flowers to his own judgment.[9]

Smith's is the first full account of the use of flowers by English printers, and this passage contains three points worth underlining: first, when he wrote, the disposition of printers' flowers was not governed by firmly established conventions, nor could he identify these with any certainty in the work of earlier printers; second, it is not clear from Smith's account who is responsible for the placement, rather than for the construction, of printers' flowers; third, Smith has seen flower borders used in miscellanies, where their function is, as he understands it, to differentiate topics.

II

While Smith is confident that the general purpose of printers' flowers is to announce divisions within a book, most particularly by marking where the 'main work' begins, it seems that no firm conventions had been established according to which this marking was undertaken. In 1723 the French printer Martin Fertel advised that flowers 'can be placed at the end of all sorts of different sections, when there is insufficient space left to begin a new title, and also at the end of a whole part, when there is not enough room for a woodcut ornament', while in 1778 Edward Rowe Mores observed: 'Metalflowers were the first ornaments used to be set at the head of the first page and at the tail of the last page, as well as at the head and tail of any separate part of the whole work. and [sic] they were sometimes used as an edging to the matter according to the taste of the author or the printer'.[10] That is, printers' flowers were used to begin, end, run alongside of, and enclose a wide variety of textual units. Although Smith saw the advantage of a standardised use of flowers it is evident, both from his own account, and from the work that survives, that such rules had not been in force, and Smith concedes that the construction of type-ornaments is and must be left to the compositor's discretion.

But is it possible that the choice and placing, rather than the construction, of flowers and other ornaments in sixteenth-century printed books did sometimes reflect what Mores described as 'the taste of the author'? John Harington's translation of Ariosto's *Orlando Furioso* (Richard Field, 1591) is perhaps the best-documented example of an Elizabethan work whose writer took a controlling interest in the details of its design and production. A surviving note from Harington, written on the manuscript from which Richard Field was working as he set the text, advising the printer where to place the 'Allegorie', suggests that it should be introduced 'with some prety knotte', and requests that it, the 'Apologie', and 'all the prose that ys to come except the table' be set 'in the same printe that Putnam's book ys'. Since, as Philip Gaskell points out, the passages specified by Harington were indeed set in the fount of pica Roman that Field had used for Puttenham's *Arte of English Poesie* (1589), it is a reasonable inference that the woodcut border used as a head-piece to the 'Allegorie' also met with Harington's approval as the 'prety knotte' he had envisaged.[11]

However, while Harington asked for a head-piece for the 'Allegorie', he did not specify which one; and it could well have been the compositor who chose to use not a piece of the flower border that frames the argument at the beginning of each alternative book of the poem, but the woodcut ornament that serves as a head-piece over its dedicatory letter to the queen. That is, while Harington had considerable input into the page design of his book, there is every possibility that the *specific* fleuron and woodcut borders used in the two editions of *Orlando Furioso* printed during his life reflected the compositor's, rather than the author's, choice.[12] Nevertheless, unless the author was the victim of concerted ill luck, the incidence of one particular flower in the published works of Richard Barnfield may suggest a different scenario. For a majority of the works published during Barnfield's lifetime (three of which appeared anonymously) were dressed with a single flower (design number 19), although each was the work of a different printer. The earliest of these, *Greenes funeralls* (John Danter, 1594) (anonymous; attributed to Barnfield and Nicholas Breton by the STC), is remarkable for the heavy use it makes of this flower, which is composed into a head-piece border for the letter, 'To the Gentlemen Readers', and then into head- and tail-piece borders for every page that follows. These borders vary in width to fill the space left by the placing of poems on the page: if there are many lines

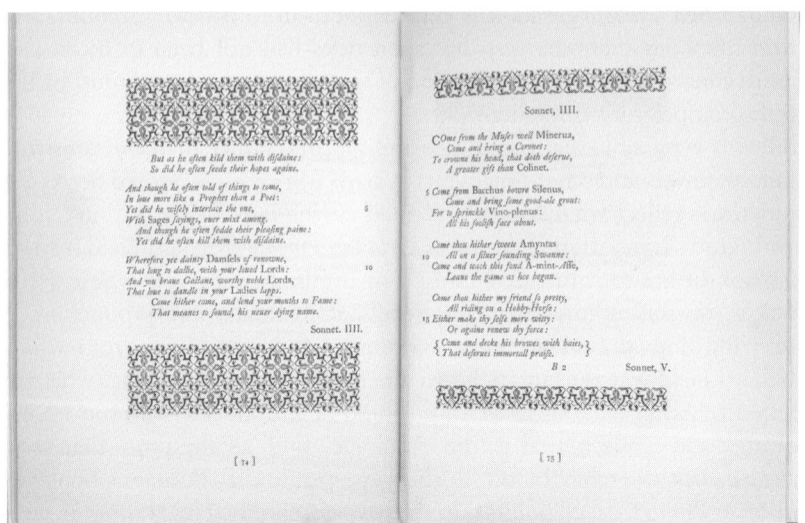

3.2 Richard Barnfield, *Greenes funeralls*, 1594, sigs. B1*v*–B2*r*.

of verse, the borders contract; if fewer, the number of lines of flowers expands, sometimes becoming so dominant on the page that they overwhelm the appearance of the poetry (Figure 3.2). And of Barnfield's remaining works, four were dressed with borders or ornaments of the same flower 19.[13] It is thus worth entertaining the thought that the author chose this flower for his published writing, and that its use reflects either his own 'taste', or his decision to have his separate and often anonymous works marked in such a way that they could appear, to those who had the eyes to see, to comprise a collective oeuvre.

If granted, the example of Barnfield renders visible the work that printers' flowers can do in local circumstances, by linking and identifying books according to a visual code that overrides, and may take no account of, their contents. Such codes were perhaps used to articulate the work of a single author (as the case of Barnfield suggests), or indeed of a coterie: in 1595 Peter Short used the same scheme of flowers to print both Spenser's *Amoretti and Epithalamion* and the Countess of Pembroke's translation of Robert Garnier's *The Tragedie of Antonie*: in 1598 he used the scheme again to print an edition of Daniel's *Delia*, and thereby gave visual articulation to the relations that bound Spenser and Daniel to their patron. But it is worth remarking that such a code may also take no account of the intentions or connections of those authors whose books are so treated. Harington wanted his *Orlando Furioso* to look a certain way, and Richard Field and his compositor apparently obliged him: nevertheless, Harington could not have prevented Field or another printer or compositor from using the same ornamental schemes in another man or woman's book, and thereby, for whatever reason, producing a work whose visual appearance allowed it to claim unauthorised relation to his own.

III

Wendy Wall's *The Imprint of Gender* is remarkable within Renaissance literary history for the energy with which it explores the work done by the typographical and physical formats of English printed books in the second half of the sixteenth century. Wall argues that, in their new material formats, these books constituted 'complicated configurations' of poetic motifs and material possibilities within which the 'idea of the book', as both a commodity and as a specific textual printed form, was negotiated in contradistinction to the material practices of manuscript circulation. She demonstrates, for example, that the concept of authorship specific to printed books was not the inherited 'residue of the dying world of manuscript culture', but was rather the 'typographical effect' of the book's new physical forms. Wall plays close attention to the ways in which texts associated with manuscript circulation, as well as texts written specifically for the new technology, were 're-formatted', and given new 'organizational frames' by print; and she is the first to have noticed, as a consequential fact, that three sixteenth-century sonnet sequences, Samuel Daniel's *Delia* (1594), Spenser's *Amoretti* (1595), and Richard Barnfield's *Cynthia* (1595), 'each framed the individual poems through a simple but uniform page border' of printed flowers.

Wall speculates that the effect of such borders was akin to that of a modern frame: she argues that, together with the numbering of individual sonnets, they 'served to create the effect of a closed and complete poetic unit, finished without the reader's collaborative aid', and that in doing so they 'strengthened the autonomy of the book artefact' while heightening the linear and asocial nature of the reading experience.[14] The format that puts one poem, with decorative borders, on each page of a sonnet sequence was, in fact, quite remarkably widespread in the printed books of early modern England. In 1592 John Charlewood printed the first two editions of *Delia* for Simon Waterstone (STC 6243.2 and 6243.3). These editions each had one sonnet per page, numbered with Roman numerals at the top: STC 6243.2 had strips of flowers at the bottom of each page, while STC 6243.3

had in their place one of three wood cut border designs. Very similar layouts, using different and varied ornaments, were in fact used for a *majority* of the English sonnet collections that were published before 1594: beyond the first two editions of *Delia* and the sequences Wall herself describes, these include Henry Constable's *Phillis* (John Charlewood for R. Smith, 1592), Giles Fletcher's *Licia* (John Legat, 1593), Thomas Lodge's *Phillis* (James Roberts for John Busbie, 1593), Richard Barnfield's *The Affectionate Shepherd* (John Danter, 1594), Michael Drayton's *Ideas Mirrour* (James Roberts for Nicholas Ling, 1594), and the anonymous *Zeperia* (the Widow Orwin for N. L. and John Busbie, 1594). An early English model for these collections is Thomas Watson's *Hekatompathia* (John Wolfe for Gabriel Cawood, 1582), which presents one numbered poem per page, with a prose explanation of its occasion above, and some form of printers' ornament below, each one: in the later collections the prose introductions are absent, and the lower ornament is always a border. These facts support Wall's thesis that by 1594 English printers were using formats that severed ties with the practices of coterie manuscript circulation, in this case by standardising the appearance of printed sonnet sequences as an emergent genre.

But Wall's argument can now be elaborated and redirected. For none of the early historians of print can be taken to suggest that flower borders were used to 'frame' textual elements, if by framing is meant the enclosure of something within a structure whose parts form an outline or 'outwork' to the thing enclosed. For it is a remarkable fact that, while border schemes are often reserved for the presentation of short individual poems within sequences, in other cases the use of borders is continued, in whole or in part, across some or all of the other textual units in the same volume, including longer poems and prefatory and concluding materials. In *Amoretti and Epithalamion*, Short used head- and tail-borders of flower 20 not only for the sonnets of the sequence, but also for the two commendatory sonnets that open it, for the nine anacreontics that close it, for the title-page and every subsequent page of the Epithalamion that follows it, and for the statement 'Imprinted by P. S. for William Ponsonby' that ends the whole volume (Figure 3.3). Such practices suggest that, even within sonnet sequences, flowers were used, not to mark the single page as the territory of a single sonnet, but to articulate the composition and identity of the entire printed volume as something more than the sum of its parts. Furthermore, although there are several late sixteenth- and early seventeenth-century English books, such as Conway's *Poesie of floured prayers*, that have a complete flower border around each page, it cannot be assumed that even these

Changed opinion as to flowers

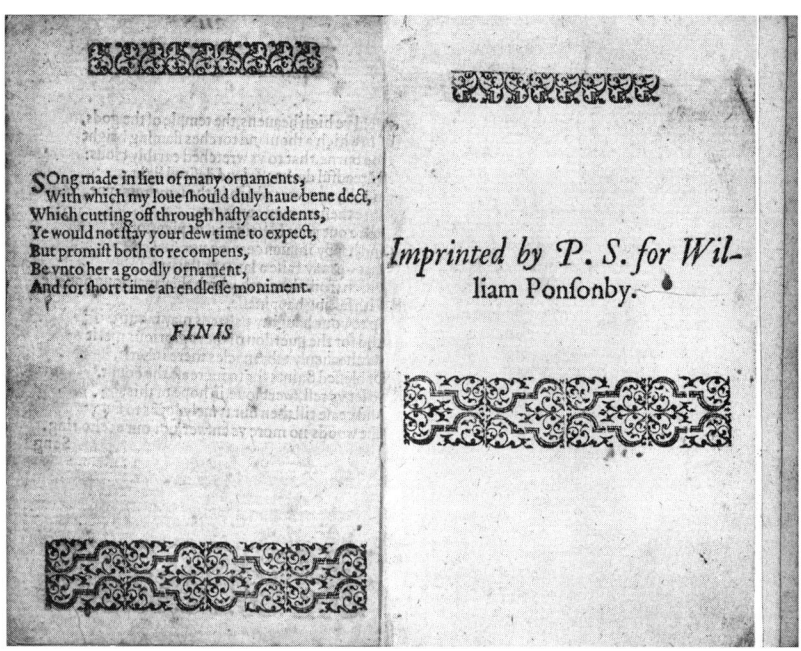

3.3 Final opening of Edmund Spenser, *Amoretti and Epithalamion*, 1595.

approximate to the modern notion of a frame. Rayna Kalas has recently argued that, in the sixteenth century, 'the word *frame* did not have as its primary sense, as it does today, the alienable quadrilateral ornament surrounding a painting ... before framing was associated with the adornment of a consummate aesthetic object, framing was about predicating the way a thing is to be wrought'.[15] To frame a house or an argument under this definition is to fit together a structure on which other materials could be hung, or, more simply, to put things in a certain order: 'all verse is but a frame of words' says Samuel Daniel in his *Defence of Rhyme* (1603).[16] To re-envision framing in this way is to discover useful ways of reconceiving the relations between the form and content of books as these were remade in the first century of print. If, following Wall, we think of the aim of a sixteenth-century printer as being not only the translation of manuscript into printed writing but also the production of a printed book – and if we give full weight to this second aim – we can begin to imagine the book as a mould into which words are poured in order to give expression to its structure as a device for reading. But here frontispieces, head- and tail-pieces and other ornaments take on a new appearance: they need no longer be seen as ornaments to embellish a book, or to mark off part of its contents for particular notice, but as part of an armature that determined the form the text would take.

Here it is worth wondering whether head- and tail-borders did not come to exert ideational pressure on the poets who undertook English sonnet sequences in the middle of the 1590s. Such a suggestion amounts to saying that some English poets may have set out to write, not sonnets, but printed sonnets – that they visualised fourteen lines of Roman type, set alone on a page, within head- and tail-borders, before they set pen to paper. The ideal form of the English sonnet in the late 1590s – the form it took in the mind before it was composed – would then have been like the view from the castle on the Isle of Shallot, whose walls 'overlooked a space of flowers'. While such a proposition will doubtless be resisted, it may at least be allowed that sixteenth-century English poets responded to visual formats that were given new articulation in the medium of print by knowing how to produce the units of writing that would fit them, and that in doing so they allowed into what Puttenham calls 'poetic making' both the labour of the technicians and the operations of the machines that constituted the work of the press.

IV

Wall uses as the illustration for her argument not the first, but the third edition of Daniel's *Delia*, which was printed by James Roberts and Edward Allde for Simon Waterson in 1594. As in the earlier sequences, each numbered sonnet occupies one page; but here a single row of printers' flowers runs along the top of each page, while the ornament at the bottom has become a double row of the same flowers – the design used is composed of the flower 19 favoured by Barnfield. As Wall's illustrations show, the same scheme, in the same flower, was used the following year, in 1595, for one of the two editions of Barnfield's *Cynthia* that were printed for Humfrey Lownes: on the evidence of the flowers we can now say that the printer of the first of these editions (STC 1483), who has not otherwise been identified, was likely to have been James Roberts. For Roberts used the same scheme of flowers several times in the next few years: for another edition of Daniel's *Delia* (James Roberts for Simon Waterstone, 1595), for Henry Constable's *Diana ... Augmented* (James Roberts for R. Smith, 1595), for Gervase Markham *The Most honorable tragedy of Sir Richard Grinuile* (James Roberts for R. Smith, 1595), for Markham's *The Poem of Poems, or Sions Muse* (James Roberts for Humfrey Lownes, 1596), for Richard Lince's *Diella* (James Roberts for Henry Olney, 1596), and for the anonymous *Anon ... or loves complaint* (James Roberts for Humfrey Lownes, 1597). In 1598 Roberts printed, for Edmond Matts, John Marston's *The Metamorphosis of Pygmalion's Image*, which doubles the upper row of flowers but otherwise leaves the scheme unchanged; five years later he printed Michael Drayton's poem *To the Majestie of King James* (James Roberts for Humfrey Lownes, 1603), which uses a single row of the same flowers as a running header throughout the text.

Roberts also used flower 19, in head- and tail-pieces, and in other formats (for example, as small ornaments, or as frontispiece borders), in many other of the books that he printed, and his work in the 1590s seems to provide a tantalising instance of a 'preference' for particular flower combinations that A. E. M. Kirwood once speculated might prove to characterise the work of individual print shops.[17] When R. B. McKerrow listed the marks and devices used by printers in England and Scotland before 1640 he admitted that there must be some uncertainty as to what a device was, since any ornament could, after all, be pressed into that service. And faced with two metal-cast crowned roses used in two sizes by Valentine Simmes from 1598 to 1603, either of which could have been 'a common ornament bought from a type-founder' (and either of which could be classified as a printers' flower), McKerrow decided to err on the side of comprehensiveness and include them as devices. That is, although he rightly felt that 'some of the commoner metal ornaments can at once be dismissed as nothing more than ornaments', others of them could not: and indeed, McKerrow also remarked a small group of designs of which it could be said that they 'were not born devices, but had deviceship thrust upon them'.[18] Flowers 12 and 16 in the work of Valentine Simmes, 19 in the work of James Roberts, and 8 and 25 in the work of Henry Denham were each used in a manner that suggests that their appearance, either on the title-page, or in the body of a book, was sometimes designed, in certain years, to substitute for, or to supplement, a device 'properly so-called', or at least to recall other books from the same printer. Although Roberts was by no means the only London printer to own a fount of flower 19 in these years, and his use of it is not sufficiently consistent to be viewed as contributing towards a putative 'house style', his setting of flower 19 into a running header and footer does seem to represent a series style for him in the 1590s, for it was in that format that he consistently set collections of poems, and thereby advertised to readers the provenance of such volumes in his own print shop. Again, however, it should be noted that Roberts was not the only printer to use flower 19 even in this characteristic way: Bartholomew Griffin's sonnet sequence *Fidessa* has the same scheme, even though it was printed by the Widow Orwin for Matthew Lownes in 1596. The third sonnet sequence illustrated by Wall is taken from Edmund Spenser's *Amoretti and Epithalamion*, as printed in 1595 by Peter Short for William Ponsonby; here too each sonnet occupies a single page with a double row of flowers as a running footer (design number 20). Each sonnet is numbered, and headed by a single row of flowers from a design not listed by Meynell and Morison, but fairly common in sixteenth-century English books, which I shall call 20a (see Figure 3.3).

V

Further investigation of the use made by English printers, during these years, of flowers 19 and 20 would surely bear further and more certain fruit than I can produce here (in particular, James Roberts's commitment to flower 19 calls for fuller investigation). A few observations can, however, be made. First, in the 1590s, English sonnet sequences were, almost without exception, printed according to the format observed by Roberts. That is, each sonnet appeared on a single page, numbered, with a head and lower border of printers' flowers or other ornaments.[19] Indeed, the only exception to this formatting convention in the 1590s of which I am aware is, provocatively enough, Philip Sidney's *Astrophil to Stella* (printed for the first time in 1591 by J. Charlewood for Thomas Newman), and we are now in a position to notice that Sidney's work ostentatiously eschewed the presentation expected of a sonnet sequence printed in the 1590s.

It can also be noted that while there clearly is a correlation between these flower schemes and sonnet sequences as an emergent printed genre, sonnets do not constitute the only object of such schemes, and their association does not govern the other generic and typographical uses to which printers' flowers were put in the sixteenth century. It is a remarkable fact that Short and Roberts each used the schemes we can now associate with their sonnet sequences to print a closet drama, Short using the same scheme of flowers 20 and 20a to print both Spenser's *Amoretti*, and the Countess of Pembroke's *Tragedie of Antonie* (Figure 3.4); while in the same year, 1595, Roberts used the scheme he had devised for his first edition of *Delia* to print (along with another edition of *Delia*, Barnfield's *Cynthia*, and Constable's *Diana*) Gervase Markham's *The Most honorable tragedy of Sir Richard Grinuile*.

The use of the same scheme of borders to print two or more books in quick succession raises the question of whether sixteenth-century English printers ever reserved the skeleton frames represented by composed flower

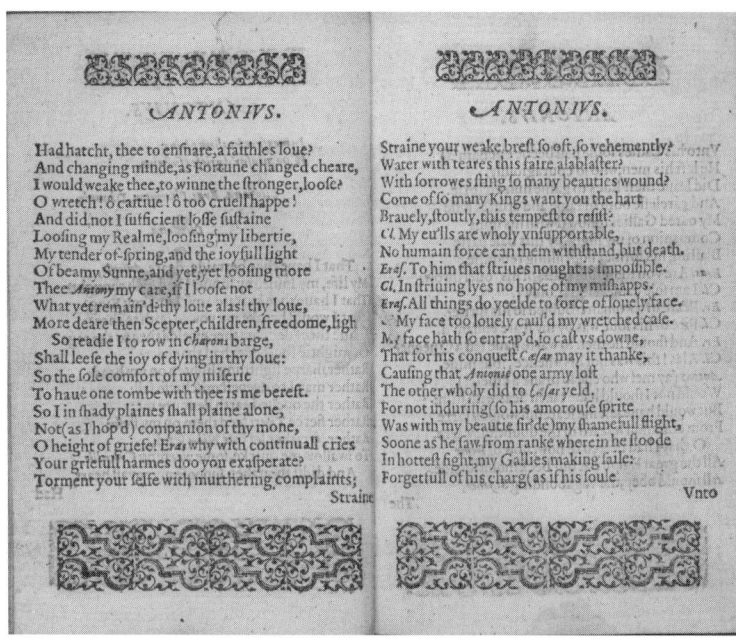

3.4 The Countess of Pembroke's translation of Garnier's *Tragedie of Antonie*, 1595, sigs. B6v–B7r.

borders for reuse in other volumes. John Smith's recommendation, made in the middle of the eighteenth century, that flower compositions be preserved and reused as a way of saving the compositor's time, now appears sensible, indeed alluring. Smith, who feared that flowers might fall out of use because of the time it takes to compose them, suggested, by way of remedy, that printers should 'preserve the substance' of the flower composition 'intire, for occasional use: being first well secured and conglutinated (by wetting it with Gum water), to keep it from breaking'.[20] Such a practice (which Smith seems to suggest was not common, but perhaps not unknown, in the eighteenth century) or the even simpler one of leaving the skeleton on the composing stone and using it for the next work printed raises the further question of whether, to meet such general purposes, texts were cut or stretched – either typographically, or by the addition or omission of written material – to fit the frames of the volumes in question (and here it should be acknowledged that a skeleton made of wood cut ornaments, such as was used by Short in 1598 to print both Abraham Fleming's *The Diamond of Devotion* and Edward Hutchins's *David's Sling against great Goliath*, might prove equally procrustean). In such cases, of course, the relation that is usually assumed to hold between what we might call the text and its paratext is reversed: the skeleton frame appears not to 'finish' the textual unit, but to dictate its extension; and the frame is preserved and reused, while the text is removed and dismantled.

To my surprise, however, I have found no evidence of the preservation and reuse of skeleton frames in sixteenth-century England. Sixteenth-century flowers proved difficult to compose, and large schemes used in English books usually display a high level of variation and error in their designs. Compositions of printers' flowers that were reused between surviving works ought, therefore, to be easily identifiable, as containing the same variants. But I have come across no such examples: indeed, the evidence points in the opposite direction. For example, of the three octavo works printed by Roberts in 1595 with upper and lower borders of flower 19 on each page, one – Henry Constable's *Diana* – has five flowers set over a rule for the header, and seven flowers without a rule for the lower border, while the other two, Daniel's *Delia* and Markham's *The Most honorable tragedy of Sir Richard Grinuile*, have the same header but only six flowers in the lower border. And the composition of the flowers between even these two works is not identical: *Delia* is set without variants, but in *The Most honorable tragedy* one of the flowers in the upper border is reversed according to a pattern of intervals that demonstrates that, for this work at least, the flower headers were reserved in position in the form while the text blocks were changed (which is to say that a skeleton frame was indeed used). Similarly, *Amoretti and Epithalamion* and *The Tragedie of Antonie*, which were both printed in octavo by Short in 1595, share an identical scheme of flowers, with eight flowers of design 20 comprising a lower border, and nine flowers of design 20a comprising an upper border, on each page, but once again the composition of the flowers is non-identical, with each work containing recurrent variants in both upper and lower borders that the other lacks. That is: *Amoretti* and *Antonie* were each set by Short, in the same year, within a skeleton frame of flowers 20 and 20a, but the composition of this frame is non-identical between the two works (see Figures 3.3 and 3.4).

One explanation of this phenomenon could be that the compositors made corrections between printing each work: successfully in Robert's case, where *Delia* would represent a correction of the *The Most honorable tragedy*; but less successfully in the case of Short, who, if he was indeed attempting correction between the printing of the two works, must have introduced new variants into the scheme of whichever one constituted the 'corrected' version. But I am grateful to Randall McLeod for pointing out to me that Short's compositor appears to have made corrections to the flowers in the middle of printing just the *Amoretti* itself, for the work displays variance in the composition of flower 20 on the same page of different copies – and here, again, it is hard (although perhaps not impossible) to tell which is the 'corrected' and which the 'uncorrected' copy, for each copy contains variants that are unique to itself.[21] A second possible explanation for the evident non-identity of flower schemes between works is that compositors dismantled them, in part or in whole, at the end of each print job, perhaps reserving certain elements as composed to be used elsewhere, otherwise distributing all the type back into its boxes.

Such facts as I have been able to assemble indicate nothing so clearly as that we know remarkably little about the composition of sixteenth-century printers' flowers. Smith's suggestion that flower compositions could be preserved between print jobs to save the compositor's time appeals to modern sensibilities that have learned to dislike wasted effort, while continuing, at some level, to distrust techniques of reproduction that do not value or preserve original forms through time. But perhaps the necessity of dismantling type-ornament, like text, as soon as the print run was taken from it, did not dismay sixteenth-century letterpress printers, for whom the movability and recomposition of type was the *sine qua non* of their practice and livelihood. Compositors may have reserved title-page frames, or parts or whole of large compositions, and may have adapted these to the exigencies of the next work printed, but they may equally well have begun each project anew with a trained and experienced eye. What is remarkable about the reiteration of flower schemes in sixteenth-century English books is, then, not that compositors reserved and reused borders and skeleton frames (which may or may not have happened), but that, without reserving these elements, they undertook to reproduce border schemes between works, deliberately, and according to a logic of convenience that is not that of a simple mechanical reproduction.

It is thus worth remaining open-minded to the possibility that sixteenth-century printers' flowers were used, in ways that may be described (although they never were, and cannot now be, codified), to mark books as belonging to a particular genre or kind, as having come from a particular print shop, as being the work of a particular author or coterie – or, alternatively, as wanting to look as if they were any of these. Much work remains to be done before the use of printers' flowers could be interpreted along these lines in anything other than an anecdotal way; and it may be that sixteenth-century fashions were often so local, and changed so quickly, that they will prove to be unrecoverable. But to continue to ignore the presence of printed flowers in sixteenth-century English books is to look away, not only from an untapped source of bibliographical evidence, but also from a feature that was valued and read, in ways we have not bothered to recover, by contemporary authors, printers, publishers, purchasers, and readers.

CHAPTER 4

The beginning of 'The End': terminal paratext and the birth of print culture

William H. Sherman

> ... print is comfortable only with finality.
> Walter Ong, *Orality and Literacy* (1982)

In Gérard Genette's foundational survey of the liminal features in texts that we now (thanks to him) call 'paratexts', he discusses book and chapter titles, authors' names, publishers' imprints, dedications, epigraphs, prefaces, footnotes, post-publication interviews and even public reviews, but he does not devote a single word to the conventional forms developed to bring books to a close. Genette never intended his account to be exhaustive: he uses his 'Conclusion' to acknowledge that 'this inventory of paratextual elements remains incomplete' and to outline some of the areas that he has knowingly ignored.[1] But conclusions themselves are not among them, nor are afterwords, postscripts, codas, epilogues, envoys, explicits, mottos, colophons, privileges, registers, errata, subscription lists, advertisements, ornaments, end-papers or any of the other features that have been used over the course of many centuries to mark the ends of books.

Genette might well be puzzled, then, by the phrase '*terminal* paratext' in my title: it would probably strike him as something of an oxymoron if not an outright contradiction in terms. Virtually all of the paratextual elements in his inventory are located at the beginnings of books, not simply outside the text proper (as the prefix 'para' implies) but before it can be said to have begun; and most of them belong to what we now tend to call the 'front matter'. Furthermore, the guiding metaphors that run throughout *Paratexts*, serving as his most interesting glosses on the term and its applications, are all essentially *preliminary*: in the introduction, paratext is described as the '*threshold*, or ... "vestibule" that offers the world at large the possibility of either stepping inside or turning back' (2), and in the conclusion it becomes the 'canal lock' that brings a text to the same level as its successive publics, and then the 'airlock that helps the reader pass without too much respiratory difficulty from one world to the other' (408). While some of these metaphors work in both directions, reversing their operations at the ends of books, none of Genette's discussions acknowledge, much less explore, the work that paratexts might do to usher readers *out of* the textual worlds they enter.

This work would, however, have been central to the textual expectations of authors, printers, and readers in the Renaissance. After all, not only were the so-called preliminary gatherings usually the *last* pages to be printed during the hand-press period[2] but, for the first century or so of printing, the 'front matter' could often be found in the *back* of the book.[3] As Elizabeth Armstrong noted in her study of French book-privileges, *Before Copyright*, 'the end of the book, rather than the beginning, was the position in which most readers at the close of the fifteenth century would expect to find if anywhere details of the place, date and circumstances of publication'.[4] Even after this information had migrated to the title-page, other preliminary material including tables of contents, addresses to the reader and dedicatory epistles or verses, could still be found in the backs of books. In Cardinal William Allen's *A true, sincere and modest defence of English Catholics* (1584), for instance, the end of the text is clearly marked with a tapered paragraph capped by the phrase 'Laus Deo' ('Praise be to God'). On the next page we find the beginning of a table headed 'The Contents of this Booke', and at least one contemporary reader was sufficiently struck by the position of this table to note on the title-page, 'The Conte*n*tes is in the Ende'.[5]

Genette's study is almost exclusively concerned with books produced after these features had moved to the opening pages where, in the Anglophone world, they have remained ever since. But the silence of *Paratexts* on the subject of endings is surprising nonetheless, and for at least three reasons: first, many continental publishers, including most French ones, continue to print much of the front matter at the back of the book; second, Genette derives almost all of his examples from prose fiction and, as one of the twentieth century's great narratologists, we would expect him to have inherited Aristotle's insistence that stories, by definition, have endings as well as beginnings and middles, endings that reveal the ultimate shape or purpose of a text; and third, he suggests on his opening page that 'the paratext is what enables a text to become a book and to be offered as such to its readers' (1). If this is true of the words that open a book, why should it be any less true of those that close it? It could be argued, in fact, that the words and signs that signal the final boundary of a text, telling its readers that it is a discrete and in some sense complete unit, do more to make it a book, and to announce it as such, than any other feature (with the possible exception of the stitching and binding). In a very real sense, a text cannot be a book until it is finished.

Perhaps Genette felt that there was simply very little to say about 'the end'. After all, very little has been said about it by other writers. There are studies of textual beginnings aplenty, but the other end of the book has been curiously neglected by critical and bibliographical scholars alike. Medievalists can now turn to D. Vance Smith's *The Book of the Incipit: Beginnings in the Fourteenth Century*, but there is as yet no *Book of the Explicit*;[6] and Edward Said's groundbreaking book on *Beginnings* has yet to be matched by a comparable study of *Endings*.[7] In a brief lecture from 1995, Giorgio Agamben observed that 'studies of the end of the poem ... are almost entirely lacking', though this genre has, in fact, fared better than others, and students of the subject can turn to I. A. Richards's 1963 essay, 'How Does a Poem Know When It Is Finished?', Barbara Herrnstein Smith's 1968 book on *Poetic Closure: A Study of How Poems End*, and now Paul Muldoon's 2006 Oxford Poetry Lectures on *The End of the Poem*.[8] When it comes to fiction, there has been very little to add to Frank Kermode's 1965 lectures on *The Sense of an Ending*.[9] All of these works have helped me to approach this subject, but they are exclusively concerned with the world of the text, whether it be story, poem or play, rather than with the paratextual devices that signal their endings. Moreover, in their choice of examples, which come primarily from modern books and editions where terminal paratext is generally at its most settled and conventional, and in their choice of methods, which rely on close readings of more or less closed texts, they may have actively discouraged later scholars from attending to the variety and complexity encountered in the long history of endings. Within the field of bibliographical or textual studies, too, there has been next to nothing to help or inspire the confused or the curious: I am not aware of any sustained attention to the range of conventions that have been developed through the centuries and across the media – from medieval manuscripts to modern printed books and beyond, into the new textual forms of the digital age, along with related developments in music, theatre, and film. This chapter offers a preliminary prospectus for the larger history the subject deserves. It focuses primarily on English and literary examples, drawing especially on Geoffrey Chaucer's texts and the works of John Taylor the 'Water Poet', and pays particular attention to the first two centuries of printing, when medieval models were giving way to those that we now expect to see when we pick up a printed book.

I

According to the *OED*, the Latin word for 'end', '*finis*', was 'formerly, and still [is] occasionally, placed at the end of a book': it was 'Almost universally used [up to] the earlier half of [the] 19th century; in recent books "End" or "The End" is substituted'.[10] Medieval manuscripts did not conclude with the phrase 'The End', but neither did they tend to end with 'Finis'. The formula most commonly used to indicate that the author, scribe or reader had reached the end of a book or any of the smaller parts it contained was '*explicit*'. In some English manuscripts the word is given in some version of its vernacular form, 'Here endeth', as a counterpart to the 'Here beginneth' found at the beginning. To take two of the best-known examples, from the most lavish manuscripts of Chaucer's *Canterbury Tales*, the Hengwrt MS begins 'Here begynneth the Book of the tales of Caunterbury' and the Ellesmere MS at the Huntington ends with 'Heere is ended the book of the tales of Caunterbury'.[11] Detailed bibliographical descriptions of medieval texts usually provide their 'incipits' (opening words) and sometimes their 'explicits' (closing words), and from the cataloguers' perspective the two simply form, as it were, the bookends of a text as it survives in any particular incarnation. But, as their etymologies suggest, they do very different work for producers and users of texts: an 'incipit' (from the Latin root '*capio*') is not just the opening of a text but a seizing or taking in hand, and an 'explicit' (from '*explicitus*') is not just the closing of a text but also its unrolling, unfolding or laying out.[12]

Any index of medieval explicits (such as the Parker on the Web project's unusual alphabetical index by last word)[13] will reveal that by far the most common final word of medieval texts is 'Amen', and in some manuscripts this takes the place and serves the function of 'explicit'. The *OED*'s first definition of the term describes it as 'a concluding formula ... = Finis'; and its detailed etymology traces it back to the Hebrew word for 'certainty, truth', suggesting that it is 'used adverbially ... as an expression of affirmation, consent, or ratification of what has been said by another'. As a 'solemn expression of concurrence in, or ratification of, a prayer, or wish' (*OED* 2a) the word can effectively mean 'Be it so' or 'It is said', and phrases along those lines, in either English or Latin, are often found in terminal paratext. But it often bears explicitly religious connotations and serves to conclude a closing prayer of some sort, one which usually looks beyond endings even as it effects them, particularly when it culminates in the conventional tag (ultimately deriving from the Nicene Creed), '*saecula saeculorum* [world without end]'.

When William Caxton first printed Chaucer's *Canterbury Tales* in 1477, he marked the ending with '*Explicit Tractatus Galfrydi Chaucer*' and not one but two prayers culminating in 'Amen': we have not travelled far from the world of the medieval manuscript in either content or form. And when Richard Pynson printed the same text in 1526, he included the same *explicit* and the same concluding prayers, but he closed his book with a new and very printerly note, tapered and centred and set apart by clusters of symbols (Figure 4.1):

Thus endeth the boke of Caunterbury tales. Imprinted at London in flete-strete / by me Rychard Pynson / printer vnto the kynges most noble grace: and finished the yere of our lorde god a[nno] M.CCCCC. and .xxvi. the fourth day of Iune.

Early printed texts, like medieval manuscripts, often end with short notes on the production of the text called the 'colophon', a word adapted from the Greek word for 'crowning moment' or 'finishing touch'.[14] In her study of the development of the title-page, Margaret Smith describes its typical placement and content:

The colophon was located at the end of a whole text ... A colophon might contain the following: the author's name, the title of the text, the scribe's name (or sometimes the rubricator's or binder's name, depending on who wrote the colophon), the date and place of the completion of the writing, and other comments, such as 'Laus deo' (praise be to God), or even comments about the difficulties of writing ... The colophon has sometimes been referred to as an 'embryo' title-page because its content could be so close to the information that eventually came to be found on the title-page.[15]

It is worth pointing out that, particularly as we move from manuscript to print culture, it is not the author him- or herself who tends to bring things to an end but rather those responsible for the book's production or reproduction. And it may be worth recalling Roger Stoddard's oft-quoted observation that, 'Whatever they may do, authors do not write books': they write texts that are made into books 'by scribes and other artisans, by mechanics and other engineers, and by printing presses and other machines'.[16] This double-agency is best captured in a case like Caxton's edition of Malory's *Morte Darthur* or Aldus Manutius's edition of the *Hypnerotomachia Poliphili*, where there are two colophons: the text is brought to a close first by an authorial colophon describing the circumstances of composition, and the book by a later one, in the voice of the printer, describing the details of production. Finally, it is worth adding that the colophon in manuscripts was very often in red ink and sometimes

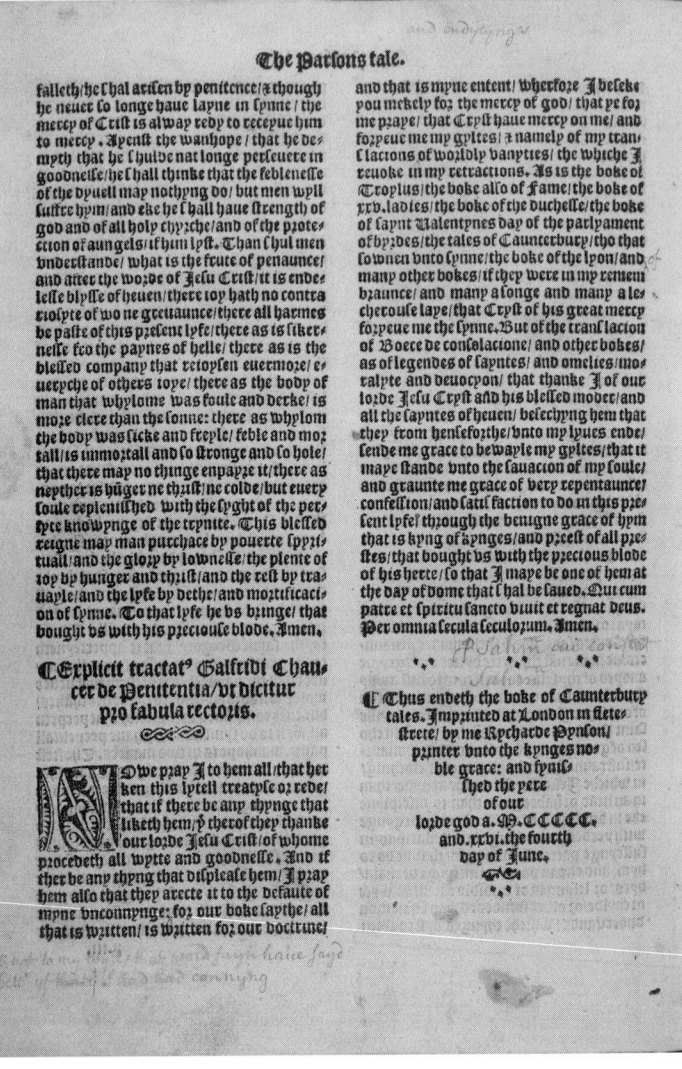

4.1 Final page of Geoffrey Chaucer, *The boke of Canterbury tales*, 1526.

set apart visually by some kind of symbol or by a change of layout. If medieval readers, as Smith suggests, could spot the beginning of the text by looking for its largest and most heavily decorated initial,[17] the colophon marked the end of the book not just by pronouncing it but also by *looking like* it.

These conventions were carried over from scribal culture to print culture, virtually from its very beginnings. But printers developed their own strategies that quickly departed from manuscript models. For instance, they often incorporated or concluded with a visual device or illustration of some sort: these could take the form of a design developed by particular printers to identify the books printed by them (for example, the twin shields used by Fust and Schöffer, the orb-and-cross design adopted by a variety of printers, the anchor and dolphin of the Aldine press, or the ornamental monogram that often served as a sort of signature or trademark for the new age of mechanical reproduction), or else of a moral or emblematic woodcut that served to round out the book (whether or not it was strictly related to the contents of the text or texts it contained).[18] A particularly interesting case is a copy of the *Chronicle of St Albans*, printed by Wynkyn de Worde in 1520 and recently acquired by the University of Notre Dame library (Figure 4.2). The text finishes as it did in the earlier edition printed by Caxton, with a paragraph beginning, 'Here endeth the descrypcyon of Brytane', and ending with Caxton's complicated note about the production of the book (underlined in red): 'I William Caxton haue them set fyrst in Imprynt accordynge to ye translacyon of Treuisa / whiche at the request of the lorde Barkeley translated the boke of Polycronycon into Englysshe'. There is then a second colophon by de Worde, who says he 'Fynyshed & Imprynted' the book in 1520. Finally, there is a version of de Worde's so-called 'Sagittarius' device, which clearly acknowledges his position as the successor to Caxton, incorporating the latter's monogram in the compartment above his name. Most interesting of all, for our purposes, is the manuscript annotation by an anonymous reader who, sometime during the sixteenth or seventeenth century, felt the need to add the word 'FINIS' between the colophon and the printer's device, as if the ensemble of other terminal forms already provided by the printer was no longer sufficient to bring the book to a close.

These particular terminal forms die out in the course of the sixteenth century, and their contents move forward to what in due course becomes the title-page, frontispiece, and copyright page; but textual endings continue to be signalled by visual as well as verbal cues. The last mark in a printed book of the sixteenth or seventeenth century is very often an ornamental tail-piece or a simple horizontal border. Early printers also frequently marked the end of a text by finishing it off with a set of symbols, most commonly a trio of asterisks in the form of an inverted triangle (following the pattern we have already seen in Pynson's colophon from 1526), but sometimes a more elaborate pattern. Robert Crowley's three 1550 editions of Langland's *Piers Plowman* end with a colophon, sandwiched

4.2 Final page of *The cronycles of Englonde*, 1520.

between a 'Finis' and a 'Cum priuilegio', and incorporating asterisks, pointing hands, leaves, and fleurs-de-lys (Figure 4.3). They also signalled the approaching ending of the text itself by centring and tapering the final sentences into an inverted pyramid or obelisk, sometimes (as we have seen) echoing the shape with a trio of asterisks or even a trio of trios of asterisks. In England, this particular convention emerges steadily during the first two or three decades of the sixteenth century and by mid-century they are an almost universal norm in printed books. It appears to be a genuinely new feature of mise-en-page in the new culture of print and does not (to my knowledge) appear at the ends of books in the three or four centuries of scribal practice preceding the invention of moveable type.

As the *OED* has already led us to expect, the vast majority of printed books from the sixteenth and seventeenth centuries end with the Latin word 'Finis'. A stark marker that shares little of the metaphorical life of an explicit, 'amen' or colophon, it simply tells us that we have hit the end of the text.[19] It does, however, constitute one of the most interesting speech acts in the history of the language. This particular form of terminal paratext constitutes a word or set of words that at once announces and effects the end of words; it usually stands outside the text and speaks in what we might call the voice of the book, which may or may not be that of the author or printer.

But once we move into the world of print, the term takes a surprisingly long time to make the leap from verb ('Here endeth') to noun ('The End') and from Latin to English. Even in thoroughly demotic and proudly vernacular productions, readers are ushered out of the text with a quick trip through a vestibule, canal lock or airlock that is stubbornly classical. The *OED* tells us that 'Finis' is the norm until the early nineteenth century, and instances of 'The End' are indeed rare during the period I am considering here. But they do start to appear in the course of the sixteenth century, and with the help of Early English Books Online's Text Creation Partnership (EEBO-TCP), it is possible to search for this phrase in the terminal paratext of English printed books.[20] I have so far identified only six examples before the end of the sixteenth century, and all but one are found in translations of foreign works into English (where it is possible that 'The End' is translated into English too). From 1600 to 1639, less than 1 per cent of the books that have been prepared by EEBO-TCP close with 'The End'; but by that period it has already emerged as a clear convention, one associated with particular authors. The first author to use the phrase with any regularity is Ben Jonson: of the seventeen works from the period currently available on EEBO-TCP, no fewer than eleven finish with 'The End'. Given that these texts represent the work of a range of printers, it is likely that the usage derives from Jonson himself – though if it does, it presents us with the

> Passus besecimus
> And walken as wyde, as the worlde lasteth
> To seke Pierce the plowman, that pryde may destroy
> And that Fryers had a findyng, ꝑ for no nede flatteren
> And cōtrepledeth me Cōscience, now kynde me aueng
> And send me hap & heale, til I haue Pyers ꝑ plowmā
> And syth he grad after grace, til I gan awake.
> Finis.

*Imprinted at London by Roberte
Crowley, dwellyng in Elye rentes
in Holburne. The yere of
our Lord M.D.L.*

Cum priuilegio ad imprimendum
solum.

4.3 Final page of William Langland, *The vision of Piers Plowman*, 1550.

ironic fact that one of Renaissance England's most learned poets and most committed Latinists was apparently the first to introduce the most familiar and vernacular form of terminal paratext.[21]

There are other forms, too, that marked the ends of books for early printers and readers, and they will be worth studying in detail when this subject gets the fuller history it deserves. The authorial motto is a particularly interesting case; so too is the list of 'errors or faults escaped in the printing' (or 'errata') that almost always follows the final 'Finis', directing readers back into the text, inviting them to rewrite it instead of ushering them out of it. These too perform the ending of the text in complex ways, raising questions of agency, temporality, and orientation.

Within poetic texts in particular, the most important genre for teasing out these dynamics must be that of the envoi or envoy (a term that might be translated as the 'sending forth'). The model has classical precedents and derives most immediately from the conventions of Provençal poetry and the lyrics of Dante and Petrarch: traditionally, they formed a concluding stanza but sometimes formed a separate poem, constituting either an epilogue or the poetic equivalent of a musical coda. In Old French poetry these verses tended to dedicate the poem to a patron or other important person; in later medieval and Renaissance examples, they typically addressed the *book* directly and sent it on its way into the world.[22] The most famous example in English comes at the end of the fifth and final book of Chaucer's *Troilus and Criseyde*, and begins 'Go, litel book, go, litel myn tragedye ...'. Following Chaucer's lead, the form is used regularly by Lydgate, and there are well-known examples by Hoccleve, Hawes, Skelton, and Spenser, in whose *Shepheardes Calender* it serves both as prologue ('Goe little booke: thy selfe present, / As child whose parent is vnkent ...') and epilogue ('Goe lyttle Calender, thou hast a free passeporte, / Goe but a lowly gate emongste the meaner sorte ...').[23] As these examples suggest, the envoi might be seen as the place where the book is transferred from the author's hands to those of its readers, and where the voice of the author gives way to what I have been calling the voice of the book. The key agents in this process are, of course, the translator and the printer; so we should not be surprised to find envois by Caxton, Copeland and others, serving as intermediaries between dead authors and living readers.

The envoi also occupies an ambiguous position between text and paratext. Sometimes it clearly falls outside the text, even when it is in the poet's rather than the printer's voice: in John Taylor's *Differing Worships* (1640), the poem ends on page 25 with an imposing 'FINIS', but if we turn the page we find a concluding poem, headed 'Lenuoy or Postscript' (27). Sometimes, following the model established by Chaucer, it constitutes all or part of a concluding section within the author's text. This should serve to remind us of the fact that we tend to know that we are approaching the end of a book before we actually reach it, especially if we are holding it in our hands and can *feel* that we are in the final pages. We may be disappointed or relieved when we hit the words that bring it to a close, but we are very rarely taken by surprise. We are often prepared by titles or chapter headings that explicitly tell us we are entering a concluding section, but there are other, more subtle, forms of closure, both narrative and poetic, that suggest we are approaching the end. As Smith suggests in *Poetic Closure*, this phenomenon depends above all on shared perception of *shape* by both writer and reader. She is not thinking so much of visual examples (such as the tapered and centred texts we have already examined), but rather of generic expectation (leading us, for example, to know that when we are in the fourteenth line of something called a 'sonnet' we should normally be in the final line) and also of rhythmic devices (such as rhyming couplets, which often conclude speeches in blank verse and even in prose).

The best way to wrap up this survey of forms and functions, before moving on to a closing section of my own, is to take a closer look at a single book with a particularly sophisticated terminal apparatus: *The essayes of a prentise, in the divine art of poesie*, published in Edinburgh in 1584 and written by the eighteen-year-old King James VI of Scotland. Among the texts in the volume is a facing-page translation of a poem to the heavenly muse Urania by Du Bartas: the preface closes with a tapered section leading to a 'faire well' and a cluster of asterisks, and the two columns of the poem itself close with a 'Finis' and tail-piece. There follows a tragic poem called 'Phoenix'; the text ends with a section labelled 'L'envoy', culminating in another terminal form (indeed, perhaps the ultimate one): the epitaph on the grave of Phoenix. Following a short treatise on the theory and practice of metre, there is then a short translation of psalms and a short poem on the nature of time, each of which end with a 'Finis'. The volume concludes, like many editions of older poets including Chaucer, with an index of obscure words and their significations; but James has also wedged in a concluding sonnet from the author to the reader, and a

> ✺✺✺✺✺✺✺✺✺✺✺✺✺✺✺✺✺✺✺✺
>
> ## I HAVE INSERT FOR THE FILLING OVT OF THIR
>
> VACAND PAGEIS, THE VERIE
> wordis of *Plinius* vpon the
> *Phœnix*,
> as followis.
>
> ✺✺✺
> ✺
>
> C. PLINII
> *Nat. Hist. Lib. Decimi, Cap. 2.*
> *De Phœnice.*
>
> * *
> *
>
> Æthiopes atq; Indi, difcolores maximè & inenarrabiles ferunt aues, & ante omnes nobilem Arabia Phœnicē: haud fcio an fabulosè, vnum in toto orbe, nec vifum magnopere. Aquilæ narratur magnitudine, auri fulgore circa colla, cætera purpureus, cæruleam rofeis caudam pennis diftinguentibus, criftis faciem, capútque plumeo apice cohoneftante. Primus atque diligentiffimus togatorum de eo prodidit Manilius, Senator ille, maximis nobilis doctrinis doctore nullo: neminem extitiffe qui viderit vefcentē: factum in Arabia Soli effe, viuere annis DCLX. fenefcenrem, cafia thurifque furculis conftruere nidū, replere odoribus, & fuperemori. Ex offibus deinde & medulla P. iiii.

4.4 James VI of Scotland, *The essayes of a prentise, in the divine art of poesie*, 1584, sig. P4r.

curious two-page section providing some of the Latin source material for the earlier Phoenix poem, 'insert[ed] for the filling out of thir vacand pageis' (Figure 4.4), at the end of which he at long last bids the reader a final 'Farevveill'.

II

I would like to begin my own ending by returning to my opening epigraph from Walter Ong and draw out the larger questions raised by the terminal patterns I have begun to trace, and to ask what exactly Ong might be claiming when he suggests that 'print is only comfortable with finality'. We have seen that there are visual and verbal conventions in terminal paratext that seem to be invented either by printers or by authors writing for print. But is Ong going so far as to claim that print culture has a fundamentally different attitude toward the end of the book and, by extension, a qualitatively different understanding of the very idea of a book?

My epigraph is lifted from a sweeping discussion of print and closure in Ong's 1982 study, *Orality and Literacy*, and it is helpful to have the larger context in which the line appears:

> Print encourages a sense of closure, a sense that what is found in a text has been finalized, has reached a state of completion ... The printed text is supposed to represent the words of an author in definitive or 'final' form. For print is comfortable only with finality. Once a letterpress forme is closed, locked up, or a photo-lithographic plate is made, and the sheet printed, the text does not accommodate changes ... so readily as do written texts. By contrast, manuscripts, with their glosses or marginal comments ... were in dialogue with the world outside their own borders. They remained closer to the give-and-take of oral expression ... Print is curiously intolerant of physical incompleteness. It can convey the impression, unintentionally and subtly, but very really, that the material the text deals with is similarly complete or self-consistent ... Manuscript culture had taken intertextuality for granted ... Print culture of itself has a different mindset. It tends to feel a work as 'closed', set off from other works, a unit in itself.[24]

Many readers have found it difficult to get past the technological determinism on display here, in which Ong assumes social or psychological effects from technological causes and attributes feelings like comfort to an entire technology like printing. Approaching this passage from the angle pursued in this chapter, however, it has become clear to me that the first two centuries of printing offer ample evidence in support of Ong's assertions. Consider, first, the transmission history of Chaucer's *House of Fame*, a poem that famously finishes in the middle of a line, just as we are introduced to the figure who will apparently deliver the final judgment or interpretation.[25] In the best manuscript, the end of the poem reads:

> Attelast, y saugh a man
> Whiche that y nat ne kan,
> But he semed for to be
> A man of grete auctorite ...[26]

In transcriptions of this text, editors tend to add these terminal ellipses, the conventional marker of omitted or missing words. But some Chaucer scholars are persuaded that this is where Chaucer intended to finish the text, and much ink has recently been spilled on the question of whether this is a finished or an unfinished work.[27] William Caxton was clearly not comfortable with this open ending, so in his 1483 edition of the poem he went ahead and closed it, adding a completely new ending that supplies the closing 'awakening' expected of a conventional dream narrative. The passage is marked by his name in the margin and followed by a characteristic colophon (Figure 4.5):

And wyth the noyse of them two   *Caxton*
I sodaynly awoke anon tho
And remembryd what I had seen
And how hye and ferre I had been
In my ghost / and had grete wonder
Of that the god of thonder
Had lete me knowen / & began to wryte
Lyke as ye haue herd me endyte
Wherfor to studye and rede alway
I purpose to do day by day
Thus in dremyng and in game
Endeth thys lytyl book of Fame
   Explicit
I fynde nomore of thys werke to fore said . . . And I humbly beseche & praye yow / emonge your prayers to remembre hys [Chaucer's] soule / on whych and on all crysten soulis I beseche al-myghty god to haue mercy Amen
            Emprynted by Wyllyam Caxton[28]

And when William Thynne printed the text in his influential edition of 1532, he adopted (and adapted) Caxton's ending, but dropped all indication that the words were the printer's rather than the author's.[29] These closing verses remained in printed editions of the work, where they were taken to be authorial, until the nineteenth century. Such an example lends support to Ong's position, suggesting that whether or not *print* was comfortable only with finality, several early *printers* seem to have been so (at least when it came to the words of Chaucer).

So too does the example mentioned above, where King James closed his envoi to his 'Phoenix' by offering an *epitaph*: there is a natural affinity, perhaps, between closing words and last words. And while Ong or Marshall McLuhan might be bold enough to venture a claim that there is an inherent connection between printing and death,[30] I would be more comfortable

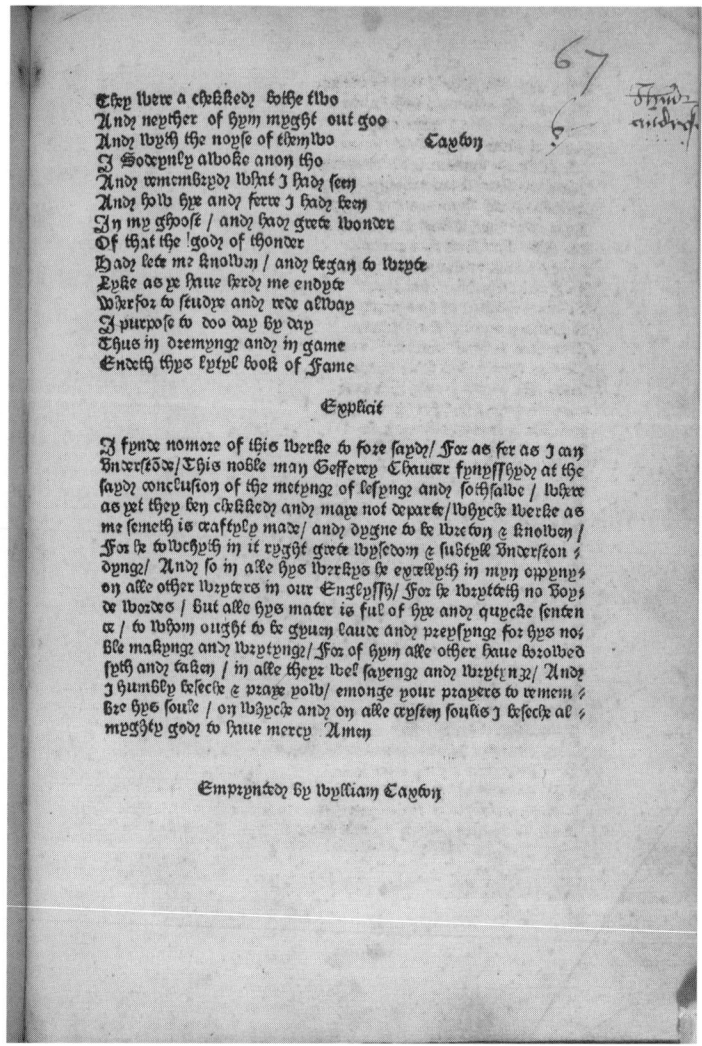

4.5 Final page of Geoffrey Chaucer, *The book of fame*, 1483.

with the more modest observation that early printers often construct or exploit parallels between the end of a text and the end of the life of its author.[31] Chaucer's fate in the first few decades of print culture is again instructive. In the course of the sixteenth century, it became traditional to end Chaucer's works with an 'Epitaph'. The last page of the various issues of his 1550 *Works* ends with a full series of terminal paratexts, including 'Et sic est finis' ('And thus is it finished'), 'Thus endeth the workes of Geffray Chaucer', the printer's colophon and 'Cum priuilegio', culminating in a Latin poem headed, 'Epitaphium Galfreidi Chaucer . . .' (Figure 4.6).

Another relevant tradition in early printing was the use of completely black pages (sometimes called 'mourning pages') in elegies commemorating the death of some important person. In John Taylor's *The Muses Mourning*, a series of sonnets paying tribute to John Moray, the blank verso of every page is covered completely in black ink, providing a negative frame or mirror for the poem it faces.[32] And in Taylor's 1612 elegy for Prince Henry, *Great Britaine, all in blacke*, the end of the poem is announced with a final 'Finis', but the black blocks that are found at the beginning of the text reappear in the final opening which offers an extraordinary pairing of epitaph and lament (Figure 4.7).[33]

It is not by chance that these examples derive from the publications of Taylor: he was perhaps the most inventive player with textual conventions before Laurence Sterne. The ability to play with conventions depends, of course, upon familiarity with those conventions; so the games Taylor plays with endings in several books might add further support to Ong's assertion. While there are very few examples of authors playing with the forms of their terminal paratexts in manuscript culture, the practice is increasingly common in print culture. Taylor's *Old, Old, Very Old Man* ends:

> And thus I lay downe the Pen, leaving it to whomsoever can, or will make more of this *Old Man*, than I have
> DONE

His 'Comparison betwixt a *Whore* and a *Booke*' ends:

> If any *Whore* be honester then mine is,
> Ile write no more, but stop my mouth with
> FINIS.

The most elaborate example of all concludes his *Taylors Motto* (Figure 4.8):

> This booke was written (not that here I boast)
> Put houres together, in three dayes at most:
> And giue me but my breakfast, Ile maintaine,
> To write another e're I eate againe.
> But well or ill, or howsoe're tis pen'd,
> Lik't as you list, and so I make an
> END.

And Taylor was not the last author to play on the comic potential of these conventions. The tradition reaches a high (or rather low) point with

Balades.

Or thoughe a man of high or lowe degre
Of Tullius had the sugred eloquence
Or of Seneca the great mozalyte
Or of Caton the forsyght and prouidence
The conquest of Charles, Arctures magnificece
Yet for al, that trust right wel this
Some wycked tonge wol say of him amis

The wyfely trouth of Penelope
Though they it had in her possessyon
Holynesse, beautie, the kyndnesse of Medee
The lyfe unfayned of Martia Caton
Or of Alcest the trewe affection
Yet dare I say, and trust right wel this
A wycked tonge wol say of her amis

Than sythen it is so, no man may eschewe
The swerde of tonge, but it kerue and byte
Ful harde it is a man for to remewe
Out of their daunger hym for to aquyte
We to the tonges that hem so delyte
To hynder or sclaunder, & set their study i this
And their plesaunces to do and say amis

Moste noble princes, cherysshers of vertue
Remembreth you of hygh discretion
The first vertue and moste plesyng to Jesu
(By the wrytyng and sentence of Caton)
Is a good tonge in his opynyon
Chastyse the reuerst, and of wisdome do this
Withdrawe your heringe fro al ȳ sayn amis

℞ Et sic est finis.

℞ Thus endeth the workes of
Geffray Chaucer.

℞ Imprinted at London by Rycharde Kele,
Dwellynge in Lombarde strete nere unto
the stockes market at the sygne
of the Egle.

Cum priuilegio ad imprimendum solum.

Epitaphiū Galfridi Chauceri, per poetā lau
reatum Stephanum Surigonum Me-
diolanensem in decretis licenciatum.

Pyerides muse si possint nu-
mia fletus
Fundere, diuinas atq; rigare
genas.
Galfridi batis chaucer crude-
lia fata
Plā gite: iit lachrimis abstinuisse nephas.
Uos coluit blues: at vos celebrate sepultum
Reddatur merito gracia digna bito.
Grāde decus vobis est docti musa Maronis
Qua didicit melius lingua latina loqui.
Grāde, nouiūq; decꝰ chaucer, famāq; paranit
Hen quātum fuerat prisca Britanna rudis
Reddidit insignē maternis versibus, vt iam
Aurea splendescat, ferrea facta prius.
Hunc latuisse virū nil, si tot opuscula vertes,
Dixeris, egregiis que decorata modis,
Socratis ingenium, vel fontes philosophie,
Quicquid et archani dogmata sacra fetūt.
Et quascūq; belis, tenuit dignissimus artes
Hic vates, paruo conditus hoc tumulo.
Ah laudis quātum preclara Britānia perdis,
Dum rapuit tantum mors odiosa virum.
Crudeles parce, crudelia filia sorores,
Non tamen extincta corpora, fama perit.
Uiuet in eternum, biuent dum scripta poete:
Uiuant in eterno tot monumenta die.
Si qua bonos tāgit pietas, si carmine dign?
Carmina qui cecinit tot cumulata modis,
Hec sibi marmoreo scribātur verba sepulchro
Hec maneat laudis sarcina summa sue.
Galfridus Chaucer vates, et fama poesis
Materne, hac sacta sum tumulatus humo.

Post obitum Caxton voluit te biuere cura
Willelmi, Chaucer clare poeta tui,
Nam tua non solū cōpressit opuscula formis
Has quoq; sed laudes iussit hic esse tuas.

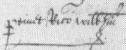

4.6 Final page of Geoffrey Chaucer, *The workes of Geffray Chaucer*, 1550.

4.7 Final opening of John Taylor, *Great Britaine, all in blacke*, 1612.

Andrew Brome's 'BVMM-FODER', a broadside ballad lampooning the so-called 'Rump Parliament' in 1660. Virtually every stanza plays in some way on the idea of endings, and the poem culminates in the terminal pun, '*FINIS*, In English, *The RVMP*'.[34]

It is tempting to stop there and rest Ong's case. But there are a number of strands in recent work by Renaissance scholars that have led them to reject some of his claims outright and to call for a more nuanced and qualified chronology for others. First, they have challenged the assumptions that lie behind Ong's contrasts between printed books and manuscripts. On the one hand, there are many examples of manuscripts that are not only comfortable with closure but insist upon it;[35] on the other, there are many kinds of evidence for printed books remaining in dialogue with the world outside their boundaries. Manuscript marginalia and other forms of customisation are only the most obvious example: we might also consider the ways in which advertisements for other books, indexes, and even notes all link books to other books rather than isolating them in ways and on a scale, in fact, that are impossible in the world of handwritten copies, and recall that printed books were often purchased unbound, which made it easier to customise them or bind them with other texts. The existence of stop-press corrections and other variants, the survival of competing versions of entire texts, and examples

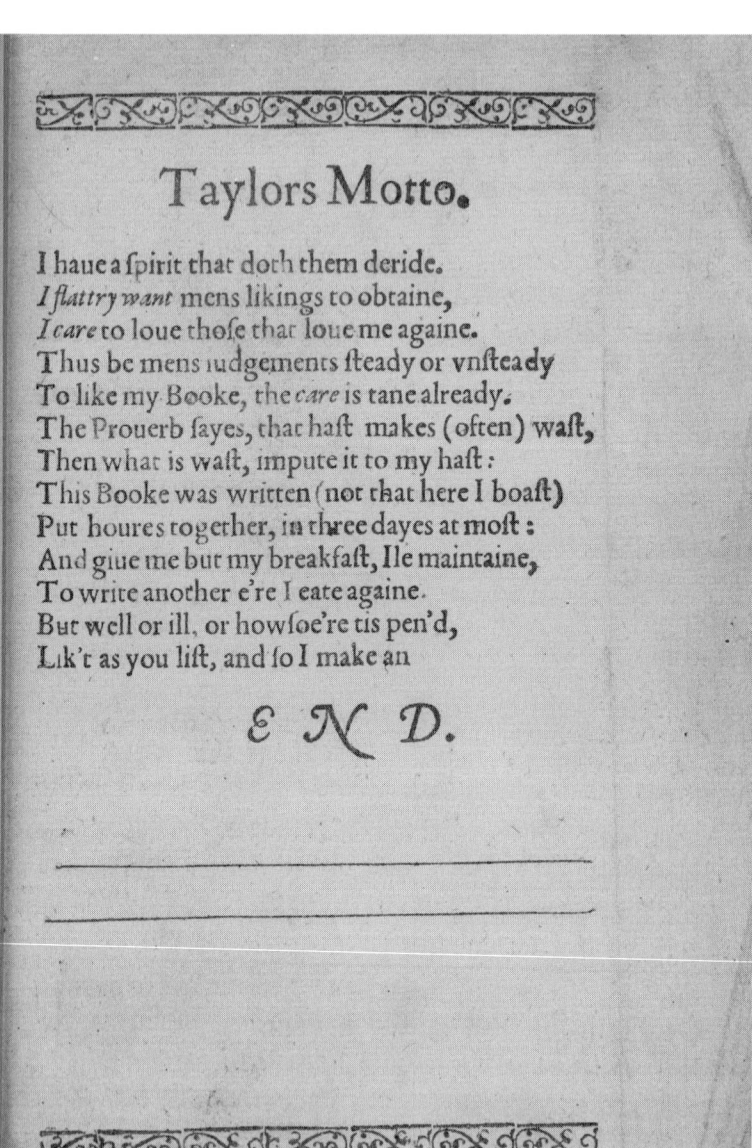

Taylors Motto.

I haue a spirit that doth them deride,
I flattry want mens likings to obtaine,
I care to loue those that loue me againe.
Thus be mens iudgements steady or vnsteady
To like my Booke, the *care* is tane already.
The Prouerb sayes, that hast makes (often) wast,
Then what is wast, impute it to my hast:
This Booke was written (not that here I boast)
Put houres together, in three dayes at most:
And giue me but my breakfast, Ile maintaine,
To write another e're I eate againe.
But well or ill, or howsoe're tis pen'd,
Lik't as you list, and so I make an

E N D.

4.8 Final page of John Taylor, *Taylors motto*, 1621.

where every surviving copy is radically different from every other copy all suggest that print may be more tolerant of openness than Ong suggests.

While Shakespeare was able to draw upon proverbial wisdom in reminding his readers that 'all's well that ends well' or that 'the end crowns all',[36] many of his contemporaries produced printed texts that finished by announcing their unfinished status. John Davies's great poem on dancing, *Orchestra* (1622), ends with a numbered stanza consisting only of 'So & c. & c. * * *' before moving into the errata list (Figure 4.9). Stephen Dobranski has recently discussed this and other examples where 'deliberate holes establish an author's authority and enhance rather than diminish meaning'.[37] One example not mentioned by Dobranski is George Gascoigne's final work, *The Grief of Ioye*, a series of four elegies offered as a New Year's gift to Queen Elizabeth in 1575. It also culminates in an incomplete final numbered stanza ending in '& c. & c.' followed by the memorable line, 'Left vnperfect for feare of Horsmen'.[38] And Abraham Cowley's unfinished *Poem on the Late Civil War* (1679) breaks off mid-sentence and finishes with the centred and italicised line, 'The Author went no further'.[39] Examples such as these suggest that print may be more tolerant of incompleteness (physical and/or conceptual) than Ong suggests. Indeed, if we consider Sir Philip Sidney's use of *aposiopesis* (where words give way to a silence meant to be filled by the thoughts or texts of others), or the 'endless work' of Edmund Spenser (whose *Faerie Queene* repeatedly undoes its gestures towards closure and finishes with the unfinished 'mutability cantos'), it looks as if Renaissance literature is peculiarly *uncomfortable* with finality.[40]

It also looks as if early modern writers and printers have more in common with their modern successors than we have appreciated. Towards the end of *Poetic Closure*, Smith identified a strong strain in twentieth-century literature that resists the emphatic closure it perceived as the inherited norm. The best-known example is James Joyce's *Finnegans Wake*, which not only ends in the middle of a sentence but finishes with a word that leads the reader back to the beginning which starts where that same sentence leaves off. But more conventional authors such as Robert Graves also reacted against the kind of closure that printed books seemed to be insisting on. He ended his *Collected Poems* of 1938 with a poem called 'Leaving the Rest Unsaid': invoking and rejecting the full range of terminal paratexts (including '*Finis*', 'fallen obelisk for colophon', 'testamentary appendices', and 'graveyard indices'), the poem finishes with a comma.[41] Finally, when I. A. Richards wrote 'How Does a Poem Know When It Is Finished?', he included a poem of his own called 'By the Pool'. He explained that he was no longer happy with the order of stanzas as printed in his *The Screen and Other Poems* a few years before, so he provides a new version of the text, with *of Dauncing.*

131

As when the Indians, Neighbours of the morning,
In honour of the Cheerefull rising Sunne,
With Pearle and painted plumes themselues ador-
A solemne stately measure haue begun.   (ning,
The God well pleasd with that faire honour done
Sheds foorth his Beames and doth their faces kis
With that immortall glorious face of his.

132

So &c. &c.   * * *

Errata in the Epistle.
Line 9. for diuinell, read Diuinest. line 13. for mooue, read moue.
Errata in Nosce teipsum.
Page 4. lin. 16. for beere, read deepe. Pag. 5. lin. 17. for It is, read Is it?
Pag. 41. lin. 9. for spring, read, bring. Pag. 47. lin. 21. for apprehension
read apprehensiue. Pag. 73. lin. 5. for vvorld, read vvould.
Jn Astræa, Hymne 18. line 10. for to, read doo.
In the Poem of Dauncing, In the 16. Stanza for imperous read im-
perious. Jn the 40. Stan. for she, read Hee. In the 74. Stan. lin. 2. for Did
read Doe, Jn the 99. Stan. lin. 6. for brothers, read brother.

4.9 Sir John Davies, *Nosce teipsum*, 1622, sig. L3r.

all the same words but in a different order. The only thing that he does not touch is the closing stanza and closing line:

> The still figure
> Beyond the flow
> Listens, listened
> Aeons ago.
> Ever a-flutter
> Must all words be.
>
> Here is an end.[42]

PART II
Making readers

CHAPTER 5

Editorial pledges in early modern dramatic paratexts

Sonia Massai

In his survey of paratexts, Gérard Genette notes that 'the publisher's peritext' may provide the 'name ... of the person(s) responsible for establishing the text and preparing the critical apparatus' and will, on occasion, indicate the 'number of printings, or "editions," or "thousands"' which the text has undergone.[1] He does not, however, discuss the early modern practice of promising readers revised or 'perfected' content. Editorial pledges on the title-pages of early modern printed playbooks have never been granted sustained critical attention.[2] This omission may be due to the fact that title-pages rarely refer to the preparation of dramatic copy for the press. A survey of the title-pages of the playbooks listed in Greg's *Bibliography of the English Printed Drama to the Restoration* shows that only twenty-four out of 836 single editions, and seven out of forty-five collections, inform their readers about the quality, provenance, and reliability of the printer's copy.[3] Probably because statistically insignificant, this type of pledge is never taken to reflect established editorial practices and is often dismissed as an unfounded marketing ploy. In this chapter I show that editorial pledges often reflect print-house practice, and that, while they may retain a marketing function, they also direct the reader's attention to a revised and improved text.

More generally, our understanding of the correction of dramatic copy for the press in the early modern period is strongly affected by the assumption that the editorial tradition of vernacular drama in England started at the beginning of the eighteenth century, when the name of the editor started to feature next to the name of the author on the title-pages of dramatic collections. The first named editors of Shakespeare reinforced the notion that his texts had progressively deteriorated as they were repeatedly reprinted in the sixteenth and seventeenth centuries. Samuel Johnson was particularly vocal in denouncing the process whereby theatrical manuscripts were transmitted from authors, to scribes, to actors, before they were eventually committed to print:

No books could be left in hands so likely to injure them, as plays frequently acted, yet continued in manuscript: no other transcribers were likely to be so little qualified for their task as those who copied for the stage, at a time when the lower ranks of the people were universally illiterate: no other editions were made from fragments so minutely broken, and so fortuitously reunited; and in no other age was the art of printing in such unskillful hands.[4]

Despite recent scholarship showing that early modern playwrights were in fact directly involved in the process of transcription and revision of their manuscripts as they were prepared or updated for performance,[5] and that they often took an active role in their transmission into print,[6] Johnson's views on the standards of early modern printing practices remain largely unchallenged. However, a survey of the dramatic paratexts of English printed drama to the Restoration offers a rather different sense of what the process of committing a dramatic text to print meant to the agents responsible for it.

The title-pages of William Davenant's and Abraham Cowley's collected *Works*, are, for example, quite explicit in pointing out that dramatic publication involved preparing the manuscript copy for its circulation in print: the first parts of these titles – 'THE / WORKS / OF / Sr William D'avenant K^t' and 'THE / WORKS / OF / Mr. Abraham Cowley' – are followed by the invariant claim that such works consist of '*Those which were formerly Printed*: / AND / *Those which he* [that is, the author] *Design'd for the Press*'.[7] Although rather generic, the term '*Design'd*' suggests an active, self-conscious effort on the part of the author to make his work suitable for circulation in print. By the middle of the seventeenth century, Sir Aston Cokain had similarly described the process whereby a theatrical manuscript was prepared for the press as a formal process, or 'method'. In 'The Authors Apology to the Reader' prefaced to his 1658 collection of 'Small / POEMS / OF / Divers sorts', Cokain makes the following announcement: 'I have made some progress into a Play, to be called the Tragedy of Ovid, which (if my *Obstinate* Lady, and *Trappolin* take) I may be encouraged to perfect, and present to you hereafter, with some other things that are not yet put into method, fit for the Press'.[8] As early as the last quarter of the sixteenth century, the verb 'to perfect' was used to suggest that a dramatic manuscript was regarded as unfinished and deficient, unless it had been specifically revised and corrected for the press. Richard Jones's 1578 edition of George Whetstone's *Promos and Cassandra* shows how both the author and the publisher felt obliged to mention the unusual circumstances which prevented the author from perfecting the copy of this play for the press while simultaneously forcing the publisher to perfect it on the author's behalf.

In the dedication, Whetstone explains why he failed to perfect the play for publication:

Syr, . . . of late I perused diuers of my vnperfect workes, fully minded to bestowe on you, the trauell of some of my forepassed time. But (resolued to accompanye, the aduenturous Captaine, Syr *Humphrey Gylbert*, in his honorable voiadge,) I found my leisure too littel, to correct the errors of my sayd workes. So that (inforced) I lefte them disparsed, amonge my learned freendes, at theyr leasure, to polish, if I faild to return.[9]

Whetstone's epistle usefully explains that the process of transferring a manuscript work into print involved a specific stage during which an 'vnperfect' work was 'polished' and corrected. In his address to the reader, Jones then reinforces the impression that even when the author is unable to perfect dramatic copy for the press, corrected copy is still preferable to what Jones refers to as the author's 'first coppy':

Gentle Reader, this labour of Maister *Whetstons*, came into my handes, in his first coppy, whose leasure was so little (being then readie to depart his country) that he had no time to worke it a new, nor to geue apt instructions, to prynte so difficult a worke, being full of variety, both matter, speache, and verse . . . so that, if I commit an error, without blaming the Auctor, amend my amisse.[10]

Overall, these references to the preparation of dramatic manuscripts for the press suggest that transmission into print, far from being a textual fall from the manuscript copy from which the printed text was set, elicited a further stage of correction, either by the author or by non-authorial agents who acted on his behalf.

Unfortunately, none of the surviving dramatic manuscripts from the period was used by an early modern printer to set a known edition of a printed playbook.[11] In other words, we have no straightforward way of assessing what perfecting dramatic copy for the press meant in practical, textual terms. However, editorial pledges often alert us to the fact that the process of perfecting dramatic copy may not have stopped at correcting a manuscript prior to its first impression but that it may have extended to the annotation of the text of a play already available in print, when readers' demand encouraged a publisher to issue a second or subsequent editions. In other words, establishing when editorial pledges occur and whether there is a correlation between such pledges and actual corrections in the text of subsequent editions of the play represents our best, and possibly our only, chance to decide what level of editorial intervention was elicited by dramatic publication and what level of editorial intervention justified the claim that a dramatic text had been 'newly corrected and emended'.

Tables 5.1 and 5.2 provide chronological lists of the earliest single and collected editions of printed playbooks whose title-pages pledge editorial intervention. The last column indicates whether changes in the text of the play are due to consultation or use of a fresh textual witness ('annotated' or 'independent copy') or to the correction of an earlier edition from which the text was reset ('corrected copy').[12] These distinctions are not always clear-cut. On some occasions, as with George Chapman's second edition of *Bussy D'Ambois*, the printer's copy seems to have been both lightly corrected and altered by reference to a fresh textual witness. On other occasions, as with the second edition of *Romeo and Juliet* or *Hamlet*, the text was reset from a fresh manuscript authority, but with occasional reference to an earlier printed edition, possibly in order to compensate for lacunæ, or to decipher obscure passages, in the manuscript. These categories are therefore distinctive, but not necessarily mutually exclusive.

The earliest instance of an editorial pledge signalling correction of copy – the generic 'Newly corrected' – is included in the title-page of the third quarto edition of Shakespeare's *1 Henry IV*, which was printed by Simon Stafford for Andrew Wise in 1599. As I explain elsewhere, the most significant substantive changes introduced in this edition can be summarised as follows:

The first quarto of *1 Henry IV* ... lacks the entry direction which in modern editions marks the beginning of Act 4. Besides, [the first quarto] uses the variant speech-prefix '*Per.*' ten times starting from G4v 27 instead of '*Hot.*', the usual prefix for Henry Percy, known as Hotspur. The second quarto ... provides an exit direction at G4v 25, which clears the stage and shifts the action from Mistress Quickly's tavern to the rebel camp near Shrewsbury, adds a new direction at G4v 28 ('*Enter Hotspur, Worcester, and Douglas.*'), and then changes all variant speech-prefixes from '*Per.*' back to '*Hot.*'.[13]

The third quarto editions of *2* and *3 Henry VI* published for Thomas Pavier in 1619 as *The vvhole contention betvveene the tvvo famous houses, Lancaster and Yorke* are also advertised as being 'newly corrected and / enlarged' on their title-pages. As with the third quarto of *1 Henry IV*, the part of the pledge which refers to the correction of copy is associated with sporadic changes to speech prefixes and stage directions. Pavier's edition of *3 Henry VI*, for example, adds three directions, including one which clarifies the stage action.[14] Pavier's *2* and *3 Henry VI* emend one further stage direction each[15] and *2 Henry VI* changes a speech prefix in connection with a variant half-line.[16] Sporadic attention is also paid to the dialogue, most prominently in *2 Henry VI*, where the emendation of York's genealogy requires complex interrelated changes to York's speech in Act 2 scene 2.

Table 5.1 *Editorial pledges on the title-pages of early modern printed playbooks (single editions).*

Bibliographical numbers	Author	Title	Printer(s) / Publisher(s)	Editorial pledge	Edition / date of publication	Type of intervention
STC 25764 Greg 104 (A)	[Robert Wilmot]	*Tancred and Gismund*	Thomas Scarlet, sold by R. Robinson	*Newly reuiued and polished according to the decorum / of these daies.*	1st, 1591	?
STC 15086 Greg 110 (a)	[Thomas Kyd]	*The Spanish Tragedy*	Edward Allde for Edward White	Newly corrected and amended of such grosse faults as / passed in the first impression	1st?, [1592]	?
STC 21528 Greg 136 (a)	W. S.	*Locrine*	Printed by Thomas Creede	Newly set foorth, ouerseene and corrected. / By VV. S.	1st, 1595	?
STC 22294 Greg 150 (a)	William Shakespeare	*Love's Labour's Lost*	W[illiam] W[hite] for Cuthbert Burby	Newly corrected and augmented	1st?, 1598	?
STC 22323 Greg 143 (b)	[William Shakespeare]	*Romeo and Juliet*	Thomas Creede for Cuthbert Burby	Newly corrected, augmented, and / amended	2nd, 1599	different copy
STC 22281 Greg 145 (c)	William Shakespeare	*1 Henry IV*	S[imon] S[tafford] for Andrew Wise	Newly corrected by W. Shake-speare	3rd, 1599	corrected copy
STC 22276 Greg 197 (b)	William Shakespeare	*Hamlet*	I[ames] R[oberts] for N[icholas] L[ing]	Newly imprinted and enlarged to almost as much / againe as it was, according to the true and perfect / Coppie.	2nd, 1604–5	independent and annotated copy
STC 17484 Greg 230 (b)	John Marston	*Parasitaster; Or, The Faun*	T[homas] P[urfoot] for W[illiam] C[otton]	And now corrected of many faults, which by reason of the Au- / thors absence, were let slip in the first edition.	2nd?, 1606	corrected copy

Table 5.1 (*cont.*)

Bibliographical numbers	Author	Title	Printer(s) / Publishers(s)	Editorial pledge	Edition / date of publication	Type of intervention
STC 1466 Greg 254 (A1)	[Barnaby Barnes]	*The Devil's Charter*	G[eorge] E[ld] for John Wright	*But more exactly renewed, corrected, and augment-/ ted since by the Author, for the more plea-/ sure and profit of the Reader.*	1st, 1607	?
STC 7243 Greg 177 (b1)	[mainly by John Marston]	*Jack Drum's Entertainment*	W[illiam] Stansby for Philip Knight	Newly corrected.	2nd, 1616	reprint
STC 1678 Greg 357 (b)	Beaumont and Fletcher	*The Maid's Tragedy*	[George Purslowe] for F. Constable	Newly perused, augmented, and inlarged, This second Impression	2nd, 1622	annotated copy
			A. M[atthewes] for Richard Hawkins	This third Impression, Reuised and Refined.	3rd, 1630	corrected copy
STC 1682 Greg 363 (b)	Beaumont and Fletcher	*Philaster*	[Nicholas Okes] for Thomas Walkley	The second Impression, corrected, and / amended.	2nd, 1622	independent and annotated copy
STC 1671 Greg 360 (b)	Beaumont and Fletcher	*A King and No King*	[John Beale] for Thomas Walkley	And now the second time Printed, according / to the true Copie.	2nd, 1625	annotated copy
STC 11069 Greg 287 (b)	John Fletcher	*The Faithful Shepherdess*	T[homas] C[reed] for Richard Meighen	The second Edition, newly corrected.	2nd, 1629	corrected copy
STC 22301 Greg 187 (d)	William Shakespeare	*The Merry Wives of Windsor*	T[homas] H[arper] for Richard Meighen	Newly corrected.	4th, 1630	reprint
STC 17891 Greg 244 (b)	[Thomas Middleton]	*Michaelmas Term*	T[homas] H[arper] for Richard Meighen	Newly corrected.	2nd, 1630	corrected copy

STC 13321 Greg 333 (b)	Thomas Heywood	*The Four Prentices of London*	Nicholas Okes	*Written and newly revised by* THOMAS HEYVVOOD	2nd, 1632	corrected copy
STC 13360 Greg 273 (e)	Thomas Heywood	*The Rape of Lucrece*	John Raworth for Nathaniel Butter	The Copy revised, and sundry Songs before omit-/ted, now inserted in their right places.	5th, 1638	corrected copy
WING C 1941 Greg 246 (b1)	[George Chapman]	*Bussy D'Ambois*	A[lice] N[Orton] for Robert Lunne	*Being much corrected and amended / by the Author before his death*	2nd, 1641	annotated and corrected copy
WING T 2018A Greg 687 (b)	The Man in the Moon	*1 New-market Fair*	Printed at *you may go look*	The Second Edition, Corrected and amended by the Author	2nd, 1649	corrected copy
WING B 1585 Greg 515 (c)	Beaumont and Fletcher	*The Elder Brother*	[?] for Humphrey Moseley	*The second Edition, Corrected and Amended*	3rd?, 1650–1	annotated and corrected copy
WING B 1609 Greg 334 (f)	Beaumont and Fletcher	*The Scornful Lady*	[William Wilson] for Humphrey Moseley	The sixt Edition, Corrected and amended	6th, 1651	annotated and corrected copy
WING B 1617 Greg 563 (b)	Beaumont and Fletcher	*Wit without Money*	[?] for Andrew Crooke	*The second Impression Corrected*	2nd, 1661	corrected copy
WING F 1229 Greg 738 (b1)	Richard Flecknoe	*Love's Kingdom*	R. Wood for the Author	Not as it was Acted at the Theatre / near Lincolns-Inn, but as it was / written, and since corrected / BY / Richard Flecknoe	2nd, 1664	independent copy

Table 5.2 *Editorial pledges on the title-pages of early modern printed playbooks (collections).*

Bibliographical numbers	Author	Title	Printer(s) / Publishers(s)	Editorial pledge	Edition / date of publication	Type of intervention
STC 11636	George Gascoigne	*Poesies* [*Jocasta* and *Supposes*]	H. Bynneman for Richard Smith	*Corrected, perfected,* / *and augmented by the Authour*	2nd, 1575	corrected copy
STC 6261	Samuel Daniel	*The Poeticall Essayes* [*Cleopatra* and *Philotas*]	I W[indet] for Simon Waterson	and now againe by him / corrected and augmented	7th, 1607 2nd, 1607	independent and corrected copy
STC 26101	William Shakespeare	*The Whole Contention*	[William Jaggard] for T[homas] [Pavier]	newly corrected and / enlarged	3rd, 1619	corrected copy
STC 22273	William Shakespeare	*Comedies, Histories, & Tragedies*	W. [and Isaac] Jaggard, Ed. Blount, I. Smithweeke, and W. Aspley	Published according to the True Originall Copies	1623	independent, annotated and corrected copy
WING C 564	Thomas Carew	*Poems* [*Coelum Britannicum*]	I[ohn] D[awson] for Thomas Walkley	*The second Edition revised and enlarged*	2nd, 1642	reprint
WING G 1006	Thomas Goffe	*Three Excellent Tragedies*	[?] for G. Bedell and T. Collins	The second Edition, carefully corrected by a friend of the Authors	2nd, 1656	corrected copy
WING R 244	Thomas Randolph	*Poems*	[Thomas Newcombe] for Francis Bowman	The fifth Edition, with several Additions, / Corrected and Amended	5th, 1664	corrected copy

Editorial pledges in early modern dramatic paratexts 99

The type of corrections introduced in the third quarto editions of *1 Henry IV* and *2* and *3 Henry VI* shows that the correctors had a level of familiarity with the text of the play which is more readily associated with annotating readers than with any other category of the agents involved in the transmission of early English drama into print. A printing-house corrector, for example, whose job was to spot typographical mistakes and to ensure that the freshly set text reproduced the printer's copy as closely as possible, was unlikely to detect wrong directions and prefixes, since their detection depends on having at least a working knowledge of the fictive world of the play. Extant proof-sheets from the period confirm that printing-house correctors were primarily concerned about the formal qualities of the text.[17] Printed playbooks annotated for performance suggest that theatrical agents were similarly unlikely to interfere with the dialogue. As Charles Read Baskerville, and, more recently, Leslie Thomson, have observed, the theatrical agents who added manuscript annotations to two copies of *A Looking Glass for London and England* (STC 16681.5) and *The Two Merry Milkemaids* (STC 4281: 1620), presumably in preparation for their revival on stage, paid no attention to the text of the dialogue.[18] The corrections introduced in Wise's edition of *1 Henry IV* and Pavier's editions of *2* and *3 Henry VI* are far from systematic. In fact, they are best described as sporadic or cursory, at most. Besides, they reveal no attempt to recover the reading which may be closest to Shakespeare's intentions by consulting earlier editions. Nevertheless, they were clearly added by annotators who were not likely to be printing-house or theatrical agents, but rather annotating readers, whose main objective was to perfect the text by removing obvious errors and by making it more consistent.

A close analysis of textual variation in the editions listed in Tables 5.1 and 5.2 shows that, contrary to the assumption that editorial pledges are generally unfounded and that they were used by early modern publishers as mere marketing ploys, the changes and corrections introduced in the third quarto editions of *1 Henry IV* and *2* and *3 Henry VI* are representative of how printed dramatic copy was prepared for its resubmission to the press. As my tables indicate, the texts of all the editions which claim to have been newly corrected and amended were indeed generally set from a lightly annotated copy, as suggested by the fact that they introduce sporadic and unsystematic changes in their speech prefixes, stage directions and the text of the dialogue, unless they were reset from, or amended by reference to, a fresh textual witness. The only exceptions are Richard Meighen's 1630 quarto edition of *The Merry Wives of Windsor*, which is set very closely from the longer version of the text as printed in the First Folio, the second edition of

John Marston's *Jack Drum's Entertainment*, where the main departure from the printer's copy is within the scope of an alert printing-house agent,[19] and *Coelum Brittanicum*, a masque included in the second edition of Thomas Carew's *Poems*.

Besides showing that editorial pledges generally signal a genuine attempt to change, update, or perfect the dramatic text for its resubmission to the press, a close analysis of the type and range of corrections introduced in editions which claim authorial involvement and editions which provide no information about the identity of the corrector reveals intriguingly similar levels of editorial commitment. A good example is the range of changes introduced in the second editions of Thomas Middleton's *Michaelmas Term*, Thomas Goffe's *The Raging Turk*, and John Marston's *The Fawn*. These three editions represent an interesting case study, because they were advertised respectively as being '*Newly corrected*', 'carefully corrected by a friend of the Authors', and 'now corrected of many faults, which by reason of the Au- / thors absence, were let slip in the first edition'. These claims reveal editorial pledges as the product of, in Genette's terms, 'the author and his allies', and suggest a concern for authorial intention. Substantive variants in these three editions suggest that differences between authorial and non-authorial corrections are best described as differences of degree rather than kind.

As Gail Paster has recently pointed out, most of the corrections in the second edition of *Michaelmas Term* are within the scope of an alert compositor.[20] However, at least two other related corrections must have been added to the printer's copy before it was set. The second edition expands the following entry direction in the first quarto, '*Enter Lethes pander, Helgill, the Coûtrie wench coming in with / a new fashion Gown drest Gentlewoman like, the Taylor pointes it, and a Tyrewoman busie about her head*', by adding the name, '*and Mistris Comings*' before '*a Tyrewoman busie about her head*'.[21] The character of the tire-woman makes her first appearance in this scene and her name is first mentioned twenty lines after this entry direction. It is highly unlikely that a compositor would have recovered the name of this character from a later section of the dialogue, and that he would have decided to add it retrospectively to a direction which he had set twenty lines earlier. Rather than acting on his own initiative, the compositor is more likely to have found a manuscript correction in his copy, which indicated that this name should be added to the entry direction preserved in the first quarto. A further manuscript correction must have alerted the compositor to the fact that the speech prefix for an isolated line spoken by this character two pages later should read '*Com.*' (for Mistress Comings), rather than '*Coin.*', as it does in the first quarto.

The mere fact that the annotator is described as a friend of the author's seems to elicit a more sustained level of intervention in *The Raging Turk*. Although, as in *Michaelmas Term*, some corrections may plausibly be compositorial,[22] other corrections seem to be beyond the scope of a printing-house agent. Cherseogles's lines – 'but you powers / That with propitious cares, tender the world / And vs fraile mortals, helpe me to preuent / A generall enemie by the fall of some' – are improved by a single, but inspired, verbal substitution of 'enemie' with 'ruine'.[23] As a result, Cherseogles is more clearly hoping to prevent the death of many by orchestrating the fall of the leaders of two large opposing armies the night before the battle. Even smarter is one correction which transforms a line where Achomates illogically calls himself a villain – '*Sely*. . . . what are thou? / *Acho*. He that vsurp's the title of a villaine' (M4ν 17–18) – into an effective indictment of his brother Selymus as a usurping villain: '*Sely*. . . . what art thou? / *Acho*. He that usurp's, hath title of a villaine'.[24] Other corrections of viable, but stylistically unsatisfactory lines, confirm the intervention of a shrewd annotating reader. Repetitions are, for example, carefully removed on at least five occasions[25] and two rhyming couplets at the end of pivotal speeches, which were originally aligned to the left margin, are indented to improve the visual layout of the verse.[26] Besides intervening to correct or improve the text of the dialogue, the annotator of *The Raging Turk* paid attention to the consistency of speech prefixes, making sure that relevant lines of dialogue were also revised when a change of speaker affects them or vice versa.[27] A considerable amount of attention is also paid to stage directions. Typical of the corrector's intervention is the ability to identify what was set as half-lines in the dialogue of the first edition as stage directions.[28] Besides, the position of some directions is changed so that their timing is improved.[29] The corrector also expanded a cluster of directions which roughly indicates the sequence in which Selymus reads three letters in the first edition.[30] Admittedly, the corrector failed to spot two wrong entry directions[31] and to add missing ones.[32] However, the corrections in *The Raging Turk* are overall more extensive than in *Michaelmas Term*.

Corrections in the second edition of *The Fawn* would seem to suggest that when an author was personally involved, the printer's copy was annotated even more thoroughly. Marston's intervention is acknowledged by a new note to the reader. In this note, the author explains why he found it necessary to correct the first edition and what type of text his readers should expect to find in the new edition: 'REader, know I haue perused this coppy, to make some satisfaction for the / first faulty impression: yet so vrgent hath been my busines, that some / errors haue styll passed, which thy discretion may amend'.³³ This seems to be a fair assessment of the improvements and the shortcomings in the text that follows. In some respects, the changes from the first edition confirm the involvement of an annotating author. A tell-tale sign is the presence of additions, which are often symptomatic of authorial intervention or consultation of a fresh textual witness. Additions in the second edition of *The Fawn* range from single words to three new lines added to a memorable *sententia* about the distasteful tendency to seek the favour of those who thrive and to shun those whom Fortune has forsaken.³⁴ While some additions are unnecessary and may have been added by Marston as he was annotating the printer's copy for this edition,³⁵ others may have been restored by consultation of the manuscript from which the first edition was set.³⁶

Another category of corrections which suggests authorial intervention is what can best be described as tinkering. On D1r alone, there are four instances of variants which improve the text without substantially altering the viable alternative preserved in the first edition.³⁷ According to recent editors and critics of Marston, several other instances of this type of editorial fussiness,³⁸ along with the additions mentioned above, bear the mark of authorial intervention. However, other changes resemble the patterns of variants observed in *Michaelmas Term* and *The Raging Turk*, thus suggesting that not *all* departures from the first edition are necessarily authorial. Only cursory attention is paid to speech prefixes and stage directions³⁹ and only some of the corrections in the dialogue reveal a detailed knowledge of the play.⁴⁰ Two variants in close proximity at G2r 6 and G2r 8, for example, are rather good: 'that *compendium* of witnes' and 'unshake the iest' become 'that *compendium* of wittiness' and 'unshale [that is, unshell⁴¹] the iest'. However, as with scores of other local corrections, it is impossible to decide whether they are more likely to be within or beyond the scope of a compositor.⁴² Another textual feature which *The Fawn* shares with *Michaelmas Term* and *The Raging Turk* is that it overlooks pretty obvious howlers. Since the whole play is set in Urbino, one wonders how Marston could possibly have missed the fact that Gonzago misidentifies himself as '*Venice* Duke' (D3v 27).

Overall, what a detailed analysis of these three editions shows is that, even when authors were personally involved, the annotation of copy was sporadic and superficial at best, and that even though the number of corrections may be more extensive, their quality is hardly distinctive enough for the majority of them to be firmly attributed to the author. Even categories which would seem to be safely associated with a correcting author are in fact very possibly the product of non-authorial intervention. The second edition of Thomas

Heywood's *The Four Prentices of London*, for example, includes no additions and no substantial rewriting, although the title-page advertises it as '*Written and newly revised* by 1THOMAS HEYVVOOD'.⁴³ Conversely, a copy of the fourth quarto of Francis Beaumont and John Fletcher's *The Maid's Tragedy* held at the Bodleian Library (STC 1680, 1638, Malone 217), which was annotated by King Charles I, adds one missing prefix (C1*r* 28) and corrects two (H3*v* 35–6), besides adding two speeches in 4.2.⁴⁴ Percy Simpson rightly interprets these two additional speeches as a critical response to two pivotal scenes, where the 'low level of intelligence in Court circles ... when the issue involved was something so serious as the murder of a king' clearly alarmed the royal reader.⁴⁵ Whatever reason may have prompted the king to add these two speeches, his annotations provide a good example of non-authorial additions, thus showing that even this type of correction is not necessarily authorial or symptomatic of consultation of a fresh textual witness.

The realisation that no category of corrections and no specific level of intervention can be firmly ascribed to authorial, as opposed to non-authorial, agents has important implications. If textual scholars like Jerome McGann and Don McKenzie have argued that editors should not attempt to 'lift the veil of print' from early modern playbooks when they re-present them to the modern reader, my work suggests that it is not so much a matter of what editors should or should not do, since it is simply impossible to disentangle the individual contributions of the multiple agents involved in the transmission and retransmission of these texts into print. In other words, editorial pledges highlight the emendation of the work, but do little to help us uncover the status of any alterations. What seemed to matter to early modern agents involved in the transmission and retransmission of dramatic texts into print was their ongoing perfection and this task, like the process of constructing a printed book more generally, was understood as inherently collaborative.⁴⁶

It is worth considering what happens when textual scholars assume that they can determine attribution, especially in relation to the type of corrections I have been discussing in this chapter. According to Nicholas Brooke, the title-page of the second edition of George Chapman's *Bussy D'Ambois* is 'certainly right in claiming much correction and amendment, but', he then hastens to add, 'whether it is right to ascribe this work to the original author is more difficult to decide'.⁴⁷ Bibliographical evidence indicates that '[the second edition] ... for all its extensive differences, is not derived directly from a manuscript, but from a corrected copy of [the first edition]'.⁴⁸ Although a manuscript was consulted, and this manuscript is likely to have been revised by Chapman himself, the annotator of the printer's copy for the second edition seems to have tampered with it and to have consulted his manuscript source only sporadically. Trying to distinguish authorial corrections from editorial tampering, Brooke sets up three categories of variants: 'a number [of variants] where the poetic quality is unmistakably Chapman; a number [of variants] where the motive is obviously "theatrical" and without poetic merit; and a number [of variants] which could easily be due to [the] copyists' who transcribed the theatrical manuscript revised by Chapman, possibly several times over the twenty-year period which intervened between Chapman's revision and the publication of the second edition.[49] Brooke is soon forced to admit that these distinctions are rather blunt and ineffective:

> I find it quite impossible to go right through the revisions assigning each one to its distinct source: the cases shade through every gradation, each source seems inextricably linked with another, as if, after all, one hand *was* responsible for all. In other words, looked at in this way, I find the problem yielding contradictory answers: it is almost equally hard to believe in one hand, and in several hands.[50]

The acknowledgement of a methodological impasse does not stop Brooke from attempting a reconstruction of the events that led to the confusing mixture of potentially authorial, but also plausibly non-authorial, corrections which found their way into the second edition of *Bussy*:

> In some places a bulky change whose character seems to me to suggest non-Chapman, contains some Chapman-like characteristic ... If Chapman revised first and did not work over his successor's version, stray lines of his authorship could not creep into the other reviser's work. It is not altogether convenient, but I am forced to postulate that the other reviser could write in Chapman's manner, and sometimes do it well ... If Chapman did not write the new scene ... in III.ii, ... then the other man could ... writ[e] ... very Chapmanesque lines.[51]

Brooke's logic is embarrassingly tenuous here: if lines which are good enough to be attributed to Chapman occur in larger sections which seem overall poetically inferior to Chapman's own style, then we are forced to assume, rather preposterously, that the corrector could write like Chapman, but only *intermittently*.

We may in fact gain a much better understanding of the complex textual make-up of early modern playbooks if we allow ourselves to step back from the imperative of attribution and if we give some serious thought to the fact that authorial intervention does not seem to have been a deciding factor in determining the type and range of corrections introduced in dramatic editions set from annotated copy. In fact, privileging authorial over non-authorial corrections, even though they cannot easily, if at all, be told apart, may misleadingly suggest that authors were the only agents responsible for, and willing to invest in, the perfection of dramatic copy for the press.

Several bibliographical and textual clues in fact indicate that publishers played a significant role in the preparation of dramatic copy for the press, especially when authors were not involved, either because they were indifferent, or openly opposed, to the publication of their works, or simply because they were unavailable or dead. Title-pages of early modern dramatic editions often record the name of acting companies, less often the name of the author, but they unfailingly record the name of the publisher. By the publisher, which is a slight anachronistic way of describing what some early modern stationers did, I mean the only agent who had a vested financial interest in the publication of any type of book, including a playbook. Before the advent of copyright legislation at the beginning of the eighteenth century, authors were only paid once, when the manuscript copy of their works was sold to a stationer willing to buy it and to shoulder the costs of having it printed. It seems therefore hardly surprising that publishers should invest money and time in the perfection of their dramatic copies for the press. The publisher Henry Herringman explicitly refers to this type of costs when he addresses the readers of his 1679 collected edition of Beaumont and Fletcher's *Works*:

Courteous Reader, The First Edition of these Plays in this Volume having found that Acceptance as to give us Encouragement to make a Second Impression, we were very desirous they might come forth as Correct as might be. And we were very opportunely informed of a Copy which an ingenious and worthy Gentleman had taken the pains (or rather the pleasure) to read over; wherein he had all along Corrected several faults (some very gross) which had crept in by the frequent imprinting of them. His Corrections were the more to be valued, because he had an intimacy with both our Authors, and had been a Spectator of most of them when they were Acted in their life-time. This therefore we resolved to purchase at any Rate; and accordingly with no small cost obtain'd it.[52]

As well as having a vested financial interest in the perfection of their dramatic copies for the press, publishers may also have been responsible for adding editorial pledges to the title-pages of their editions. The formulaic quality of at least some of the editorial pledges discussed in this chapter suggests that they may indeed have been phrased and added by the publisher rather than the author. This certainly seems to have been the case with the identical pledges found on the title-pages of Davenant's and Cowley's collected works, since both Davenant and Cowley were dead by the time Herringman published these collections in 1673 and 1693. Even more crucially, publishers may have annotated the printer's copy themselves, as suggested by the fact that editions published by the same stationer often introduce similar types of corrections. It is, for example, significant that the Pavier Quartos, besides introducing sporadic corrections to speech prefixes, stage directions, and to the dialogue, also include instances of slight, but fairly idiosyncratic, revisions, which are shared by earlier dramatic editions also published by Pavier at the beginning of his career.[53]

More generally, focusing on publishers as key agents in the transmission of early English drama into print has led me to believe that although the occurrence of editorial pledges on the title-pages of early modern printed playbooks may be statistically insignificant, the preparation of dramatic copy for the press must have been a more widespread practice, since editions published by stationers committed to dramatic publication, like Andrew Wise, Thomas Pavier, Isaac Jaggard, include corrections even when editorial intervention is *not* advertised on their title-pages.[54] It therefore seems reasonable to conclude that, although informed by different principles and carried out anonymously, dramatic copy was often, if not routinely, corrected for the press, even before the official rise of the editorial tradition of vernacular drama at the beginning of the eighteenth century. As this chapter has shown, editorial pledges reflect printing-house practice and are not merely marketing ploys. We should thus read them as part of the paratextual apparatus of interpretation and emendation of an early modern playbook rather than as a merely sales-orientated peritext.

CHAPTER 6

Status anxiety and English Renaissance translation

Neil Rhodes

When we use the term 'Renaissance' for early modern, one thing we might have in mind is translation. Translation represented a process of cultural transmission from the classical to the modern world and a process of exchange within the modern world. Texts were converted from Greek into Latin, from the classical languages to the modern vernaculars and then from one modern language to another. About 20 per cent of the entire book production in England during Elizabeth's reign, amounting to over a thousand separate items, consists of translation.[1] F. O. Matthiessen observed that, 'A study of Elizabethan translations is a study of the means by which the Renaissance came to England', while more recently Warren Boutcher has suggested that we should try to 'read Renaissance translations as "original" works by those who happened to be translating'.[2] Modern readers would certainly regard works such as North's Plutarch, Chapman's Homer, or Florio's Montaigne as classics of English literature in their own right, but even at the time translation was recognised as a distinct literary form. In his well-known advertisement for the Elizabethan literary revival in *Palladis Tamia*, Francis Meres included translators alongside his other lists of successful modern English emulations of classical authors, citing Golding and Chapman as well as the translators of Seneca's tragedies, Harington's Ariosto, and Thomas Watson's version of *Antigone*.[3] Meres's point is not just that these writers deserve praise for enriching the store of literature in English, but also that they are comparable with the best Roman translators of Greek texts into Latin.

All this would seem to present translation as a high-status activity and change of status is indeed at the heart of the concept of 'translation' itself. In one sense of the word this can involve an elevation: when a clergyman is 'translated' to a bishopric, for example; but in its more usual sense of a conversion from the language of the author into another language any additional suggestion of a change of status is more likely to be downward. Translations are always inadequate, while translations from Latin or Greek into the vernacular also risk the charge of commonness, dumbing down. Despite Meres's claims to the contrary, this is especially true in the case of translations into English during the sixteenth century, since the language itself was held to be inferior and unfit for serious literary purposes, even by native speakers, up to about 1580. For non-native speakers who were obliged to use it, like John Florio, it was an object of disdain: 'It is a language that wyl do you good in England, but passe Douer, it is woorth nothing', he wrote in his Italian language manual, *Firste fruites*.[4] In 1614, when the Earl of Arundel went on a cultural tour of Italy with Inigo Jones, he is reported by Camden to have spoken only in English. How successful this was is not recorded, though Camden explains that he did so not out of ignorance but 'for the honour of our native tongue'.[5] Even though England could now boast its own national literature there is still a kind of combative defensiveness about the language itself. In Arundel's case he would also have been conscious of the discrepancy between his high social status and his rather lower cultural status as an Englishman. The point of his tour was, after all, to drink at the well of the Renaissance. The subject of translation is fraught with status anxiety, and this is particularly evident in the paratextual material that accompanies printed translations, which often presents complex and interesting negotiations between cultural and social status.

Gérard Genette specifically excluded translation from his account of what he termed 'paratexts', while agreeing that 'its paratextual relevance seems ... undeniable', because this would have required a book in itself.[6] The present chapter is a small step in that direction, and we could begin by asking whether translations might themselves be classed as paratexts. That would seem to be impossible, but the familiar example of the Loeb edition gives pause for thought. Here is a printed book in which every page of text is literally pre-faced by a page of the text from which it is translated. However, since the pre-facing material comes from original or authorial text it would be counter-intuitive to designate this as paratextual. But what if the relationship between verso and recto is switched so that the translation appears on the left-hand side and the original text on the right? An early modern example of this is Sir Francis Kinaston's Latin version of Chaucer's *Troilus and Criseyde* published in 1635. The printed version consists of the first two books only, taking Chaucer's text from Thomas Speght's 1598 edition of the *Workes*, but Kinaston went on to complete his translation of the whole poem, intending to publish it if the first instalment proved successful. He died before he was able to see his plan through, but the complete translation survives in manuscript and has on-page glossing of words in English with more substantial commentary at the end in Latin. We do not know whether this format would have been reproduced in print. The book we have presents three numbered stanzas on each page, the English on the right in black letter and a Latin rhyme-royal version in italic on the left. Kinaston's Chaucer is a fascinating textual case study in all sorts of ways and is significant here because it runs contrary to the principle that translations are, in more than one sense, inferior to the authorial text. The point of Kinaston's translation was to convert this jewel of a poem into a timeless language, and so save it for posterity, since the language of the original was antiquated and already scarcely intelligible.[7] One conclusion we might draw in the case of this particular print convention is that the high-status text tends to appear on the left.

Nevertheless, that would not address the question of how we might describe the phenomenon of parallel text. It is not discussed by Genette in *Paratexts*, but it might nonetheless fit somewhere into his five-part scheme of intertext, paratext, metatext, hypertext, and architext. One characteristic of paratexts is that they are situated on a horizontal plane: this is implied in the metaphor of the threshold. As with other 'para-' formations, such as 'paramilitary' and 'paramedic', their situation is one of adjacency and their function auxiliary. But although you might say that the physical construction of the printed book creates an impression of adjacency in the case of the Loeb edition, or Kinaston's Chaucer, this is not the actual relationship between left-hand and right-hand pages. The relationship here is not horizontal but vertical: translation adds the third dimension. Genette acknowledges that paratexts may be situated temporally as well as spatially, as in the case of prospectuses or later prefaces,[8] but these do not have quite the same relationship with the main text as translations do with their authorial predecessors. The appropriate way to describe translations would probably be as metatexts in the sense that they represent something of a second-order kind. By analogy, a metalanguage is a language or set of terms that we use to describe another language, so the two languages operate on different levels. A paralanguage on the other hand is adjacent and auxiliary, as in the case of gesture and other bodily movements: in rhetorical terms, the *actio* that accompanies *elocutio*. Genette offers literary commentary as his principal example of metatext, but translation should also be placed in this category. Nor do we need to describe translations only as second-order texts, since they may be third order or beyond. North's Plutarch was translated from Amyot's French translated from Plutarch's Greek, and there are many other Renaissance examples of texts reaching English either through an intermediary Latin version or through a second European vernacular. Spanish romances, for example, were often translated into English from French versions rather than from the original language.[9] What we have in these cases is a kind of textual genealogy and inevitably (even with two texts) a hierarchy – which brings us back to the question of status, and with it, status anxiety.

If translations are metatexts, then translators' prefaces are the paratexts of metatexts. Do they have any distinctive features? One obvious consequence of status anxiety is apology, and apology is indeed a characteristic feature of the translator's preface. Again, this is something that Genette says relatively little about. He has one page in *Paratexts* on what are called 'lightning rods' in the English translation, which is a term he borrows from Lichtenberg.[10] But this rather underestimates the frequency of apology in prefaces both in the everyday sense of the word and in its more formal sense of *apologia* or defence. North's preface to his translation of Plutarch, for example, offers a passionate defence of history. The most famous English critical text of the period (by Sidney) is known alternatively as an 'apology for' or 'defence of' poetry. Apologies for translation are in the first place extensions of the apology for poetry in general and this is how Harington styles the preface to his translation of Ariosto. Most of this paratext is devoted to praise of the 'sweet statelinesse' of heroic poetry and of Ariosto in particular.[11] Reaching the point where he feels obliged to comment on his own inadequacy as a poet, he agrees that this has 'most need of an Apologie both large & substantiall' and confesses that readers may find 'that my verse is vnartificiall, the stile rude, the phrase barbarous, the meeter vnpleasant'.[12] More usually, however, English Renaissance translators produce prefaces of a different kind because they are suffering from a three-fold dose of status anxiety. First, all translations are necessarily inadequate renderings of their originals; second, in the case of English they are being turned into a language which is itself felt to be poorly equipped for literary purposes; and third, by making texts more easily accessible they carry the taint of commonness.

Translators' prefaces deal with these problems in various ways. Philemon Holland argued pugnaciously in the preface to his translation of Pliny that if English people who objected to translation thought more of their own language and nation they would welcome this opportunity 'to triumph now over the Romans in subduing their literature under the dent of the English pen'.[13] But a rather more effective response to the first two anxieties about English translation is offered by Chapman in the prefaces to his translations of Homer. In the 1611 *Iliad* he counters the argument that translation necessarily involves loss by pointing out that it is over-literal, word-for-word renderings that are more likely to be inadequate. Authors who attempt this might as well 'make fish with fowl, Camels with Whales engender; / Or their tongues' speech, in other mouths compell'.[14] As for the second anxiety, in his earlier preface to *Achilles shield*, Chapman had defended English by arguing that the language was 'more conformable, fluent, and expressiue' than other modern languages. Besides – and here both anxieties are swept away – he claims that Homer wrote 'from a free furie' and 'would scorne to haue his supreme worthinesse glosing in his courtshippe and priuiledge of tongue'.[15]

The last response to the burden of anxiety felt by many translators is to reject the charge of dumbing down by arguing for the cultural benefits of translation in general. This is what Thomas Hoby does in the paratexts to his English version of Castiglione's *Courtier*, which contain an epistle to Lord Henry Hastings, son of the Earl of Huntingdon, a suitably noble figure whose family had hosted Castiglione on his visit to England in 1506.[16] Although he tells Hastings that the work is designed for gentlemen such as himself, he then argues that it should be made available for the 'commune benefite' rather than remain a 'private commoditie' for those who know Italian.[17] This spurs him on to a polemic against scholars who labour over foreign-language texts only to keep the knowledge to themselves so that others will have to go through the same drudgery. England is inferior to other nations in encouraging translation, he claims, whereas in Italy, 'where the Sciences are most tourned into the vulgar tungue, there are best learned men'. He then argues, somewhat provocatively, that 'the translation of Latin or Greeke authours, doeth not onely *not* hinder learning [my italics], but it furthereth it, yea, it is learning itself, and a great staye to youth'.[18] Commonness, then, according to Hoby, becomes a virtue.

This argument is likely to have been received with mixed feelings by Sir John Cheke, the celebrated Greek scholar, whose response to the preface is printed at the very end of the book. Hoby was an undergraduate at St John's College, Cambridge in Cheke's time and had sent him his translation, seeking his approval for the preface in particular. Although Cheke was sympathetic to the development of the vernacular, as a scholar who had been much concerned with the correct pronunciation of Greek he would surely not have welcomed being told by a former student that 'profounde learned men' such as himself should be devoting their efforts to English translation, as Hoby urges.[19] And although Cheke's circle at Cambridge had been responsible for planning the first 'serious' translations,[20] it is difficult to imagine him agreeing with Hoby's claim that translation 'is learning itself'. His own translations of Chrysostom had been from Greek into Latin, a rather small step towards commonness. Cheke's laconic reply to Hoby is polite enough, but deliberately ignores the very argument that Hoby was presumably hoping he would endorse. Instead he gives him a brief lecture on pure English, which is broken off with the lame excuse, 'But I am called awai, I prai you pardon mi shortnes'.[21] His views on Hoby's claim for the academic status of translation remain unknown.

The case of Castiglione's *Courtier* is complicated by the fact that it was translated into Latin by another Englishman, Bartholomew Clerke, in 1577 *after* the publication of Hoby's version.[22] The object of doing so was clearly not the same as Kinaston's when he produced his Latin Chaucer: Castiglione's Italian was far from obsolete. Nor would it seem to us that Clerke was making the work more accessible. Nonetheless, it was Clerke's Latin *Courtier* that stayed in print the longest. While Hoby's version went through three editions (1561, 1577, 1603), with an additional parallel-text edition in Italian, French and English issued by John Wolfe in 1588, Clerke's was reprinted five times up to 1612. It was the Latin version that Gabriel Harvey, a professor of rhetoric at Cambridge like Clerke himself, recommended to his pupil Arthur Capel.[23] The superior status of the translation is signalled by its being printed in italic in contrast to Hoby's more demotic black letter, and while Hoby's dedicatees are gentlemen, Clerke caps him by dedicating his version to Queen Elizabeth herself. Appropriately enough, the one dedicatee shared by both Hoby and Clerke, Thomas Sackville, had been translated to the peerage by the time the Latin version came out, where he appears as Lord Buckhurst.

Perhaps the most complex set of paratexts to precede an English Renaissance translation, and certainly the most revealing in terms of status anxiety, is the introductory material to Florio's 1603 Montaigne. This is a highly elaborate document with several different components. After the title-page, the first image that meets the reader's eye is a vertical arrangement of three 'consecrated Altares', each bearing the names of two noble ladies; adjacent to this is an 'Epistle Dedicatorie' addressed to Florio's first pair of patrons, Lucy, Countess of Bedford, and her mother, Lady Anne Harrington; this is followed by two sonnets from the pen of 'Il Candido', an address to the reader, two further sonnets by 'Il Candido', and finally a poem by Samuel Daniel. This sequence of paratexts has a number of functions, each responding to different but closely related anxieties about the status of the author/translator and Florio's own social and cultural status.[24]

The epistle to Lucy and her mother begins with some Baroque wordplay based on rhetorical figures of doubling and pairing, inspired, no doubt, by the doubling up of the dedicatees. The dedication itself is to 'my best-best

Benefactors, and most-most honored Ladies', which sounds more like an affected stammer than a polite intensifier. But in view of the fact that Florio is speaking to a mother and daughter (who was herself a mother), what follows is much stranger. He describes his previous literary labour as his 'last Birth', designating this 'masculine' on account of its being primary and independent and therefore of high status. The analogy he draws is with the mythological loosing of Bacchus from Jupiter's thigh. Embedded in parentheses here is a reference to Montaigne's essays themselves as also representing a masculine birth, even though they were made by 'collecting'. His translation of Montaigne, however, is a 'defective edition' and therefore a female birth, 'since all translations are reputed femalls, delivered at second hand', and Florio's role as translator is comparable with Vulcan's in hatching Minerva from Jupiter's brain. Florio's metaphors are a little confused, first because it is not clear whether it is the parturition or the progeny that is being gendered here, and second because he immediately goes on to characterise his role in the Montaigne translation as that of 'fondling foster-father' by contrast with the true fathering of his previous offspring.[25] He has 'transported it from *France* to *England*; put it in English clothes; taught it to talke our tongue [and] ... would set it forth to the best service I might'.[26] The confusion is an indicator of Florio's anxiety about quite what status his translation of Montaigne has as an authored work.

It would be interesting to know how the two mothers received Florio's account of his English Montaigne as a defective female birth. The convoluted opening to his dedication does make a little more sense, however, if we recognise that the 'last Birth' which Florio refers to is his Italian–English dictionary, *A worlde of wordes* (1598), and if we read the Montaigne paratexts alongside the paratexts to the earlier work. We can see from these that the later dedication is an elaborate play on the notion of the authored book as brainchild: 'my riper yeeres affoording me I cannot say a braine-babe *Minerua*, armed at al assaies at first houre; but rather from my Italian *Semele*, and English thigh, a bouncing boie, *Bacchus*-like'.[27] Florio evidently finds his mythological metaphors easy to take apart and reassemble. Here, the brainchild Minerva is presented as the high-status, primary birth, while Bacchus, the offspring of Jupiter and Semele (whose role is suppressed in the Montaigne dedication), becomes a lesser creation, born from the copulation of English and Italian. In both cases, of course, Florio is employing the modesty topos: he does not want to claim too much for his achievement and certainly not before these exalted patrons who are acting as godparents to the book. The dedicatees of the dictionary were the Earl of Rutland, the Earl of Southampton and, as for the Montaigne translation, Lucy, Countess of

Bedford, and Florio fairly grovels before them: 'The retainer doth some seruice, that now and then but holds your Honors styrrop, or lendes a hande over a stile'.²⁸ This is what he meant when he said of the Montaigne translation that it was sent into 'the best service'. There is a difference, however, in the assignment of quasi-paternal roles. While Florio presented himself as the foster-father of the English Montaigne, in the case of the *Worlde of wordes* it was the dedicatees who were invited to act as godparents, and not just to the book. The dedication ends with Florio describing himself as 'borne, bred, and brought foorth for your Honors chiefe seruice' and observing hopefully that sometimes parents make as much 'of adopted, as begotten children'.²⁹

The remainder of the Montaigne dedication adopts a different and even more exaggerated style of self-abasement, that of the desperate Petrarchan lover. Providing his six female patrons with consecrated altars takes the Petrarchan language of worship to a new level of hyperbole, and towards the end of the dedication he does indeed say that he will outdo the tributes of Petrarch to his mistress.³⁰ In-between we are treated to a display of simpering rhetorical antics in which Lucy Russell, the first of the dedicatees, is likened to various kinds of dominatrix. It is just about possible to extract from the high camp of Florio's prose style the circumstances that led to his producing an English Montaigne. Sir Edward Wotton had commissioned a translation of one essay, which Lucy had read, and as a result she had decided to get Florio to do a complete English version of the three books. The work was done while he was a guest at her house. This sounds like a fairly comfortable billet, but Florio's account of the sufferings inflicted on him by his task-mistress is hair-raising: she was 'without pitty of my failing, my fainting, my labouring, my languishing, my gasping for some breath (O could so Honorable, be so pitty-lesse? Madame, now doe I flatter you?)'. He was like her hart (pun intended) with a collar around his neck, risking strangulation: 'I sweat, I wept, and I went-on, til now I stand at bay'. And in a bizarre conjunction of metaphors he was her 'blacke ... seruant' and 'a captived Cannibal fattend against my death'.³¹ The last image probably echoes Montaigne's essay, 'On the Cannibals', but it seems also to refer to the ample dinners he had enjoyed in the Bedford household in compensation for the terrible stress that Lucy had put him under.

It is difficult not to enjoy the absurdity of Florio's self-presentation in the 'Epistle Dedicatorie'. What it underlines, to put it more soberly, is the way in which anxieties about the status of the translator combine with a high degree of self-consciousness about social status. The address to the reader, however, is specifically concerned with the status of translation and it takes the form of an apology, beginning, with unexpected simplicity: 'Shall I apologize translation?'. Since Florio had been so dismissive of English twenty-five years earlier, he might well have felt the need to defend the Montaigne project. But the status of English had changed. That quarter of a century from *Firste fruites* to the death of Elizabeth, or from *The Shepheardes Calendar* to the first quarto of *Hamlet*, represents the coming of age of English as a literary language. Florio's change of heart was evident in the preface to the *Worlde of wordes* where he explains that:

If in these rankes the English out-number the Italian, congratulate the copie and varietie of our sweete-mother-toong, which under this most Excellent well-speaking Princesse or Ladie of the worlde in all languages is growne as farre beyond that of former times, as her most flourishing raigne for all hapines is beyond the raignes of former Princes.[32]

Now it is only translation in general that Florio needs to defend, and his first concern in the Montaigne paratexts, like Hoby's in the preface to his *Courtier*, is with those who say 'that such conversion is the subversion of Universities'. Not so, he counters, because 'my olde fellow *Nolano* tolde me, and taught publikely, that from translation all Science had it's ofspring'.[33] This is very similar to Hoby's argument, except that here he claims the authority of 'Nolano', a name for Giordano Bruno, who had become friendly with Florio while staying at the French embassy in London in the 1580s. His statement also makes a contribution to the English language: Frances Yates notes that this is the first usage of the genitive neuter pronoun (it's) and it contains what we should perhaps now call the florist's apostrophe.[34] But Florio's translation also makes more substantial contributions to the 'copie and varietie' of English, including the words 'conscientious', 'facilitate', 'amusing', 'regret', and 'emotion', which he records at the end of his address to the reader. These would have disgusted Cheke, who told Hoby to stick to 'the old denisoned wordes' as far as possible in his own translation and not to 'boldly venture of unknown wordes'.[35]

Florio's next move in the defence of translation is to try an analogy. If we think of original texts in terms of source rather than ancestry, then we have the image of a well; so how 'can the wel-springs be so sweete and deepe; and will the well-drawne water be so sower and smell?', he asks rhetorically. The analogy is ingenious because it preserves the vertical relationship between text and metatext but at the same time transforms it from the process of handing down, with its inevitable associations of loss and decay, to one of drawing up. Carried away, perhaps, by the success of the image, Florio then fatally extends it. Addressing the point that learning should not be made common, he agrees that no man would wish his mistress to be a prostitute. But, he continues, 'this Mistresse is like ayre, fire, water, the more breathed the clearer; the more extended the warmer; the more drawne the sweeter'.[36] In the last part of this analogy the mistress has become the well, but quite how this image is to work is mysterious. What is evident, though, is that Florio is anxious to create some sort of alignment between the status of translation and social status. The latter is then given a sexual dimension in the antithesis between the elevated Petrarchan object of desire and the prostitute. The stated terms of dispute here concern 'commonness'; the unstated ones concern 'purity', verbal as well as sexual, as the sweet water of the well transmutes into the idealised mistress. In this respect, at least, Cheke would have approved, since 'purity' was very much a watchword in language debates among his Cambridge circle.

Status anxiety in all its forms is the connecting thread of the paratexts to Florio's Montaigne, and there is good reason for this. The forthright tone of Hoby's epistle to Hastings and the reply from Cheke is that of a gentleman speaking to other gentlemen about a text that is concerned with gentlemanly conduct. As far as the issue of English translation is concerned, all three are native English speakers, so they share the same cultural as well as social status. These paratexts represent a form of conversation between men who are, in the most important respects, equals. Florio's situation, and the relationships on display in the paratexts of the 1603 Montaigne, are very different. He was the son of an Italian Protestant asylum seeker, and although probably born in England he spent his childhood in an Italian canton of Switzerland where his father had fled on the accession of Mary in 1553. When he returned to England in the mid-1570s he paid his way through Oxford by giving Italian lessons. His social standing in the university as a servant to Emmanuel Barnes (brother of the poet, Barnabe Barnes) at Magdalen College was certainly lowly. The duties he would have performed were far beneath a gentleman, as an undergraduate at Corpus Christi College recorded some years later: 'should I have carried woode and dust and emptied chamber pots and no man, no scholler so doing but myselfe, it had been intolerable and to[o] base for my minde'.[37] Florio's experience at Oxford was very different from Hoby's experience at Cambridge. Where most young men acquired effortless superiority, Florio learned obsequiousness. This is all too evident in the dedication of the manuscript collection of proverbs that he wrote from Oxford to Sir Edward Dyer in 1582, which begins: 'My most honourable and illustrious lord, whose virtues shine like stars in the sky, and whose nobility resounds everywhere, I know will wonder how so base a person as Florio can presume to address him'.³⁸ This may sound less abject in the original Italian, but the fact of his having written to Dyer in that language underlines the point that his cultural identity, too, was uncertain – hence his assertion of Englishness in the lines beneath his engraved portrait in the second edition of the *Worlde of wordes*: '*Italus ore, Anglus pectore*' (Italian by country, English at heart).³⁹

But while Florio's social position was precarious and his cultural identity ambiguous, his first language, and the cultural capital he was able to offer by teaching it, had real class.⁴⁰ Italian was the premier language of the Renaissance, as he noted in his dedication to Dyer, and it was also the only modern language with a 'classical' tradition, based on the style of the canonical authors, Dante, Boccaccio, and Petrarch.⁴¹ This was acknowledged by Meres when he presented his 'comparative discourse of our English poets with the *Greeke, Latine, and Italian poets*'.⁴² So when commissioned by an English aristocrat to translate the works of a Frenchman into English twenty-five years later, although the status of his adopted language had risen considerably by then, Florio would still have been conscious that the end-product of his labours would be made out of relatively poor-quality material. This is why he constantly seeks to beautify and elaborate on the original text in his translation. But the language of the Montaigne dedication is so absurdly extravagant on account of insecurity as well as pride. The highly wrought façade of flattery and self-abasement (he deliberately exaggerates both his foreignness and his lowliness by casting himself as a black servant and a cannibal) is a defence mechanism designed principally to conceal his anxiety about his cultural and social status. It is also in striking contrast with Montaigne's own preface to the reader, which in its English version forms part of these paratexts, where in a single paragraph Montaigne presents himself in 'simple and ordinary fashion', adding that if he had been born in a more primitive country, he 'would most willingly have pourtrayed my selfe fully and naked'.⁴³ Montaigne was, of course, a nobleman.

So what kind of paratext is the preface to Florio's Montaigne? It does, of course, have several constituent parts and these fall roughly into two classes: one, as we have seen, is apology, which is a generic feature of translators' prefaces; the other is a species of self-accreditation, which advertises the status of the translator himself. Alongside the obeisance he does to his female patrons, he acknowledges the help of male friends: two from Oxford days – Matthew Gwinne, who is 'Il Candido', and Samuel Daniel, who was also his brother-in-law⁴⁴ – and a third, Theodore Diodati, another Italian Protestant and the father of Milton's friend. The commendatory poems from Gwinne and Daniel constitute the last part of the Montaigne paratexts, standing alongside the 'Epistle Dedicatorie', the address to the reader and the translation of Montaigne's address to the reader. This mixture of tributes to rank and thanks to friends, who then reciprocate with commendatory poems, is designed to ground Florio personally, socially and professionally, just as the ridiculous hyperbole and conceits of his dedicatory style are deployed to camouflage his anxiety about personal status. As a form of self-accreditation, this other kind of paratext has the same function as the modern Acknowledgements page in academic monographs. Genette devotes a chapter of *Paratexts* to dedications but does not discuss the Acknowledgements page as such. Yet it is a distinct paratextual genre, waspishly outlined by Mark Bauerlein in an article published in the *Times Literary Supplement*. After naming and quoting a long list of academic authors' lavish exhibitions of gratitude – variously boastful, obsequious, gratuitous and always exquisitely self-conscious – Bauerlein sums up: 'At stake is the author's standing ... A successful Acknowledgements page presents him as in-the-know, well-connected, heavily subsidized and hard-working.'[45] Florio's concern with status, his profusion of gratitude and the elaborate chronicling of his labours make him the definitive exponent of the Renaissance version of this genre. He was indeed renowned for it, and widely mocked, as Frances Yates records.[46] The most devastating parody was produced by Donne, who invented this characteristically florid book-title in *The Courtier's Library*:

The Ocean of Court, or, The Pyramid, or the Colossus, or the Bottomless Pit of Wits: in which, by sixty thousand letters sent and received by the Milords of every Nation invariably in the vulgar tongues to avoid display, anything that can be propounded is propounded on the subject of tooth-picks and nail-parings: Collected and reduced into a corpus and dedicated to their individual writers by John Florio, an Anglo-Italian: the chapter headings of those included in Book 1. are contained in the first seventy pages; the diplomas of Kings with their titles and the attestations of licensers in the next one hundred and seven pages; poems in praise of the Author in Books I–XCVII, which follow.[47]

As well as lampooning Florio's snobbery and tireless self-promotion, Donne neatly catches this particular translator's dilemma in the phrase 'invariably in the vulgar tongues to avoid display'. Donne's own text was in Latin.

But the final elements in the Montaigne paratexts extend the function of these preliminaries beyond the kind of social and professional endorsements supplied by the Acknowledgements page. They do so in a way that addresses both the ambiguous status of translation as a literary genre and the equally ambiguous cultural status of the translator himself. Matthew Gwinne gestures in this direction by contributing poems in both English and

Italian, but his principal role is to collude with Florio in flattering his distinguished female patrons. It is Daniel's poem that provides the most revealing paratextual commentary on translation and the translator, and it is particularly significant because, as Florio's brother-in-law, he represents family as well as friends. Daniel observes that Montaigne's essays are unique in their degree of self-presentation: '[he h]ath more adventur'd of his owne estate / Then ever man did of himselfe before'. This corresponds to Florio's depiction of the essays in terms of masculine birth. He then applauds Florio's enablement of the French writer's 'happie setling in our land' and says that he has 'Plac'd him in the best lodging of our speech. / And made him now as free, as if borne here'. This observation on the naturalisation of Montaigne as a 'free' English citizen prompts Daniel to reflect on the greater freedom of the international community of letters where 'th' inter traffique of the mind' is not impeded by national boundaries. This celebration of the literary global village is the well-known part of Daniel's poem,[48] but it is in fact the domestic sphere that he returns to at the end, echoing the earlier metaphor of 'the best lodging of our speach' with the reminder that 'as a guest in gratefulnesse, / For the great good the house yeelds him within' does not complain about the 'convayances', so, 'while England English speakes' we should not complain about the inadequacy of English translation.[49]

The conclusion of Daniel's poem, and of the Montaigne paratexts, takes us back to our starting point, but in a way that indicates something of the multi-dimensional character that paratexts acquire when their accompanying main text has the status of translation. Daniel was an outspoken advocate of English. In the same year that Florio published his Montaigne he was fulminating in the *Defence of ryme* against writers who introduce foreign words into the language and 'without a Parliament, without any consent, or allowance, establish them as Free-denizens in our language'.[50] But the poem for his brother-in-law's translation follows an address to the reader where, as we saw, Florio admits to having done exactly that. Daniel's response is to use the same political language of birthright and naturalisation but with a quite different spin. Here the foreign settler is welcomed as an enfranchised Englishman, for Daniel is well aware that the terms he uses of Montaigne apply equally to Florio; the allusion to the grateful guest, too, refers to Florio's situation as he worked away at his translation in the Bedford household. Daniel's poem offers an endorsement of Montaigne and of translation, but it also aims to reinforce his brother-in-law's own sense of cultural identity.

Taken as a whole, the paratexts to Florio's English version of Montaigne transfer the kind of textual relationships described by Genette into social terms; for transmission and textual status (metatext, epitext, and so on) read lineage and kinship. The indeterminate textual status of translation, in this case compounded by the uncertain social and cultural status of the translator, extends the conventional idea of the book as the author's baby or brainchild into an extraordinarily complex set of social ramifications based on parentage, meta-parentage (godfathers, foster-fathers), kinship, patronage, and hospitality. Florio's figuring of his translation as an adopted child in a foreign country seems almost to be a meditation on his own homelessness, while Daniel's final poem offers the reassurance of belonging. Although Florio is something of a special case, his predicament draws together many of the status anxieties that frequently attended English Renaissance translations and which were then transferred to their accompanying paratexts on publication. There is, of course, much more to say on the subject of the paratexts to translation, but Florio's 'discountryed' condition, to borrow a term from Chapman,[51] seems a good place to start.

CHAPTER 7

Playful paratexts: the front matter of Anthony Munday's Iberian romance translations

Louise Wilson

When translations of Iberian romances first appeared in England in the late sixteenth century, their reputations preceded them. From the initial printing of the first and most ubiquitous of the romances, Garci Rodríguez de Montalvo's *Amadís de Gaula*, in Zaragoza in 1508,[1] these texts had been the subject of controversy throughout Europe. The Spanish and Portuguese romances were undisputedly popular reading matter, spawning numerous reprints, translations and appropriations, and were occasionally cited as models of eloquence or pleasant diversions, particularly in their French and Italian translations. More frequently, they were considered to be dangerous texts, likely to lead the reader into an idle or unrestrained life and containing little in the way of pragmatic lessons to be studied, commonplaced and reproduced by a humanistically trained reader. In the course of the sixteenth century, the terms 'Amadis' and 'Palmerin' (the names of the protagonists of the two main Iberian chivalric cycles) came to stand metonymically for the kind of frivolous or harmful text which humanist and religious writers counselled against.[2] However, more thorough debates on the aesthetic and moral merits of romance fiction were conducted through the romances' paratexts;[3] this front matter, in particular, helped to shape and reshape the publication and reception of the texts as they were translated first into French and then from French into English. When translations from the *Palmerin* cycle arrived in the English marketplace of the 1580s, their front matter bore the weight of almost a century of criticism and apology. Sensitive to widespread charges of immorality and inelegance, Anthony Munday's English peritexts (those paratexts which Genette defines as part of the material object of the book) participate in an intricate, tongue-in-cheek rebuttal of accusations of the unworthiness of the genre; these pseudo-humanist preliminaries, which engage with humanist concerns about the proliferation and popularity of the chivalric romance texts, expose a playful attitude to the function of the peritext among a close network of agents in the printing trade connected both personally and professionally.

The sophisticated intertextual allusions in Munday's prefatory material which are the focus of this chapter challenge Genette's argument that paratexts act as a benign zone of transition between the reader and the text, facilitating movement into the text and governing readerly responses to it. As Munday's practice shows, the paratexts can instead be disruptive or obscuring, serving as interpretative obstacles; they are sites which contest the value of reading for pleasure as they engage with the generic rhetorical addresses of early modern prefaces and epistles and involve the reader in humanist debates on profitable texts and reading practices. Recent critical work on the paratexts of early modern fiction argues that these prefatory addresses are predominantly transactional spaces between the writer and reader, to be understood in terms of the economic imperatives of the development of professional writers in the early modern book trade.[4] While they undoubtedly serve in part as advertisements to the widening readerships of the period, they also maintain a private and exclusive system of address for a small number of readers in Munday's circle.

Munday, the 'versatile Elizabethan',[5] translated from French editions all but one of the Iberian romances which were printed in England between 1588 and 1619. Only Margaret Tyler's *The mirrour of princely deedes and knighthood*, printed by Thomas East in 1578, was independent of his work; it was translated directly from the Spanish of Diego Ortúñez de Calahorra's *Espejo de príncipes y caballeros*. Munday's initial ventures into the mode were *Galien of France* (now lost) and *Palmerin d'Oliva* and *Palladine of England* published in 1588. His translations appeared over a period of almost forty years, as Donna B. Hamilton tells us, with printing and reprinting taking place during 1588–92, 1598, 1602, 1609, 1615–19, and, posthumously, in 1637 and 1639.[6] Munday was in the habit of announcing his forthcoming translations in his various dedications and prefaces to the readers; for example, in *Palmerin d'Oliva*, he writes in his dedicatory epistle to Edward de Vere, the Earl of Oxford, that the text is a 'New yeeres gift', and that the second instalment will follow shortly: 'the second part, now on the presse, and well neere finished, I will shortly present my worthie Patrone';[7] and in his preface, 'To the courteous Readers', he reminds the reader, 'When I finished my seconde parte of *Palmerin* of *England*, I promised this worke of *Palmerin d'Oliva*'.[8]

Munday had a varied career as a writer and translator, and would have been acquainted with both sides of the textual and paratextual arguments surrounding the translation and reading of the texts in contemporary France. In 1589, he translated a text by one of the most vocal French opponents of Iberian romances, the Huguenot soldier, François de la Noue: *The Politicke and Militarie Discourses of the Lord de la Noue* was printed in England by John Wolfe in 1589, one year before Munday's translation of *Amadis de Gaule* appeared in print; evidently he was translating the two texts at the same time. La Noue's text, *Discours politiques et militaries*, published in Geneva by François Forest in 1587, attacked Iberian chivalric romances for their redundancy, as their unrealistic depictions of battles were of no use in teaching young soldiers the way of the modern battlefield, and recommended that they read classical writers for instruction instead. Munday's English translations of the various volumes of the *Amadis* and *Palmerin* cycles were produced from the French translations of, among others, Nicolas Herberay, Seigneur des Essars. Herberay's first translation of *Amadís de Gaula*, commissioned by François I, was published in 1539, and he translated a subsequent book every year until 1546. The translations of later books were undertaken by a number of different French translators, including members of the Pléiade, until, in 1574, Antoine Tyron translated Book XIV, the last book of the original Spanish cycle. The romance was immediately popular with French readers, and was reprinted three times in its first year. Because of the sustained popularity of the cycle, French publishers turned to its Italian continuations to provide translations of Books XV to XXI, which were published in France between 1576 and 1581.

While immensely popular with readers, the Iberian romance translations attracted a large amount of criticism in France. One of the chief protagonists in the vehement attacks against the unprofitability of chivalric fiction was the French educator and churchman, Jacques Amyot. Amyot's early career was as a tutor, notably to the young Charles IX and Henri III. He became a priest at Bellozane in 1548, *Grand Aumônier* of France in 1560, and Bishop of Auxerre in 1570. His first translation was of Heliodorus's *Æthiopica* in 1547, completed while he was still a lay professor at Bourges University and presented to François I, and he subsequently devoted much of his time to translating classical texts. He also translated Longus's *Daphnis and Chloe* as *Les Amours pastorals de Daphnis et de Chloé* in 1559. He was the translator of both Plutarch's *Lives* as *Les Vies des homes illustres grecs ou romains* (1559) and his *Moralia* as *Les Œvres morales et mêlées* (1572). Amyot's translations of Plutarch's exemplary texts are perhaps standard material for a humanistically educated churchman, but his choice of classical fiction is less predictable given the vitriol with which he attacked contemporary Iberian romances. However, like many sixteenth-century commentators, Amyot drew a distinction between classical and contemporary fiction and viewed classical texts as inoffensive and, therefore, permissible recreation.

Genette cites Amyot's preface to his translation of *Théagène et Chariclée* as an example of the allographic preface, that is, a preface composed by someone other than the author. Genette writes:

> In 1547, Amyot heads his translation of *Théagène et Chariclée* with a kind of manifesto in support of the Greek romance, regarded as a salutary moral and aesthetic antithesis to the shapeless nonsense of chivalric romances. Amyot's prefaces to his translations of Diodorus (1554) and Plutarch (1559) also become manifestos, in support of History.[9]

The 'History' of which Genette writes can be, for Amyot, either true or fictional as long as it provides valuable examples for the reader. In the same vein, Amyot's preface to his translation of the *Histoire éthiopique d'Heliodore* acknowledges that human nature renders impossible the constant reading of instructive books and that suitable literary diversions must be provided to refresh the mind for more serious study. He accordingly allows the reading of fiction if it resembles nature. In the same preface, he claims that he translated the Greek text specifically to counterbalance the trend at court of reading *Amadis*. Nicolas Herberay, the first and most prolific French translator of *Amadis*, appears to have responded to the views of Amyot since, as Marc Fumaroli points out, the seven books of *Amadis* which were printed before the publication of the *Histoire éthiopique* had no apologetic preface while those that appeared after it included paratextual material which engaged with Amyot's criticisms.[10]

In the context of such attacks on the romance mode, contemporary French humanist translators of the Iberian romances included protestations of the profit these texts afforded the individual reader and the commonwealth in their front matter. François de Vernassal, the translator of *Il Primaléon de Grèce*, printed in 1550 and later translated into English by Munday, explains in his preface that he has augmented the Spanish and Italian editions of the romance by the addition of various educative rhetorical features:

> [t]he better to express and render more honorable the reading of it, I have described some passages according to true cosmography, brought to bear many authorities and comparisons (both from history and the fables of poetry) and often made use of sententia, explanations, metaphors, similes, notes, letters, verses, speeches, orations, and long decorations of my own finding in those places where I saw the little that I know to be proper and suitable.[11]

This extensive list of profitable features appears to be an attempt to counter the accusations of writers such as Amyot who criticised the texts for being devoid of such beneficial material. Vernassal explains that he is enhancing the original Spanish, providing a set of rhetorical embellishments which aim to inform the reader at the same time as they enhance the pleasure of reading.

The claims to exemplary history and pragmatic reading which characterise the prefatory material of French translations and defences of romance material are reproduced and subverted in the front matter of their English translations. In his preliminary addresses, Munday adopts a strategy which appears to camouflage the narratives as the more profitable humanist genre of exemplary historiography. The paratexts protest that the pleasure engendered by reading the romance is linked to the humanist mode, after Horace, of teaching through delight. The third book of *Palmerin of England* printed by James Roberts for William Leake in 1602 contains a commendatory poem by John Webster which details the fantastic nature of the narrative: 'The sighes of Ladies, and the spleene of Knights, / The force of Magicke, and the Map of fate: / Strange Pigmey-singlenes in Giant-fights'. At the same time it protests: 'Not for the fiction is the worke lesse fine: / Fables have truth and morall disciplined'.[12] The poem revisits the humanist claim that fiction can instruct as well as a true or verisimilar narrative, although the fiction that the humanists have in mind is very different from that of the Iberian romances, being instead that of moral fable or exemplary 'life'. Munday's front matter to the first book of *Amadis of Gaule*, conjectured to have been printed by Edward Allde in 1590,[13] offers stock humanist arguments attesting to the moral worth of the narrative. In his dedicatory epistle to Philip Herbert, Earl of Montgomery, he writes:

Right honourable, according to the saying of Cicero, writing in the commendation of Histories, he avoucheth them to be the Treasure of things past; the patterne of those that are to come, and the picture of mans life; the touchstone of our actions, and the full perfecter of our honour. And Marcus Varro saith: They are the witnesses of Times, the light of Truth; the life of Memorie; the Mistresse of life; and the Messenger of Antiquitie. And in very deede (Noble Lord) Histories cause us to see those things without danger, which millions of men have experimented with losse of their lives, honour and goods, making many wise by others peril and exciting imitation of precedent mens virtues, only to reach the like height of their unconquerable happinesse.[14]

Munday cites classical precedent to add an ostensibly profitable veneer to his translation. All that he writes is familiar to the reader aware of the instructive function of poetry. The first part of this passage reflects on the uses of history as a spur to worldly honour, through the performing of good deeds imitated from texts. The second part reiterates the common argument made, for example, by Erasmus in *The Education of a Christian Prince*, that reading classical texts is a means to knowledge without arduous or dangerous practical experience.

In his dedicatory epistle to Francis and Susan Young in *Palmerin of England*, Part 2, printed by Thomas Creede in 1596, Munday writes:

> I must needs thus confesse with *Aristotle*, that History is the Schoolemistresse of Princes, and the onelie Trumpet that soundeth in the eares of all noble personages, the famous deeds of their worthy progenitors. *Plato* likewise affirmeth, that the name of History was given to this end, that by recording matters of antiquity, our fleeting memories might be stayed, which otherwise would soone be lost and retaine little.[15]

As with his treatment of *Amadis of Gaule*, we might imagine that the text which this extract precedes is a 'matter of antiquity' recorded to be relevant to 'the learned sort'. However, these peritextual excerpts bear virtually no relation to the texts they accompany; their humanist commonplaces could have been written for any history aiming to persuade the reader of its worth; the romance genre and the text's fictitiousness are not acknowledged at all. It is unlikely that any early modern reader would be unaware of the genre and subject matter of the text, given the popularity of the romances and the widespread familiarity of the titles, *Palmerin* and *Amadis*, as generic signifiers; therefore, the insistence on instruction through fruitful engagement with the text conceivably becomes an ironic enticement to the narrative thanks to the disjunction between the goals of reading set out in the front matter and the well-known delights of the narrative.

In 1596, the *Palmerin* romances which had already been printed and dedicated to Edward de Vere, the Earl of Oxford began to be reprinted, this time with dedications to Francis Young and occasionally also to his wife, Susan; Munday's customary paratextual promises of translations in progress were also now addressed to Young.[16] While Young, a merchant, was of a lower social rank than de Vere, there is little sense that the paratexts are recast for a different readership; indeed, in some of them, the two names are merely substituted before reprinting.[17] The project of reprinting seems to have been to place the romances in their correct order according to the Spanish originals, rather than the order in which they were translated and printed in English. Furthermore, this project coincided with the point in Munday's publishing career when he was more concerned with seeking patronage in non-aristocratic circles.[18] It appears from the prefatory material that Munday knew Francis and Susan Young personally. In his dedication of the first part of *Palmerin of England*, 'To the Right worshipfull and his approued good friend, Maister Frances Young... and to the most kind Gentlewoman, Mistresse Susan Young, his louing wife and my Mistresse', he writes:

This first part is but to relish your tast, how yee can like of such worthy Knights loues, and memorable aduenture, whereof, at last being with you in the Countrie, I saw yee vse no mislike. Then finding such gentle entertainement, as I make no question of, the second part shall bee with you verie speedilie after.[19]

In the dedication to the 1616 edition of *Palmerin d'Oliva*, Munday writes again to them: 'Being indebted to you both for your manifold kindnesses, I am bold to continue my labour begun, concerning the course of my promised Histories'.[20]

It is in a dedicatory epistle to Francis and Susan Young that Munday's most flagrant appropriation of humanist arguments on the benefits of reading for instruction occurs. The epistle, 'To the Worshipfull Maister Fraunces Young, of Brent Pellam, in the Countie of Hertford Esquire, and to Mistresse Susan Young his wife, and my kinde Mistresse', accompanies the second edition of *Palmerin of England*, Part 2; the first edition, now lost, is thought to have been printed between 1580 and 1587. It includes the salutary tale of King Alphonsus of Naples being healed of his sickness by reading Quintus Curtius's life of Alexander the Great:

ALFONSVS King of *Naples*, (right worshipfull) a King renowmed in sundrie volumes of antiquitie, for his wisedome, bountie, and affabilitie of nature, lying verie sore sicke in the Citie of *Capua*, hauing tried the very vtteremoste cunning his Phisitions could vse on him, yet all would not helpe to recouer his health; determined with himselfe to take no more medicines, but for his recreation caused the Storie of *Quintus Curtius* (concerning the deedes of *Alexander* the great) to be read before him, at the hearing wherof he conceiued such woonderfull pleasure, as nature gathered strength by it, and chased away the frowardnesse of his disease. Whereupon, hauing soone recouered his health, hee discharged his Phisitians, with these wordes: *Feast me no more with* Galene, *and* Hippocrates, *sith all their skill would not serue to asswage my sicknesse: but well fare* Quintus Curtius *that holpe mee so soone to my health*.[21]

This example was common in early modern exemplary writing; it appears in a Latin text with commentaries on the life of Alphonsus, written by Antonio Beccadelli (known as Panormita): *De dictis et factis Alphonsi Regis Aragonum libri quatuor*, first printed in Basel in 1538,[22] and a copy of this text in the British Library bears the initials and crest of Robert Dudley, Earl of Leicester, suggesting that it was still current reading matter in England in the late sixteenth century. Beccadelli's 'life' of Alphonsus is followed by '*scholia*' by Jacobus Spiegel and then a commentary by Enea Silvio

Piccolomini (later Pope Pius II) which was later published separately in the collected works of Piccolomini. Both text and commentary assert the importance of reading profitable texts studiously. There is also an allusion to the same example of Alphonsus in Sir Edward Hoby's translation, *Politique discourses upon trueth and lying*, printed by John Windet for Ralph Newbery in 1586, from the French writer Matthieu Coignet's *Instruction aux princes pour garder la foy promise*; it is mentioned in a section on the use of classical historiographers as exemplars for battle: 'For this cause *Alphonsus* sayd of *Qu. Cursius*, that he was soner healed by his history, then his Phisitions'.[23] In this context, Munday's use of this particular example at first seems to be a further instance of his paratextual mode of claiming classical authority for his texts, but in fact its significance is highly specific. While Munday, as usual, is able to exploit the generic nature of humanist exemplary discourse and highlight its ironic disjunction with the romance narratives it accompanies, the more pertinent feature of this passage is that it echoes the words of Sir Thomas North's translation of Jacques Amyot.

Amyot's 'Epistle to the Readers', accompanying his French translation of Plutarch's *Lives*, sets out to defend the inclusion of invented details in historiography or life-writing while simultaneously denouncing romances. He identifies a hierarchy of genres, with historiography at the top, and is careful to distinguish between the 'reformed' moral fable, which illustrates the truth of human nature despite being fictional, and the romance, which affords no moral benefit to the reader. The epistle is reproduced by North in his translation of Plutarch's *Lives* from Amyot's French edition. He translates Amyot's preface as 'Amiot to the Readers', placing it after his dedication to Princess Elizabeth, and his brief epistle 'To the Readers'; it makes up the most substantial part of the *Lives*' prefatory material. North's translation of the example reads:

Also it is seene that the reading of histories doth so holde and allure good wits, that diuers times it not only maketh them to forget all other pleasures, but also serueth very fittely to turne away their griefes, and sometimes also to remedie their diseases. As for example, we find it written of Alphonsus King of Naples, that Prince so greatly renowmed in Chronicles for his wisedom and goodnesse, that being sore sicke in the citie of Capua, when his Phisitions had spent all the cunning that they had to recouer him his health, and he saw that nothing preuailed: he determined with him selfe to take no mo medicines, but for his recreacion caused the storie of Quintus Curties, concerning the deedes of Alexander the great, to be red before him: at the hearing whereof he tooke so wonderfull pleasure, that nature gathered strength by it, and ouercame the waywardnes of his disease. Whereupon hauing soone recouered his helth, he discharged his Phisitions with such words as these: Feast me no more with your Hippocrates and Galene, sith they can no skill to helpe me to recouer my helth: but well fare Quintus Curtius that could so good skill to help me to recouer my helth.[24]

North's translation concludes this passage with the words: 'Now if the reading and knowledge of histories be delightfull and profitable to all other kind of folke: I say it is much more for great Princes and Kings, because they haue to do with charges of greatest weight and difficultie, to be best stored with giftes of knowledge for the discharge of their dueties'.[25] North wrote, in his own brief epistle, 'To the Reader', that he had little direction to give on the text he had translated because: 'THE profit of stories' is 'sufficiently declared by Amiot, in his Epistle to the Reader'.[26] For more mischievous reasons, Munday appears to think the same way.

Munday's subtle use of an example from one of the most prominent opponents of the Iberian chivalric romance tells a complex story of both highly localised and continental intertextual and paratextual conversations: well versed in French opinions on Iberian romances, he adopts an ironic strategy of defence in his romance preliminaries, seeking to clothe them in humanist arguments on the profit of reading valuable texts. It would take a particularly attentive reader to spot the similarities between his and North's writing so it seems rather that Munday included this witty misappropriation for the benefit of his patrons and friends, the Youngs, in particular. He was also part of a circle of printing-house associates who revelled in the opportunities for irreverence afforded by the seemingly strict conventions of paratextual address in the rapidly expanding marketplace of print.

Throughout his varied career, Anthony Munday maintained his attachment to the printing trade of early modern London. His father, Christopher, had been a member of the Drapers' Company and a stationer, one of a number of freemen of the Drapers' Company who earned their livings as stationers.[27] Following him, Munday was apprenticed in 1576 to John Allde, a printer, stationer, and charter member of the Stationers' Guild, and received the freedom of the Drapers' Company by patrimony on 21 June 1585. Throughout his working life, he appears to have associated with only a small group of printers and booksellers: John Charlewood printed Munday's first book in 1577 and continued to print the majority of Munday's books until his death in 1593, after which, the printer and bookseller James Roberts took over Charlewood's printing materials and shop when he married Charlewood's widow, Alice, and continued to print Munday's texts. When William Jaggard in turn took over Roberts's printing materials in 1606, he also printed Munday's work.[28] It is Munday's relationship with Henry Chettle, however, that is particularly significant. Chettle was, at various points in his career, a pamphlet writer, dramatist, printer, stationer, stationer's agent for the printer, John Danter, a compositor, and a reader. Charlewood appears to have been instrumental in helping both Munday and Chettle in the early stages of their careers; he licensed and printed Chettle's *The Pope's pittiful lamentation, for the death of his deere darling Don Ioan of Austria* (c. 1578).[29] This text, claiming to be a translation from a possibly fictitious French source and ironically attributed to Pope Gregory XIII, is an early indication of the irreverent approach to authorial attributions and paratextual apparatus that Chettle shared with Munday.

Much critical attention has been paid to Munday's use of the pseudonym, Lazarus Pyott, which he employed in a number of translations including the second part of *Amadis de Gaule*, printed for Cuthbert Burby in 1595, and Alexander Silvayn's *The Orator*, printed by Adam Islip in 1596.[30] In 1963, Turner Wright broke with the earlier twentieth-century scholarly tradition of regarding Pyott and Munday as separate authors and identified them as the same person.[31] Since its publication, most critics have followed her lead in accepting that Munday and Pyott were one and the same. Turner Wright describes Munday's use of the pseudonym in his translation of Book 2 of *Amadis de Gaule* as 'a most necessary cloak', since he was working on it for the printers Cuthbert Burby and Adam Islip instead of his usual associate, John Wolfe.[32] Donna B. Hamilton argues instead that the pseudonym served a political purpose as the romances were problematic in England since, although Munday eliminated many of the Catholic references, the plots remained 'unifyingly Catholic'.[33] John Jowett, however, details the distinctive printing-house culture which gave rise to Munday's deployment of the pseudonym, regarding it as part of a wider scheme of mischievous authorial misattributions and paratextual mock-insults common among his associates. Henry Chettle in particular 'played fast and loose with the identities of his acquaintances'[34] and initiated a paratextual mode of address which is directed to his friends rather than exclusively to the reader.

Chettle provided an epistle and a commendatory verse to Munday's translation of *The second booke of Primaleon of Greece*, printed by John Danter for Cuthbert Burby in 1596. In the epistle, 'To his good Friend M. *Anthony Mundy*', he teasingly acknowledges Munday's use of the pseudonym, Lazarus Pyott, by figuring Pyott as a contrary and self-regarding translator dismissive of Munday's skills: 'the Translator of *Amadis de Gaule* his second Part, (seeming to dwell farre from neighbors) speaking in his owne praise saith, That betweene the first Part which you translated, and that of his, there should be found more than a dayes difference'.³⁵ In the commendatory verse, Jowett observes that in the penultimate line, 'Peace chattring *Py*, be still poore *Lazarus*',³⁶ 'Chettle publicizes the joke behind the name, that the supposed rival is a chattering magpie and a corpse risen from the dead',³⁷ as '*Piot*' or '*piau*' was a diminutive of the early modern French word, '*pie*', meaning 'magpie'.³⁸ Chettle had previous form in such matters: Jowett, in an earlier article, goes so far as to say that Chettle participated in 'various kinds of literary fraud' when he argues that Chettle, and not Robert Greene, was the author of *Greene's Groatsworth of Wit* (1592).³⁹

It seems, then, that Munday and Chettle were involved in mischievous games of paratextual authorial attributions: they appear to have colluded in the misattribution of an epistle written to Munday by Chettle, entitled 'To his good friend Ma: A. M.', and prefixed to Munday's translation of Etienne de Maisonneufve's *Gerileon of England*, Part 2, printed for Cuthbert Burby in 1592; this epistle, which ends with 'Your friend, T. N.' (i.e. Thomas Nashe) was, in fact, by Nashe's friend, Chettle himself.⁴⁰ Chettle claims authorship of the epistle in his epistle 'To the Gentlemen Readers' prefixed to his *Kind-Heart's Dream*. He jokingly blames the 'error' on the printer, writing: 'Neither was he [i.e. Nashe] the writer of an Epistle to the second part of Gerileon, though by the workemans error T. N. were set to the end. That I confesse to be mine, and repent it not.'⁴¹ While Joseph Loewenstein ascribes the substituted initials to 'a compositor's error' and notes that in such circumstances '[t]he personal claims on discourse are fragile',⁴² it seems rather to have been part of the elaborate scheme of fictionalised agents in book production which Chettle manufactured.

This working relationship between Munday and Chettle results in a playful attitude to paratexts and a delight in the misdirection of readerly expectations. Tracey Hill is perhaps euphemistic in her description of Munday as 'unabashedly pragmatic'⁴³ in his writing career; he was not averse to redeploying the texts and techniques of others and this is clear in his magpie-like skill in appropriating a passage from North's translation of Amyot's preface in his epistle to the second part of *Palmerin of England*. Conversing with North's text, Munday's dedication is at once a peritext and an intertext. For the reader who does not recognise the provenance of the translation, it is merely a further example of the humanistic gloss which Munday assigns to his paratextual material, ostensibly conferring classical authority and a pragmatic function on the text; but the reader who is well versed both in the preliminaries of North's Plutarch and in Munday's fondness for misappropriating paratextual markers is invited to appreciate the incongruity of this particular exemplary tale as a defence of the chivalric romance it precedes. This subversion of humanist discourses on the importance of reading exemplary texts and on the hazards of reading unprofitable romance fiction results in the paratexts assuming an elaborate rhetorical function. By attending to the controversial status of the romance in sixteenth-century Europe as well as highlighting the playfully ambiguous paratextual strategies fostered in Munday's printing-house relationships, the prefatory matter of Iberian romance translations transcends the reductively economic terms in which these romance paratexts are commonly discussed. The peritext, in Munday's hands, is instead a space in which readerly approaches to the text can be constructed in inventive ways; in this case, it provides the educated and vigilant reader with a supplementary source of entertainment in an intertextual moment which, with supreme irony, turns the argument of a humanist commentator for profit over pleasure against itself.

CHAPTER 8

'Signifying, but not sounding': gender and paratext in the complaint genre[1]

Danielle Clarke

Might gender be considered as a paratext? Or might paratext be gendered? These questions require a consideration of the construction and functions of gender in relation to the material and spatial elements of text. These elements are often considered to be extraneous to the formation of gender, perhaps because of their physical objectivity within a paradigm of modernity that privileges the written, the graphic, as signifying presence. Where texts are explicitly read and received through the framework of gender – where, for example, gender is thematised in the shape of a female speaker – it seems legitimate to ask how the reader finds and identifies these clues (or cues), and in what circumstances he/she is able to resist or ignore them. If paratext is indeed 'a zone not only of transition but also of transaction', might this zone not play a crucial role in inaugurating the play of gender within a given text or genre?[2] How does a reader identify gender textually? Is gender integral to a text, or does the reader ascribe gender to given aspects of that text? If the former, by what kinds of textual or paratextual signs can this be identified? If the latter, what elements of the text signal to the reader that this is the code by which it might generate certain kinds of meaning? This essay will argue that a series of broadly paratextual elements play a crucial role in facilitating the reader's identification of and response to female speech, that these are variable across genre and time, and that they tell us much about how the relationship between gender and print was understood.

I

I want to suggest that the ways in which we create relationships between the concept of 'gender' and a given text are not obvious. The 'space' in which these convoluted transactions take place is – amongst other things – the transitional 'zone' of paratext. Alongside the aids to reception defined by

Genette as epitexts, these 'codes' are equally important to the production of gender within texts and as uncertain in their effects.[3] These transactions are particularly pertinent to the early modern complaint genre: a genre that has its origins in the circulation of masculine cultural capital yet uses the female voice as its 'currency', and the inscription of femininity as a sign of negotiated textual authority. The ground of the competition is imitation, not in the realist mode, but in the rhetorical mode, as befits the early modern transmission history of Ovid's *Heroides*.[4]

The texts examined in my essay reveal a consistent interest in 'femininity' as performance, as an effect of textual production that has its origins not only in source texts (which create one kind of authority for these voices), but in cultural contexts (the generic affiliation of female voices with certain speech genres), and, crucially for this essay, in paratexts which frame and facilitate these voices and enable their gendered transaction with a reader. Genette asserts that '[a] final pragmatic characteristic of the paratext is ... the *illocutionary force* of its message' (10), and that some elements, notably dedications, 'entail ... the power logicians call *performative*' (11). In other words, paratext works not so much by what it 'says' – indeed, many paratextual elements are not verbal as such – but by 'what it is or does'.[5] In a similar but not identical fashion, gender is something that is enacted, rather than simply stated, in complaint; the female speakers of these poems perform their own lack of agency, giving their social and cultural construction the persuasive force – perhaps even illocutionary – of selfhood, of authenticity, of the free unfettered voice. Yet, as I will argue, these voices are both explicitly and implicitly produced by pretexts, contexts, and paratexts that position them as secondary, imitative, despite their rhetorical claims to presence, and the investment of early modern poets in the illusion of oral presence in print. These include the various thresholds of interpretation, as well as material and spatial qualities of the printed text, such as the use of printers' flowers as ways of demarcating and differentiating speakers, the deployment of different typographies, and the use – or not – of punctuation as a marker of the transition between speakers: of what Renaissance grammarians and rhetoricians term 'division', and the meanings that can be inferred from strategies of differentiation signalled by the use of space. Questions of textual spatialisation are, as Jonathan Hope points out, historically contingent: 'we take the representation (writing) for the thing itself (speech), and thus take as essential, features which are accidental fabricants of writing (for example, orthographic spaces which allow us to see "words" on the page, standardised spellings which distinguish phonetically identical words)'.[6] As Cathy Shrank has recently argued: 'the early moderns subscribed to a *rhetoric* of presence that they developed, perpetuated and manipulated'.[7] Such 'presence' was predicated upon the ability of the text to embody and to express the authority of *speech*; it is the attempt to produce this artificial effect in the medium of print culture, deploying the figure of woman, often assumed to be closer to a 'pure' form of language, that I am concerned with here.[8] Shrank's insight that the hand or typeface has power to alter the character of the text (297) will – extended to the spatial organisation of the page – prove fruitful, bearing in mind that '[t]he typesetting – the choice of typeface and its arrangement on the page – is obviously the act that shapes a text into a book ... typographical choices may provide indirect commentary on the texts they affect'.[9]

II

The literary territory that I am defining using the labile but diffuse term 'complaint' is a ragbag of traditions, myths, historical scraps, and texts. Although it originates with Ovid's *Heroides*, for many early modern writers, Ovid's basic model bequeathed a series of generic markers that proved highly amenable to adaptation and transformation.[10] The hybridity of complaint is symptomatic of early modern humanist practice, in particular, the tendency to incorporate and reanimate so-called 'native' forms as readerships broadened and the social range of these texts increased. Complaint has affinities not only with the 'high' tradition deriving directly from Ovid (and from Virgil before that), but also with vernacular medieval texts, the *de casibus* tradition and chronicle histories, and it is articulated via a range of pre-existing forms, genres, and modes: ballads, collections of 'epistles', the single-voiced lament, the complaint appended to a sonnet sequence, and complaints or epistles interpolated into other kinds of texts, notably prose romance. Given this multiplicity, how does a reader identify what it is that he or she is reading? By what means does the reader understand which generic parameters to bring into play?

There is little doubt that by the sixteenth century, poetic complaint is closely identified with the female voice, although not exclusively confined to it;[11] Drayton's *Englands heroicall epistles* (1597, seven editions, 1597–1603) is modelled generically on Ovid's *Heroides*, but includes epistles from male respondents. The complaint form has to guide the reader to find the appropriate framework for interpretation, and does so by using titles in a number of different ways: firstly to provide a 'genre indication' (Genette, 57) and secondly to link the text to its historical (if often distant) relatives. These functions are frequently fulfilled by the simple expedient of using a woman's name as the title, following the post-classical tradition in the reception of Ovid's *Heroides*, hence the speaker's name functions metonymically to conjure up a series of generic expectations that certain tropes will be present.[12] The titles typical of complaint might be said to be, in Genette's term, *parageneric*, in that they innovate, and function as 'a key to interpretation' (86). There is an immediate difference in readerly expectation between a text entitled *The complaint of Elstred* (Lodge, 1593), *The complaynt of Phylomene* (Gascoigne, 1576) or *The complaint of Rosamond* (Daniel, 1592), and one which gestures explicitly towards its Ovidian predecessor, like Drayton's *Englands heroicall epistles*.[13] A title like Shakespeare's *A Lover's Complaint* (1609) does not appear to suggest anything about the gender of its speaker ('lover' being used of either sex, then as now); but a reader will quickly confirm her or his suspicion that 'complaint' indicates a genre marked by the presence of a female speaker. This is in the absence of any other epitext and relies upon the confirmatory 'tropic attributes' that the reader finds in the text: the riverine setting, the presence of letters and love tokens, the maiden's dishevelled appearance and so on.[14]

Other forms of complaint dispense entirely with the generic 'indication' *qua* indication, and rely instead on the device of the *copula* to do the connective work; thus, Drayton's *Endimion and Phoebe* (1595), Weever's *Faunus and Melliflora* (1600), and Heywood's *Oenone to Paris* (1594). Prepositions and conjunctions matter almost as much as proper names: 'and' implying a narrated text with speeches from both named parties, whilst 'to', combined with the allusiveness of the proper names, here suggests a direct link to Ovid's Epistle V.[15] Rather than being titles in their own right, many that I have cited constitute one part of 'a rather complex whole' (Genette, 55). Printed complaints rarely stand alone as single texts; they are either organised into encyclopaedic (and imitative) volumes, like Drayton's *Heroicall epistles*, or they are elements in a volume composed of distinct but related textual artifacts, like Spenser's *Colin Clouts come home againe*, or Daniel's *Delia and Rosamond augmented Cleopatra*; in the case of collections of sonnets this usually entails the positioning of the complaint at the end of the volume. In the case of a linear reading (and linearity should not be assumed), this means placing the female voice in the secondary position, yet the evidence of many title-pages suggests that the presence of these intriguing poetic texts was central to both the meanings and the appeal of these volumes.[16] Shakespeare's *A Lover's Complaint* is unusual, in that the inclusion of this text is not flagged on the title-page; by contrast, Daniel, Drayton and Lodge's sonnet sequences carry title-pages that suggest the integral importance of these poems to the volumes (Figure 8.1(a) and (b)).[17]

Gender and paratext in the complaint genre

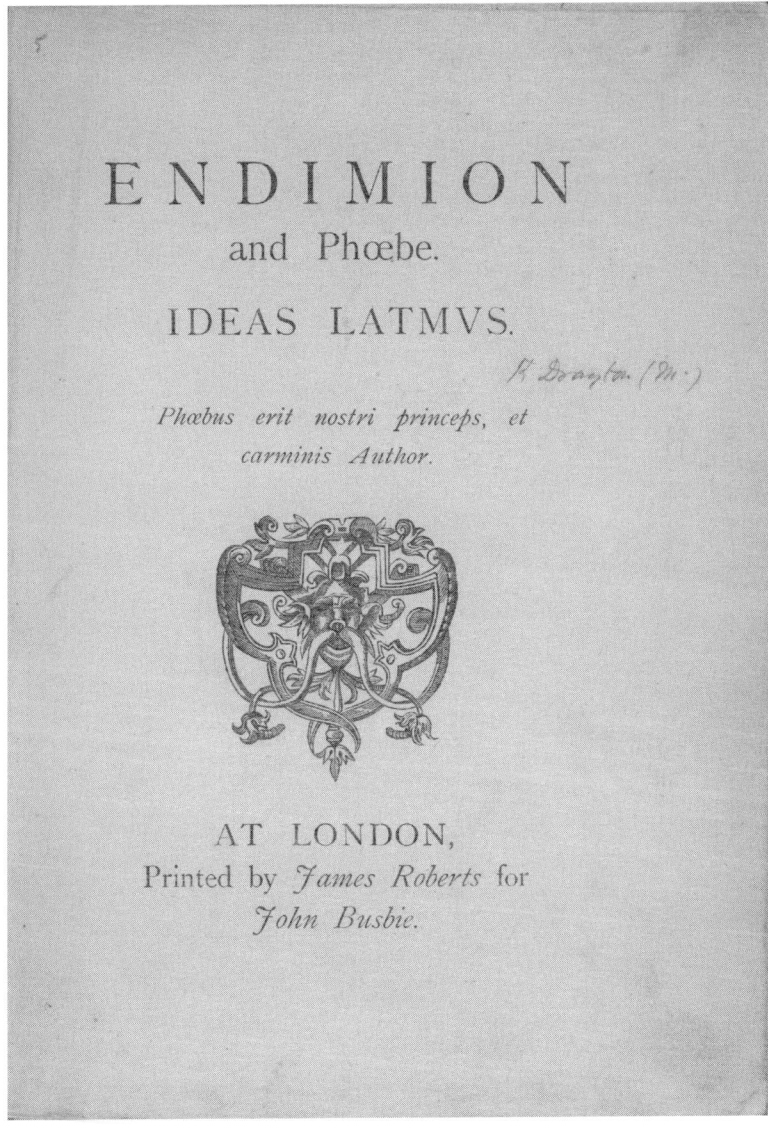

8.1a Title-page to Michael Drayton, *Endimion and Phoebe* 1595.

Here Genette's analysis that 'if the text is an object to be read, the title . . . is an object to be circulated' (75) seems entirely appropriate, but in many cases, the epitextual 'work' done by a given title or sequence of titles is dispersed throughout the volume. Sub-, secondary, and, sometimes (as

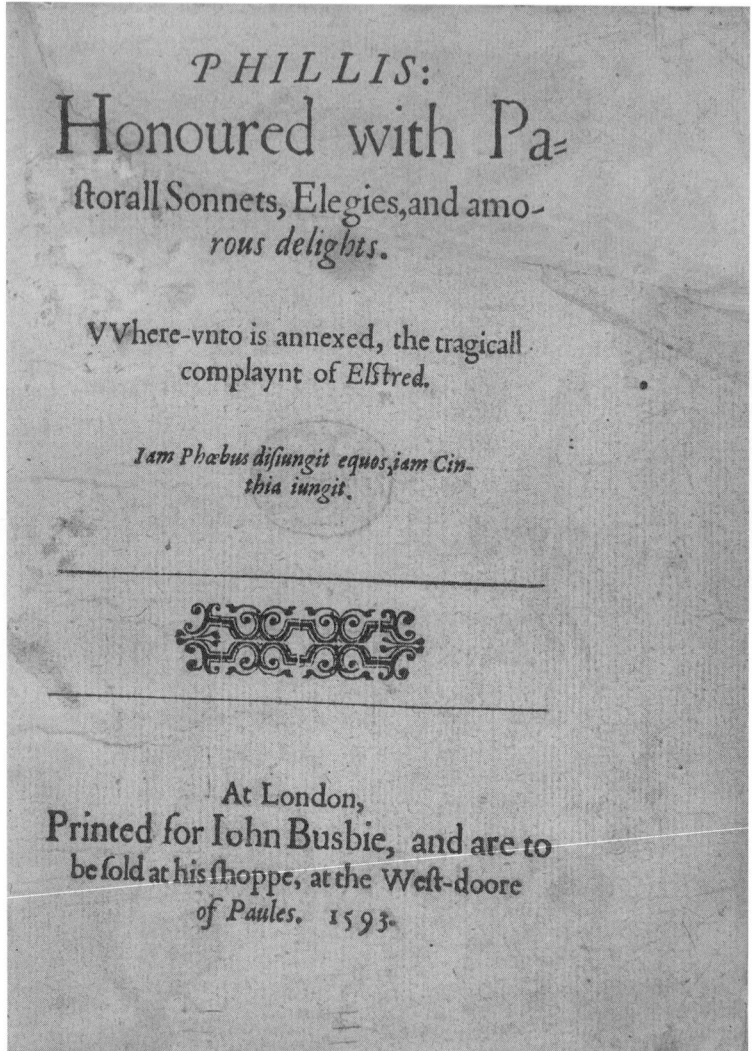

8.1b Title-page to Thomas Lodge, *Phillis*, 1593.

Matthew Day points out in Chapter 2), running titles have a range of functions, one of which is that of enabling clear distinctions to be made between voices to allow their difference – gendered or otherwise – to come to the fore. The effect is to create structural patterns, signalled visually rather than verbally. Titles have a spatial function in addition to their referential value, they demarcate and distinguish, and what they distinguish often turns out to be the gender of speakers, upon which other kinds of thematic, moral, and structural distinctions then hang.

In addition to the metonymic and generic functions of the proper name in the title of these texts, they posit a point of origin, an apparently authentic ontology which operates alongside the textual and rhetorical game of imitation, the degree of recognition of which often demarcates one readership from another.[18] These origins may be unspecified (Shakespeare), classical – either directly Ovidian (Gascoigne, Heywood) or not (Weever, Drayton, Barnfield), or real – either historical (Drayton, Lodge) or living (Spenser). But these figures are supposed to be recognised, and thus to inaugurate, through the invocation of the proper name, a set of ideas, a body of knowledge and expectation. How these posited speakers are presented to the reader has a direct bearing on how they are understood, and how the voice of the poem is received: the key aspect of this is how an individually voiced text is positioned in relation to the volume as a whole.[19] The encounter with a speaker/new text might be announced by means of an intra-textual title. In the case of Shakespeare's *A Lover's Complaint* this suggests a breach between the sonnets and the complaint, implying that the two works might work contrastively rather than connectively. The title, along with the spatial organisation (the final page of the *Sonnets* concludes with a solid 'FINIS', *A Lover's Complaint* opens with a new title, in lower case and in smaller point size than the title-page of the volume, and a reannouncement of Shakespeare's authorship), points to a topical or thematic relationship, rather than one based upon continuity of speakers.[20] Sometimes these transitions are not marked by titles at all, as is the case in Spenser's volume of elegies for Philip Sidney, *Colin Clouts come home againe* (1595), where a poem ascribed within the text to 'his sister that *Clorinda* hight' is introduced without any title to match that which introduced *Astrophel* (Figure 8.2). The division *is* marked by a printer's flower.[21]

Daniel and Drayton provide illuminating examples of the intra-textual functions of titles because of their investment in fashioning an authorial identity through the medium of print, and due to the fact that their texts went through several editions, and were frequently revised.[22] Furthermore, the texts under discussion (*The complaint of Rosamond* and *Englands heroicall epistles*) were produced by a network of printers and booksellers who worked together repeatedly: Simon Waterson in the case of Daniel, and James Roberts and N. Ling in the case of Drayton.[23] Daniel's *Delia* (1592, STC 6243.2) uses an internal title to signal the transition to an apparently

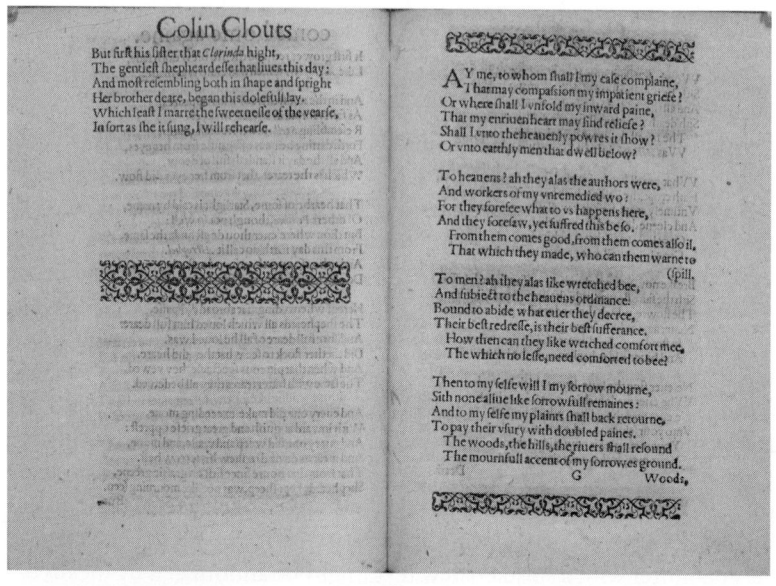

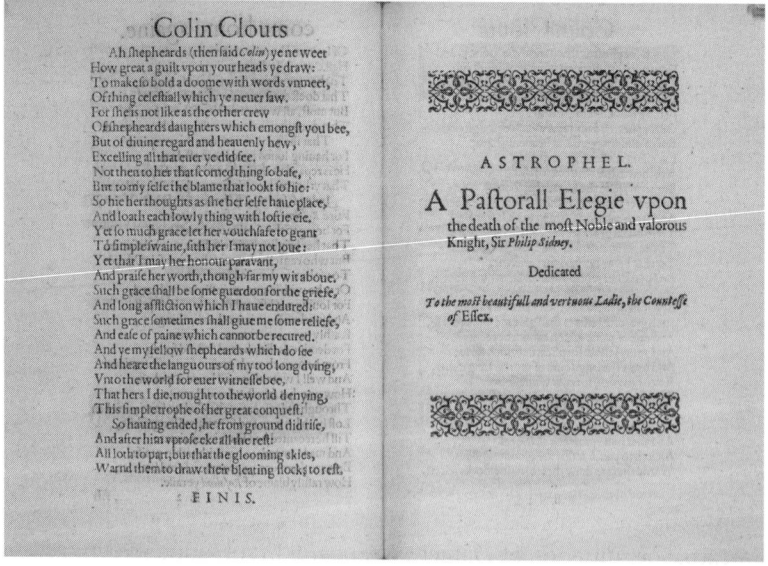

8.2 Edmund Spenser, *Colin Clouts come home againe*, 1595, F4v–G1r. Compare the lack of title to that which introduces 'Astrophel' on E2v–E3r.

Gender and paratext in the complaint genre 141

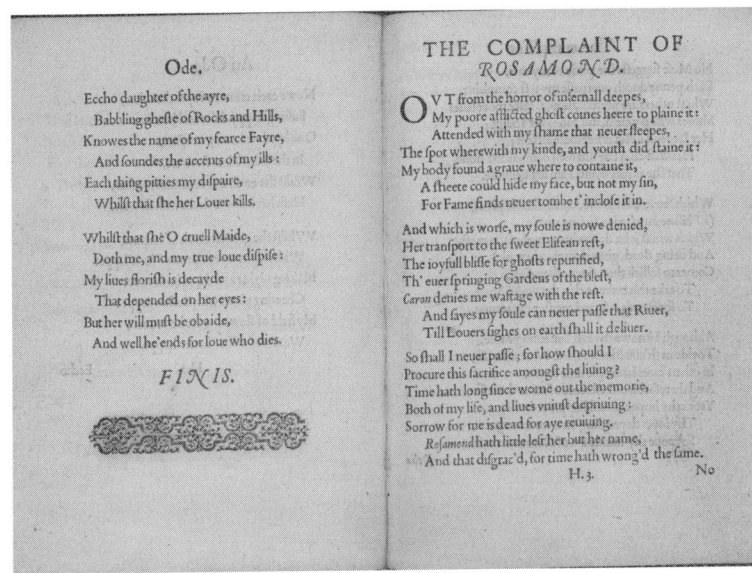

8.3 Samuel Daniel, *Delia. Contayning certayne sonnets: vvith the complaint of Rosamond*, 1592, H2v–H3r.

unmediated voice (Figure 8.3); the texts are presented as parts of a whole, despite the lack of any obvious linkage of speaker or person between the two.

A further edition of 1592 (STC 6243.3), however, gives Rosamond equal billing on the title-page and drops the framework of 'complaint', presumably because the popularity of the poem meant that both character and genre were instantly recognisable.[24] Within the volume itself, 'Rosamond' gets its own title-page, which echoes the classically modelled main title-page (and this was clearly used by Daniel's printer to impose some sort of authorial identity on his works), before reusing the opening page with *The complaint of Rosamond* from STC 6243.2. Equal weighting on the title-page (Delia *and* Rosamond) is followed by a stronger division between sonnet sequence and complaint, which raises the intriguing possibility that the more integrity a textual unit has – or the extent to which it is signalled to the reader as an entity that might possibly be separated from the larger corpus – the greater its authority. These two editions set the pattern for the paratextual organisation of Daniel's *Complaint* in subsequent editions, even where other texts are introduced. The 1594 edition, for example, uses the same title-page and typesetting, but adds *Cleopatra* as 6243.3; the 1595 edition replicates STC 6243.2. It is indicative of the relative marginality of paratextual elements that the *Short-Title Catalogue* deems the two 1595 editions to be effectively the same text, when, as I have attempted to suggest, their use of titles and title-pages put in place divisions that imply rather different relationships between the textual units within the volumes.

Drayton's collection, *Englands heroicall epistles*, suggests a conscious process of authorial self-fashioning, of a piece with his apparent desire to construct himself as a learned laureate figure.[25] The seven editions of the *Heroicall epistles* ally themselves visually with the textual apparatus of an edition of a classical text, and with the kinds of laureate claims that Spenser had attempted to make, ludically, through the medium of *The Shepheardes Calendar* a generation before – not through direct poetic imitation, but through aping that volume's paratextual practice.[26] Everything about the *Heroicall epistles* aims to suggest its connection to an Ovidian source, although this is more heavily influenced by the typesetting of classical texts in the earlier part of the sixteenth century than by any quality of Ovid's *Heroides* themselves. These claims begin with the title, which evokes the only available English translation, by George Turberville, printed in 1567 and reprinted in 1584: *The heroycall epistles of... Publius Ovidius Naso*. Drayton's substitution of 'England' for the name of Ovid is both deliberate and powerful, as is the explicit claim not to be *imitating* Ovid, but to be writing *as* Ovid, and his appropriation of the term 'heroicall' is highly self-conscious. The use of the term 'heroical' entails a telling reorientation away from the specifically feminine connotations of the Latin term *heroides*, one that is underpinned by Drayton's adoption of the pattern of paired epistles which characterise *Heroides* XVI–XXI but have long been regarded as somewhat dubious inclusions in the Ovidian canon.[27]

Unlike the paired epistles in *Heroides*, where the male voice is *always* the primary one, Drayton does not entirely invert the basic emotional and stylistic logic of Ovid's texts; in almost every case, the woman speaks first. The gender politics of the volume and the semiotics of the page can be seen to cohere, and the use of titles as ways of differentiating voice is evident here, not least in the use of dedications for each *pair* of texts, which are then titled separately, using the standard epistolary formula, 'x to y/y to x'. These are used to evoke Ovid as generic precedent, and the epistles display many of the tropes of the *Heroides*: lament, performance of the (female) speaker's connection to the beloved, self-consciousness about speech, writing and language, the articulation of desire. Like them, Drayton's texts ultimately demonstrate the dependence of the female voice on the male term. Each pair of 'letters' is opened by an Argument, and each individual epistle is followed by 'Notes of the Chronicle historie', some of which are 'more poetical then historicall'.[28] The internal logic of the text is to treat the paired epistles simultaneously as a single semantic unit, and to view them as independent of one another. As with other aspects of paratext, titles can be seen to have multiple functions, they do indeed 'indicate the text's form, either in a traditional and generic way ... or in an original way' (Genette, 77), not simply by generic or descriptive evocation, but by creating and articulating a visual and spatial economy for the inter-relationship of disparate parts of a text. In this sense, paratext is integral to the text, not in the service of that text.

III

There is no greater difference betwixt a civill and brutish utteraunce then cleare distinction of voices: and the most laudable languages are alwaies most plaine and distinct, and the barbarous most confuse and indistinct : it is therefore requisit that leasure be taken in pronuntiation, such as may make our wordes plaine & most audible and agreable to the eare: also the breath asketh to be now and then releeved with some pause or stay more or lesse: besides that the very nature of speech ... requireth some space betwixt them with intermission of sound, to th'end they may not huddle one upon another so rudly & so fast that th'eare may not perceive their difference.[29]

Puttenham's analysis of division, or distinction, is typical of early modern views as to how texts might properly be divided into logical units of analysis. What he has in mind is a written text being read aloud. How are these transitions to be represented, textually speaking, and more broadly, how is it that print can represent the integrity of a given voice? The patterns and practices that we find in early modern texts tend to support the view that male appropriations of the female voice are exactly that, and that what is at stake is less the authenticity or integrity of that voice, than the display of the poet's rhetorical skills. The use of paratextual features, on the whole, reinforces and underlines this practice. The representation of division tends to marginalise women's connection with the voices by which they are represented, and to confirm early modern conventions surrounding female speech. Whilst there is wide variation in practice amongst the complaint texts I have examined, these paratexts of division can be classified into three main groups: the uses of printers' flowers; the use of white space, positioning, and typography; and punctuation and other diacritical marks.[30]

I alluded above to the fact that in Spenser's *Astrophel* the transition between the male speaker of the main elegy and the female speaker of 'The Doleful Lay of Clorinda' is signalled not by a new title, nor a change in typeface, but by a textual boundary marked by a printer's flower (see Figure 8.2). By 1611, however, the presentation of this text has changed (Figure 8.4). The 'Lay' is presented as an integral textual unit by its

8.4 Edmund Spenser, *Colin Clouts come home againe*, 1611, B2v.

positioning on the page, but the spatial logic suggests that the poem has been incorporated into the preceding elegy: the typeface is identical, there is no mark to signal a distinction, and the running head gestures to include, or, perhaps, to appropriate, this female-voiced text.

By contrast with the 1595 edition, there is nothing beyond the playful voice of the poet-narrator to indicate that this might be a distinct text in its own right, despite the use of a different rhyme scheme. This may be related to the change of printer from Ponsonby to Lownes, and to the fact that in the same year, Lownes printed an edition of *The Faerie Queene* including most of Spenser's other works; it was thus a volume intended to authorise Spenser as a national poet. In this light, it seems entirely appropriate that a poem that may have been in some sense authored/authorised by the Countess of Pembroke should be presented in a way likely to disguise this fact. Spenser was dead by 1611, and no longer in a position to attempt to negotiate the Countess's pre-eminent position as Sidney's heir, so there was no need to suggest that 'Ay mee' might have some authority derived from the speaker's position as chief mourner, or her proximity to Sidney's poetic authority.[31]

Flowers were often used 'to articulate the composition and identity of the entire printed volume as something more than the sum of its parts' (Fleming, 56). In marking transitions between one text and another, and in the case of complaints attached to sonnet sequences, from a male to a female voice, they often serve to differentiate related parts of the whole. In Lodge's *Phillis* for example, the presentation of the sonnets suggests the kind of combinatorial pattern that Fleming proposes above, along with the use of different flowers for poems that depart from the sonnet form within the sequence. The transition to 'The complaint of Elstred' is marked by a mediating 'Ode', and the use of a different flower, but is concluded not with another flower, but with 'FINIS'. In this way, the female-voiced text is presented as having a coherence and integrity of its own, and as having a loosely defined relationship to the rest of the volume. A similar pattern can be observed in Barnfield's *Cynthia* (1595), where the sonnets are marked by a printer's flower at the top and bottom of each, again, there is a mediating ode, and then 'Cassandra', which uses the same arrangement of printers' flowers as the sonnet sequence, thus implying the overall coherence of the volume. There is a certain irony in the fact that the running title on each page of the complaint is marked 'Cassandra', in that the female character in Barnfield's poem speaks rarely. She is surely a textual and a paratextual creation.

Generally speaking, complaints that use direct speech are registered materially on the page as autonomous texts, even where these are tenuously linked to other poetic units within a volume. Daniel's *Complaint of Rosamond*, for example, explicitly and self-consciously makes reference to the volume of which it is a part:

> Tell *Delia* now her sigh may doe me good,
> And will her note the frailtie of our blood.
>   And if I passe unto those happy banks,
>   Then she must have her praise, thy pen her thanks.[32]

Different editions of the text use varied means to signal its relationship to the evolving volume of which it is a part; nevertheless, these paratextual elements symbolise both connection *and* separation, in a way which ultimately serves to propose *The complaint of Rosamond* as a male-authored text, and thus as a particularly impressive and influential sample of Daniel's poetic skill. An analysis of five editions containing 'Rosamond' reveals some variation in its relationship both to *Delia* and, after 1594, to a decidedly feminocentric volume, now expanded to include *Cleopatra*. Each text deploys some kind of paratextual device to signal division, and all use running heads to create a sense of the *Complaint* as a single extended unit; one of the 1592 texts uses a title-page, the other uses a flower; both conclude with 'Finis' and neither use flowers at the end of the volume (the 1595 text does not depart from this practice). The 1594 text uses a recto title-page, followed by a blank verso, running heads, and a printer's flower at the bottom of each page of the complaint. By contrast, *Delia* has flowers at both the top and the bottom of each poetic unit, but those at the bottom appear throughout the volume (including *Cleopatra*), with the exception of dedications and arguments. In other words, these devices signal a kind of provisional poetic unity.

By 1598, the flowers are only used for *Delia*, although the opening of *The complaint* is marked with a different flower from the sonnets, which is unique to it. The earlier title-page is absent, although *Cleopatra* now has its own title-page. The use of paratexts presents 'Rosamond' as an individually voiced poem, enfolded into the overall poetic agenda of the volume as a whole: it thus might be said to mirror the practice of Shakespeare's 1609 *Sonnets*, Lodge's 1593 *Phillis* and Spenser's 1595 *Colin Clouts come home againe*. As such, paratextual arrangement can once again be seen to reflect the gendering of textuality more generally, as material and spatial elements of the text reinforce the fact that these voices are constructed, and always allied to and mediated through male poetic authority and agency; this is a feature of the genre of 'amorous complaint', namely the performance of a gender identity that posits an authentic ontology, which turns out itself to be produced, constructed.

The use of paratextual features in Drayton's *Englands heroicall epistles*, whilst not entirely consistent, imposes an overall shape on the text, grouping the epistles together to suggest particular kinds of relationships. The seven reprints provide a useful body of evidence with which to compare the practice associated with the presentation of female voices in the more diffuse complaint, as opposed to the Ovidian tradition, not least because Drayton generally presents a pair of epistles (a letter and a reply) as a discrete unit, even taking account of the various elements of additional textual apparatus (dedication, argument, notes). There appear to be no presentational differences that align with the sex and order of the speakers, although there is a tendency to dedicate those poems that open with the female speaker to a female patron. The textual apparatus is signalled as falling outside the text proper, which is defined here by its capacity to capture the idea of the voice, or to reproduce aspects of oral delivery rhetorically: this in itself is a defining trope of the genre, and as such is a heavily textual phenomenon.

It is fascinating that a poet as conscious of the potential of print as Drayton should produce texts that are so finely tuned to the ways in which spatial and paratextual presentation may reinforce the internal logic and poetic dynamics of a self-consciously designed collection. The 1597 edition uses printers' flowers to demarcate the address to the reader, and then to delineate the beginning of each new pair of epistles; the flowers appear above the individual dedications that accompany each paired epistle. In this sense, once again, the epitext (if we assume that the dedication had a prior life outside the book) is asserted as an integral part of the text itself. The dedications are in italic type, the body of the text in roman, and each epistle is further demarcated within the macro unit of the pair: there is usually a single line following the dedication, a space (sometimes a new page), the epistle itself, another single line, 'Notes', a further single line and then the response, which follows the same pattern. The paired epistles find closure as a unit through the use of 'FINIS' after the notes, and a final single line. What is interesting about this arrangement is the fact that the poetic epistles themselves are presented as the *texts* (along the lines of the classical editions that Drayton, or his printer, had in mind), with all the other apparatus clearly signalled as such by paratextual means: the epistles are printed in a slightly bigger point size than the notes, and the ruled lines segment the text in such a way as to create a hierarchy of meaning and to represent this spatially.

The consistency of this method creates a degree of coherence from diverse and scattered material, and draws attention to Drayton's inventive and rhetorical skill in (re)producing these narratives from the interstices of the chronicle record, much as Ovid had done from classical myth. Later editions maintain this consistency of presentation (with a few minor variations which probably reflect conditions in the print shop rather than any concerted effort to alter the design), even though the addition of new epistles required some degree of internal rearrangement, given the use of chronology as an additional organisational principle. In the 1598 edition, for example, Drayton adds paired epistles between Edward, the Black Prince and Alice, Countess of Salisbury, which to preserve the chronological arrangement have to be positioned after Isabel and Mortimer, and before Isabella and Richard II; it is introduced without the apparatus that accompany the other epistles, probably because it lacks a dedication; this is not corrected until the edition of 1602.

Questions – paratextual and otherwise – about the transition between speakers are more contested in complaints that mix direct and indirect speech. Shakespeare's *A Lover's Complaint*, with its nested speakers and narratives, is a good example; modern editions usually deploy both single and double quotation marks to signal who is speaking, and the status (reported speech, or not) of what they are saying. Where even a sophisticated reader might struggle to follow the structure of the spoken sections in *A Lover's Complaint* without the guidance of editorial punctuation marks, an early modern reader must have been able to follow these complex syntactical twists without any great difficulty. This suggests that in the late sixteenth century, printed texts were still being understood primarily as being dominated by oral habits, such that transitions between speakers would have been thought of as literally marking a change of voice (and this change might be grammatical and/or tonal). This is represented in Lodge's *Elstred* where a portion of dialogue (rare enough in complaint) is laid out using the regular conventions for the presentation of dramatic speech:

> *Sabrine.* Then you and *I* sweet Mother were led forth,
> *Elstred.* We were led foorth sweet daughter to our last;
> *Sabrine.* Our words, our beauties had but little worth,
> *Elstred.* So will the heavens: that purest, soonest wast.[33]

The use of single or double commas to denote direct speech is not a consistent feature of early modern printed texts; where they are used, it is generally to highlight a passage of particular import or sententiousness, not to indicate which parts approximate most closely to the spoken voice.[34] A range of different typographical and paratextual features were used to signal shifts and distinctions between speakers, all of which, in varying ways, work towards a spatial representation of rhetorical style; often these reveal a great deal about how the English Renaissance viewed the status of female speech,

Gender and paratext in the complaint genre 149

namely as having a contingent and uncertain authority. Transitions between speakers were frequently marked typographically as well as spatially, particularly by the use of italic typeface.[35] Malcolm Parkes states that the use of type to signal *lemmata* or quotations in this way was introduced in the sixteenth century, and that it was very much a humanist practice.[36] What is interesting about this practice is its adaptation for the presentation of vernacular and largely non-scholarly texts, and that readers were clearly acquiring new kinds of spatial, typographical, and paratextual literacy.

Like other aspects of the language, punctuation in early modern English reflected older oral and manuscript conventions and this is apparent in the notation of direct speech. Writers on grammar in the English Renaissance, whether reformist or conservative, assume that the purpose of notation by 'characts' is to indicate the duration of sound and stress and to underline where pauses and distinctions should be made. This is only coincidentally logical or grammatical, and is asserted as primarily rhetorical: 'for the plainer deliverance of the things spoken'; 'all in all to the right and tunable uttering of our words and sentences'.[37] Verbs of speaking, as Parkes notes, were separated from the main text by parentheses, and this is common practice in complaint poems.[38] As Mulcaster notes:

Parenthesis is expressed by two half circles, which in writing enclose som perfit branch, as not mere impertinent, so not fullie concident to the sentence, which it breaketh, and in reading warneth us, that the words inclosed by them, are to be pronounced with a lower & quicker voice, then the words either before or after them.[39]

Daines suggests that the parenthesis requires 'rather a distinction of *tone*, than a distance of *time*'.[40] This parenthetical method of indicating who is speaking can have the overall effect of subordinating the individual speaker to the poem (or poetic style); this is particularly powerful in the context of a poetic tradition where access to speech and to language is a key trope. Whilst many complaint poems do place verbs of speech in parenthesis (he saith; she spake), more often, speech is endlessly deferred, surrounded by numerous pre-conditions, in such a way as to literally reinforce the parenthetical nature of gender in these texts. Sometimes other punctuation marks are used to mark a switch of speaker; for modern readers, used to rather more definite (and frequent) symbols, these can be easy to miss:

> But such a vow devoutly have I made
> To die a virgin: scarce the halfe word said,
> His wit and senses by desire set open.
> Sweet Saint (quoth he) that vow must needes be broken,

It is not lawfull you should make a vow,
The which Religion cannot wel allow:[41]

Here the 'stay', as Jonson calls it, 'as well for the speakers ease, as for the plainer deliverance of the things spoken', indicated by the colon, also marks the period to what Melliflora says.[42] More frequently, women's words are introduced by means of a series of conditionals, or contexts, that tend to render them less authoritative: 'But now sad sorrow hath her language choked' (Heywood, B2r); 'Fresh she begins, thinking that word to alter, / The more she speakes, the more her tongue doth falter' (Weever, Cv); 'There (like a lambe,) she stoode,/ And askte with trembling voice,/ Where *Progne* was' (Gascoigne, Mv).

Paratext allows us to analyse a variety of textual, material, and spatial features, and to consider how they work both independently and collectively to produce gender as an interpretative category. Whilst it would be hard to argue that paratexts are in themselves gendered, the evidence of this essay shows that paratexts can play a crucial role in constructing and determining how a reader might position gendered speakers in relation to the overall dynamic of a poetic volume. Rather like the performative aspects of paratext itself, gender in complaint as articulated through spatial arrangement, the use of divisions and distinctions, titles and other epitexts, is registered via the representation of the female voice, which in turn proves to be not just a rhetorical effect, but a material effect produced by the material text and its conventions.

PART III
Books and users

CHAPTER 9

Unannotating Spenser

Jason Scott-Warren

What can early modern paratexts contribute to the way we think about 'the early modern period'? It would be easy to assume, from a too-casual reading of recent studies such as Rhodes and Sawday's *Renaissance Computer* or Cormack and Mazzio's *Book Use, Book Theory*, that this period indeed represented – as was once widely believed – a Renaissance.[1] Thanks to print, as Walter Ong suggested several decades ago, words were technologised; they became newly manipulable, whether in terms of their spatial organisation on the page, or through the ramifying paratextual apparatus that surrounded them.[2] Prefaces, tables, marginal annotations, and indices opened books up to ever more sophisticated kinds of engagement, making the multiple-entry-point technology of the codex ever more useful, allowing the resources of this unique tool to be harnessed to the full.[3] This is certainly one way of understanding what was happening in the sixteenth and seventeenth centuries. It is, however, only one way, grounded in a rather partial selection from the evidence. Here, I want to focus on a book that would probably get left out of the master-narrative; a case of paratextual breakdown and technological failure, which has never been sufficiently recognised and pondered. My chapter sets out from a virtual exhibition of four books, one of which stands out as particularly problematic and unusual.

Exhibit A is Edmund Spenser's *Shepheardes Calender*, first published by Hugh Singleton in 1579. As has long been recognised, the *Calender* was not just a richly innovative sequence of poems; it was also a landmark in book design, amalgamating visual elements from several sources: native almanacs (the illustrated *Kalenders of Shepardes* that were reprinted throughout the sixteenth and seventeenth centuries); editions of Virgil (such as Abraham Fleming's 1575 translation of Virgil's *Eclogues*, with its black-letter text prefaced by arguments in roman); the publications of French poets like Marot and Ronsard (the latter's *Amours* annotated by Marc-Antoine de Muret just as the mysterious 'E. K.' annotated Spenser); and later Italian editions of Sannazaro's *Arcadia*, which S. K. Heniger has identified as perhaps the key design influence.[4] The complexity of the 1579 volume, with all its paraphernalia of illustration and annotation, must have made it a nightmare to print; it also makes it near-impossible to edit, since these words really are at their best when locked into this bibliographical form.

Exhibit B is Spenser's *Faerie Queene*, the first three books of which were printed by John Wolfe for William Ponsonbie in 1590. A six-book edition was printed by Richard Field for the same publisher in 1596.

Exhibit C is John Harington's translation of Ariosto's *Orlando Furioso*, first published by the same Richard Field in 1591. Scholars disagree about the quality of Harington's translation, but they have been unanimous in hailing this as another landmark in Elizabethan book design. Imitating the most sumptuous of the available Italian editions, Harington ushered his folio volume into the world with an orgy of paratexts. He provided an emblematic title-page; a prefatory apology for poetry; full-page illustrations preceding each canto; extensive marginal annotation; and notes on Ariosto's moral, historical, allegorical and allusive matter, following each canto. To wrap things up, he appended to the poem 'A briefe and summarie allegorie' explaining what it was about; a life of Ariosto, 'briefly and compendiously gathered out of sundrie Italian Writers'; a 'table' or index, listing the characters and helping the reader to locate their stories; and a list of 'the principal tales' in the *Orlando* 'that may be read by themselves' (the poem's numerous inset narratives).[5] So many and various are the volume's paratexts that Harington felt obliged to produce a *para*-paratext, entitled 'An Advertisement to the Reader before he reade this poeme, of some things to be observed, as well in the substance of this worke, as also in the setting foorth thereof', which tells the reader how to use the marginal notes, the arguments, the pictures, and so on.[6] The *Orlando* is, like the *Shepheardes Calender*, a book that forms such a tightly knit graphic entity that it is difficult to re-edit it today, especially after the bibliographical interventions of Randall McLeod.[7]

Exhibit D is what I take to be the standard scholarly edition of *The Faerie Queene*, edited by A. C. Hamilton and published by Longman in 1977, with a second edition in 2001. This is a triumph of scholarship and (if not a landmark) at least an achievement in book design; above all, through its strategic use of very small type, it manages to cram several stanzas of text and several centuries of editorial wisdom onto each page, and to wrap these up in a finished product which is (to quote Martin Marprelate) 'a portable booke / if your horse be not too weake'.[8] In its latest manifestation it is graced by a portrait of Elizabeth I on the cover, and a fulsome dedication to Elizabeth II inside.[9]

The odd one out here, as the abruptness of my comments on it will have suggested, is Spenser's *Faerie Queene* as it first appeared in 1590. It is possible to survey this book's paratexts and to find fault with almost all of them. We might begin at the beginning with the book's format: it is a thick quarto, an undistinguished block of paper that looks certain to contain a stodgy theological treatise rather than a masterpiece of poetry. The English national epic deserved better, but it was not promoted to folio format until 1609, a decade after the poet's death. Then there is the startlingly uninformative title-page, which neglects to name the author, fails to mention that this is a poem (indeed, rather implies that it will be a treatise, 'fashioning XII. Morall vertues'), and fails to mention that the volume it heralds will contain three books, not twelve. Turn the page, and the next thing you find is the oddly four-square dedication to 'the most mightie and magnificent empresse Elizabeth', with its elaborate display of obeisance; the poet's name is relegated to the foot of the page, as though kissing the ground at the monarch's feet.[10] Or perhaps you don't – because some surviving copies lack the dedication altogether. (You can re-create the effect via *Early English Books Online*, by flipping between the Huntington and the Folger copies.[11]) The small matter of the dedication of the *Faerie Queene* to the Faerie Queene may have been something of an afterthought.

The next problem lies in the front matter, which (as several commentators have noted with bemusement) is all at the back.[12] The 'Letter to Ralegh', in which the author expounds 'his whole intention in the course of this worke, which for that it giueth great light to the Reader, for the better understanding is hereunto annexed', is relegated to the quire signed 'Pp'. The possibility that an early reader might have chanced upon this explanatory epistle *after* s/he had struggled uncomprehending through all three books would be too ghastly to contemplate, were it not for the fact that the letter is notoriously inaccurate, and occasionally shifty, in its description of the poem that precedes it. To quote the *Spenser Encyclopedia*: 'No part of the 1590 edition of *The Faerie Queene* has puzzled readers more than the appended Letter to Raleigh'.[13] The letter creates an insuperable headache for editors, as Gordon Teskey has shown, because it was not reprinted with the six-book edition of the poem in 1596, and when it did reappear in the later folios, it migrated far from the *Faerie Queene*, usually turning up (nonsensically) somewhere in the midst of Spenser's shorter poems, and thereby offering a kind of parable about the irrelevance of 'The Authors Intention' to textual interpretation.[14] Where should it go in modern editions? After Book 3? Following Book 6, or the 'Mutabilitie Cantos'? Or should we, perhaps, follow Spenser's example and banish it from view altogether? The author's intention regarding this expression of his intention is entirely unclear.

The Pp gathering also contains commendatory poems by Ralegh, Gabriel Harvey, and three unidentified well-wishers, and Spenser's dedicatory poems to a host of late-Elizabethan worthies. Here again, the story is complicated. Spenser originally wrote ten dedicatory sonnets, which the printer set on leaves 6r–8r of the 'Pp' gathering, concluding with a final-looking 'FINIS' and (on 8v) a list of 'Faults escaped in the Print'. Then something happened that prompted the printer to produce a four-leaf, unpaginated gathering that contained eight of the original sonnets (the sonnets that had appeared on Pp6 and Pp7) intermingled with seven extra sonnets to assorted high-ranking courtiers. The new gathering has usually been taken to be a last-minute 'cancel' or substitute for Pp6–7; and the supposition has traditionally been that Spenser originally intended to omit William Cecil, Lord Burghley, from his pageant of dignitaries, but later thought better of this rebellious gesture, and took the opportunity to add in Burghley and six further dedicatees on the insert. Unfortunately, the compositor signed that insert 'Qq', with the result that binders took the replacement sonnets to be additional material, and usually included both sets of sonnets, one after the other. And so, far from being covered up, any offence that Spenser may originally have intended to Burghley was visible for all to see.[15]

Clearly, a lot went wrong in the publication of Spenser's poem in 1590. The cheeky typesetter who came up with this headline to the 1596 version of the text:

was understating the case quite considerably; the *Faerie Queene* had by this time acquired many 'boobes'.[16] And we have not yet mentioned the text of the poem, which offers versified arguments at the head of each canto, but no annotation, no typographical play, and only one illustration, a woodcut image of St George and the Dragon, recycled from John Wolfe's French newsbooks of the 1580s.[17] Take everything together, and you have a book that appears oblivious to the significance of its physical form. This obliviousness is all the stranger given that Spenser had, in 1579, shown himself to be so sensitive to the possibilities of bibliographical invention, recycling old forms of textual presentation to create a product whose cultural innovation sang out.

Having made this bald statement, the preceding comments need to be nuanced and in some cases rejected. Firstly, it may well be unreasonable to wonder why the would-be laureate Spenser failed to produce a 'laureate' folio text in 1590. In 1590, English or *Englished* poets (with the notable exception of Chaucer) had not yet arrived in folio.[18] Translations of Virgil had been in quarto throughout the century, with no reissues of Caxton's folio *Aeneid* of 1490. Hall's Homer of 1581 was a quarto, and Chapman's Homer remained in quarto until 1609. Sidney's *Arcadia* appeared initially as a quarto in 1590, going into folio in 1593. Samuel Daniel's *Works* first made it big in 1601. So it would seem that Harington's 1591 Ariosto translation was doing something new; it was followed by Fairfax's folio Tasso in 1600. For Spenser's poem, the original work-in-progress of a living author, to have appeared in folio might have been a serious act of presumption (something akin to Ben Jonson's presumption in publishing his folio *Workes* in 1616). There may also have been issues of cost (Harington may well have financed all or part of the *Orlando*), or of practicality: as a folio, the first three books of the *Faerie Queene* might have looked implausibly svelte.[19] And then, it is probably wrong to object to the unprepossessing physical format of the 1590 quarto: the copies that survive today are usually much cut-down from the far larger and more graceful beasts that hit the bookstalls in the 1590s, a few of which survive in their original bindings.

It was, of course, no crime in this period for books to omit the author's name on their title-pages, or for them to be altogether anonymous. Recent studies, mainly focused on Shakespeare, have pointed out that authors' names were often little more than commodities in the hands of publishers; they appeared on title-pages when they could contribute to a text's marketability.[20] More surprisingly, it seems that it is unfair to criticise a book for not telling you on its title-page that it contains a poem. It is fairly easy to find examples of earlier books that omit this information, suggesting perhaps that publishers relied on word-of-mouth to circulate news about poems, or that they expected their readers to be quite as comfortable with verse as prose.[21] Finally, we should also acknowledge the fact that Queen Elizabeth liked the *Faerie Queene*. No presentation copy of the work survives, but we have the evidence of Spenser's £50 pension to suggest that it was well received – which is more than we can say for Harington's Ariosto.[22]

Still, having conceded those points, much of the case for the prosecution stands. So how can we explain the *Faerie Queene*'s failure to make something of itself, what we might call its dereliction of bibliographical duty? Why does Spenser un-paratext, un-illustrate and unannotate himself at this key moment in his career? This question may be unanswerable. Were I, like S. K. Heninger, convinced that the elaborate design of the *Shepheardes Calender* was forced upon a more-or-less unwilling poet by his overbearing friend Gabriel Harvey, the early printed form of the *Faerie Queene* might look like the casting off of a bad influence, a sign of Spenser's ascension from the sphere of the courtier *manqué* into the sphere of a genuine courtier, Sir Walter Ralegh.[23] But I find it hard to believe that the earlier text was not collaborative from start to finish, Spenser and Harvey confecting their publication together with all the alacrity of Erasmus and More sixty years earlier. Alternatively, if you follow the arguments of Evelyn Tribble and Wendy Wall, and see *The Shepheardes Calender* as an attempt to import into print something of the coterie chic of the manuscript medium, then the *Faerie Queene* might look like a proper transition to print culture, embracing the newer technology in all of its impersonality; Spenser almost forgets to add the dedicatory trimmings that will insert the text into the dying structures of the patronage system.[24] For me, such a reading is too teleological, effacing both the print-dependency of the earlier, and the coterie elements of the later work.

And so I am left, bereft of explanations, gazing at the blank paper that opens up around Spenser's stanzas. It is blank paper that aches with a sense of absence; there is something missing here. Flanked by my other exhibits, it would be difficult to deny that the *Faerie Queene* is a poem that craves annotation. But these margins are of course not always blank. Indeed, they are sometimes crowded with words: the marginal commentaries of the poem's early readers. Without wishing to make any inflated statistical claims, it is striking how many annotated early copies of the *Faerie Queene* survive. The annotators range from the very famous to the unknown, from Ben Jonson to the Kentish yeoman John Dixon; many more are anonymous. Are these readers simply adding something more to the book, or are they responding to a sense of lack? Might they have something to tell us about the *Faerie Queene*'s paratextual malaise?

Firstly, they tell us that a lack of signposting really can be a problem. Stephen Orgel has described the annotations of an early reader who gets the first book of the *Faerie Queene* marvellously wrong.[25] The problems begin with the invocation of the 'holy Virgin, chiefe of nine' in the proem to Book I, which moves our reader to scorn: 'heere hee invocates one of the 9 Muses, as the heathen poetes did, & so is an idolater'. The Catholic trappings of the Legend of Holiness evoke comparable ire in this stridently Protestant reader; so the Redcross Knight's red cross is 'not the way to adore [Christ]', the 'fayeries are [div]ells', 'this comendation of an heremiticall lyfe, is naught', and St George of Merry England is 'a popish saint devised by idle Monks'.²⁶ You would never guess from this reader's comments that he and Spenser were, however broadly speaking, on the same side. When the annotator begins to wake up to the fact that this is an allegory, and an anti-Catholic one at that, he (the confident secretary hand suggests that it is 'he') lashes out at allegory itself. The Redcross Knight kills Sansfoy, and the reader glosses: 'The good knight should have saved him, & not killed. you will say heere is a mysticall meaning. I think so, but all know not that, & therefore it is not safe to teach murther under such pretenses'.²⁷ Moral matter cannot excuse the sinfulness that lies on the surface.

But no other documented reader is led astray in this way. John Dixon, our Kentish yeoman, surprised everyone when his annotations were published by Graham Hough in 1964.²⁸ Utterly alert to the allusiveness and allegorical density of the poem, he read the first book of the *Faerie Queene* with one finger in his Geneva Bible, noting copious references to the Book of Revelations. So Error's 'darksom hole' (A5*r*) is 'the lake which burneth with fier and brimstone, for the utter distruction of such as loue The world's vanities reuela: 21: 8:', while the two 'sprights' that Archimago sends to Orpheus (A8*v*) are 'spirits of diuills to worke miracles on the kynges of the earth which are false profits to hinder the kingdome of Christe reue: 16:14'.²⁹ And this committed Protestant was also a patriotic antiquarian, pulling out a copy of Fabyan's chronicles to expand upon the British history charted in the poem's second and third books. Thus, when Spenser specifies that Brutus's progeny ruled for 'seuen hundred yeares' (Y1*r*), Dixon notes '704: yeares', and when the poet glides over 'eleuen descents' (Y2*v*) of the crown, the annotator adds: 'from the laste ye: of Elidur to the laste ye: of Hely are 166: ye: in which time hath raingned 33 kinges albeit for their ill gouerninge their is no mention made of them'.³⁰ Another forward-Protestant reader, Thomas Posthumus Hoby, the son of the translator of Castiglione's *Courtier*, produced yet another kind of reading.³¹ Notably, he read for the plot, offering brief summaries of events that strive to make sense of Spenser's endless proliferating narrative: 'Archymago bryngs Gyon / to the syght of the red= / cross knyght'; 'Gyon chargeth yᵉ red= / cross knyght'; 'they meet'; 'theyr Communica= / tion'; 'Gyon shewes to yᵉ red= / cross knyght howe Archymago and Du= / essa had deceyved hym'.³² Hoby is clearly aware of the allegory, but he delights in the story, and his marginalia work to render it more conspicuous to the eye.

Such a pattern of diversity might seem to verge on the purely random, but I am struck by the fact that both Dixon's and Hoby's approaches to the text are anticipated by the notes that Harington added to his 1591 *Orlando*.

There he expands on allusions to factual historical sources; he points out religious and moral allegories; and he makes visible the pleasures of the plot, adding copious marginal notes and an index of characters that allows the reader to thwart Ariosto's playful *entrelacement*, following individual narratives to their conclusion.[33] Given the literary consanguinity of Spenser and Ariosto, could we argue that many of these readers' annotations are being *invited* by the text? The same would go for other kinds of marking, the most common of which is the noting of epic similes and moral commonplaces. Spenser provides a simile or a commonplace; the reader responds with a marginal cross or line or flower.[34] Or there is the noting of 'the woman question'. Spenser provides a stanza that touches on the *querelle des femmes*; the reader provides a marginal pointing hand, or an injunction: 'lege maid lege' ('read, girl, read!') (Figures 9.1 and 9.2). The annotations in Harington's Ariosto are ever-alert to such matters.

What I am trying to capture is the combination of spontaneity and predictability in early annotations to the *Faerie Queene*; while each reader draws out different aspects of the text, and by different means, they collectively adumbrate a rather familiar set of interests and concerns. This is not to say that readings are 'hard-wired' into the text, but rather to suggest that the poem was pitched quite precisely to its readers' competences, so that annotators found themselves doing certain recognisable things in the margins.[35] Although the *Faerie Queene* is unannotated, we can without too much difficulty imagine what an annotated edition might have looked like. And perhaps annotation is ultimately redundant, if the poem turns out to contain its own implicit paratext, a set of unspoken cues for annotation.

If it is true that the *Faerie Queene* unsettles the distinction between text and paratext, this unsettling reflects the broader problem of how far we can apply Genette's terms to the poem in the first place. Where does text end, and paratext begin, in a work which is only ambiguously fictional, only playfully and tenuously sealed off from the world? One reason, after all, why Spenser might have forgotten to dedicate the *Faerie Queene* to Elizabeth was that his poem was, in itself, one long dedication to Elizabeth. Like many other early modern texts, this poem seems to be in danger of becoming *all* paratext: of becoming consumed by the negotiation of relationships with its audiences. Genette's distinction comes under severe pressure in the performative textual culture of the early modern period.

A final question: can handwritten annotations be paratexts? For those of us who are interested in reading, Genette's big idea is a frustrating one; although paratexts are at every point involved in negotiating the relationship between books and readers, they are produced by authors and publishers,

> *Cant.V.* **FAERIE QVEENE.** 245
>
> So being clad, she brought him from the field,
> In which he had bene trayned many a day,
> Into a long large chamber, which was field
> With moniments of many knights decay,
> By her subdewed in victorious fray:
> Amongst the which she caus'd his warlike armes
> Be hang'd on high, that mote his shame bewray;
> And broke his sword, for feare of further harmes,
> With which he wont to stirre vp battailous alarmes.
>
> There entred in, he round about him saw
> Many braue knights, whose names right well he knew,
> There bound t'obay that Amazons proud law,
> Spinning and carding all in comely rew,
> That his bigge hart loth'd so vncomely vew.
> But they were forst through penurie and pyne,
> To doe those workes, to them appointed dew:
> For nought was giuen them to sup or dyne,
> But what their hands could earne by twisting linnen twyne.
>
> Amongst them all she placed him most low,
> And in his hand a distaffe to him gaue,
> That he thereon should spin both flax and tow;
> A sordid office for a mind so braue.
> So hard it is to be a womans slaue.
> Yet he it tooke in his owne selfes despight,
> And thereto did himselfe right well behaue,
> Her to obay, sith he his faith had plight,
> Her vassall to become, if she him wonne in fight.
>
> Who had him seene, imagine mote thereby,
> That whylome hath of *Hercules* bene told,
> How for *Iolas* sake he did apply
> His mightie hands, the distaffe vile to hold,
>
> Q 3

9.1 Trinity College, Cambridge, shelfmark VI 2 63, f. Q3r (a copy of the 1596 *Faerie Queene*, Books 4–6; there are comparable manicules on K5r and P1v).

not by readers. They exist at a very precise point on what Robert Darnton has taught us to think of as the communications circuit: that point where the text teeters on the brink of publication, arming itself to encounter the public.[36] Indeed, Genette appears reluctant to credit publishers with much responsibility for the paratext; rather, as the introduction to the present volume suggests, he privileges authorial intention. I propose that we should

> Cant. I. *the Faery Queene.* 405
>
> Faire Ladies, that to loue captiued arre,
>   And chaste desires doe nourish in your mind,
>   Let not her fault your sweete affections marre,
>   Ne blott the bounty of all womankind;
>   'Mongst thousands good one wanton Dame to find: *Lege maid / lege*
>   Emongst the Roses grow some wicked weeds;
>   For this was not to loue, but lust inclind;
>   For loue does alwaies bring forth bounteous deeds,
> And in each gentle hart desire of honor breeds.
>
> Nought so of loue this looser Dame did skill,
>   But as a cole to kindle fleshly flame,
>   Giuing the bridle to her wanton will,
>   And treading vnder foote her honest name:
>   Such loue is hate, and such desire is shame.
>   Still did she roue at her with crafty glaunce
>   Of her false eies, that at her hart did ayme,
>   And told her meaning in her countenaunce;
> But *Britomart* dissembled it with ignoraunce.
>
> Supper was shortly dight and downe they satt,
>   Where they were serued with all sumptuous fare,
>   Whiles fruitfull *Ceres,* and *Lyæus* fatt
>   Pourd out their plenty, without spight or spare:
>   Nought wanted there, that dainty was and rare;
>   And aye the cups their bancks did ouerflow,
>   And aye betweene the cups, she did prepare
>   Way to her loue, and secret darts did throw;
> But *Britomart* would not such guilfull message know.
>
> So when they slaked had the feruent heat
>   Of appetite with meates of euery sort,
>   The Lady did faire *Britomart* entreat,
>   Her to disarme, and with delightfull sport
>   Cc 4   To

9.2 Cambridge University Library, sss 22 27, f. 2c4r. The inscription is the work of a highly responsive reader who also urges 'disce boy disce' at 2A1r (the '*Whirlepoole of decay*') and 'lege non crede' at 2N6r (a reference to Jove's rape of Leda in the guise of a swan).

think of early modern printed texts in the same way that we have come to think of manuscripts from the same period. Just as the readers of manuscript material were encouraged by the nature of the medium to become writers themselves, and to engage in onward circulation or 'publication' of texts, so the annotators of printed books were marking their texts up for future readers. The work of Lisa Jardine, Anthony Grafton, and William Sherman has demonstrated how interpersonal early modern reading practices could be.[37] Annotation, in their analyses, becomes one of the means by which a semi-professional reader made a text's insights available to the community of scholars, diplomats, and politicians who might need them. A wealth of annotation in early modern books suggests that readers' marks were imagined as public or semi-public statements, rather than purely private ruminations or soliloquies.

So it is that one early reader pens an abusive verse for the flyleaf of his copy of Pietro Martire d'Anghiera's *Decades of the Newe Worlde* (1555), translated by Richard Eden:

> As in Christmas men eate pies
> so in lent you maie reade lies
> whereof this booke hath cruell store
> And therefore poetes I implore
> Yf they to these some more maie add
> and make another booke so badd
> Then farewell frost, & welcome raine
> God send good chese all kinde of graine
> ....
> Dick Eden did this booke translate
> and I beshrewe his heade & pate[38]

In a comparable spirit of detraction, the lawyer Edward Coke embellished the title-page of his presentation copy of Francis Bacon's *Instauratio Magno* with a tart distich:

> It deserveth not to be read in schooles,
> but to be fraughted in the ship of fooles

Playing on the title-page image, which depicted the ship of knowledge passing beyond the Pillars of Hercules, Coke placed his annotation just below the title: branding the book on the forehead or slitting its nose, somewhat in the manner of the symbolic shaming rituals so widespread in early modern Europe.[39] Both of these interventions blur the boundaries between print and manuscript culture, suggesting that we need to think more fluidly about the relationship between the two media. And both interventions constitute paratexts; although they are prompted neither by the author nor by the publisher, these are 'accompanying productions' which aim to influence how a copy of the text will be interpreted by the readers who will later share, or borrow, or buy, or steal, or inherit it.[40] The same could be said about the annotations we surveyed earlier; as readers break into the margins in order to stage conversations ('you will say heere is a mysticall meaning') or to issue instructions ('lege maid lege'), they create a frame for future readers of that volume. In this light, one of the most striking aspects of Gabriel Harvey's annotations has to be the hand he employs to write them. His marginalia are typically penned in his best set italic; these words are visibly designed for display, and for consumption by the many readers who might borrow the book from his (only semi-) private library. Paratexts in this period do not stop at the publisher's front door.

CHAPTER 10

Reading the home: the case of The English Housewife

Wendy Wall

> A print manual must be pedagogically complete, or else point readers toward practical – even psychological – ways of compensating for its incompleteness.
>
> Sandra Sherman[1]

In 1615 soldier, writer, and horse-breeder Gervase Markham published a comprehensive estate guide that became an enduring bestseller in seventeenth-century England. First appended to a book about men's rural sports, *The English Housewife* pointedly took issue with other fashionable cookery books encouraging hospitality, shopping, and leisure activities for women. With chapters detailing medical care, cooking, distilling, brewing, dairying, and textile-making, Markham instead promoted the path of home-grown practice and thrift for his national home-worker, and he did so by linking the virtues of womanhood to tasks important for the 'generall good of this kingdome' (Figure 10.1).[2]

So popular that it went through ten editions in the seventeenth century, *The English Housewife* remained on booksellers' stalls long after fashions in domestic advice had strayed towards continental cuisine or female-authored guides, manuals that largely staked their value on the appeal of exoticism or the claim to first-hand experience. Even in its first publication, parts of *The English Housewife* might have seemed out of date. By 1695, the book was positively a dinosaur, yet still appealing enough to warrant reprinting.

When republished throughout the seventeenth century, the format and presentation of Markham's text altered in subtle though significant ways. *The English Housewife*, I argue, shifted its focus away from confirming tried-and-true 'native' experience and towards the project of rationalising domestic processes, a venture carried out through both textual and technical features of the book. Examining the publication history of Markham's text over the course of a century, with an eye to understanding the paratextual matter of the book – its typographical features and preliminary materials – I

THE ENGLISH Huſ-wife,

Contayning,

The inward and outward vertues which *ought to be in a compleat woman.*

As, her skill in Phyſicke, Cookery, Banquetingſtuffe, Diſtillation, Perfumes, VVooll, Hemp, Flax, Dayries, Brewing, Baking, *and all other things belonging to an Houſhould.*

A Worke very profitable and neceſſarie, gathered for the generall good of this kingdome.

Printed at London by *Iohn Beale*, for *Roger Iackſon*, and are to bee ſold at his ſhop neere the great Cunduit in Fleet-ſtreete. 1615.

10.1 Title-page to Gervase Markham, *The English Hus-wife*, 1615.

The case of The English Housewife 167

find that this guide increasingly organised the reading experience so as to model methodical practice. My intuition is that conventions of print and household practice partook of a shared and evolving system of knowledge. I thus position my analysis at the intersection of histories of the book and histories of the *domus*, and I see it as a preliminary study in which I address the mystery of the book's enduring success. Namely, does this book's modality of reading offer some compensatory household expertise? What would this proficiency be? Can the answer to the question of why *The English Housewife* remained so popular be found, in part, in its history as a material artifact?

HOW DO YOU READ RENAISSANCE HOW-TO BOOKS?

When approaching a cookery book today, how does a modern person expect to navigate through the text? Historians of media often foreground the fundamental divide when the scroll gave way to the codex, with its new invitation for discontinuous reading.[3] Anecdotal evidence suggests that cookery-book readers take advantage of random access to forge one of two primary routes through the text. One might leaf through the book, gazing voyeuristically at pictures of dripping roasts and exquisitely decorated tarts, sampling the cookery book as an artifact to be relished. Yet many people are compelled to read pragmatically. Desperate to find something for dinner, one searches for particular recipes and relies on the table of contents, chapter headings, page runners, and indices as entry points to the material, features that generate a technology of reading. While I hardly see functionalism and fantasy as mutually exclusive, cookery books might be seen as falling nearer the functionalist end of the spectrum in terms of the goals of their readers.

In order to understand how early modern readers used this type of guide, we might turn to one of the first printed recipe books in England, John Partridge's *Treasurie of commodious conceites & hidden secrets* (1573).[4] Unlike his continental counterparts or earlier English writers, Partridge did not offer a print version of a medieval 'order of serving' book catering to male servants in great households. Instead he took the risk of addressing his book centrally to women and he assumed a readership of people from different social classes. Modern readers might find this book, one indebted to the genre of the 'book of secrets', unusual on several fronts: first, pre-modern recipe books fully intermix desserts and medicines, blending curatives with culinary advice. Finding what to make for dinner also constituted, for the early modern reader, the quest for a diet emanating out of the Galenic theory of the balance of humours. After Partridge explains how to make conserves of strawberries, for instance, the reader is informed of the healing 'virtues' of the recipe, namely that it is 'good against a hot liver or burning of the stomach'.[5] But even in recipes that are not explicit about their health benefits these can be assumed to be important to the reader. Typical for the pre-modern world as well but perhaps surprising for modern readers is the fact that this text is often vague about amounts for ingredients, cooking times, and precise instructions: it relied on the reader's existing knowledge or supplementary apprenticeship. Finally, the modern reader might not expect to find highly seasoned meat dishes calling for fruits and an array of spices imported from the East, a fare typical of medieval cuisine but far from the common conception of plain British food that would develop later in time.

The treasurie of commodious conceites orientates its reader to the material by grounding its advice in privileged erudition rather than common experience. The frontispiece (see Figure 10.2) displays an elegantly dressed man writing in a closet. Wearing a ruff and stockings tied with a floret, he pens with his quill a version of the book that the reader plans to consume. This image authorises domestic advice as the product of the circulation of texts; the recipes travel through the hands of the distinguished author who creates a manuscript derived from an existing text. The title-page offers a clue about what book the esteemed author copies. Its advice is 'Gathered out of sundrye Experiments lately practised by men of Great knowledge' and recommended by the unnamed gentlewoman who supposedly urges Partridge to publish it. After a quaint rhymed envoy familiar to students of literature (which begins: 'Goe forth my little booke / That all on thee may look') the reader discovers a dedicatory letter to a member of the Company of Barber Surgeons and two commendatory poems. It is only at this point that the text offers the tool that modern readers of English books see as indispensable, the table of contents, a book feature which later would be expected to offer a concise prologue and some sense of how information in the text is organised. But Partridge's table consists merely of a five-page list of all recipes in the somewhat miscellaneous order in which they fall in the book, with each title followed by a chapter denotation rather than page number. The entries are marked with alternating paragraph marks and asterisks, symbols that one might expect to be functional but that are used here for decoration. The list begins: 'To Bake a Capon with Yokes of Eggs', 'To Bake a pheasant or capon instead of a pheasant'. The reader then encounters yet another poetic envoy before arriving at any specific kitchen advice. Such is the paratextual matter that one has to traverse as part of the journey towards recipes.

10.2 Frontispiece to John Partridge, *The treasurie of commodious conceits*, 1573.

In order to appreciate early modern recipe books, we should first note that early modern tables and indices were not distinct. Modern tables of contents typically precede the text and group information chronologically, while modern indices of English books follow the text and provide other points of entry, usually by recourse to alphabetic order. Indices are designed to enable efficiency, so that the reader can access information in ways other than that suggested by the book's narrative logic or chronology, yet these features interchanged to varying degrees in the early modern period. Printers shifted the table, alternately called the 'table' or 'index', from back to front or front to back when reprinting a text. While recipe books typically did not have alphabetical indices at all until the mid-seventeenth century, other types of books did, though these features were more or less helpful to practically minded readers. Robert Burton's index for the *Anatomy of melancholy* obligingly offers topics such as 'guts described' but it also includes 'All are melancholy' under the letter 'A'; 'Best site of an house' under 'B'; 'How to resist passions' under 'H'; and 'Who are most apt to be jealous' under 'W'. Such designations might allow what could be considered to be the 'main subject' to be overlooked.[6] Interpretative indices, on the other hand, explicitly aim to educate readers about proper classification. One case in point is William Prynne's *Histrio-mastix*, which lists under the entry 'Women – Actors', 'notorious whores', a gloss that apparently gave offence to some at court.[7]

The first printed recipe books in England, such as Partridge's, however, provide only an introductory list rather than any sort of index. What was the contemporary reader of *The treasurie of commodious conceits* to do? Pore through the entire book, attempting to remember roughly where that coveted oil of roses recipe was when one needed to use it in making preparations for dinner, or more urgently when required for a medicinal cure? Skim the entire preliminary list before each use of the book and approximate where a recipe might fall in the volume? In its indifference to offering a navigational system, this recipe book emphasised the social and literary features of the guide over and above its functionality. With multiple prefaces and dedicatory poems and little in the way of a navigational system, the supplemental knowledge it provides seems to have been class savviness.

The treasurie of commodious conceits was not idiosyncratic. It launched a significant publishing event in the dissemination of culinary knowledge, making England the most active site of cookery publication in Europe between 1570 and 1650, and the only country in which such texts catered to housewives. Scholars estimate that 14,500 copies of different cookery books circulated around 1600, in this 'second wave' of cookery publication.[8]

The case of The English Housewife   171

Such texts tended to present either a bare list of contents or no indexical feature at all: for example, *The good huswifes jewel* (1587), *The good huswifes handmaide for the kitchin* (1594), *The Widdow's Treasure* (1595), *A closet for ladies* (1608), and John Murrel's *A newe book of cookery* (1615).⁹ Many of these books were strikingly decorative, with attention given to aesthetic pleasure rather than expediency. As book objects, they encouraged leisurely reading and viewing, the delight of detouring to gaze at ornate printers' flowers, borders, and engraved capitals.¹⁰ The wave of recipe books published at the turn of the century promulgated an ideology of domestic work as enjoyment.

If we move forward in time, leaping past the publication of Markham's text, we find that domestic guides published after mid-century were quite different in terms of their 'usability'. Elizabeth Grey's *A choice manual of rare and select secrets*, a medical book bound with a guide for conserves, includes an alphabetised table that precedes the text, one in which all recipes beginning with the same letter are grouped together.¹¹ Hannah Woolley, the most popular domestic writer of late seventeenth-century England and the first woman to publish a cookery book, offers alphabetical tables for most of her works, including her *Queenlike closet or Rich Cabinet*, as did subsequent cookery writers such as Elizabeth Raffald, Eliza Smith, and Martha Bradley.¹² By 1650, it was the norm for cookery-book producers to classify material alphabetically and to enable readers to access information somewhat efficiently. By the time we get to Hannah Glasse's famed *Art of cookery* (1774), with its table of contents offering elaborate chapter headings and its hyper-extensive table of contents spanning twenty-three pages, it had become absolutely standard for cookery books to use the combined table and index as the equivalent of a mouse clicker on the computer screen.¹³ From kitchen miscellanies to a systematised reference world: such is one part of the history of recipe collections.

ARE YOU OUT OF YOUR ELEMENT? ENTER
MARKHAM IN DIGESTIVE MODE

Famous for books on husbandry, veterinary care, and estate management that placed a premium on tested practice, Markham ventures into the realm of housewifery in 1615 by including *The English Housewife* in his book *Country Contentments*. In the preface to the sporting manual to which this domestic guide is appended, he promises to deliver, first, efficient methods, or what he calls 'a plaine forme of doing things by a neerer and ... easie way'. Markham then typically privileges the importance of hands-on verification when he lauds 'our latest experiments'.[14] The prefatory materials for the companion text, *The English Housewife*, however, offer somewhat contradictory justifications. After an obsequious letter to a past and would-be patron, Sir Theodore Newton, an epistle in which Markham identifies the book as the product of his experience when serving Newton, the text presents printer Roger Jackson's address to the reader, which is frankly sceptical that a man could know anything about this subject:

> Thou mayst say (gentle Reader) what hath this man to do with Hus-wifery, he is now out of his element; and to be so generall for all the qualities, is to expresse more in one Booke then can be found exprest in two women. I shall desire thee therefore to understand, that this is no collection of his whose name is prefixed to this worke, but an approved Manuscript which he happily light on belonging to an honorable Personage of this kingdome ... This only he hath done, digested the things of this booke in a good method, placing every thing of the same kind together.[15]

Jackson reassures readers by cancelling the claims that Markham has just made to learning his trade by experience. Dismantling the personified scene in which Markham's relations with Newton and his immersion in life practices produce knowledge, Jackson locates the book's value as resting in Markham's arrangement of material, his ordering – rather than authoring – of 'an approved Manuscript ... belonging to an honorable Personage of this kingdome'. His expertise rests in his ability, in fact, to put the contents of the book 'in good method'.

In *The English Housewife*'s next edition, issued in 1623, the printer's disclaimer about knowing women's work disappears, but the problem of experience as opposed to taught authority resurfaces. Now dedicated to the Countess Dowager of Exeter, whom the preface states cannot learn from the book because she needs no instruction, Markham freely admits his lack of expertise and retreats to his former publisher's claims:

> I doe not assume to my selfe (though I am not altogether ignorant in abilitie to judge of these things) the full invention and scope of this whole worke: for it is true (great Lady) that much of it was a Manuscript which many yeeres ago belonged to an Honorable Countesse ... and were the opinions of the greatest Physicians.[16]

Markham *downplays* experience (though he is not altogether 'ignorant' of such matters) and instead emphasises origins and transmission: a countess's private recipes sent to another countess, to inspire countess-like qualities in readers. Domestic advice is approved by noblewomen and physicians though reordered, or reconsumed, by men like Markham.

When the final edition of *The English Housewife* published in Markham's lifetime appears in 1631, Markham specifies that he has garnered medical

The case of The English Housewife 173

information largely from two popular doctors, Dr Burket and Dr Bomelius. As such, remedies formerly described as common or well known in the kingdom are now attributed to specific professional sources.[17] The disavowal of authorship, now more pronounced, is evident in the text as well in the paratext, for instance, in the section on wine-making where Markham confesses that he merely reproduces a vintner's handbook. Part of the initial rationale for *The English Housewife*, as preserving tried-and-true national practice, fades as the story of how Markham chiefly reassembles and digests previous texts is amplified. According to the *OED*, to 'digest' could mean to 'dispose methodically according to a system; to reduce into a systematic form'.[18] With this disavowal of a traditional notion of authorship, experience does not underwrite advice; strangely enough, book preparation does.[19] Taxonomy, not readiness, is all, for making both books and dinner.[20]

SETTING THE TABLE OF CONTENTS

Of what did Markham's *digestion* consist? Although Markham cites the manuscript of a noblewoman and two physicians and although some of his recipes correspond to those found in dainty books or French estate guides, many recipes are taken verbatim from the popular *Bankes* herbal, a book that presents its lore by elaborating on the properties of plants which are arranged in alphabetical order.[21] Markham's chief concern in organising and transmitting information can be seen in the strategies that he used to reclassify this material: he first parsed advice into clearly demarcated sections that extracted medical care from cookery and other tasks. In a first section devoted to *physic* he gathers all herbs that helped similar ailments, so that the primary principle of organisation becomes the illness rather than the herb. By emphasising the home-worker's use of the herbs rather than the natural characteristics of plants, flora, and fauna, Markham renders this knowledge more domestic than botanical. He then secondarily arranges cures so that they follow an imaginary spatial movement *down* the body. He begins with recipes for diseases of the head (including a cure for the 'frenzy' or brain inflammation, deafness, and headache). The text then offers remedies for problems in the abdomen and lungs (such as stomach ache, pleurisy, shortness of breath) before moving to the privy parts and ending with the feet. The reader is thus to traverse the book fantasising that one is performing a diagnostic blazon of the body, much like those commonly found in lyric poetry but with diseases rather than Petrarchan compliment as the subject. Although the *ad capite ad calcem* (or head-to-toe order) structures some fifteenth-century medical manuscripts, it was not a feature of household manuals in Markham's time.[22] This rough spatial classification is hardly fool-proof since at points Markham throws in miscellaneous cures, and it is never clear where one would locate something like skin or joint diseases. Yet this structure offers the reader an approximate and *unannounced* guidance system for locating recipes in the book. To find a treatment, the reader might use the table, but this apparatus simply condenses an imaginative stealth structure: that of the body.

Each edition of *The English Housewife* marshals the resources of print to make the stealth classifications neater and the classificatory principles explicit. The table for the 1615 edition is not much of a table (see Figure 10.3).

10.3 Gervase Markham, *Country contentments, in two books* ... *The second intituled, The English husvvife*, 1615, Q2r.

The Table.

	Page		Page
For the falling of the fundament	35	To boile a Mallard	49
For sinewes cut or shrunk	35	How to make an excellent olepotrigo	50
Of the outward and actiue knowledges of the Husewife, and first of her skill in Cookery, (shee must know all hearbes.	36	To make the best white broath	50
		To boile any wilde-fowle	51
		To boile a legge of mutton	52
		An excellet way to boil chickens	52
Her skill in the garden	37	Broth for any fresh fish	52
Transplanting of hearbes	38	Roast-meats and Carbonadoes	53
Choice of seeds	38	Obseruations in roast meats	53
Prosperity of seeds	38	Temprature of fiers	53
Gathering of seeds	38	The complexions of meate	54
Cookery and the parts thereof	39	The best basting for meate	54
Of Sallads	39	The best dredging for meate	54
Simple Sallads	39	To know when meate is enough	54
Compound Sallads	40	Rosting mutton with oysters	55
Another compound sallad	40	How to roast a legge of mutton curiously	56
An excellent boiled sallad	40		
Preserued sallads	41	To roast a gigget of mutton	57
Making of strange sallads	41	Roasting Oliues of veale	57
Sallads for shew only	42	How to roast a pigge	57
Frycase and quelque choses	42	To roast a pound of butter well	58
Simple fricafes	43	Roasting a pudding on a spit	58
Best collops and egges	43	To roast a chine of beefe, a loine of mutton, a capon and a larke all at one instant and at one fire, & to haue all ready together and none burnt.	58
Compound fricafes	43		
How to make the best Tansey	43		
To make the best fritters	44		
To make the best pancake	45		
To make Veale toasts	45	To roast venison	59
The best Panpardie	46	To roast fresh Sturgion	59
To make any quelque chose	46	Ordering of meats to be roasted	59
Of ordinary boiled meates	47	Sauce for a Capon or Turquie	60
Pottage without sight of hearbs	48	Sauce for a Hen or Pullet	60
Pottage without any hearbes	48	For Chickens	61
Pottage with whole hearbes	48	For Pheasant or Partridge	61
To make ordinary stew'd broth	48	For Quaile, Raile or big birds	61
A very fine boil'd meate.	49	For Pigeons.	61

10.3b (cont.), Q3r

It offers a fairly undifferentiated list much like that found in Partridge's guide, with each recipe, medical or culinary, appearing in the order in which it falls in the text. The recipes, 'For the headache' and 'For the frenzy', are indexical in the sense that they offer page numbers to the reader, but there is not much efficiency enabled by the list. Recipes for similar cures are not grouped together; for instance, the entry entitled 'A powder for the Collicke & stone' is, like many others, simply followed by the bare word, 'Another' (Q2r). Nor is much labour expended to allow the reader to conceptualise the organisation of the book itself. The visual architecture of the page layout does not demarcate chapter divisions through spacing or numeration (in fact, where chapter breaks seem to be indicated by blank space, these are instances in which the type ran over from one line to the next). Although the word 'Table' is displayed as a running header for these pages, it does not exhibit the modern features of a table in one of its definitions ('an arrangement of numbers, words, or items ... in a compact form, so as to exhibit a set of relations in a distinct way').[23]

When reprinted in the 1623 edition of *The English Housewife*, the table notably consolidates multiple recipes under a single group header and indicates the relationship of the particular cure to a general principle of organisation (see Figure 10.4).

10.4 Gervase Markham, *Countrey contentments, or The English husvvife*, 1623, A3r.

The Table.

For the bloody Flux.	28.29	To helpe the skarres of the small Pox.	46
For Costiveneſſe.	29.30	For the French Pox.	46.47
For all sorts of Wormes.	29	For pricking with a thorne.	28
For hardneſſe of the belly.	30	For any Ache or swelling.	49
For the Rupture.	30.34	For bruſes.	49
For the Stone.	31.32.33	For bones broke or out of ioynt.	50.51
For the Cholick and Stone.	31	A Bath to comfort the body.	50
To helpe the Vrine.	33.34	To make oyle of Swallowes.	52
For the Strangullion.	33	The oyle of Camomile or Lauender.	53
For the Gonorea.	34	To make oyle of Roſes or Violet.	55
For the Emorods.	35	Oyle of Nutmegs.	55
For diſeaſes in the fundement.	35	Oyle of Spike or Maſtick.	56
For the greene ſickneſſe.	35	Oyle to make ſmooth hands.	53
To increaſe milke.	36.37	Of Doctor Steuens water.	53
To drie vp milke.	36	A Reſtoratiue of Roſa-ſolis.	54
For ſore breſts.	36.38		
For eaſe in child-bearing.	36	Chap. 2.	
Child dead in the wombe.	36.37		
For aptneſſe to conceiue.	37	The outward and actiue knowledge of the	
To ceaſe the Termes.	37	Houſ-wife.	57
Helpe for the Matrix.	37	The knowledge of Hearbs and Garde-	
Helpe in the childbed.	37	ning.	57.58.59
For Morphew of both kinds.	38	Of Cookerie and the ſeuerall parts.	59
For the Gout.	38	Of Sallets ſimple and compound.	60.61
For the Siatica.	38.49		62.63
For the ſtinging of venemus beaſts.	39.45	Of Fricaſes ſimple and compound.	63.64
For ſwellings in the leggs.	39.49	Of Collops and Eggs.	63
For old or new ſores.	39.40.41.42.43	The beſt Tanſey.	64
	44.45.47.48	Fritters of all ſorts.	65.68
For Scabs or Itch.	40.45.46	To make Pancakes.	66
For the Leproſie.	40	Veale toaſts.	66
Priuie parts burnt.	41	To make any Quelquechoſe.	67
For any burning.	41.42.43	To make all ſorts of Puddings.	68.69.70
For Scaldings.	41	To make Linkes	72
To eate away dead fleſh.	41.44	To make all ſorts of boyld-meates or pot-	
For Sinews cut or ſhrunke.	42.48	tage.	from 71 to 79
To helpe Impoſtumes.	42	To make Oleopotrigo.	74
			To

10.4b (cont.), A3r

Eight recipes fall into a single group labelled for 'fevers', and the table groups multiple page numbers after entries (for example, cures 'for a canker' can be found on pages 15, 18, and 19). Not only does the table generate more indexical function, it also uses blank space and numeration

The Table.

To make Broth for fresh-fish.	77	A proportion for expence in Feasts.	125
To make all sorts of Roast-meats.	80	Of all sorts of Distillations,	116
81.82.83.84.85.86		117.129.130.131.132	
The obseruations in Rost-meates.	80.85	133.137.141	
Spitting of Rost meates.	80	The natures of Waters.	129
The temperature of the fire.	81	Hipocrates fixe famous Waters.	133
The complexion of meates.	81	Waters for Perfumes.	137
The best basting and dredging.	81	To perfume Gloues, Ierkins, &c.	137
To know when meate is enough.	82		138.142
All sorts of Sauces.	86.87.88.89.90	To make washing Balls.	138
To make Gallantines or Chauders.	90	To make Muske Balls.	138
To make all sorts of Carbonados.	90	To make perfume to burne.	139
	91.92	To make all sorts of Vinegar.	139.141
Tosting of Mutton.	91	To make verinyce.	140
Rashers of Mutton or Lambe.	92	To make all sorts of sweete Baggs.	140
The dressing of all kind of Fish.	92.93.94	To make Powder for Baggs.	140
Sauce for any Fish.	92	The ordering, choyce, helping and curing	
To make Pastery and all sorts of Bak't-		of all sorts of Wines. from 143 to 153	
meates.	from 94 to 110	The notes and markes for gadging of all	
The mixture of Pasts.	95	Wines, oyles or liquors.	149
To make a Norffolke Foole.	101	The contents of Wines.	151
To make a Trifle.	101		
To recouer Venison that is tainted.	103	Chap. 3.	
To preserue Quinces to bake all the yeere.			
	105.123.121	Of Wooll and woolling cloth.	154
Tarts of als sorts.	from 105 to 110	Dying of Wooll.	155.156.157
To make a Florentine.	107	The mixing of colours.	157
To make a Whitepot.	111	The oyling of Wooll.	158
To make all sorts of Banqueting stuffe		The tumming and spinning Wooll.	159
and conceited dishes.	from 111 to 124		160
To make all sorts of Conserues.	119	Of winding, Waping and weauing.	160
	120.122		161
To make Wafers.	120	The ordering of Flaxe, Hempe, and ma-	
To make a fine bread.	121	king of all kind of Linnen cloth, from	
To make Ipocras.	112.121	page 162 to page 173.	
To make all sorts of Preserues.	121		
The ordering of great Feasts.	124	Chap.	

10.4C (*cont.*), A4r

to subdivide chapters and thus expose the organisational framework for the book. After sections on physic and cookery, chapter descriptions shrink to a single heading with the result that the first two chapters are privileged because of the specificity offered by the table. Thirty-nine individual entries about making cheese are listed simply as 'Of dairying' in this edition. In the body of the text, where Markham has added remedies for ailments including headache and eye problems, book producers make the corporeal infrastructure evident through marginal glosses. For instance, when the reader sees 'additions to diseases of the belly' in the margin, he or she becomes glaringly aware that *this* is the part of the book where diseases of the belly are located. The structural platform on which Markham's advice is arranged is thus displayed as it is made more consistent. Readers could thumb through a more user-friendly book, one in which domestic work was afforded the prestige of a Ramus-like visual arrangement of knowledge.[24]

The 1631 edition continues the process of digesting information. This text deploys small printed pointing hands in the margins. 'Manicules', as William Sherman terms them, were the most common symbol produced for and by readers in manuscripts and printed books between 1200 and 1800.[25] Also known as a digit, fist, hand, mutton fist, or index, the pointing hand functions as a highlighter, in this case calling attention to a fresh or especially successful recipe. The 1631 table not only achieves its goals by marking the onset of a chapter with large capitals and printed lines but strikingly employs manicules *within* the table, an addition that creates a potentially confusing double-referencing system. Known as the *index*, the little printed hand reduplicates itself, indexing the index through a pictorial figure that sifts information through a different mechanism. As a well-known symbol used in many types of books to call attention to noteworthy items, the manicule has the general effect of signalling several taxonomic systems at work. It calls attention to the tactile act of holding the book in hand, reduplicating the reader's finger as it rests on the page; in doing so, it self-consciously foregrounds the interface between the reader's prerogative in annotating and the book producers' accenting of information. As such, the 1631 *English Housewife* moved into what might be called the *digitary*, if not digital, world of information technology. While the book is organised primarily through an imaginative logic of the body, this added feature introduces a rival readerly path that sorts the information using a feature unique to writing. As it was republished, *The English Housewife* was subject to a page layout that increasingly denoted hierarchies of information and amplified the book's utility.[26]

The cookery section for *The English Housewife* also underwent an editorial makeover when republished. Imitating manuscripts that follow the order of serving at the table, Markham innovates this conventionally medieval framework by sub-arranging courses by method of cooking (boiled, baked, roasted) rather than by food type (beef, fish, poultry). He begins by warning his housewife that she should have a 'quick eye' and not be 'butter-fingered, sweet-toothed, nor faint-hearted'.[27] But his advice about character gives way to an account of his system of organisation: 'Now for the substance of the *art* itself, I will divide it into five parts: the first, sallats and fricassees; the second, boiled meat and broths; the third, roast meats, and carbonadoes; the fourth, baked meats and pies, and the fifth, banqueting and made dishes, with other conceits and secrets'.[28] Arranging dishes by method of cooking, Markham invites the reader to conjure up the household space or tools needed to prepare a dish rather than the animal eaten or the dining experience. The text calls to mind the implements of the kitchen – the pot, kettle, pipkin, spits, cobirons, and chafing dish – as the principle of unity for seemingly disparate recipes. In modern terms, a cookery book organised around 'barbecuing' would follow roughly the same principles. But modern cookery books tend *not* to rely on a taxonomy resting principally on the method or site of cooking: on, for instance, 'dishes cooked in the oven' regardless of whether they are sweet or savoury (such as roasted lamb, apple pie, and quiche).

In his recent book, *Aguecheek's Beef, Belch's Hiccup, and Other Gastronomic Interjections*, Robert Appelbaum argues that one change in culinary taste and its representation in technical guides in the seventeenth century was the shift to 'modular' recipes. Writers newly provided 'basics' that could be mixed and modified. Markham does precisely this when he observes that he can eliminate 'further repetition' because he has furnished 'the art of seasoning' for baked meats.[29] Previous texts relied sometimes on 'mnemonic clusters'.[30] As Markham systematised by designating techniques of cookery as 'basics', he eliminated the miscellaneous air of other cookery books. *The English Housewife*'s formatting gradually made this framework explicit, emphasising the imposed structures of print over and above imagined domestic practice. In the 1623 table, five recipes become simply 'Of Sallats, simple and compound', and the text uses typography to signpost principles of classification. One might say that the table of contents overtook the dinner table. But I might articulate this claim more deliberately by arguing that the imagined body or kitchen space is increasingly a *product* of the reader's engagement with the physical book.

If, as Sandra Sherman argues, early cookery books had not 'accommodated cognitive models adapted to teach cooking in a print environment',[31]

English domestic guides did certainly offer a vexed expertise. In addition to relieving the burden of memory and providing some still vital advice, Markham's book inaugurates the reader into a newly systematised *habitus* of the household.[32] His texts trained the reader to experience home practices as sophisticated cognitive acts – involving processing, ordering, and prioritising – skills helpful in many domains but certainly crucial to home economics. *The English Housewife* everywhere insists on the significance of sequential and rationalised learning. 'There followeth now in his place after these knowledges alreadie rehearsed, the ordering and government of Dairies', Markham writes, outlining the importance of establishing a clear hierarchy of household tasks. 'When our *English Hous-wife* knowes how to preserve health by wholesome Physick . . . she must not then . . . bee ignorant in the provision of bread and drinke', he advises.[33] Markham's text *formats* such lessons, materialising kitchen proficiency out of book conventions; it translates the household into a specific object of (readable) knowledge. As Markham tenders a nostalgic vision of an English community deeply tied to land, this vision is marked on the surface of the book so as to emphasise newly important taxonomies for managing home economics.[34] It was a matter of setting the table properly, of creating a domestic reading ethic.[35]

It is worth remembering that books activate fantasies for readers as part of these frameworks for cognition. Markham's *English Housewife* appeared when recipe books typically sought to frame domestic knowledge as part of the civilising process. The cookery books discussed earlier did so precisely by playing on the reader's elitism and penchant for voyeurism. Publishers and writers used conceits to describe book objects that suggested the elite status of their content: *The closet for ladies*; *The good huswifes jewel*; *The treasurie of commodious conceits*; *The queen-like closet*. To consume such books was to enter a private space harbouring precious riches supposedly newly released to a wider and more heterogeneous public. Promising cultural capital and pleasure, recipe books value profusion, abundance, and plenitude.[36] Markham's guide, by contrast, offers a nationally moral housewife whose person exemplifies the modesty and order that should pervade domestic work. Discriminating reading was a mental habit and disposition as important as the work ethic that the book recommends.

THE INDEXICAL DOMESTIC IMAGINATION

Historians of English household life have argued that the seventeenth century witnessed several important transformations in marriage, architecture, the structural relations of family to state, and ideologies of work.[37] In doing so, they have found some points of consensus about economic life. The first is that production gave way slowly to consumption, such that the consumerism and the organisation of goods were emphasised over and above the sheer tasks of making. Natasha Korda, Susan Cahn, Alice Clark, and Amy Erickson narrate this evolution largely as a decline in the housewife's power. One might quibble about whether nostalgia pervades such accounts, but the basic story of professionalisation that they evidence remains unchallenged.[38] The second point of consensus is what Lena Cowen Orlin describes as the 'exploding availability of consumer goods' in the early modern household.[39] The proliferation of luxury goods and necessities was evident in homes at all socioeconomic levels, and produced a newly fuelled drive for organisational frameworks to account for these goods.

In the domain of literature, there is abundant evidence that writers represented household space and objects as potentially out of control, with the mechanisms used for ordering them subject to mockery. Let me point to two examples. In Shakespeare's *The Merry Wives of Windsor*, Mrs Ford plaintively observes that she cannot hide Falstaff because her jealous husband obsessively searches his own home: 'He will seek there, on my word. Neither press, coffer, chest, trunk, well, vault, but he hath an abstract for the remembrance of such places, and goes to them by his note. There is no hiding you in the house.'[40] Seething jealousy inspires a pathological form of husbandry, in both meanings of the word. Small-town citizen Ford compulsively makes a mental inventory of goods and spaces, an 'abstract' that allows him to account for every object in which his wife might hide a potential lover. Searching his house is a hobby that he misunderstands as the sign of smart house-holding. Mrs Ford's description of her husband's quirky behaviour as an 'abstract' renders it both a parody of recommended accounting methods and a perverse memory system: a mini-version of the elaborate memory arts described by classical and medieval thinkers. (Rather than using furniture as a trigger for remembering a ten-part argument, Ford retains only the catalogue and the heightened affect necessary for burning the argument in one's memory.) In this instance, *Merry Wives* presents a dystopian domestic world of *loci* out of control, a playful send-up of the organisational frameworks that guide writers earnestly promoted as the basis for the state.

For another example, we might glance at Thomas Dekker's 1599 play *The Shoemaker's Holiday*, where a foreman named Firk offers a faux-inventory as he imagines kitchen fare taking over the streets:

O my brethren! There's cheer for the heavens – venison pasties walk up and down piping hot like sergeants, beef and brewis comes marching in dry-fats, fritters and pancakes come trolling in in wheelbarrows, hens, and oranges hopping in porters' baskets, collops and eggs in scuttles, and tarts and custards come quavering in in malt shovels.[41]

In Firk's imagination, the absence of any human labour that might regulate goods signals prosperity as frightening as it is utopian. As the cupboards unleash food that comes alive in city streets, these items assume the bodies of soldiers and labourers. The rhetorical excess of the passage combined with its military references reveal as much anxiety about how bounty will be controlled as delight. The fact that the play ends with the threat of war only plays out the undercurrent of tension in this scene of bounty. In general, Firk offers a catalogue of a world out of order: 'brewis', a broth common in household books, could not be housed in 'dry-fats', for these were barrels used to contain dry goods; fried bacon and eggs would not be found in a 'scuttle', which was a large basket; and custards would never be shovelled like barley. Obviously nothing except the hen should be alive. Hopping with, and heaped with, the oranges, the hen confuses the line between animal and vegetable. Firk's cornucopia of the kitchen marks a category crisis.

In imaginative writings of many eras, the household is portrayed as a site of potential disorder. In early seventeenth-century England, however, such representations took particular meaning from the fact that the family economy was changing to a market economy and the proliferation of goods required new systems of classification. It is not surprising that the dissemination of domestic knowledge also took various and competing forms. *The English Housewife* might be said to respond to this moment of transition not with panic or parody but by offering the compensatory moral skill of reading methodically.[42] It tapped into features of the book newly accessible as part of print culture, promoting a more systematised mode of reading now internalised as natural. Here is one site where the history of the book meets housework, with both steeped, in my view, in a kind of fantasy that often goes unacknowledged. It is true that critics have speculated readily on the phantasmatic nature of how-to books, asking whether Markham's patriotic self-sufficiency was a nostalgic fantasy, or how we square his injunction not to shop with his own exotic recipes that required a trip to the market. Questions about the content, I argue, might fruitfully be expanded to consider the book's format. Once we extend our enquiry to the book's material features, we see that the text does not simply verify the triumph of Ramist thought or confirm the inherent features of print technology but shows an active choice on the part of the book publisher. Markham's *English Housewife* puts the fantasy of the indexical domestic imagination into print.

CHAPTER 11

Pictures, places, and spaces: Sidney, Wroth, Wilton House, and the Songe de Poliphile

Hester Lees-Jeffries

Critics have often been drawn to metaphors of space and place to describe both families and the genre of romance, speaking of households, networks, and cycles. Recently Helen Cooper has persuasively adopted the idea of the meme, derived from genetics, to discuss the transformations of romance motifs in medieval and early modern England;[1] as she observes: 'The romance genre – any genre, indeed – is best thought of as a lineage or family of texts rather than a series of incarnations or clones of a single Platonic idea. A family changes over time as its individual members change, but equally, those individuals can be recognized through their "family resemblance"'.[2] There are not enough surviving portraits to ascertain whether the Sidney family resembled one another physically, but the repetition of names across the generations certainly emphasised their relationships: Mary Wroth was named after her aunt, Mary Sidney Herbert, whose mother had also been a Mary; Philip's brother Robert was named after his uncle, Robert Dudley, Earl of Leicester; he named his own youngest son Robert, and one of his daughters was Philippa.[3] These ties of kinship were paratextually re-created in the Sidneys' own publications: Philip Sidney dedicated his romance to his sister, locating its composition within her household and describing her as his first reader in his preface; it was published, after his death, as *The Countess of Pembroke's Arcadia*. A generation later, Mary Wroth or her printer also located her romance firmly within kinship networks, using its title-page to announce it as *The Countesse of Mountgomeries Urania. Written by the right honorable the Lady Mary Wroath. Daughter to the right noble Robert Earle of Leicester. And neece to the ever famous, and renowned Sr. Phillips Sidney knight. And to ye most exele[n]t Lady Mary Countesse of Pembroke late deceased.*

The importance of place to the writings of the Sidney family, both actually and metaphorically, is not an original concern: writers and critics from Ben Jonson onwards have tied the family to Penshurst and Wilton.[4]

Marion Wynne-Davies has described Penshurst and Wilton as 'safe houses' which gave the Sidney women in particular rooms of their own; she has also considered the landscape of Penshurst in relation to the Sidneys' own writings. For Wynne-Davies, the writings of the Sidney family are no longer an 'edifice', but 'a range of rooms with parallel forms and features'.[5] Don Wayne too has discussed Penshurst, largely in relation to Jonson's poem,[6] and Gary Waller includes a useful, if brief, psychoanalytically inflected consideration of place in the Sidney family romance, suggesting (for example) that the conventions of Petrarchanism provided writers like Sidney with 'a space in which the poet could experiment . . . a psycho-erotic model in which ideological and social tensions were acted out. The sonnet itself is such a space – a stanza, a small room'.[7] In one of the few full-length studies of Wroth's *Urania*, Sheila Cavanagh discusses the text's 'emotional geography', noting 'the primacy of place in the conceptualization of the romance's key characters'; her second chapter is entitled '"None can run so far, that shall not some time to return", or, there's no place like home'.[8] *The Countess of Pembroke's Arcadia* is, of course, named for the country in which it is set as well as for Sidney's sister, and Virginia Woolf described the *Arcadia* as 'one of those half-forgotten and deserted places'.[9] Woolf is a writer to whom Gérard Genette refers on a number of occasions,[10] and, given my concerns here with the shared experiences of writing and reading, mediated by specific copies of books in particular places, it is useful to note that Woolf begins her short essay on the *Arcadia* by considering 'the ghosts of those old readers who have read their Arcadia from this very copy', and she concludes it by returning the book 'to its place on the bottom shelf'.[11]

Genette's account of the paratext is largely a linear one as, particularly in the first part of his book, he articulates the way in which a book works as a series of textual frames, encountered in sequence and establishing particular expectations for a subsequent engagement with the text. Yet a concern with sequence, priority and lines of descent, or with the points of interplay between strands of text, perhaps obscures the interstices, the spaces between and the different ways in which they might be read: the paratext can also be described in terms of interpenetrating, contiguous, mutually informative spaces, more experiential than the implicit linearity of intersection. What might it mean to read, or to write, a particular text in a particular place? How might illustrations and ekphrasis be read differently from, or indeed in similar ways to, more obviously paratextual elements? What if the page is envisaged as being somehow coextensive with, as well as informed by and informing, where it is read or written, so that a text's relationship with other texts (and so writers with other writers, readers with other readers) is mediated visually and spatially by both reader and writer? In his foreword to *Paratexts*, Richard Macksey quotes Genette's description of the paratext as being 'neither on the interior nor on the exterior: it is both; it is on the threshold; and it is on this very site that we must study it, because essentially, perhaps, *its being depends on its site*', and Macksey adds that '*Paratexts* is itself a resolutely liminal book ... it broaches issues related to the adjacent realms of fiction and fact'.[12] These spatial metaphors are characteristic of Genette's own discussion; as Macksey goes on to note, an attention to the categories of time and space is one characteristic of the Structuralist discourse upon which Genette ultimately draws.[13] One of my concerns here is to show how these two dimensions in particular might be both vastly extended and brought to bear upon each other, as I construct a hypothetical three-way relationship between texts, readers and writers, across time, and within a particular space that is at once inter- and extra-textual.[14]

This chapter is based upon the hypothesis that both Philip Sidney in his revised *Arcadia* and his niece Mary Wroth in her *Urania* drew on a late fifteenth-century Italian romance, the *Hypnerotomachia Poliphili*, and specifically on its mid-sixteenth-century French translation, the *Songe de Poliphile*. It also posits the existence of a copy of this book at Wilton House, in Wiltshire, which both Sidney and Wroth knew well, and suggests that in addition to influencing the two writers, the *Songe* also influenced the gardens at Wilton, which in turn influenced, or were influenced by, Wroth's *Urania*. In particular, I explore an additional paratextual genre neglected by Genette, images, arguing that both Wroth's and Sidney's readings and consequent appropriations of the *Songe* were shaped by its lavish illustrations. Illustrations, I argue, can provide alternative points of entry to the text, as well as points of exit from it into other texts and experiences for both readers and writers. Wroth was born almost exactly a year after her uncle's death, but their shared reading of the *Songe* (and not simply that they read it, but how they apparently read it) and their common experience of Wilton forms a kind of conversational, paratextual space between the writers and their works, which overcomes temporal distance and offers a different model of intertextuality. The *Urania* is clearly influenced by the *Arcadia* but, as this chapter will suggest, the relationship between them can also be considered as one that is not simply dyadic, but more or less triangular, in that both bear traces of a third text, the *Songe de Poliphile*, which could have been encountered by both writers in a specific copy at a particular place, Wilton House.

Of the three texts with which this discussion is concerned, Philip Sidney's *Arcadia*, Mary Wroth's *Urania*, and the *Songe de Poliphile*, Sidney's romance is by far the best known. Its first version, now commonly known as the *Old Arcadia*, was written largely at Wilton, or nearby, at Ivychurch, when Sidney was staying there with his sister Mary Sidney Herbert, Countess of Pembroke, between about 1578 and 1580. The second version, now somewhat misleadingly referred to as the *New Arcadia*, was begun by Sidney in about 1580 and worked on until about 1582; it was unfinished at the time of his death. The composite version, known as the *Countess of Pembroke's Arcadia*, was published in 1593.[15] Mary Wroth's romance was clearly modelled on her uncle's, but it is not simply derivative of it. The first part, entitled, in an obviously imitative fashion, *The Countess of Montgomery's Urania*, was published in 1621, taking its title from a minor character in Sidney's romance who becomes one of the main figures in Wroth's. The central characters (although the cast runs into the hundreds) are the lovers Pamphilia and Amphilanthus, she faithful, he faithless, and doomed never to be united. The second part of the romance, which was unpublished until 1999, prior to that existing as a single authorial manuscript, continues the story into the next generation.[16] It is unfinished. The romance is in some respects a *roman à clef*:[17] the faithful Pamphilia at times is Wroth herself, while Amphilanthus is her cousin, William Herbert, son of Mary Sidney Herbert and eventually the third Earl of Pembroke and the father of her two illegitimate children. But a number of the other female characters are also versions of Wroth and such correspondences are only rarely exact.

The third text is perhaps the least familiar of the three. The *Hypnerotomachia Poliphili* was one of the first and most lavishly illustrated books of the Renaissance, published by Aldus Manutius in Venice in 1499. Its apparent author was a Dominican monk, Francesco Colonna. The French version, the *Songe de Poliphile*, in part a translation, in part a redaction, with redrawn woodcuts (including some not appearing in the Aldine edition) was published in Paris in 1546, with a second edition in 1561.[18] It seems likely (for reasons outlined below) that it was this French version to which Sidney and Wroth had access. Although a partial English translation, *The Strife of Love in a Dreame*, probably by Robert Dallington, appeared in 1592, dedicated both to the Earl of Essex and to Sidney's immortal memory, the *Hypnerotomachia* as a whole was not translated into English until 1999.[19] The reasons for this lack of an English translation are straightforward: in addition to the text's length, lack of narrative and character interest and esoteric nature, Colonna wrote his romance in a language that was a hybrid of Latin and Italian, stuffed with neologisms (many of them Greek in origin) and extremely heavy-going. The French translation did not attempt to reproduce this feature of the original. The *Hypnerotomachia* is an erotic architectural dream-vision romance, its first book telling the story of Poliphilus's search for his beloved Polia, and their eventual reunion and subsequent unions first at the Temple and then at the Fountain of Venus on the island of Cytherea. It is full of elaborate and lengthy descriptions of temples, palaces, gardens, triumphs, rituals, and costumes, most of which are illustrated.

Sidney was a fluent linguist and Wroth was well educated by the standards of the time, but the *Hypnerotomachia* is not a book that lends itself to reading from beginning to end, even in its French redaction as the *Songe de Poliphile*; it is simply too long, with pages and pages of description and nothing much happening. Its pictures, however, are immediately beguiling, and it appears that both Sidney and Wroth were drawn (as one is, when leafing through a book) first to the illustrations and then from them into the surrounding text. Sidney often refers to his dual roles as reader and poet: *Astrophil and Stella* opens with the poet seeking 'fit words to paint the blackest face of woe, / Studying inventions fine, her wits to entertain; / Oft turning others' leaves'.[20] In sonnet 11 he employs a vivid simile of leafing through an illustrated book to suggest an inferior form of both loving and reading: 'like a child, that some fair book doth find, / With gilded leaves or coloured vellum plays, / Or at the most on some fine picture stays, / But never heeds the fruit of writer's mind'.[21] The point here is that this way of reading is limiting only if it is an end in itself, rather than a beginning. As several striking examples in the *Arcadia* and the *Urania* show, however, illustrations can function as dynamic points of entry into a text. It is above all the illustrations of the *Songe de Poliphile* that both Sidney and Wroth draw on in their own romances, so bringing its heady eroticism and exploration of the powers of love and imagination and of the dynamics of visual pleasure to bear on their own romances.

The second book of the *Songe* is narrated by Polia, as the lovers sit beside the Fountain of Adonis. It is a scenario familiar from many medieval texts: you go and sit beside a fountain to tell stories about love. Polia tells the story of the lovers' courtship from her point of view, and what becomes apparent is that she is in fact telling the same story as has been presented in the first book of the romance, but in a different narrative mode: it could be called Boccaccian. This is part of the description of the Fountain of Adonis, around which they sit (Figure 11.1):

On the tomb[22] the goddess Venus was sculpted in the round, as large as life, from a fine sardonyx stone in three colours, sitting on an antique chair, in the form of a woman who had recently given birth. The goddess's body was completely naked,

11.1 The statue of Venus and Cupid on the Fountain of Adonis. *Songe de Poliphile*, 1561, f. 131.

carved from a white vein in the onyx and only ornamented with a little cloth, carved from a red vein in the same stone, which covered her below her navel and part of her thigh. It passed over her left breast, which seemed to thrust against it. Venus had thrown it over her shoulder, so that it hung down behind the fountain, and on the other side as far as the base of her seat. Certainly, it was constructed and draped with such skill that one could easily see all the muscles, joints and movements of her body. She held her son in her arms, and he suckled at her left breast, looking at his mother, and she at him, so gracefully that they each took great pleasure in it. The cheeks of the goddess and her child, together with her nipple, were rosily tinted, thanks to a convenient vein in the stone. It was, you may believe it, an excellent work, and one might well call it miraculous, because in these two bodies nothing was lacking but the soul.[23]

Both structurally and thematically, the Fountain of Adonis acts like a mirror, reflecting the two halves of the romance onto each other. Here, in

Sidney, Wroth, Wilton House, and the Songe de Poliphile

this reflecting fountain, there is a paradox – the surface of the water becomes somehow permeable – and it is unclear which is the real story and which is the reflection. It is this fountain of Colonna's that Sidney borrows for Kalander's garden:

> They came into a place cunningly set with trees of the most taste-pleasing fruits; but scarcely they had taken that into their consideration but that they were suddenly stept into a delicate green; of each side of the green a thicket, and behind the thickets again new beds of flowers, which being under the trees, the trees were to them a pavilion and they to the trees a mosaical floor, so that it seemed that Art therein would needs be delightful by counterfeiting his enemy Error and making order in confusion. And in one of the thickets was a fine marble fountain made thus: a naked Venus made of white marble, wherein the graver had used such cunning, that the natural blue veins of the marble were framed in fit places to set forth the beautiful veins of her body. At her breast she had her babe Aeneas, who seemed, having begun to suck, to leave that to look upon her fair eyes which smiled at the babe's folly, meanwhile the breast running ... In the midst of all the place was a fair pond whose shaking crystal was a perfect mirror to all the other beauties, so that it bare show of two gardens; one in deed, the other in shadows.[24]

One is unavoidably reminded of Genette's own quotation of J. Hillis Miller's description of the prefix 'para-' as 'not only simultaneously on both sides of the boundary line between inside and out. It is also the boundary itself, the screen which is a permeable membrane connecting inside and outside'.[25] The debt of Sidney's fountain to the *Songe*'s is clear, and specifically its borrowing from the *Songe* the detail of Venus and her child looking at each other, not present in the Italian text. His substitution of an infant Aeneas for Cupid is crucial. Sidney essentially describes an illustration in the *Songe* (see Figure 11.1), borrowing details such as the coloured veins in the stone from the surrounding text. He also adds a reflecting pool, which becomes an image for love, fiction, and imagination; it has an ethical and aesthetic function akin to the structural, reflecting function of its counterpart in the *Hypnerotomachia*.[26] As an imperfect mirror (the crystal is 'shaking') it suggests, as we might expect from the author of the *Defence of Poesie*, a certain ambivalence about the mimetic capacities of art and fiction. Like Miller's permeable membrane, it points beyond itself, and in many directions: back to the *Songe de Poliphile*, forward to the *Urania*.

It appears that Mary Wroth also drew on these particular illustrations, as well as the text adjacent to them, not for a description of a fountain but for two of her fullest evocations of the many arbours and idyllic gardens found in her romance. The garden surrounding Colonna's Fountain of Adonis (Figure 11.2) is described thus in the *Songe*:[27]

11.2 The Fountain of Adonis. *Songe de Poliphile*, 1561, f. 130.

Then there was a hedge of orange and lemon trees, both flowering and laden with fruit ... The hedge of orange trees was fenced on the inside by an arbour of crimson sandalwood, a foot and a half in height, latticed like a trellis, skilfully cut in a pattern of leaves in a Moorish style, through the holes in which were interlaced roses and jasmine, without covering or obscuring the sight of such rare work, and among the trees, all sorts of birds were singing ... At the entrance adjoining the fountain was an arbour as broad and as high as one of the aforesaid six sides [of the fountain], made of stone. The rest was two feet high, that is to say one for the upright and one for the arch. It was twelve feet long. That which would ordinarily have been made of wood in the trellis was made of pure gold. But the roses which covered it were real, although far more scented than is usual. The pavement beneath was mosaic, made of precious stones in all colours imaginable, illustrated with beautiful stories.[28]

In the first book of the *Urania*, the lovelorn prince Dolorindus wanders away from his companions Amphilanthus, Steriamus, and Ollorandus, who

Sidney, Wroth, Wilton House, and the Songe de Poliphile 193

have taken the paths that lead, in the approved romance fashion, straight ahead, to the left and to the right. Passing, like Polia and Poliphilus, through a mixed wood, he arrives at 'a rare meadow', where:

> He found a delicate Fountaine circled about with Orenge, and Pomegranet trees, the ground under them all hard sand, about the Fountaine (as next adjoyning) was a hedge of Jesamins mingled with Roses and Woodbines, and within that, paved with pavements of divers colours, plac'd for shew and pleasure; on the steps he sate downe beholding the worke of the Fountaine which was most curious, being a faire Maide as it were, thinking to lade it drie, but still the water came as fast, as it past over the dish she seemd to lade withal. (1.135–6)

The fountain here is different from both Colonna's Fountain of Adonis and Sidney's Fountain of Aeneas, but the setting is strongly reminiscent of that which surrounds Colonna's fountain: the circular citrus grove, the hedge of roses – only in the French text are the roses intermingled with jasmine – and the mosaic, or at least multi-coloured, paving. (In Sidney's description, the flowers are described as being a 'mosaical floor' to the trees.) Wroth more or less repeats the description of the arbour-like setting in the second part of the romance, here conflating the two elements of the citrus hedge and the trellis covered with roses and jasmine, when the heroine Pamphilia's brother Philarchos describes seeing the princess whom he loves by moonlight:

> In an Arbour in the midst wherof was a rare wrought fountaine, and of that curiousitie as a man might justly say, non but the master of curiosities could have had such an other. The topp of itt was covered with most curious fruict trees (some ripe, some growing towards itt, some greene, som in blossome). Over which, as if a vaile, was a blushing rose, an innosent Jessimine, and an ambitious-inloving woodbine. (II.123)

In this case Wroth does not describe the fountain at all, other than that it is 'rare wrought', like most of her fountains, and like Colonna's, delicate and curious. It is tempting to imagine Wroth leafing through the *Songe de Poliphile* and finding illustrations not only enticing in themselves (one of which even depicts a woman telling a story) but also so clearly reminiscent of her uncle's work, subsequently reading around and through them.

There are other passages in the *Urania* which also recall other illustrated parts of the *Songe*. One of the climactic episodes in the first part of Wroth's romance, for example, takes place in a 'round building like a theatre, carved curiously, and in mighty pillars' (1.372). Wroth's editors suggest analogues in *Amadis de Gaule* and in Jonson's *Masque of Queens*, but there is also a striking illustration, and lengthy description, of the amphitheatre which contains the Fountain of Venus in the *Songe* (Figure 11.3). Wroth describes a

11.3 The 'theatre' of the Fountain of Venus. *Songe de Poliphile*, 1561, f. 123.

group of lovers as being 'all chain'd one unto another with linkes of gold, enamuled with Roses and other flowers dedicated to Love' (1.169); in the French edition, the description of Poliphilus and Polia as being 'menés après attachés à liens de fleurs et de cordes faites de roses' (led bound with cords of

Sidney, Wroth, Wilton House, and the Songe de Poliphile 195

11.4 Poliphilus and Polia bound with chains of roses and led in the Triumph of Cupid. *Songe de Poliphile*, 1561, f. 121v.

flowers and ropes made of roses)[29] appears immediately under its illustration (Figure 11.4), which is not the case in the Italian text.

Perhaps most striking is the first sonnet of *Pamphilia to Amphilanthus*, the sequence which was appended to the 1621 edition of the *Urania*, which closely recalls two illustrations in the *Songe*:

> When night's blacke Mantle could most darknesse proue,
> And sleepe (deaths Image) did my senses hyre,
> From Knowledge of my selfe, then thoughts did moue.
> Swifter then those, most swiftnesse neede require.
> In sleepe, a Chariot drawne by wing'd Desire,
> I saw; where sate bright Venus Queene of Loue,
> And at her feete her Sonne, still adding Fire
> To burning hearts, which she did hold aboue.
> But one heart flaming more then all the rest,
> The Goddesse held, and put it to my breast,
> Deare Sonne now shut,[30] said she, thus must we winne;
> He her obeyd, and martyr'd my poore heart.
> I waking hop'd as dreames it would depart,
> Yet since, O me, a Louer I haue beene.[31]

11.5 Polia's vision of Venus and Diana. *Songe de Poliphile*, 1561, f. 146v.

Similar details can be found in Petrarch, Sidney's *Astrophil and Stella*,[32] and Jonson's *Celebration of Charis*,[33] but two illustrations in the *Songe de Poliphile* are far closer than any of these. Both in the second part of the romance, that told by Polia, the first shows Polia's vision of Venus chasing away Diana after she has abandoned her life as a vestal in order to be united with Poliphilus (Figure 11.5); the second shows the penetration of the lovers' hearts by a golden arrow, which occurs as the erotic climax of both parts of the romance, but is illustrated only in the second. It is plausible, therefore, that not only was Mary Wroth, like her uncle Philip Sidney, influenced by the *Songe de Poliphile*, but she also, like him, approached it initially via its illustrations, sometimes reading from them into the surrounding text and evoking illustrations, more than text, in her borrowings and adaptations.

Some of the limitations of the terms in which Genette delicately avoids 'illustration' have by now become apparent. As he notes in the rather hurried discussion of illustrations in his conclusion (a subject that he terms, in a characteristically spatial metaphor, 'an immense continent'), illustration as a practice has 'value as commentary, which sometimes has great force'.[34] The illustrations of the *Songe de Poliphile*, both of themselves and as they were apparently read by Sidney and Wroth, are not simply illustrations in the sense of the plates that might illustrate a classical French novel, for 'illustration' is not a transhistorical category. Rather, they have a generic, aesthetic, and ethical functionality akin to those elements, such as printed marginalia, that Genette is happy to label 'paratextual'. Complementing, rather than merely illustrating, the text, they draw attention to the *Songe*'s exploration of visual pleasure; they add immeasurably to its discourse of desire by making the book itself, as an entity separate from its interminable narrative, an object of desire for reader or even collector. They encourage the reader to linger, and to look, not least at naked nymphs, beautiful gardens, elaborate buildings, to consider the erotics of reading as something greater than merely the desire to know what happens next. It is not simply a matter of being able to decode the iconology of an emblematic frontispiece, an activity which apparently 'exceeds the means of a plain "literary person"',[35] but concerns a different concept of the relationships between text and image.

The elaborate frontispieces of Sidney's *Arcadia* and especially Wroth's *Urania*, both of which test the boundaries of Genette's definitions in terms of the possible involvement of the authors in their production, have far more in common with the lavish woodcuts illustrating the *Songe de Poliphile* than they do with the specific cover illustrations cited by Genette. To think simply in terms of 'decoding' is reductive in the extreme: such frontispieces do not illustrate, but rather establish an expectation as regards the *modus legendi* that the texts themselves will solicit or compel, whereby meaning can be spatially mediated (what is happening on this page *qua* page, in this place *qua* place as I read it?) as well as temporally (what will happen next?). As text and image, description and narrative share the same space of the page, so the text/narrative is not necessarily prior or secondary to the image/description as they are experienced and interpreted by the reader, the assumption implicit in both the idea of 'illustration' itself and in Genette's brief discussion. Mary Wroth in particular seems to have read outwards, from image into text; her passages of ekphrastic description, and Sidney's, can be read both onto each other and onto Colonna's text and images. Miller's image of the *doubly* permeable membrane is again a useful one. Moreover, as with more conventional paratexts, illustrations such as those of the *Songe* invite, even impel, a certain kind of reading. While Genette's avoidance of illustrations may be understandable, at the same time his implicit treatment of them as a *single*, or a simple category is misleading. As Sidney's and Wroth's treatment and adaptation of the *Songe*'s illustrations shows, even in their (largely) unillustrated texts passages of ekphrastic description themselves readily take on an ethical dimension: the reader becomes at once actively involved, even implicated, in the texts' projects, and is simultaneously invited to scrutinise that involvement.

What, then, of the fourth element in this hypothesis, Wilton House and its gardens? No library records survive for Wilton, or, for that matter, for Penshurst, for the late sixteenth or early seventeenth centuries. A mid-seventeenth-century catalogue for Penshurst does; it does not include the *Hypnerotomachia*.[36] A copy of the *Hypnerotomachia* (presumably the Italian version) was in the Wilton library until 1914, when it was sold at Sotheby's.[37] Its binding was early eighteenth century and it had been most likely acquired, according to the 1914 catalogue, by the eight earl of Pembroke at a roughly similar date. That the library must have been impressive is suggested by a passage in the unpublished portion of the *Urania*; the young prince Rosindy visits the court of the true Sophy of Persia, and is invited to make use of her library, which is described as

the most sumptious in the world for a woeman to have, and the rarest, since non butt the rarest of bookes were permitted to bee ther (all chosen ones, and as choisely chosen and as truly used and imployed by ther owner), she beeing exactly and parfectly learned in all siences, and learning well bestowed on her, who honored learning for the truth of learnings sake, perfect knowledg.[38]

This is not inconceivably a tribute to Mary Sidney Herbert and her 'academy' at Wilton. Wroth appears to have spent less time there than her uncle, although she is known to have visited on a number of occasions, and presumably spent time there not only with her aunt Mary Sidney Herbert as a child, but also with William the third earl, her cousin and lover, the Amphilanthus of the *Urania*. Wilton is much changed since the days of Sidney and Wroth, thanks largely to a fire in 1647; its gardens, too, were famously redesigned in the 1630s.[39] Yet there were already elaborate gardens at Wilton by the 1620s, and several of their features are particularly relevant here.

One of the earliest descriptions of Wilton was written by the indefatigable John Taylor the 'Water Poet', who travelled by sea from London to Salisbury in 1623. Unusually, he particularly named and praised the gardener, Adrian Gilbert, who:

(much to my Lord's cost and his owne paines) vsed such a deal of intricate Setting, Grafting, Planting, Innoculating, Rayling, hedging, plashing, turning, winding, and returning circular, Trianguler, Quadranguler, Orbiculer, Ouall, and euery way curiously and chargeably conceited: There hath he made Walkes, hedges, and Arbours, of all manner of most delicate fruit Trees, planning and placing them in such admirable Artlike fashions, resembling both diuine and morrall remembrances, as three Arbours standing in a Triangle, hauing each a recourse to a greater Arbour in the midst, resembleth three in one, and one in three ... [he] hath made his Walkes most rarely round and spacious, one Walke without another, (as the rinds of an Onion are greatest without, and lesse towards the Center) and withal, the hedges betwixt each Walke are so thickly set, that one cannot see thorow from the one walke, who walkes in the other: that in conclusion, the worke seems endless, and I thinke that in *England* it is not to be fellowed, or will in haste be followed.[40]

Arbours, hedges and walks were the norm in sixteenth- and seventeenth-century gardens, and they remained a feature of the redesigned gardens at Wilton. The idea that they could resemble 'both diuine and morall remembrances' is perhaps less common – it suggests topiary or *parterres de broderie* – and these are both devices notably illustrated in the *Songe de Poliphile*. More intriguing, however, is Taylor's description of a Trinitarian arbour, for this seems closely reminiscent of an illustration that is found only in the *Songe*: it depicts a curious construction of an obelisk, cube and sphere, located in a leafy, possibly triangular, arbour, which is explained in the text as an emblem of the Trinity (Figure 11.6).

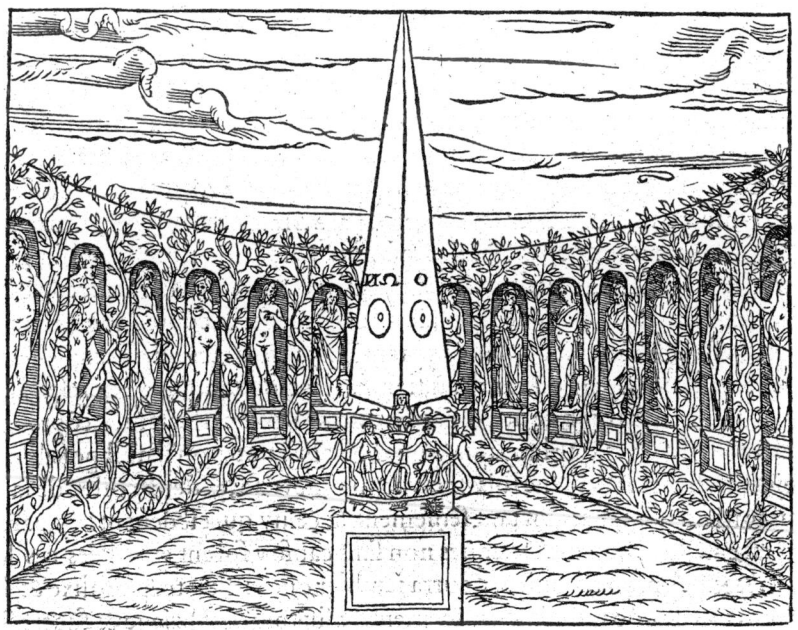

11.6 The 'Trinitarian' arbour. *Songe de Poliphile*, 1561, f. 44.

On the obverse of the page illustrating the arbour of the Trinity in the French edition but not the Italian, there is a labyrinth, albeit a water labyrinth, described as an allegory for human life (Figure 11.7); a figure of the labyrinth marks the first and last lines of Wroth's crown of sonnets, part of her 'Pamphilia to Amphilanthus' sequence: 'In this strange labourinth, how shall I turne?' The description of the 'Walkes' at Wilton, made by Adrian the gardener 'most rarely round and spacious, one Walke without another, (as the rinds of an Onion are greatest without, and lesse towards the Center)'[41] seems closely reminiscent of this illustration in the *Songe*, especially the description of it being like an onion. Alas for Adrian the gardener, that in barely a decade a great deal of his careful work must have been cleared away.

A feature of the gardens at Wilton after they had been redesigned were two tall fountains, set in rectangular pools, which consisted of tall columns topped with crowns: these are clearly visible in De Caus's design, *c.* 1633. The crowns have gone but the columns survive at Wilton; they were originally *giocchi d'acqua*, or water jokes: a description from the 1630s records that 'by turning of the Cockes [taps] that are close by, the water flyes spouting out, at the top of the Rockes; turning and whirling the Crownes'. These appear in De Caus's book about fountains, and they

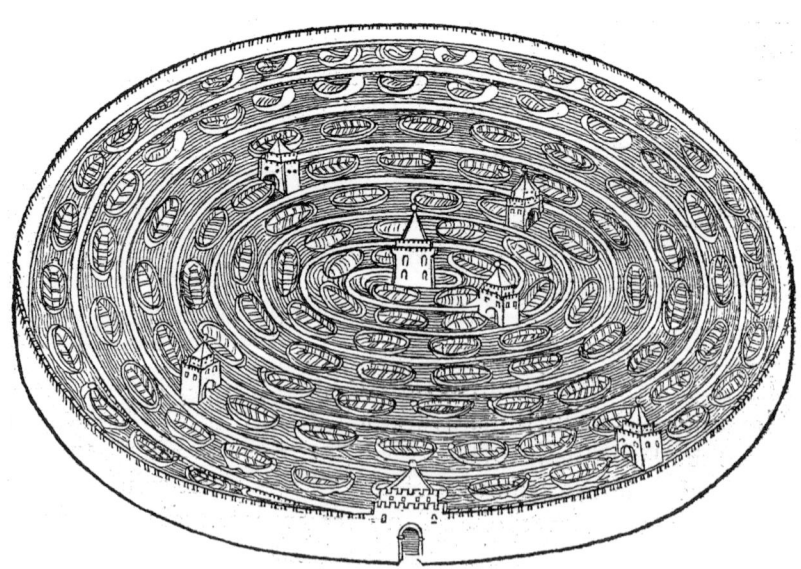

11.7 The 'water labyrinth'. *Songe de Poliphile*, 1561, f. 43.

were certainly at Wilton by 1635, when this description was written and they also appear in Wroth's *Urania*. The knight Leonius, brother of the hero Amphilanthus, on meeting his beloved Veralinda for the first time, walks with her

> Into a little Grove, where he heard as at her comming exquisite Musique, drawing neerer he discerned a Fountaine made in the fashion of an Emperiall Crowne with a Globe on the toppe, out of which like a full shower of raine the water came so plentifully, and showringly, as it resembled such plenty, so finely was it counterfeited, and the trees grewe so, as who hadde stood in the wood would not suddenly have knowne whether it had rayned or no.[42]

There is a clear relationship between Wroth's fountain in the *Urania* and the fountains at Wilton, but its nature is unclear. Wroth's romance was printed in 1621, De Caus's design made in about 1633 and the fountains described in 1635. Was Wroth describing existing features of the Wilton gardens with which she was familiar, merely relocated when the gardens were redesigned? Or were the fountains at Wilton made in accordance with her description? It is impossible to know. There are, it should perhaps be pointed out, no crowned columns in the *Hypnerotomachia*. There are no records as to who was responsible for the design of Wilton's gardens prior to Isaac de Caus's redesign in the 1630s – one might suspect William Herbert, the third earl, who was intensely interested in art and architecture, as well as literature – and it is tempting to think that he too, like his uncle Philip and his cousin Mary, might have leafed through a copy of the *Songe de Poliphile*.

This circle cannot be completed by pointing to elements of Wilton's gardens that appear in Sidney's *Arcadia*, nor yet passages of his romance that were re-created in the gardens; the wall paintings in the great 'Single Cube' room which do depict scenes from the *Arcadia* were not added until the 1650s. Nevertheless, the idea that the physical environment of Wilton can be approached as being in some ways analogous to the textual and especially visual space of the *Arcadia*, the *Urania*, and the *Songe de Poliphile* is an immensely attractive one. That texts can be thought of in terms of circulation, as objects of exchange and trade, has become a commonplace. Yet books as material objects could also surely remain in the same place for long periods of time. (This is especially true of folios, the antithesis of the 'pocket-size' book considered by Genette.)[43] This association of a particular text with a specific place is a construct which is more familiar in discussions of manuscripts, customarily identified by their location. Yet in some cases (this surely being one) it is a habit of mind that could well encompass printed books too. That a book such as the *Songe de Poliphile*, highly visual, sensually and experientially appealing even to a reader unable or unwilling to read it in its entirety, might have been consumed by two writers a generation apart in an environment similarly stimulating to all the senses, in turn having some influence upon both that environment and those two writers, is an exciting thought. It makes both text and environment places of conversation, spaces shared by those two writers; as such, it perhaps suggests new ways of thinking about influence and intertextuality as the contiguity and elision of spaces rather than the intersection of texts. 'In principle, every context serves as a paratext.'[44]

Fountains or pools combine surface and depth, and being reflective surfaces, they can be inscribed over and over again, becoming infinite numbers of surfaces and spaces; like the surface of water, illustrations can be looked both *at* and *through*. It is particularly suggestive that the word customarily used to describe a gap in a text or narrative is *lacuna*, borrowed from the conventions of manuscript transmission and description. *Desunt caetera*; it is assumed that something which was once there has been lost, never to be recovered. Yet *lacuna* is ultimately derived from the Latin 'lacus', meaning pit or pool. If *lacunae*, gaps, are thought of in this sense, then they become spaces not where something is lost but spaces where something could be; not that something is missing, but that an infinitude of co-existent perspectives and narratives is possible. They connote not loss, but potentiality. Both Sidney's revised *Arcadia* and Wroth's *Urania* famously break off mid-sentence, giving rise in the case of the former to continuations by other writers.[45] Wroth supplied her own continuation, in the form of the unpublished second part, and in her sonnet sequence, printed with the romance in the 1621 edition, but the second part also breaks off in mid-sentence. The *Songe de Poliphile*'s readers imagine their own erotic epiphanies; Wroth and Sidney's broken sentences allow others to take up the story; Wilton is still there and its gardens can be, must be reimagined: as Henri Lefebvre put it, 'No space ever vanishes utterly, leaving no trace'.[46] This story about Sidney, Wroth, Wilton, and the *Songe de Poliphile* is an invention: it may never have happened, but it could have. Texts, pictures, and spaces interpenetrate, blend into one another and suggest strategies of interpretation to one another; they are, in the image that Genette adopts from Philippe Lejeune, on the 'fringe'[47] not simply in their liminality but in the full force of materiality, movement, experience, interpenetration that the word suggests. The interrelationships of Sidney's *Arcadia*, Wroth's *Urania*, the *Songe de Poliphile*, and the gardens of Wilton House are paratextual in its deepest and most suggestive sense; they are each other's paratext as much as each other's intertext, and more, because those interrelationships can be best conceived in spatial terms, and sometimes the spaces are left blank. In the Renaissance, therefore, it cannot be assumed that the paratextual is coextensive with the text, the page, or indeed the book; it can also be, on occasion, that which is seen when the reader lifts his or her eyes from the page, the places and spaces where he or she walked in the intervals in between reading and writing.

Afterword

Peter Stallybrass

In a famous formulation, Gérard Genette wrote: '*Paratext = peritext + epitext*'. By 'peritext' Genette means all the additional materials (prefaces, notes, indexes) that are printed in the same volume as 'the text itself'; by 'epitext' he means 'all those messages which are situated, at least originally, outside the book', including advertisements, prospectuses, interviews, rough drafts, and reviews. As Genette was fully aware, 'the ways and means of the paratext change continually, depending on period, culture, genre, author, work, and edition, with varying degrees of pressure'.[1] One feature of this collection, concerned as it is with Renaissance paratexts, is that the great majority of the chapters focus on peritexts rather than epitexts. Without the full apparatus of newspaper and magazine reviews on the one hand and archives collecting authorial manuscripts on the other, epitexts had nothing like the determining function on Shakespeare in the early seventeenth century that they had on Walt Whitman in the late nineteenth century.

Within weeks of publishing *November Boughs* in 1888, Whitman was being reviewed, often at length, in major papers throughout the United States and in Europe. He was already notorious for his activities in publishing self-reviews anonymously (epitexts) and for developing new ways of packaging his books (peritexts), including printing a puff from a personal letter from Thoreau on the spine of the second edition of *Leaves of Grass*. The nine volumes in which Horace Traubel recorded the daily conversation of Whitman during the last years of his life reveal the extent to which the poet planned his poetry in relation to specific reviewers. At the same time, Traubel's extraordinary record is itself testimony to the archival fever in which famous nineteenth-century authors participated. Three separate copies of the printed proofs of Whitman's 'Shakspere-Bacon's Cipher' survive, marked with the same emendation in the author's own hand, correcting 'anthor' to 'author' in purple crayon. It is difficult to account for the survival of three such proofs unless Whitman was beginning to manufacture his own archival legacy, in full awareness that every last scrap of his writing would be collected, as indeed it was. In addition to Traubel's massive collection of autograph materials and memorabilia, Whitman's doctor, Richard Maurice Bucke, published *Notes and Fragments* of the great poet after his death. They were transcribed, according to Bucke, from 'loose sheets and small pieces of paper of endless sizes, shapes, shades and qualities, (some even written on the back of scraps of wall-paper!)'.[2]

But if Genette's epitext is largely absent in this collection, the peritext is expanded to include an extraordinary range of materials that structured Renaissance books. Above all, many of the contributors challenge both the centrality that Genette gives to the author as the controller of the paratext and his notion that the paratext is a 'portal' through which one enters the text. In their introduction, Helen Smith and Louise Wilson pick up Genette's suggestion that the paratext could be thought of as a 'fringe' in which, as in a rug, one can see the 'constitutive structures that run throughout the length of the work, but that can also be perceived as distinct elements' (6). And where Genette focuses upon the threshold of a work, and above all the preface, William Sherman illuminates the complexity of how endings are staged in Renaissance books. This afterword is itself, of course, a modern form of exit strategy. But I want to use it to show how the authors of this book have suggested new beginnings, above all in relation to visual paratexts and to the function of authorship.

VISUAL PARATEXTS

In her essay, Hester Lees-Jeffries emphasises the inadequacy of Genette's account of illustrations as supplements whose value is simply to reinforce a pre-existing textual message. And this volume as a whole provides multiple examples of how printers and publishers, and occasionally authors, framed, segmented, and interpreted texts through running titles (Day), printers' flowers (Fleming), and spatial divisions (Clarke). To these fine readings of the function of visual paratexts I would add two more: 'illustrations' that directly contradict the text and indeed can have the power to predetermine how a reader recalls that text; and 'ornaments' that move in and out of focus in the course of reading.

For images that contradict the text, I will take two illustrations of the expulsion of Adam and Eve from Paradise. Illustrating the third chapter of Genesis in the 1539 Great Bible is a woodcut that depicts a winged and clothed St Michael, with sword held aloft, who banishes the fleeing Adam and Eve. They are naked. An engraving of the same scene was added to the fourth edition of *Paradise Lost* in 1688 – a scene that is reproduced on the front cover of David Scott Kastan's 2005 edition.[3] But here Adam and Eve are no longer naked: they wear woven branches of fig leaves around their waists, concealing their genitals.

So which illustration of the text is 'correct': were Adam and Eve naked or were they wearing fig leaves when they were expelled? In fact, both 'illustrations' directly contradict the two texts that they illustrate. In the Great Bible, verse 21, preceding the woodcut, reads: 'Vnto the same Adam also & to hys wyfe dyd the Lorde God make lethren garmentes, & clothed them'.[4] It is only *after* God has reclothed them that 'the Lorde God sent them furth from the garde*n* of Eden'. And in *Paradise Lost*, Christ, 'pittying' how Adam and Eve 'stood / Before him naked to the aire', covers them 'with Skins of Beasts':

> Nor hee thir outward onely with the Skins
> Of Beasts, but inward nakedness, much more
> Opprobious, with his Robe of righteousness,
> Araying cover'd from his Fathers sight.[5]

In other words, in both cases, the 'illustrations' oppose the texts that they supposedly illustrate. And so powerful has the visual tradition been that most readers remember the expulsion, however often they have read it, not through the biblical text or Milton's reworking of it but through the visual tradition of Massaccio, Michelangelo, Holbein and the hundreds of named and unnamed engravers who have repeatedly depicted Adam and Eve at the moment of expulsion as either naked or wearing fig leaves.

But illustrations are only one form of visual paratext in Renaissance books. By the sixteenth century, printing houses throughout Europe were stocked with miscellaneous collections of woodblocks, made at different periods and for different books, many of them inherited along with presses and type from earlier printers. Compositors had to learn how to find not only the right metal type to compose words but also the decorative initials and ornaments for the beginnings and ends of books, chapters, and other important textual divisions. The compositors of the 1574 Bishops' Bible, for instance, could choose from thirteen decorative capital 'I's.[6] Most of these 'I's belonged to different alphabetic sequences, the images including depictions of foliage and flowers, a lion, a centaur being ridden by a woman, and a depiction of St John the Evangelist, with his symbol, the eagle, opposite him, and Christ revealed to him in the sky. Only the last image has any specific relation to the Scriptures. As for the centaur ridden by a woman, to a modern eye at least it looks quite inappropriate for a text that claims to be the word of God.

These decorative letters were used to mark textual divisions, the particular choice often depending upon how many letters had already been used by the compositor for the sheet being printed, and the size of the initial. Compositors were paid according to the speed, as well as the accuracy, with which they worked and we can rarely presume that a compositor even looked at a specific letter as opposed to choosing it by touch from the appropriate compartment of a case. Whether you get St John or a centaur ridden by a woman appears to be largely random. But the actual size of the letter did matter. And the larger the image, the more likely an attempt to make at least some correlation with the text.

The compositor was always constrained by the capitals that were available to him, so readers had to get used to arbitrary conjunctions of word and image. The 1625 edition of the Book of Common Prayer includes several large Ovidian capitals.[7] One is a 'C', used as the first letter of 'Christ'. But the scene depicted within the 'C' is the pagan god Mercury and, even more astonishingly, Jove fondling Ganymede. Another is an 'I/J', used as the first letter of 'Iesus'. But on one side of the 'I', we see Apollo, and on the other, Daphne being transformed into a laurel tree. Do these letters participate in the long tradition of the *Ovide moralisé*, in which translators interpreted the *Metamorphoses* as a Christian allegory? Or are they blasphemously inappropriate to the sacred name of the Son of God? No doubt both readings were and are possible. But the recycling of such letters in an extraordinary variety of textual contexts suggests that they usually functioned less as narrative scenes than as letters that, through their visual density, segmented the text. In this volume, Juliet Fleming and Helen Smith explore the overlapping fields of the text as something to look at and as something to read. Judging from how rarely readers censored these decorative initials, one must presume that the semantic and grammatical functions of the letters usually trumped their visual and symbolic meanings. The initials could be *read* as letters without being *seen* as images.

Take, for instance, the beginning of the New Testament in the first edition of the King James Bible, printed in 1611. This was a translation that had been prepared with extraordinary care by teams of translators. Why then does the New Testament begin with a woodcut 'T' of Neptune riding on a hippocamp? Here, in fact, a specific choice was involved, but not because the image was textually appropriate. The compositors of the 1611 King James Bible set their text not from a manuscript but from printed sheets of the 1602 Bishops' Bible that the translators had marked up with their revisions. The 1602 Bishops' Bible had used the same woodblock with a Neptune 'T' to begin the New Testament. The compositors of the 1611

King James Bible were thus following their 1602 copy, selecting the 'I' that had been used eight years earlier. Here, at this most important division in the Christian Bible, the compositors did indeed use their eyes and not just their hands. But they were not looking for meaning but for the reproduction of an earlier visual effect.

The reuse of decorative initials, irrespective of context, was the norm. But a reader who treated all decorative letters as equally arbitrary would be missing the rare but important occasions when a specific letter was chosen for a specific context. An 'I/J' depicting St John, for instance, was used only a single time in the 1574 Bishops' Bible: at the beginning of the Gospel of St John. Indeed, the image recapitulates the text: 'In the beginning was the Word, and the Word was with God, and God was that word'. On the right of the decorative initial, St John looks up into the sky where he reads the Word, depicted as the tetragrammaton. There can be no question of this being mere coincidence. The other three gospels all begin with decorative initials depicting the relevant evangelists with their symbols: Matthew (with an angel), Mark (with a lion), and Luke (with an ox).

But one cannot conclude from this that the distinction between relevance and irrelevance is simply reuse – the reused images being arbitrary, the images used only once being selected for their appropriateness to specific passages. Most of the decorative capitals in the 1611 King James Bible are used more or less randomly as far as what they depict is concerned, although with attention to size and abstract visual effect. But there is nothing arbitrary about the decorative 'I' at the beginning of Genesis. At first sight, the capital appears to have only decorative appeal, since it is composed of intertwining flowers. But these flowers are not just any flowers: they are thistles and roses, to this day the emblems of Scotland and England. In the 1611 Bible, there was indeed a programmatic attempt to compose Great Britain: an entity that would not officially exist for another century. The union of England and Scotland is visually materialised at the very beginning of the Old Testament not only in the 'I' of 'In the beginning' but also in the cuts of a rose and a thistle at the top of the page.

Not only is the union of England and Scotland repeatedly made visible through ornamental cuts; so too is the claim that James maintained to rule France and Ireland. 'The Translators to the Reader' is preceded by a block composed of the rose of England, the thistle of Scotland, the harp of Ireland, and the fleur-de-lis of France. All of these blocks celebrating King James's kingdoms were reused in other places in the 1611 Bible, where they were relevant to the royal dedicatee without having the specific textual relevance that the image of St John did in the 1574 Bishops' Bible. But, like the cut of St John, these decorations and images are meant to be *seen* – otherwise why go to the trouble and expense of adding new woodblocks to a large existing stock that would have been quite adequate for the decorative needs of the 1611 Bible?

In the case of printed books, then, the visual paratext was determined by the variable circumstances that led to a specific printer accumulating old and new woodblock initials. Even in as elaborate a production as the King James Bible, the programmatic attempt to stage Britain was a small part of the material process of printing. Most of the woodblocks employed were recycled from earlier projects. Like every other printing house, the King's printing house, where the 1611 Bible was created, was the repository of letters and images from different periods and countries. A single page might be composed of metal type made in the Low Countries in the 1580s, German decorative initials made in the 1550s, and ornamental head- and tail-pieces made in England in the 1600s. As a result, one can move on a single page from a carefully chosen, custom-made emblem of Britain to an arbitrarily recycled initial depicting a satyr with an erection. Most of the decorative letters and ornaments help the reader to navigate the text, making visible the hierarchy of divisions, from the various prefatory materials to the two Testaments (and the Apocrypha, when included) to books and chapters. They function, in other words, as a kind of metapunctuation, abstractly visible but often textually distracting when they are seen as specific images in themselves.

One of the most interesting features of visual paratexts in the Renaissance is how they can move in and out of focus. Among the capital 'I's that the compositors of the 1574 Bishops' Bible could choose from was a small decorative letter with an image of St John, much more crudely cut than the larger letter that was used a single time at the beginning of the Gospel of St John. This smaller capital was reused multiple times but not once does it appear in the places that connect the image to the text, namely, St John's Gospel, his three Epistles, or his Revelation. Given the number of times that the compositors were reusing this smaller 'I', it must surely have seemed as generic as the 'I's with foliage and flowers or, for that matter, as the 'I' with a centaur ridden by a woman. But during the printing of the Prophets, something very curious happened. The small capital with St John ceased to be generic. Between chapters 20 and 27 of Isaiah, the compositor for the first time must actually have seen the letter; seen the letter, that is, not just as being a suitable size for the beginning of a chapter but also as a particular image. The image clearly offended him, because he got out a knife and excised the image of Christ at which John is gazing. Why? The head-note to chapter 27 reads: 'A prophecie of the commyng of Christ, *and destruction of idolatrie*' [my emphasis].

In the 1570s, Protestant iconoclasm was in its most militant phase in England, and visual representations of the godhead were increasingly interpreted as a sign of Catholic idolatry. The image of Christ, once seen, had to go. Indeed, the image had already gone in the larger decorative 'I' at the beginning of St John, where Christ had been replaced by the tetragrammaton. Yet a trace of the excised image remains as a haunting presence in the rays of light whose reason for existence has ceased to exist. Throughout the rest of the bible, the compositors continued to reuse the 'I/J' of John for 'In', 'Iudith', 'Iudge', 'It', and so on. The letter becomes once again generic. Yet the presence of an absence, materialised by the few remaining rays of light, marks the contradictory claims of a reading that doesn't see and a seeing that doesn't read, of a visual paratext that moves in and out of focus.

THE AUTHOR AS PARATEXT

As Jason Scott-Warren reminds us, 'Edmund Spenser' appears nowhere on the title-page of the 1590 edition of the *Faerie Queene*. That authorship is a form of ascription rather than a determinate origin is further illuminated by Neil Rhodes's account of translation and Louise Wilson's exploration of the playful prefaces to translations of Iberian romances. Can translations themselves be considered paratexts? Different editions of John Florio's translation of Montaigne suggest different answers. The title-page of the 1603 edition names only 'Lo: Michaell de Montaigne' as author of these *Essayes*. Montaigne's authorship is not supported/divided by any translator, printer, or publisher. But when one turns the page, one finds not only the name of the translator ('IOHN FLORIO'), of the publisher ('Edward Blount') and of the printer ('Val. Sims') but also of the six women, their names inscribed on three tombs, who, as the book's dedicatees, could also be interpreted, as its 'onlie begetters'. The authorial text (on a recto) and the translation (on the verso) both materially and ideologically face in opposite directions. But the title-page of the second edition of Florio's translation could not be more different. Now, although Montaigne's name precedes the translators, they share equal billing (the same size of type being used for 'MICHAEL' and 'IOHN FLORIO'), and the translator has acquired his own aristocratic position to set beside Montaigne's. If the latter is '*Knight of the / Order of* S, Michael, *Gentleman of the French* / Kings Chamber', the former is '*Reader of the Italian tongue vnto the Soueraigne* / Maiestie of ANNA, Queene of England, / Scotland, France and Ireland, / &c.'. The claim that Queen

Afterword

Anne is Queen of France as well as of England etc. gives a curious twist to the precedence granted to the English translation over the French original that reverses the precedence given to author and translator:

> DONE INTO ENGLISH,
> according to the last French edition

But far and away the most striking feature of the second edition of Florio's translation is the engraved author-portrait facing the title-page. For here, the author has been displaced by the translator. It is Florio, not Montaigne, who gazes out at the reader, accompanied by a Latin quatrain that puns upon the flourishing flower who is Florio.

But the problems of the authorial paratext are perhaps most clearly seen when we turn to the translated text that was far and away the best-selling text in sixteenth- and seventeenth-century England: the psalms. And no book could better reveal the fact that authorship is a form of ascription. It was conventional to ascribe authorship of the psalms to David, and David kneeling in penitence or lasciviously gazing at Bathsheba frequently appeared in manuscripts and printed books alike at the beginning of psalters or before the penitential psalms in Books of Hours. But David's authorship is explicitly contradicted by the headings to many of the psalms, which gave an astonishing range of other authors: Solomon (Psalms 72, 127); Moses (Psalm 90); the Korahites (Psalms 42, 44–9, 84–5, 87), Asaph (Psalms 50, 73–83); Heman the Ezrahite (Psalm 88), Ethan the Ezrahite (Psalm 89); 'the lowly man' (Psalm 102). Indeed, one ancient tradition was that David was the scribe who first wrote down the psalms rather than the author who composed them. The multiple attributions of authorship were acknowledged by T. W. in 1586 at the very beginning of his '*right godly and learned exposition, vpon the whole booke of Psalmes*': 'The penners of the Psalmes were diuers men, as *Dauid, Moses,* &c.'. At the same time, T. W. draws attention to the fact that the paratexts that are the headings to the psalms are usually not concerned with authorship at all; if some 'containe the name of the writer of that Psalme', more refer to 'the instrument whereon [the psalm] was sung', or 'the end whereunto it was appoynted', or 'the principle matter therein contayned'.[8]

But should the headings of the psalms be treated as paratexts? This was itself a cause of dissension. Catholic bibles had traditionally included the headings in numbering the verses of the psalms. So (following the King James translation), the first verse of Psalm 3 for Catholics was 'A Psalme of Dauid when he fled from Absalom his sonne', whereas for Protestants it was 'Lord, how are they increased that trouble mee?' How sensitive the question of where a psalm begins, whether with the heading or the first line of verse, is revealed by the commentary to Psalm 3 (the first psalm with a traditional heading) in the first Catholic translation of the complete bible to be printed in English. The Rheims-Douai translation self-consciously followed the Protestant system of numbering, starting with the first line of verse, because it was an explicitly polemical translation, a weapon to be used in the battle against the heretical versions that preceded it. The 'annotations' to the Catholic translations of Psalm 3 begin with a concession: 'Al Interpreters agreably teach, that king Dauid made not the titles, which are before the Psalmes'. So the Protestants are right in their numbering? Well no, because '[n]euertheles [the headings] are authentical, as endited by the Holie Ghost'.[9] Here, the Catholic annotators are in agreement as to the ultimate authorship of the psalms with the Protestant T. W., who wrote that although the 'penners' of the psalms were 'diuers men', they were 'all led by one and the same spirit so that the holy Ghost may rightlie be said to be the Author of this Booke'. But the question of just where that authorship begins, with the heading or with the first line of verse, remains in dispute. Is the heading a paratext that has been added by a later editor or is it an 'authentical' part of the psalms, 'endited by the Holie Ghost'? As Danielle Clarke argues, in her chapter in this volume, 'voice' is both paratextually marked and paratextually produced in ways that can render authority and authorship difficult to locate.

If authors are produced paratextually, so too, as Matthew Day demonstrates, authors may produce paratexts usually ascribed to printers. But one point that Genette both knows and constantly forgets is that many authors were dead when their texts were printed. This is not just true of the ascribed authors of the Bible. By far and away the most popular author to be printed between 1450 and 1470 was Cicero (first century CE). Thirty-seven editions of his works survive from this period. Other popular authors were St. Augustine (fifth century CE) with thirteen editions, Donatus (fourth century CE) with seven editions, and St Thomas Aquinas (thirteenth century CE) and St Chrysostomus (fourth century CE), each with six editions. The only living 'authors' were high-ranking members of the Church and State, who had to pay printers to have their decrees, indulgences, and polemics published. The debates that by the late eighteenth century led Kant to affirm the rights of authors and the centrality of intellectual property would have made less sense to a publisher in 1470 whose textual negotiations were with the dead – and, judging by the reprintings of Cicero compared even to any of the Church Fathers, the deader the better. Living authors would come to play an increasingly significant role during the eighteenth century. But we should not forget that some of the most important eighteenth-century debates about authorship in England concerned the rights to reprint Shakespeare and Milton: writers who had died a century before.

Moreover, from a publisher's perspective, the first edition of any book is in an important sense the least significant. Publishers don't sue each other over books that don't sell or that only go through a single edition. But books in their tenth and their hundredth edition (like Foxe's *Actes and Monuments* in the seventeenth century and Shakespeare's plays in the eighteenth century) are a different matter. And the further a text gets from the authorial manuscript, the more diverse the forms in which it is likely to appear, although, as Sonia Massai persuasively argues, the claim to an authorial connection could lend credibility to claims of emendation and 'improvement'. On the one hand, the publisher's hand may be most marked in cheap abridgments. The fragmentation of 'works' into selections was common practice in the case of the canonical Bible. Throughout the late Middle Ages and the Renaissance, books of hours and psalters massively outsold bibles both in manuscript and print. But abridgments (and where do they fit into Genette's typology?) did not necessarily correspond to a reduction of paratext. In 1643, the Bible was published in the form of a sixteen-page pamphlet: *The Souldiers Pocket Bible*. In addition to being cheap, this pamphlet had two other advantages, both of which were advertised on its title-page: it '*reduced* [the Scriptures] *to severall heads, and fitly applyed [them] to the souldiers severall occasions, and so may supply the want of the whole Bible*'; and it was small and light enough for a soldier to '*conveniently carry about him*'.[10] In this case, it is the imagined *reader*, not any concept of a divine or inspired author, who determines both the textual selections and the paratextual apparatus.

But if canonical texts are subject to abridgment, they are equally subject to massive editorial elaboration. Take, for instance, Harold Jenkins's 570-page Arden edition of *Hamlet*. Its list of contents include 'Preface' (pp. vii–x), 'Abbreviations and References' (pp. xi–xvii), 'Introduction' (pp. 1–159, divided into 'The date', 'Publication', 'The texts', 'The editorial problem and the present text', 'Sources', '*Der Bestrafte Brudermord*', 'Critical Introduction'), '*The Tragedy of Hamlet Prince of Denmark*' (pp. 161–419), 'Longer Notes' (pp. 421–571), and 'Appendix' (pp. 573–4). And the list of contents effaces the fact that *The Tragedy of Hamlet* is prefaced by a list of '*Dramatis Personae*' and an interpretation of that list, and that the pages dedicated to 'the play itself' contain footnotes that are considerably lengthier than the play, not to mention textual collations. I both admire and depend upon Jenkins's edition and its impressive successor, edited by Ann Thompson and Neil Taylor. My dependency is in direct relation to the paratexts that now appear to be so conspicuously missing in the case of *The Tragicall Historie of Hamlet, Prince of Denmarke* as it was printed in 1603 and 1604–5.[11]

Just how radical the significance of the author's name as a paratext can be is revealed by the changing fortunes of what were perhaps the two most widely copied manuscript poems in the seventeenth century: 'What is our life?' and 'Even such is time'. Both poems circulate today under the authorial name of Sir Walter Ralegh and both regularly appear and are analysed in biographies and critical works about Ralegh. But that is not how they circulated in the seventeenth century. Or rather, it is only how 'Even such is time' circulated and then in what I would call an 'over-authored' form, related to a specific time and place, even if there was some disagreement about both. The first printed version appeared in Richard Brathwaite's *Remains After Death*, only a couple of months after Ralegh's death, where it was printed under the title 'By Sir *W. R.* which he writ the night before his execution'.

It was under similar titles that 'Even such is time' circulated throughout the seventeenth century. In the last century, the poem, while still universally attributed to Ralegh, has usually appeared under more modest titles and sometimes with no title at all. But in the seventeenth century, it was not just associated with Ralegh but with the specific moment of his execution. From the poem's earliest circulation, the emphasis was on the exact place and time of writing. As for place, it was 'found in S*ir* Walter Raleighs Bible in the Gatehowse'; 'Found in his *Bible* in the *Gate-house* at *Westminster*'; 'written in his byble a lyttell before his deathe'.[12] As for time, it was written 'the night before his execution'; 'the night before he was beheaded'; 'the night before he dyed'; 'the night before his death'; 'the night before his death at the gate house'; 'the nighte before he suffred'; 'giuen to one of his the night before his sufferinge'; 'the nighte before he was beheaded in London 1619 [*sic*]'; 'Nox ante obitum. S*ir* W: R: 29 October. 1618'.[13] But several manuscript copies claim that Ralegh wrote the poem on the morning of his death: 'the morning before his death and deliuerd to the deane of Westminster a littell before his ende'; 'the morn a little before he was ledd from ye Gatehouse'; 'a little before he was ledd from the Gatehouse'; 'in the prison of the Gatehouse, the same morneing hee suffered'; 'The morneing before his execuc*i*on'; 'but twoe howers before his death'; 'a little before his death'; 'at his beheading'.[14] The differences are less striking than the desire to use the title as a paratext that *locates* the poem above all in time.

That we get so much information in the titles of 'Even such is time' emphasises Ralegh's fame/notoriety as a public figure rather than his reputation as a poet. Indeed, the poem circulated less among other poems than as a memorial to Ralegh in state and family papers. Of ninety-one known manuscripts (including inscriptions on tombs), more than half (fifty-six) appear in such papers, compared to thirty-six in literary miscellanies. And when the poem appears in state papers, it usually appears as the *only* poem attributed to Ralegh (and often as the only poem in the whole collection). To put it another way, Ralegh's 'Even such is time' was attached to his life (and death) in the seventeenth century, whereas Shakespeare's life was attached (if and when it was) to his poems and plays.

But there is a stark contrast between the circulation of 'Even such is time' and 'What is our life?' The latter, universally ascribed to Ralegh today, was never ascribed to him in print in the seventeenth or eighteenth centuries, and it was never to my knowledge copied into a collection of state papers. Of the seventy manuscript copies that Peter Beal records, fifty-eight are anonymous. The twelve copies whose authors are named are attributed to no fewer than seven different authors: John Donne, Thomas Dodd, Ben Stone, William Strode, Thomas Harding, 'g.s.', and Sir Walter Ralegh. The poem was first printed anonymously in 1612 as the lyrics to one of Orlando Gibbons's songs. While there is no direct attribution of any of the lyrics in *The First Set of Madrigals and Mottets of 5. Parts: apt for Viols and Voyces. Newly Composed by Orlando Gibbons*, the collection as a whole was dedicated by Gibbons to 'my much Honoured friend, Syr *Christopher Hatton*' (this Hatton was not the famous Elizabethan statesmen but a country gentleman with a passion for music). In his dedication, Gibbons writes that the songs '*were most of them composed in your owne house, and doe therefore properly belong vnto you, as Lord of the Soile; the language they speake you prouided them, I onely furnished them with Tongues to vtter the same*'.[15]

'The language' the songs 'speake' was, Gibbons claims, 'prouided' by Hatton. That may mean that Hatton actually wrote the words, but it is equally possible that he commissioned or compiled the lyrics for Gibbons to set to music. My point, though, is that no one, either in the seventeenth or the twentieth centuries, felt any need to print 'What is our life?' under the name of an obscure gentleman by the name of Hatton any more than they needed to ascribe it to Ralegh. The modern compulsion for authorial origins, though, has constructed a Ralegh manuscript that precedes any of the printed editions. The manuscript is not a forgery but it does not tell the story that modern editors of the poem want it to tell. In the introduction to his excellent edition of *The Poems of Sir Walter Ralegh*, Michael Rudick writes:

While the preponderance of attribution to Ralegh is no guarantee of his having either written either a hypothetical 'original' version or any of the variant versions, there exists in this case one source for which unusual claims can be made. The Marsh's MS [in Dublin] collects Elizabethan and early Jacobean writing. In the Elizabethan verse miscellany which opens its collection, twenty poems are attributed by name and each attribution can be verified from independent sources; this is a rare record for any miscellany. 'What is our life?' appear in the company of some unattributed epigrams of indeterminate date, though the manuscript was complete by about 1615. The copy is headed with the one word 'Rawley', and this is as near as we can come to documentary certitude ...[16]

Now it is perfectly true that 'the preponderance of attribution' is to Ralegh, if Rudick means that the six attributions to Ralegh outweigh the single attributions to each of six other authors. But all these attributions are heavily outweighed by the fifty-eight manuscript copies and the two early printed copies that are anonymous. The weight of anonymity is all the more impressive, given how strong the temptation was to attribute *any* plausible poem or text to Ralegh after his death. The printer of a 1650 collection that included some of Ralegh's works noted: 'Raleigh's very Name is Proclamation enough for the Stationers advantage'.[17] Printed collection after printed collection appeared of Ralegh's political and personal papers, many ending with his epitaph, 'Even such is time'. But not once was 'What is our life?' attributed to Ralegh in print.

So a lot rests upon the Marsh Manuscript. Rudick's claim depends upon two arguments: first, that the paratextual attributions at the beginning of the Marsh Manuscript are accurate, and so tend to make the attribution of 'What is our life' to Ralegh more trustworthy; second, that this copy of the poem was written before 1615. To take the reliability of the copyist's attributions first, the Marsh miscellany is in several different hands and the hand in which the 'Ralegh' poem is written has nothing in common with any of the Elizabethan hands in the early pages of the manuscript. Indeed, unlike the early pages, which only contain poems, the later part of the volume is increasingly miscellaneous. But crucially, 'What is our life?' occurs immediately after, and in the same hand as, a poem on a 1619 court scandal concerning Lady Mary Lake. It thus postdates Ralegh's death by some months at the least and it postdates the first anonymous printing of the poem by at least seven years.

But it is by no means clear that the Marsh Manuscript ascribes 'What is our life?' to Ralegh anyway. Everything depends upon how one reads the paratext. Here is the poem as in appears in the manuscript:

> Rawley.
> What is o*ur* life? it is a play of passion
> what is o*ur* mirthe? the musicke of diuision
> Our mothers they the tyringe howses be
> wheare we are drest for times short tragedye
> Earthe is the stage, heaue*n* the spectator is
> who dothe behould who heare dothe act amisse.
> The graues w*hi*ch keepe vs fro*m* the parching sunne
> are as drawne curtaynes till the play be done.

Rudick assumes that 'Rawley' means that Ralegh is the *author* of the poem. But although many of the poems in this miscellany are ascribed to authors, the ascriptions come *after* the poems. 'Well shoes the tyme in this compassion spent' *concludes* with 'Goodyer the penchon*er* beinge prisoner in the towere', Woe, woe, to hir yt made him goe awrye' with 'T. B. finis', 'Amarillis was full fayre' with 'G: Dier:', 'Loue Compared to a Tennis playe' with 'Made by the Earle of Oxeforde'.

There is a much stronger reason for believing that 'Rawley' is the *title* of the poem, not the name of its author. For in a book dated 1618 (i.e. published before 25 March 1619), 'What is our life?' had been printed with, for the first time, some connection to both 'Even such is time' and to Ralegh's death. The book, in which it appeared anonymously, as it had in its first printing, was Richard Brathwaite's *Remains After Death* ('Imprinted at London by John Beale, 1618'), where it bears the title 'Vpon the life of Man'. It is immediately followed by two poems on Sir Walter Ralegh. The first is an anonymous poem 'On Sir *W. R.*'; the second is 'Euen such is time' under the title 'By Sir *W. R.* which he writ the night before his execution'. Now, for the first time, one can quite plausibly read the poem as the first of a sequence of three poems commemorating Ralegh's death:

'Vpon the life of Man' ('What is our life?')
'On Sir *W. R.*' ('The life of Man is like the moouing hand/ Of euery Clocke')
'By Sir *W. R.* which he writ the night before his execution' ('Euen such is time')

'Vpon the life of Man' is echoed in the combined title and opening phrase of the following poem: 'On Sir *W. R.*'. 'The life of Man . . .'. In other words, two anonymous poems, the first possibly, the second definitely *about* Sir Walter Ralegh, followed by a poem *by* Ralegh. The differences between the texts of the 1619 printed text and the Marsh Manuscript are too significant to suppose that the former was the source of the latter. But it was almost certainly the printed text that suggested the connection that later copyists made between 'Even such is time' and 'What is our life?' And it is not surprising, given

Ralegh's fame, that a few copyists did indeed attribute both poems to Ralegh. In a composite scrapbook including poems from the sixteenth to the eighteenth centuries, for instance, 'What is our life?' appears under the title 'Verses Syr Walt. Rauleigh made the same morning he was executed'.[18] Given that this copy was written after Brathwaites printed version, there is no reason to give its attribution any authority, even if its full claim were not manifestly false. Ralegh could not have written 'What is our life?' on the morning of his execution in 1618 because it had already been published anonymously six years before in Orlando Gibbons's 1612 *The First Set of Madrigals*.

It is highly improbable that Ralegh wrote 'What is our life?' But for this volume on paratexts, the more significant point is that the poem circulated throughout the seventeenth century in print entirely and in manuscript dominantly as an anonymous poem. Vice versa, the titles given to 'Even such is time' in printed and manuscript texts alike insisted not only on Ralegh's authorship but on the specific occasion when the poem was written: the night before or the morning of his execution. Both poems occur in manuscript miscellanies although never together, but 'Even such is time' more frequently occurs in state and family papers. Two different notions, both modern, come together in Michael Rudick's otherwise superb edition of Ralegh's poems to obscure the difference between the two poems. The first is that it always matters who the author is, whereas the different manner in which the two poems circulated reveal the extent to which authorship was a variable practice of ascription in the seventeenth century. The second is the desire to find a manuscript that precedes print.

This second assumption is the outcome of literary archives that, from the eighteenth century, began preserving authorial manuscripts at the same time that they inscribed new notions of originality and literary property. In the process, printed books have increasingly been treated as the posthumous epitexts of the author's holograph, while 'manuscript' takes on a new aura of authenticity. Michael Rudick thus prints no fewer than three versions of 'What is our life?' from manuscript miscellanies, all three of which postdate the first two printed versions of the poems. He ignores the latter, I suspect, both because they are anonymous and because, being printed, they appear, from a modern perspective, to be both belated and secondary. Against such a view, it is worth recalling not only that the massive majority of medieval manuscripts are copies of copies of copies of . . ., but also that the concept of 'manuscript' is itself parasitic upon printing. Before printing, there was writing, no end of writing, but no manuscripts. It made no sense to speak of writing *by hand* before printing. The first recorded use of 'manuscript' in English is in fact from the 1590s, nearly a century and a half after the invention of moveable type.[19]

CONCLUSION

What are the limits to the significance of the paratext? First, insofar as we are talking about what Genette calls the peritext, there is the simple question of how a reader approaches a text. The codex form enables random access. There is no reason why a reader should read the preface to a book first, or even at all. If I were teaching a course on how books end, I might run my eyes over the list of contents of this volume until I came to Bill Sherman's 'The beginning of the end' and then turn to page 65 without further ado. Or suppose I am teaching a course on lyric poetry and want to see if there is anything in this book about sonnets, I might first turn to the index to see whether or not anyone addresses the topic. I could then turn to Juliet Fleming's fascinating argument about the framing of sonnets. In both cases, the paratextual material would play a crucial role, enabling me to find what I wanted. Indeed, to take the second example, if there were no index to this book or if the indexer had failed to add an entry for 'sonnets', that lack might determine my non-reading of the book. A totalising view of paratexts, in which each element is added up, misrecognises how one paratext can be used to skip or evade another. Indexes, above all, enable a reader to ignore prefaces, and even title-pages and tables of content, so as to get as rapidly as possible to what he or she wants.

The importance of indexes to how a book is used is central to Wendy Wall's illuminating analysis of *The English Housewife*. Being a book of recipes, a modern reader would expect to find an index so as to find a suitable recipe for an evening meal. But early editions of Markham's text frustrate any such reading, not only because they do not have indexes but also because they intermix culinary and medical recipes, making it hard to know where one should begin looking. But, as Wall shows, 'domestic guides after the middle of the seventeenth century were quite different in terms of their "usability"'. As a result of the addition of thorough tables of contents and indexes, kitchen miscellanies were transformed into systematised reference books. It is difficult to imagine a more powerful example of how paratexts can reshape the function of a book.

If paratexts make readers, so readers both negotiate paratexts and make new ones. My own afterword is the product of a reading of the chapters which go before it. Jason Scott-Warren shows us readers engaged in acts of marking and interpretation. The paratexts – both epitexts and peritexts – of this book will proliferate, taking in underlinings and the residue of post-it notes, the ownership marks of libraries and individuals, reviews, and citations. Each of these alterations will not only add to the complex life of the printed volume but will themselves prompt and guide interpretation. Paratexts do not just mark the book; they make it what it is.

Notes

INTRODUCTION

1. Gérard Genette, *Paratexts: Thresholds of Interpretation*, trans. Jane E. Lewin (Cambridge University Press, 1997).
2. Richard Macksey, 'Foreword' to Genette, *Paratexts*, xviii. For a full discussion of *Paratexts* in relation to Genette's other works, see Graham Allen, *Intertextuality* (London: Routledge, 2000), 98–197, and Macksey, xii–xx.
3. Jerome McGann, *The Textual Condition* (Princeton University Press, 1991), 13.
4. Some of this history is charted in Bill Bell's review essay, 'Victorian Paratexts', *Victorian Literature and Culture*, 27 (1999), 327–35.
5. John Taylor, *Verbum Sempiternæ* (London: Jo. Beale for John Hamman, 1614). See P. J. Anderson, 'Thumb Bible, by John Taylor', *Notes and Queries*, s10-ix (1908), 366.
6. Homer, *Achilles shield Translated as the other seuen bookes of Homer, out of his eighteenth booke of Iliades* (London: Iohn Windet, 1598), B3r.
7. William Turner, *The first and seconde partes of the herbal of William Turner Doctor in Phisick, lately ouersene, corrected and enlarged with the thirde parte* (Cologne: Heirs of Arnold Birckman, 1568), *iir.
8. Edmund Coote, *The English schoole-maister teaching all his scholers, the order of distinct reading, and true writing our English tongue* (London: the widow Orwin, for Ralph Iackson, and Robert Dextar, 1596), F2v.
9. For work on editorial practice and the new bibliography see, for example, Margreta de Grazia and Peter Stallybrass, 'The Materiality of the Shakespearean Text', *Shakespeare Quarterly*, 14 (1993), 255–83; Laurie Maguire and Thomas L. Berger (eds.), *Textual Formations and Reformations* (Newark: University of Delaware Press, 1999); Randall M Leod (ed.), *Crisis in Editing: Texts of the English Renaissance* (New York: AMS Press, 1994); and Andrew Murphy (ed.), *The Renaissance Text: Theory, Editing, Textuality* (Manchester University Press, 2000). For work on material culture, see Margreta de Grazia, Maureen Quilligan, and Peter Stallybrass (eds.), *Subject and Object in Renaissance Culture* (Cambridge University Press, 1996); Patricia Fumerton and Simon Hunt (eds.), *Renaissance Culture and the Everyday* (Philadelphia: University of Pennsylvania Press, 1999); and Natasha Korda and Jonathan Gil Harris (eds.), *Staged Properties in Early Modern English Drama* (Cambridge University Press, 2006). For 'thing theory', see Julian Yates, *Error, Misuse,*

Failure: Object Lessons from the English Renaissance (Minneapolis and London: University of Minnesota Press, 2003).
10. Seth Lerer, 'Errata: Print, Politics and Poetry in Early Modern Europe', in Kevin Sharpe and Steven Zwicker (eds.), *Reading, Society and Politics in Early Modern England* (Cambridge University Press, 2003), 41–71; William Slights, *Managing Readers: Printed Marginalia in English Renaissance Books* (Ann Arbor: University of Michigan Press, 2001); Evelyn Tribble, *Margins and Marginality: The Printed Page in Early Modern England* (Charlottesville: University of Virginia Press, 1993); Thomas Corns, 'The Early Modern Search Engine: Indices, Title Pages, Marginalia and Contents', in Neil Rhodes and Jonathan Sawday (eds.), *The Renaissance Computer: Knowledge Technology in the First Age of Print* (London: Routledge, 2000), 95–105; Peter Stallybrass, 'Books and Scrolls: Navigating the Bible', in Jennifer Andersen and Elizabeth Sauer (eds.), *Books and Readers in Early Modern England* (Philadelphia: University of Pennsylvania Press, 2002), 42–79; Ann Blair, 'Annotating and Indexing Natural Philosophy', in Marina Frasca-Spada and Nick Jardine (eds.), *Books and the Sciences in History* (Cambridge University Press, 2000), 69–89; and Anthony Grafton, *The Footnote: A Curious History* (Cambridge, Mass.: Harvard University Press, 1999).
11. Michael Saenger, *The Commodification of Textual Engagements in the English Renaissance* (Aldershot: Ashgate, 2006); Heidi Brayman Hackel, *Reading Material in Early Modern England* (Cambridge University Press, 2005), 88.
12. The Utopia Project Team, 'Preface' to Terence Cave (ed.), *Thomas More's Utopia in Early Modern Europe: Paratexts and Contexts* (Manchester University Press, 2008), xiii. A broad-ranging taxonomy of early English dramatic paratexts will be provided by Sonia Massai and Thomas L. Berger (eds.), *The Paratext in English Printed Drama to the Restoration* (Cambridge University Press, forthcoming).
13. Genette seizes on J. Hillis Miller's discussion of the prefix 'para-', which draws heavily on the term's biological significance, rather than its more usual meaning of something which is 'analogous or parallel to, but separate from or going beyond, what is denoted by the root word' (*OED* para-, *prefix* 1, def. A1). According to Hillis Miller: 'A thing in "para", moreover, is not only simultaneously on both sides of the boundary line between inside and out. It is also the boundary itself, the screen which is a permeable membrane connecting inside and outside. It confuses them with one another, allowing the outside in, making the inside out, dividing them and joining them' ('The Critic as Host', in Harold Bloom *et al.* (eds.), *Deconstruction and Criticism* (New York: Seabury Press, 1979), 219 (cited in Genette, *Paratexts*, l, n. 1).
14. Jacques Derrida, *The Truth in Painting*, trans. Geoff Bennington and Ian McLeod (Chicago University Press, 1987), 9.
15. John Earle, *Micro-cosmographie. Or, A peece of the world discouered in essayes and characters* (London: William Stansby for Edward Blount, 1628), F12v–G1r.

16. Francis Lenton, *Characterismi: or, Lentons leasures Expressed in essayes and characters, neuer before written on* (London: I[ohn] B[eale] for Roger Michell, 1631), E3v–E4r.
17. For a survey of marginalia in printed books, see William H. Sherman, *Used Books: Marking Readers in Renaissance England* (Philadelphia: University of Pennsylvania Press, 2007).
18. For a useful summary of this field, see Heather Hirschfeld, 'Early Modern Collaboration and Theories of Authorship', *Proceedings of the Modern Language Association*, 116 (2001), 609–22.
19. See especially Mark Rose, *Authors and Owners: The Invention of Copyright* (Cambridge, Mass.: Harvard University Press, 1995).
20. Arthur F. Marotti, *Manuscript, Print, and the English Renaissance Lyric* (Ithaca: Cornell University Press, 1995), 222.
21. Zachary Lesser, *Renaissance Drama and the Politics of Publication* (Cambridge University Press, 2004).
22. For a clear statement of the relevant distinctions, see Peter Blayney, 'The Publication of Playbooks', in John D. Cox and David Scott Kastan (eds.), *A New History of Early English Drama* (New York: Columbia University Press, 1997), 383–422.
23. Henry Burton, *A divine tragedie lately acted, or A collection of sundry memorable examples of Gods judgements upon Sabbath-breakers, and other like libertines* (Amsterdam: J. F. Stam, 1636), H2r.
24. Stephen Orgel, 'Margins of truth', in Murphy (ed.), *The Renaissance Text*, 91–107: 91.
25. Burton, *A divine tragedie*, H1v.
26. Huntington Library, Rare Books 61542.
27. John Jowett, 'Henry Chettle: "Your Old Compositor"', *Text*, 15 (2003), 141–61: 144.
28. Marie Maclean, 'Pretexts and Paratexts: The Art of the Peripheral', *New Literary History*, 22 (1991), 273–80: 274.
29. Lerer, 'Errata', 42.

1 'IMPRINTED BY SIMEON SUCH A SIGNE': READING EARLY MODERN IMPRINTS

1. Thomas Nashe, *The terrors of the night* (London: Printed by *Iohn Danter* for *William Iones*, and are to be sold at the signe of the Gunnenere [*sic*] Holburne Conduit, 1594), A4. Since this chapter argues for the importance of imprints as interpretative sites, I have reproduced early modern imprints in full throughout, though this practice is not in line with modern paratextual conventions.
2. Lotte Hellinga, '"Less than the Whole Truth": False Statements in 15th-Century Colophons', in Robin Myers and Michael Harris (eds.), *Fakes and Frauds: Varieties of Deception in Print and Manuscript* (Winchester: St Paul's Bibliographies, 1989), 1–27: 4.
3. Gérard Genette, *Paratexts: Thresholds of Interpretation*, trans. Jane E. Lewin (Cambridge University Press, 1997), 33.

4. W. W. Greg, *Some Aspects of London Publishing Between 1500 and 1650* (Oxford: Clarendon Press, 1956), 82.
5. On decorative frontispieces, see Margery Corbett and Ronald Lightbowm, *The Comely Frontispiece: The Emblematic Title-Page in England, 1550–1660* (London: Routledge, 1979); on title-pages, see Margaret Smith, *The Title-Page: Its Early Development, 1460–1510* (Delaware: Oak Knoll Press, 2000).
6. In 1597, *A most strange and wonderfull herring,* marked on one side with pictures and on the other with text, was discovered in Rotterdam, and its providential implications were anonymously translated and printed by John Windet for John Wolfe in 1598. Thomas Lodge and Robert Greene's *A looking glasse for London and England* (London: Printed by Thomas Creede, and are to be sold by William Barley, at his shop in Gratious streete, 1594) features the stage direction 'Ionas the Prophet cast out of the Whales belly vpon the Stage' (F3v). A fourth quarto, probably contemporary with Taylor's text, has been marked up by the prompter, who noted 'whale' in the margin against the stage direction. For details, see C. R. Baskerville, 'A Prompt Copy of *A Looking Glass for London and England*', *Modern Philology*, 30 (1932), 29–51.
7. See Bernard Capp, *The World of John Taylor the Water-Poet* (Oxford: Clarendon Press, 1994), esp. 14–15. Tiffany Stern also gives an account of this combat in '"On each Wall and Corner Poast": Playbills, Title-Pages, and Advertising in Early Modern London', *English Literary Renaissance*, 36 (2006), 57–89.
8. William Fennor, *Cornu-copiae, Pasquils night-cap* (London: Printed for THOMAS THORP, 1612), H1v.
9. Cuckold's Haven, also known as Cuckold's point, lies on the south side of the Thames, to the east of London, and was supposed to be the site at which King John cuckolded a London miller.
10. The Dekker texts are: *Newes from hell* (1606), *A knights coniuring* (1607), *Northward hoe* (1607), *West-ward hoe* (1607), *The ravens almanacke* (1609), and *The Owles almanacke* (1618). Other uses include Edward Sharpham's *Cupid's Whirligig* (1607), Robert Daborne's *A Christian turn'd Turke* (1612), and Sir John Harington's *The most elegant and witty epigrams* (1618).
11. Greg, *Some Aspects*, 89.
12. Genette, *Paratexts*, 31.
13. W. W. Greg, *A Bibliography of the English Printed Drama to the Restoration*, vol. IV (London: Oxford University Press for the Bibliographical Society, 1959), clxiii.
14. M. A. Shaaber extends and corrects Greg's taxonomy in 'The Meaning of the Imprint in Early Printed Books', *The Library*, 4th series, 24 (1943–4), 120–41.
15. Roland Barthes, 'The Reality Effect', in Tzvetan Todorov (ed.), *French Literary Theory Today: A Reader* (Cambridge University Press, 1982), 16.
16. Folger MS G.b.10, f. 105v.
17. Cited in Arnold Hunt, 'Book Trade Patents, 1603–1640', in Arnold Hunt, Giles Mandelbrote, and Alison Shell (eds.), *The Book Trade and its Customers, 1450–1900* (Winchester: St Paul's Bibliographies, 1997), 32.

18. For a discussion of claims to amplification and correction in early modern playtexts, see Sonia Massai, 91–106 below.
19. The most notorious example is the case of the 'wicked bible', so called because the word 'not' was omitted from the seventh commandment.
20. As Lotte Hellinga makes clear, this imprint was part of a long-established tradition of false or fictive colophons and imprints. It is different from most of its predecessors, however, in making its fictional status so explicit.
21. Marcy N. North notes the prevalence of false, though not directly satirical, colophons during the 1540s and 50s, and notes of Tyndale's 1530 *Genesis* that: 'in manipulating a convention with an extensive history in the scribal period and early print culture, Tyndale and his printers made the most of its standardised features. They retained the structure but altered the contents, a process that concealed the printer's name by seeming to follow the convention's rules' (*The Anonymous Renaissance: Cultures of Discretion in Tudor-Stuart England* (University of Chicago Press, 2003), 64). Joad Raymond notes that John Field's 1572 *Certaine articles* ('Imprinted we know where, and whan, judge you the place and you can: J. T. J. S.') is one of 'very few satirical imprints' to predate the Marprelate tracts (*Pamphlets and Pamphleteering in Early Modern Britain* (Cambridge University Press, 2003), 40).
22. Thomas Doughty, *The practise how to finde ease, rest, repose, content, and happines* (AT DOVAY [i.e. England] By IOHN HIGHAM, with permission of Superiors [i.e. English secret press], 1618; later ed. (AT ROAN [i.e. England] By *Iaques Foüet*, with permission of Superiors [i.e. English secret press], 1619).
23. Patrick Collinson, *The Elizabethan Puritan Movement* (London: Jonathan Cape, 1967), 391.
24. For further examples of this kind of 'onomastic play', see Laurie Maguire, *Shakespeare's Names* (Oxford University Press, 2007), esp. 34–5.
25. Peter W. Blayney, 'The Publication of Playbooks', in John D. Cox and David Scott Kastan (eds.), *A New History of Early English Drama* (New York: Columbia University Press, 1977), 389.
26. Tiffany Stern reaches a similar conclusion in '"On each Wall and Corner Poast"', 79, n. 64.
27. On the 'paradox of initials' which 'hang in balance between naming and authorial discretion', see North, *The Anonymous Renaissance*, 67.
28. See Peter W. M. Blayney, 'The Bookshops in Paul's Cross Churchyard', *Occasional Papers of the Bibliographical Society*, 5 (1990), and Adrian Johns, *The Nature of the Book: Print and Knowledge in the Making* (University of Chicago Press, 1998), esp. ch. 2.
29. Lawrence Manley, *Literature and Culture in Early Modern London* (Cambridge University Press, 1995), 127.
30. Cynthia Wall makes a similar point in her investigation of seventeenth- and eighteenth-century imprints, but her assertion that this level of topographical detail was a novelty in 'the decades of the most culturally and textually visible anxiety about urban navigation as witnessed by the vast new production of city maps, guidebooks, imprints, and urban fictions' ignores the copious evidence

of the fifteenth and sixteenth centuries ('"At *Shakespear's-Head*, Over-Against *Catharine-Street* in the *Strand*': Forms of Address in London Streets', in Tim Hitchcock and Heather Shore (eds.), *The Streets of London from the Great Fire to the Great Stink* (London: Rivers Oram Press, 2003), 10–26: 17.

31. John Stow, *A Suruay of London* (Imprinted by Iohn Wolfe, Printer to the honorable Citie of London: And are to be sold at his shop within the Popes head Alley in Lombard Street, 1598), G8r.
32. Ibid., C7r.
33. STC 9494.9, 16703, 16703.5, 16717. For a detailed discussion of city and civic printing in London, see Charles Welch, 'The City Printers', *Transactions of the Bibliographical Society*, 14 (1919), 175–241, and Mark Jenner, 'London', forthcoming in Joad Raymond (ed.), *The Oxford History of Popular Print Culture*, vol. 1 (Oxford University Press, 2011).
34. See Benedict Anderson, *Imagined Communities: Reflections on the Origin and Spread of Nationalism*, rev. edn (London: Verso, 1991), esp. ch. 3.
35. Brian Stock, 'Reading, Community and a Sense of Place', in James Duncan and David Ley (eds.), *Place / Culture / Representation* (London: Routledge, 1993), 314–28.
36. Stern, '"On Each Wall and Corner Poast"', 87.
37. Juliet Fleming, 'How to Look at a Printed Flower', *Word & Image*, 22 (2006), 165–87: 171.
38. Joseph Loewenstein, 'Personal Material: Jonson and Book-burning', in Martin Butler (ed.), *Re-presenting Ben Jonson: Text, History, Performance* (Houndmills: Macmillan Press, 1999), 93–113: 98.
39. Ben Jonson, *The Alchemist* (London: Printed by *Thomas Snodham*, for *Walter Burre*, and are to be sold by *Iohn Stepneth*, at the West-end of Paules. 1612), F2r.
40. See, for example, STC (2nd edn) 22237; 19054; 31.5; 19494.7; 25644; 25196.
41. William Hawkins, *Corolla varia contexta* (Cantabrigiae: Apud Tho: Buck 1634. Venundatur autem Londini apud Rob. Milbourn in Coemiterio Paulino ad [illustration of a sign of a greyhound], [1634]).
42. According to Ben Weinreb and Christopher Hibbert (eds.), *The London Encyclopedia*, 2nd rev. edn (London: Macmillan, 1993), it was not until 1765 that an act was passed requiring the Court of Common Council to affix street names to the corner of each street, square, and lane. See also Ambrose Heal's discussion of street-name history in his introduction to *The Signboards of Old London Shops: A Review of the Shop Signs Employed by the London Tradesmen During the XVIIth and XVIIIth Centuries* (London: Batsford Press, 1947, rpt New York: Blom, 1972).
43. Mark Jenner, 'From Conduit Community to Commercial Network? Water in London, 1500–1725', in Paul Griffiths and Jenner (eds.), *Londinopolis: Essays in the Cultural and Social History of Early Modern London* (Manchester University Press, 2000), 254. This information also marked Jones's premises as distinct from Edward White, who sold books at another sign of the gun, next to the little North door in St Paul's Churchyard.
44. John Taylor, *The pennyles pilgrimage, or The money-lesse perambulation, of Iohn Taylor, alias the Kings Majesties water-poet* (London: Printed by *Edw*:[ard] *All de*, at the charges of the Author, 1618), A4v.

45. Stow, *Suruay*, H4r–v.
46. *A declaration of the Parliament of Scotland, to all his Majesties good subjects of this kingdom concerning their resolutions for religion, King and kingdoms, in pursuance of the ends of the Covenant* (Imprinted at *Edinburgh* by *Evan Tyler*, and reprinted at London for *Robert Bostock*, at the King's head in *Pauls* Church-yard, 1648); Edward Reynolds, *The shields of the earth* (London: Printed for *Robert Bostock*, and are to be sold at his Shop in *Paul's* Church-yard, at the signe of the Kings Head, 1636).
47. See David Garrioch, 'House Names, Shop Signs and Social Organization in Western European Cities, 1500–1900', *Urban History*, 21 (1994), 20–48. Richard Wrigley discusses the aesthetics of shop signs in 'Between the Street and the Salon: Parisian Shop Signs and the Spaces of Professionalism in the Eighteenth and Early Nineteenth Centuries', *Oxford Art Journal*, 21 (1998), 45–67. Yu-Chiao Wang examines the promotional overlap between shop signs and printers' devices in 'The Image of St George and the Dragon: Promoting Books and Book Producers in Pre-Reformation England', *The Library*, 7th series, 5 (2004), 370–401.
48. John Bidwell, 'French Paper in English Books', in John Barnard and D. F. McKenzie (eds.) and Maureen Bell (assistant ed.), *The Cambridge History of the Book in Britain*, vol. IV (Cambridge University Press, 2002), 583–601: 585.
49. Garrioch, 'House Names', 32.
50. Richard Steele and Joseph Addison, *Selections from* The Tatler *and* The Spectator, ed. Angus Ross (London: Penguin, 1988), 284. I thank Alison O'Byrne for drawing this to my attention.
51. William Goddard, *A mastif vvhelp and other ruff-island-lik* [sic] *currs fetch from amongst the Antipedes* (Imprinted amongst the *Antipides* [i.e. Dordrecht: By George Waters], and are to bee sould, where they are to be bought, [1616]), A2v.
52. Cited in Annabel Patterson, *Censorship and Interpretation: The Conditions of Writing and Reading in Early Modern England* (Madison: University of Wisconsin Press, 1984), 92.
53. John Ainsworth, *The trying out of the truth begunn and prosequuted in certayn letters and passages between Iohn Aynsworth and Henry Aynsworth* ([Amsterdam: Giles Thorp], Published for the good of others by E. P. in the yeare 1615).
54. Natalie Zemon Davis, 'Rabelais Among the Censors (1940s, 1540s)', *Representations*, 32 (1990), 16.
55. Thomas Nashe, *Martins months minde that is, a certaine report, and true description of the death, and funeralls, of olde Martin Marreprelate, the great makebate of England, and father of the factious* ([London: Printed by Thomas Orwin], 1589), D2v–D3r.
56. R. B. McKerrow, 'Booksellers, Printers, and the Stationers' Trade', in *Shakespeare's England* (Oxford: Clarendon Press, 1916), II, 231.
57. Folger Shakespeare Library, STC 11944.
58. Oxford, Bodleian Library, Savile 1 23 (4).
59. William Fennor, *Fennors defence: or, I am your first man VVherein the VVaterman, Iohn Taylor, is dasht, sowst, and finally fallen into the Thames* (London:

Printed [by G. Eld] for *Roger Barnes*, and are to sold at his shop in S. *Dunstans* Church-yard in Fleetstreet, 1615), c3v.

60. John Taylor, *A cast over the vvater, by John Taylor. Giuen gratis to William Fennor, the rimer, from London to the Kings Bench* (Printed at London [By G. Eld] for *William Butler*, dwelling in the Bulwarke neere the Tower, and are to be sold by *Edward Marchant*, in Pauls Church-yard, 1615), d2v, d3r.
61. Kathryn Perry, '"I do it onely for the Printer's sake": Commercial Imperatives and Epigrams in the Early Seventeenth Century', *Entertext*, 3 (2003), 204–26. http://people.brunel.ac.uk/~acsrrrm/entertext/3_1_pdfs/perry.pdf.
62. See Kathleen Lynch, '*Vox Piscis*: Dead Men Shall Rise Agayne', *Shakespeare Studies*, 28 (2000), 154–9.
63. Thomas Mall, *A cloud of witnesses, or, The sufferers mirror. made up of the swan-like-songs and other choice passages of several martyrs and confessors to the end of the sixteenth century* (*London*: Printed for the Author and are to be sold by *Robert Boulter*, 1665), 87.
64. K. K. Ruthven, *Faking Literature* (Cambridge University Press, 2001), 121. See, however, Hans J. Rindisbacher, *The Smell of Books: A Cultural-Historical Study of Olfactory Perception in Literature* (Ann Arbor: University of Michigan Press, 1992).
65. Alexandra Walsham notes that 'reports reached Sir Julius Caesar in 1609 concerning a fisherman of Barking who conducted a profitable sideline in "papistical" literature concealed beneath his smelly catch' ('"Domme Preachers?" Post-Reformation English Catholicism and the Culture of Print', *Past and Present*, 168 (2000), 72–123: 85).
66. See Alexandra Walsham, '*Vox Piscis: or The Book-Fish*: Providence and the Uses of the Reformation Past in Caroline Cambridge', *English Historical Review*, 114 (1999), 574–606.

2 'INTENDED TO OFFENDERS': THE RUNNING TITLES OF EARLY MODERN BOOKS

1. David McKitterick, 'Obituary, Katharine F. Panzer, 1930–2005', *The Library*, 7th series, 7 (2006), 87–8.
2. McKitterick, 'Obituary', 88; A. W. Pollard and G. R. Redgrave (eds.) revised and expanded W. A. Jackson, F. S. Ferguson, and Katharine F. Panzer, *A Short-Title Catalogue of Books Printed in England, Scotland, & Ireland and of English Books Printed Abroad, 1475–1640*, 2nd edn, 3 vols. (Oxford University Press, 1976–91), II, 340.
3. Gérard Genette, *Paratexts: Thresholds of Interpretation*, trans. Jane E. Lewin (Cambridge University Press, 1997).
4. Eleanor Shevlin has recently observed that running titles, like titles of works themselves, had a role in marketing books in the early modern period, but her observations are made *en passant* as she explores the link between titling, entitlement and the rise of copyright. Similarly Elizabeth Eisenstein has suggested that the wider availability of running titles in the era of print helped,

along with other paratexts, to structure thought but her emphasis again is on their functionality. See Eleanor Shevlin, '"To Reconcile Book and Title, and Make 'em kin to one another": The Evolution of the Title's Contractual Function', *Book History*, 2 (1999), 42–78; Elizabeth Eisenstein, *The Printing Revolution in Early Modern Europe* (Cambridge University Press, 1993), 73.

5. Philip Gaskell, *A New Introduction to Bibliography* (1972; reprinted Winchester: St Paul's Bibliographies, 1995), 110. See also Fredson Bowers, 'Notes on Running-Titles as Bibliographical Evidence', *The Library*, 4th series, 19 (1938–9), 315–38; Thomas L. Berger 'Running Title Variants in Chapman's *Caesar and Pompey*', *Papers of the Bibliographical Society of America*, 70 (1976), 399–403; D. F. McKenzie, 'Printers of the Mind: Some Notes on Bibliographical Theories and Printing House Practice', *Studies in Bibliography*, 22 (1969), 1–75. Randall McLeod has devised an ingenious method for collating and comparing running titles for those of us unfortunate enough not to have access to a collating machine. See Randall McLeod, 'A Technique of Headline Analysis with Application to Shakespeare's *Sonnets, 1609*', *Studies in Bibliography*, 32 (1979), 197–210.

6. Ronald B. McKerrow, *An Introduction to Bibliography for Literary Students* (Oxford: Clarendon Press, 1927), 26–7.

7. Michael Siedel, 'Running Titles', in David Galey (ed.), *Second Thoughts: A Focus on Re-reading* (Detroit: Wayne State University Press, 1998), 34–51. The 'running head' in STC actually comprises the STC numbers printed centrally above a ruled line on every page, which denote the first and last entry for each page. Thus, the 'running head' or, using Jennett's terminology, in this case 'page headline' for ii, 340 of STC reads '22720–22764'.

8. *OED running* ppl.a. iv. 16. b.

9. Seán Jennett, *The Making of Books* (London: Faber and Faber, 1964), 277–8.

10. Unfortunately, Jennett's clarity about the different forms of headline has not been shared by other scholars. Compare, for example, the definition given in John Carter and Nicolas Barker (eds.), *ABC for Book Collectors* (London: British Library, 2004), 121, under 'Headline': 'The Cambridge University Press's manual, *Preparation of Manuscripts and Correction of Proofs*, distinguishes usefully between *page heads*, for book-title, section-title or chapter-title, and *running heads* for those headlines, usually on the right-hand page and changing with each turn-over, which indicate the contents of the two pages under view'.

11. John Cameron, *An examination of those plausible appearances which seeme most to commend the Romish Church, and to preiudice the Reformed* (Oxford: John Lichfield and William Turner for Edward Forrest, 1626), *4r.

12. John Wallis's letter to Collins, 25 August 1668, in Stephen Jordan Rigaud (ed.), *Correspondence of Scientific Men of the Seventeenth Century, Including Letters of Barrow, Flamsteed, Wallis and Newton Printed from the Originals in the Collection of the Right Honourable the Earl of Macclesfield*, 3 vols. (Oxford University Press, 1841), ii, 492.

13. Samuel Purchas, *Purchas his pilgrimes*, 5 vols. (London: for Henry Fetherstone, 1625), ¶ 6r.
14. Joseph Mede, *The works of the pious and profoundly-learned Joseph Mede, B. D., sometime Fellow of Christ's Colledge in Cambridge* (London: for Richard Royston, 1672), *3r.
15. Jennett, *Making of Books*, 280.
16. John Gauden, *A discourse concerning publick oaths, and the lawfulness of swearing in judicial proceedings* (London: for R. Royston, 1662), B1v–G4r.
17. Samuel Fisher, *The Bishop busied beside the businesse* (London, 1662), B3v.
18. Anthony à Wood, *Athenae Oxoniensis* (London: for Thomas Bennet, 1692), 2N3r. Significantly, the five different section headlines do not separate chapters, for the text is continuous. Indeed, the work has six different page ones and six signature Bs, because there are fifty pages which have no headline at all. The alternating section headline titles involved Moulin in a complex system of referencing. See Louis De Moulin, *Patronus bonae fidei in causa puritanorum contra hierarchicos Anglos* (London, 1672).
19. Edward Stillingfleet, *A discourse concerning the idolatry practised in the Church of Rome* (London: for Henry Mortlock, 1671), 2N8v.
20. John Sergeant, *Errour non-plust, or Dr Stillingfleet shown to be the man of no principles* (London, 1673), D1v–D2r.
21. George Wither, *The schollers purgatory* (London, 1625), H5v, cited in Shevlin, 'To Reconcile Book and Title', 52–3. See also John Freeman, *A sermon preached without a text* (London, 1643) where the address 'To his friends, & c' ascribes the title to the printer (no sig.).
22. Jerónimo Osório, *An epistle of the Reverend Father in God Hieronimus Osorius Bishop of Arcoburge in Portugal, to the Most Excellent Princesse Elizabeth*, trans. Richard Shacklock (Antwerp, 1565), A5r–K6r.
23. John Payne, *Royall exchange: to suche worshipfull citezins/marchants/gentlemen and other occupiers of the contrey as resorte therunto* (London, 1597), B1v–F4v.
24. William Perkins, *The true gaine: more in worth then all the goods in the world* (Cambridge, 1601), A1v–F3v.
25. Jan Orlers and Henrik van Haestens, *The triumphs of Nassau*, trans. W. Shute (London, 1613), A1v–3D2v.
26. Anonymous, *A certaine relation of the hog-faced gentlewoman called Mistris Tannakin Skinker* (London, 1640), A2v–B4v.
27. William Burkitt, *The peoples zeal provok't to an holy emulation by the pious and instructive example of their dead minister* (London: M. W. for Ralph Smith, 1680), B2r–E3v.
28. Nicholas Culpeper, *A physicall directory or, A translation of the London dispensatory* (London: for Peter Cole, 1649), C1r.
29. Nicholas Culpeper, *Pharmacopoeia Londinensis: or the London dispensatory* (London, 1655), title-page.
30. Robert Crowley, *Fryer John Frauncis of Nigeon in Fraunce* (London, 1586), A1v–K3r.

31. Robert Crowley, *A deliberat answere made to a rash offer, which a Popish Antichristian Catholique, made to a learned Protestant (as he saieth) and caused to be published in printe: Anno Do. 1575* (London, 1588), A2r.
32. Crowley, *Deliberat answere*, A2r. In fact, the tract never quite uses this exact phrase but many passages do end with a promise to recant. See Jean d'Albin de Valsergues, *A notable discourse plainlye and truly discussing who be the right ministers of the Catholique Churche*, trans. Edward Rishton (London, 1575).
33. Crowley, *Deliberat answere*, A2r.
34. John Evelyn, *The moral practice of the Jesuits* (London: for Simon Miller, 1670), F2r. It is possible that since the reference is not explicitly to 'running titles', Evelyn is referring to some other practice. I have been unable to identify an edition of Calvin's *Institutes* which uses the arrangement Evelyn describes. However, his own copy seems to have been an extremely rare one. The *Evelyn Library Sale Catalogue* notes that the only copy other than that in Evelyn's library was at Oberlin College. I have not been able to see this copy. The edition was Calvin's own French translation of his initial Latin work, Jean Calvin, *Institution de la religion Christienne* (Geneva, 1545). See *The Evelyn Library Sale Catalogue*, 4 vols. (London: Christie's, 1977), I, 86. The practice of putting 'Jesus' at the top of each page to indicate a Jesuit text appears to be confirmed by Samuel Purchas. Speaking of a manuscript that had come into his hands, he comments: 'The name Jesus divers times on the top of the page, and often mention of the Fathers and societie maketh me thinke him a brother of that order'. Purchas, *Purchas his pilgrimes*, IV, vii, 1289.
35. Thomas Day, *Wonderfull straunge sightes seene in the element, over the Citie of London* (London, 1583), [no sig.] 4.
36. William Cecil, Lord Burleigh, *The execution of justice in England for maintenance of publique and Christian peace, against certaine stirrers of sedition* (London, 1583), A2v–E4v. I am grateful to Helen Smith for drawing this example to my attention following a seminar by Professor Bill Sherman in which he discussed the tract and alluded to its running title.
37. The versions were Richard Schilders, *D'Executie van justitie* (Middleburgh, 1584) which read 'Executie om verraderije, (verso) and 'ende niet om de Religie.' (recto); Anonymous, *Atto della giustitia d'Inghilterra* (London, 1584) which replaced the running titles with page number in brackets; and Anonymous, *L'Execution de justice faicte en Angleterre* (1584) in which the running title read 'L'EXECUTION DE JUSTICE' (verso) 'EN ANGLETERRE' (recto).
38. Robert Crowley, *A briefe discourse against the outwarde apparell and ministering garments of the Popishe Churche* (London, 1566), A3v–C5r.
39. John Barthlet's *The pedegrewe of heretiques wherein is truely and plainely set out, the first roote of heretiques begon in the Church* (London: Henry Denham for Lucas Harryson, 1566), title-page; A1v–Z1v.
40. de Valsergues, *Notable discourse*, A1v–N2v.
41. Anonymous, *Our ancient testimony renewed concerning our Lord and Saviour Jesus Christ* (London, 1695), *passim*.

42. Thomas Nashe, *Strange newes* (London, 1592), B4*v*–M2*r*.
43. Bartolomé de las Casas, *The Spanish colonie, or Briefe chronicle of the acts and gestes of the Spaniardes in the West Indies*, trans. M. M. S. (London: for William Brome, 1583), A1*v*–N4*v*.
44. George Ker, *A discoverie of the unnaturall and traiterous conspiracie of Scottish Papists* (Edinburgh, 1593), title-page; A4*v*–D4*v*.
45. Anonymous, *A free conference touching the present state of England* (London: for R. Royston, 1673), A5*v*–A6*r* and *passim*.
46. William Tyndale, *The souper of the Lorde* (Nornburg, 1533).
47. John Frith, *A book made by John Frith while he was prisoner in the Tower* (London, 1533), B2*v*–B3*r*, B4*v*–B5*r*, C2*v*–C3*r*, C8*v*–D1*r*, D3*v*–D4*r*, G2*v*–G3*r*.
48. George Joye, *The subversio[n] of Moris false foundacion* (Emdon, 1534), A7*v*–A8*r*, C3*v*–C4*r*, F2*v*–F4*v*, F5*r*–F6*r*.
49. Martin Marprelate, *Oh read ouer D. Iohn Bridges for it is worthy worke* ('On the other hand of some of the Priests', 1588), B4*v*, E1*v*, C1*r*, E1*r*, E3*r*, E2*v*, and E1*v*.
50. *Ibid.*, F2*r*, F2*v*, and G1*r*.
51. Susan Felch, 'Shaping the Reader in the *Acts and Monuments*', in David Loades (ed.), *John Foxe and the English Reformation* (Aldershot: Scolar Press, 1997), 52–65: 64.
52. John Foxe, *Actes and monuments of these latter and perillous dayes, touching matters of the Church* (London, 1563), C1*v*–4P7*r*.
53. For discussion of the bibliographic history of *Actes and monuments* see, in chronological order, L. M. Oliver, 'Single-Page Imposition in Foxe's *Acts and Monuments*, 1570', *The Library*, 5th series, 1 (1947), 49–56; P. S. Dunkin, 'Foxe's *Acts and Monuments*, 1570, and Single-Page Imposition', *The Library*, 5th series, 2 (1948), 159–70; and Julian Roberts, 'Bibliographical Aspects of John Foxe', in Loades (ed.), *John Foxe and the English Reformation*, 36–51. For the debate about how much control Foxe had over the second edition, see Elizabeth Evenden and Thomas S. Freeman, 'John Foxe, John Day and the Printing of the "Book of Martyrs"', in Robin Myers, Michael Harris, and Giles Mandelbrote (eds.), *Lives in Print: Biography and the Book Trade from the Middle Ages to the 21st Century* (London: British Library, 2002), 23–54; and Evenden and Freeman, 'Print, Profit and Propaganda: The Elizabethan Privy Council and the 1570 Edition of Foxe's "Book of Martyrs"', *English Historical Review*, 2004 (119), 1288–307; for a different view, see Devorah Greenberg 'Community of the Texts: Producing the First and Second Editions of *Acts and Monuments*', *Sixteenth Century Journal*, 36 (2005), 695–715.
54. Dunkin, 'Foxe's *Acts and Monuments*', 168.
55. See Evenden and Freeman, 'Print, Profit and Propaganda', *passim*.
56. Pamela Neville-Sington, 'A Primary Purchas Bibliography', in L. E. Pennington (ed.), *The Purchas Handbook*, 2 vols., 2nd series (London: Hakluyt Society, 1997), II, 528. Neville-Sington details the corrected running titles and notes that it was only presentation copies that seem to have had them.
57. *Ibid.*, II, 529.
58. *Ibid.*, II, 537.

3 CHANGED OPINION AS TO FLOWERS

All early modern editions are published in London, unless otherwise stated.

1. Francis Meynell and Stanley Morison, 'Printers' Flowers and Arabesques', *The Fleuron*, 1 (1923), 1–46.
2. Juliet Fleming, 'How to Look at a Printed Flower', *Word and Image*, 22 (2006), 165–87.
3. Juliet Fleming, 'How Not to Look at a Printed Flower', *The Journal of Medieval and Early Modern Studies*, 38 (2008), 345–70.
4. The designs used in the sixteenth century comprised westernised 'arabesque' patterns, in a variant that is sometimes called 'vegetal', in that its forms are ultimately derived from those of plants. These forms are, however, deliberately stylised, and transformed into interpenetrating shapes that confound the distinction between figure and ground and suggest, to European eyes, a deliberate turn away from mimesis.
5. Edward Rowe Mores, *A Dissertation Upon English Typographical Founders and Founderies* [1778], ed. Harry Carter and Christopher Ricks (London: Oxford University Press, 1961), 39–49.
6. 'In 'The Serpentine Progress of the STC Revision', *The Papers of the Bibliographical Society of America*, 62 (1968), 297–311, Katharine F. Pantzer noted that 'around 1635 . . . type ornaments (printers' "flowers") changed from large and relatively lacy designs' (that is, from arabesque designs) 'to blacker, blunter, and usually smaller designs' (that is, to single 'spot' designs unsuitable for composition into large ornaments or borders), 308–9.
7. The edition of 1569, printed by H. Wykes, uses flower number 20; those of 1571 and 1572 by William How use number 8; and that of 1611 by T. Purfoot for Valentine Simmes uses flower number 19.
8. Joseph Moxon, *Mechanick Exercises on the Whole Art of Printing* [1683–4], ed. H. Davis and H. Carter (London: Oxford University Press, 1962), 25–6.
9. John Smith, *The printer's grammar* (London, 1755), 135–9.
10. Martin Fertel, *La Science practique de l'imprimerie* (Paris, 1723), 55; Mores, *A Dissertation*, 37.
11. Philip Gaskell, *From Writer to Reader: Studies in Editorial Method* (Oxford: Clarendon Press, 1978), 24. I am grateful to Jason Scott-Warren for drawing this to my attention.
12. Nevertheless, Field himself seems to have had little 'taste' for flowers in the first few years of his career, preferring woodcut borders and ornaments. When he began printing in 1588 he owned a font of flower 6, which he used only five times before 1591; and he further had – or could borrow – a font of the flower Yamada lists as Short's ornament 134, and a font of 19, each of which Field used once. That is, the use of flower 19 in *Orlando Furioso* is uncharacteristic of Field's other work to this date, and could possibly reflect the promptings, if not the specific choice, of Harington himself. See also Simon Cauchi, who notes that the borders surrounding the verse arguments in Harington's book are of two kinds: 'one, a frame of type ornaments' (that is, of a double row of flower 19), 'the other, a compartment made up of four head-pieces, i.e.: ornamental

woodblocks'. The two borders alternate in regular sequence, with 'a change of step at Book 24', which marks the middle of the poem. Cauchi argues that this feature of alternating borders (though not the use of type ornaments to compose some of these borders) was imitated from the Valgresi edition of 1556, or one of its reprints, and that 'we may take it that Harington either suggested or at least approved the imitation'. Simon Cauchi, 'The "Setting Foorth" of Harington's Ariosto', *Studies in Bibliography*, 36 (1983), 137–68: 148.

13. In 1595, two editions of Barnfield's *Cynthia, with certaine sonnets, and the legend of Cassandra* were printed for Humfrey Lownes: in one of these, STC 1484, head- and tail-borders are composed of flower 12; but the other, STC 1483, uses flower 19 in a scheme characteristic of the work of printer James Roberts. Barnfield's next published works were *The encomion of Lady Pecunia* (G. Shaw for Richard Jaggard, 1598), which uses flower 19 as head- and tail-piece borders, as well as woodcut head-pieces, throughout the volume; and a second edition, *Lady Pecunia, or the praise of money* (Richard Jaggard, 1605), which is not designed in imitation of the previous edition, but retains its use of head- and tail-pieces of the same flower. The last work attributed to Barnfield is an anonymous broadside, *A lovers newest curranto* (printed by M. Flesher for I. W., 1625 [author, printer's name and date of publication from STC]), which has a long strip of flower 19 running down the middle of the page.

14. Wendy Wall, *The Imprint of Gender: Authorship and Publication in the English Renaissance* (Ithaca: Cornell University Press, 1993), 70–4.

15. Rayna Kalas, 'The Language of Framing', *Shakespeare Studies*, 28 (2000), 240–7.

16. Samuel Daniel, *A panegyrike congratvlatory . . . with a defence of ryme* (London: Edward Blount, 1603), F2r.

17. A. E. M. Kirwood, 'Richard Field, Printer 1589–1624', *The Library*, 4th series, 12 (1931–2), 1–39.

18. R. B. McKerrow, *Printers' and Publishers' Devices in England and Scotland, 1485–1640* (London: Illustrated Monographs of the Bibliographical Society, 1913).

19. Examples by printers other than Roberts include William Percy's *Sonnets to the fairest Coelia* (Adam Islip for William Ponsonby, 1594), which has varied borders composed from three different flowers (designs 19, 20, and 12); another edition of Richard Barnfield's *Cynthia* (STC 1484), which was printed by an unknown printer for Humfrey Lownes in 1595, with head- and tail-borders of flower 12; and Sir John Davies, *Hymns of Astrea* (Richard Field for I. Standish, 1599), which contains twenty-six poems to Queen Elizabeth with head and bottom borders of flowers 19, 20, and 12.

20. Smith, *The printer's grammar*, 137.

21. It may be noted here that flower 20, which Short used for the lower borders of both *Amoretti* and *Antonie*, admits variance in its composition more readily than does Robert's favoured flower 19; and while Short's composition of flower 20 in both volumes is highly irregular, and at first glance unpleasing, it is likely I think that at least some of this variety was intentional, and represents a

deliberate exploration of the compositional possibilities of flower 20. The same cannot be said for flower 20a, however, which Short used for the upper border of both volumes, and here there does seem to be a high incidence of compositional error.

4 THE BEGINNING OF 'THE END': TERMINAL PARATEXT AND THE BIRTH OF PRINT CULTURE

1. Gérard Genette, *Paratexts: Thresholds of Interpretation*, trans. Jane E. Lewin (Cambridge University Press, 1997), 407.
2. 'The preliminaries were not included in the main signature series of new books because it was usual to print them last' (Philip Gaskell, *A New Introduction to Bibliography* (Oxford: Clarendon Press, 1972), 8). They could be left unsigned, given symbols rather than letters, or lower-case rather than upper-case letters, and in some cases the printer began the sequence of gatherings in a text with B, reserving A for the dedication or any other prefatory matter that came in. D. C. Greetham has described the 'embarrassing example' of Mary Wroth's *Urania* (1621), 'where the printer began the text with B on the assumption that laudatory introductory materials from noble personages would arrive for the A gathering, only to have none turn up, and thus to [have to] do without an A gathering or any prelims' (*Textual Scholarship: An Introduction* (New York: Garland, 1994), 133).
3. This is by no means to suggest that Renaissance authors, printers, and readers did not invest a special – and spatial – sense in the front entrances of books. This is clearest, perhaps, in the architectural frontispieces or title-page borders that quickly became the norm for printed books: see my essay, 'On the Threshold: Architecture, Paratext, and Early Print Culture', in Sabrina Alcorn Baron, Eric N. Lindquist, and Eleanor F. Shevlin (eds.), *Agent of Change: Print Culture Studies After Elizabeth L. Eisenstein* (Amherst: University of Massachusetts Press, 2007), 67–81. Indeed, that essay and this one can be seen as a diptych on the order of the early modern book.
4. Elizabeth Armstrong, *Before Copyright: The French Book-Privilege System, 1498–1526* (Cambridge University Press, 1990), 140.
5. Henry E. Huntington Library, Rare Book 6060. We have come to see the current paratextual structure, with the table of contents at the beginning and the index at the end, as natural but there is no inherent reason why these or other sections need to be where they are, and even today readers may prefer the navigational aids offered by the index and turn to the back of the book first.
6. D. Vance Smith, *The Book of the Incipit: Beginnings in the Fourteenth Century* (Minneapolis: University of Minnesota Press, 2001).
7. However, Said's final essays, *On Late Style*, were published posthumously in 2003, and there is now an extensive literature on 'lateness' in Shakespeare, Beethoven, and others.
8. Giorgio Agamben, *The End of the Poem: Studies in Poetics*, trans. Daniel Heller-Roazen (Stanford University Press, 1999), 112; I. A. Richards, 'How Does a

Poem Know When It Is Finished?', in Daniel Lerner (ed.), *Parts and Wholes: The Hayden Colloquium on Scientific Method and Concept* (London: Macmillan, 1963), 163–74; Barbara Herrnstein Smith, *Poetic Closure: A Study of How Poems End* (University of Chicago Press, 1968); Paul Muldoon, *The End of the Poem: Oxford Lectures* (London: FSG, 2006). Agamben is surely going too far when he claims that 'the end' is 'a poetic institution that has until now remained unidentified' (109).

9. Frank Kermode, *The Sense of an Ending: Studies in the Theory of Fiction* (Oxford University Press, 1967). For an extension of Kermode's and Smith's ideas to the field of drama, see June Schlueter's *Dramatic Closure: Reading the End* (Cranbury, NJ: Associated University Presses, 1995).
10. *OED, finis* 1.
11. Aberystwyth, National Library of Wales, Peniarth MS 392 D (olim Hengwrt MS 154); Henry E. Huntington Library, MS EL 26 C9. Each prologue and each tale also contains its own incipit and explicit.
12. Smith, *The Book of the Incipit*; G. A. Glaister's *Encyclopedia of the Book* explains that 'explicit … is contracted from the Latin "Explicitus est liber", *i.e.*, "it is unrolled to the end", a phrase which originated when the form of a manuscript was a roll or *volumen*' (Cleveland: World Publishing Company, 1960), 127.
13. Parker on the Web (http://parkerweb.stanford.edu) offers digital images of the manuscripts in the collection of Archbishop Matthew Parker (d.1575): it is a collaboration between the Parker Library at Corpus Christi College Cambridge and Stanford University.
14. Alfred W. Pollard, *An Essay on Colophons, with Specimens and Translation* (Chicago: The Caxton Club, 1905). The fastest way to survey scribal colophons is to consult the massive collection compiled by the Bénédictins du Bouveret, *Colophons de manuscrits occidentaux des origines au XVIe siècle*, 6 vols. (Fribourg: Éditions universitaires, 1965–82). I owe this reference to Christopher de Hamel.
15. Margaret M. Smith, *The Title-Page: Its Early Development, 1460–1510* (London: British Library, 2000).
16. Roger Stoddard, 'Morphology and the Book from an American Perspective', *Printing History*, 9 (1987), 2–14. Alex Gillespie rightly reminds me that 'authors in the Middle Ages did make books … That changes with print; a writer only makes his text into the thing in which it will be read if he works in a coterie context. This change must also change endings … But … the gap between the activity of literary production and the making and dissemination of texts as objects, could be imagined before printing' (personal communication).
17. Smith, *The Title-Page*, 30.
18. Glaister, *Encyclopedia of the Book*, 103–4.
19. Alan Cromartie has, however, suggested to me that, for Renaissance readers, the word may well have carried Aristotelian connotations, where it implied not just completion but *perfection*.
20. I am extremely grateful to two members of the TCP team, Emma Huber (Oxford) and Paul Schaffner (Michigan), for their assistance in searching for 'The End' using their mark-up tags rather than the more general fields

available on EEBO's public interface – though it has since become possible for all users to search for this and other phrases using the new field for 'trailers'.
21. These calculations were reported by Paul Schaffner (personal email, 16 November 2007). The other authors who come to use the phrase regularly include Philip Massinger, Francis Quarles, Thomas Nabbes, and John Milton. It is important to note that only a fraction of the texts on EEBO have been converted, and there is presently a strong bias towards literature (broadly defined) since the authors selected to date have largely been drawn from the Cambridge Bibliography of English Literature.
22. R. J. Schoeck, '"Go Little Book": A Conceit from Chaucer to William Meredith', *Notes & Queries*, 16 (1952), 370–2. I am grateful to Tony Edwards for reminding me of this tradition and for bringing this short essay to my attention.
23. Edmund Spenser, *The Shepheardes Calender* (London: Hugh Singleton, 1579), 1v and N4r.
24. Walter J. Ong, *Orality and Literacy: The Technologizing of the Word* (London: Methuen, 1982), 132–3.
25. Geoffrey Chaucer, *The House of Fame*, ed. Nicholas R. Havely (Durham Medieval Texts, 1994).
26. Bodleian Library, MS Fairfax 16, lines 2155–8.
27. Important discussions include Kay Stevenson, 'The Endings of Chaucer's House of Fame', *English Studies*, 59 (1978), 10–26; John Burrow, 'Poems without Endings', *Studies in the Age of Chaucer*, 13 (1991), 17–37; and Rosemarie P. McGerr, *Chaucer's Open Books: Resistance to Closure in Medieval Discourse* (Gainesville: University of Florida Press, 1998). Several of Chaucer's Canterbury Tales (those of Sir Thopas, the Squire, and the Cook) are also evidently unfinished. I am grateful to Derek Pearsall, Linne Mooney, Dan Mosser, and Alex Gillespie for their guidance on this subject.
28. Caxton's 1483 edn (STC 5087), lines following 2094.
29. Thynne's 1532 edn (STC 5068), lines following 2094.
30. They could point to the fact that the earliest printed representation of a Renaissance printing house is the famous Dance of Death woodcut included in a *Danse Macabre* edition printed in Lyon by Mathius Huss in 1499/1500 (see www.bl.uk/treasures/caxton/workshop.html). I am grateful to Sophie Oosterwijk for pointing me to the source of this image.
31. In a few cases, the author him- or herself was able to play with this parallel. The most obvious examples from the Renaissance are the 'scaffold speeches' that were published after the executions of famous people. But the most extraordinary example I have encountered (and the one that plays most powerfully with the conventions I have been exploring in this essay) is the letter Robert Louis Stevenson wrote to W. E. Henley on the night of 2 May 1884, as he was suffering a massive haemorrhage. While the blood poured from his body, he wrote a delirious last will and testament in rhyming quatrains which began by declaring, 'Of many letters, here is a Full End ... My indefatigable pen I here lay down forever'. The final stanza asserts, 'I now write no more' and the fanciful signature of 'Richard Lefanu Stevenson' is followed by that of his

fictional 'Secretary', Mark Tacebo [I will be quiet]. The letter concludes with a final line reading only 'The finger on the mouth', and the entire production is surrounded by a series of terminal formulae, written lengthwise in the margin, including 'Here endeth the Familiar Correspondence of R.L.S.', 'Explicuerunt Epistolae Stevensonianae', 'Terminus: Silentia', and 'FINIS Finaliter finium' (Ernest Mayhew (ed.), *Selected Letters of Robert Louis Stevenson* (New Haven: Yale University Press, 1997), 260–1). Stevenson went on to add another decade of letters to his voluminous familiar correspondence before dictating a final letter to Edmund Gosse on 1 December 1894, which he concluded, in his own hand, '(Matter petered out.) Yours ever, R. L. Stevenson' (608).

32. John Taylor, *The Muses Mourning, or funerall sonnets on the death of Iohn Moray Esquire* (London: s.n., 1615).
33. John Taylor, *Great Britaine, all in blacke* (London: Edward Allde, 1612). These examples bring to mind the infamous black page in the middle of *Tristram Shandy*, which follows the line 'Alas Poor YORICK!' on a page that also mentions an inscription serving as both 'epitaph and elegy'.
34. Andrew Brome, 'BVMM-FODER or, Waste-Paper Proper to wipe the *Nation's RVMP* with, or your Own' (Wing B4648A). I owe this example to Mark Jenner.
35. This is particularly true of legal documents or letters, where seals of various sorts were used to prevent the loss or transformation of the author's words. But it is also true of literary manuscripts that, while falling under the category of 'miscellany' or 'anthology', have a clear and closed programme, such as the so-called Bannatyne Manuscript, compiled by the young George Bannatyne in the face of a plague epidemic in 1568. It assembled Scottish poetry from a range of manuscript and printed sources and ended on its final page with two poems, each given a terminal 'ffinis', one 'Off begynnyng and ending', and one from 'The wryttar to the redare': see *The Bannatyne Manuscript, National Library of Scotland Advocates' MS 1.1.6*, ed. Denton Fox and William A. Ringler (London: Scolar Press, 1980).
36. Studies of Shakespearean closure include Schlueter's *Dramatic Closure*, Barbara Hodgdon's *The End Crowns All: Closure and Contradiction in Shakespeare's History* (Princeton University Press, 1991), and Richard Meek's 'The Promise of Satisfaction: Shakespeare's Oral Endings', *English*, 56 (2007), 247–63.
37. Stephen B. Dobranski, *Readers and Authorship in Early Modern England* (Cambridge University Press, 2005), 2.
38. British Library, MS Royal 18.A.lxi, f. 38r. The ending (which Mike Pincombe brought to my attention) is clearly a literary conceit: there is nothing rushed about the presentation of this manuscript, which is very carefully written and embellished in gold leaf.
39. I owe this example to Maria Fanchini.
40. Gavin Alexander, *Writing After Sidney: The Literary Response to Sir Philip Sidney, 1586–1640* (Oxford University Press, 2006); Jonathan Goldberg, *Endlesse Worke: Spenser and the Structures of Discourse* (Baltimore: Johns Hopkins University Press, 1981).

41. Robert Graves, *The Complete Poems*, ed. Beryl Graves and Dunstan Ward (London: Penguin, 2000), 386. I would like to thank Tom Cain for bringing this extraordinary poem to my attention. A similar poem begins the recent edition of selected poems by the Polish writer Julia Hartwig: see the title poem in *In Praise of the Unfinished* (New York: Knopf, 2008).
42. Richards, 'How Does a Poem Know When It Is Finished?', 172–3.

5 EDITORIAL PLEDGES IN EARLY MODERN DRAMATIC PARATEXTS

1. Gérard Genette, *Paratexts: Thresholds of Interpretation*, trans. Jane E. Lewin (Cambridge University Press, 1997), 24.
2. Even recent scholars interested in the transmission of early vernacular drama into print stop short of testing this type of pledge; see, for example, Julie Stone Peters, *The Theatre of the Book, 1480–1880: Print, Text, and Performance in Europe* (Oxford University Press, 2000), 57.
3. A further edition is mentioned by John Nicholas, who, after reprinting the first quarto of *The Entertainment at Elvetham* (1591) in his *Progresses of Elizabeth* (1778), reports to have come across a different early quarto, which claims to have been 'Newlie corrected and amended' on its title-page; in W. W. Greg, *A Bibliography of English Printed Drama to the Restoration*, 4 vols. (London: Bibliographical Society, 1939–59), 1, 176. These figures do not include references to the addition of new material to the printer's copy.
4. Samuel Johnson, *Proposals for printing, by subscription, the dramatick works of William Shakespeare* (London, s.n., 1756), 3–4.
5. See Grace Ioppolo, *Dramatists and their Manuscripts in the Age of Shakespeare, Jonson, Middleton and Heywood: Authorship, Authority and the Playhouse* (London: Routledge, 2006).
6. See Joseph Loewenstein, *Ben Jonson and Possessive Authorship* (Cambridge University Press, 2002); Lukas Erne, *Shakespeare as Literary Dramatist* (Cambridge University Press, 2003); Henry Woudhuysen, 'The Foundations of Shakespeare's Text', The Shakespeare Lecture, *Proceedings of the British Academy*, 125 (2004), 69–100.
7. Sir William D'Avenant, *The works of Sr. William Davenant, Kt.* (London: by T. N. for Henry Herringman, 1673); Abraham Cowley, *The works of Mr. Abraham Cowley* (London: for Henry Herrringman, 1693).
8. Sir Aston Cokain, *Small poems of divers sorts written by Sir Aston Cokain* (London: by Wil. Godbid, 1658), A5*v* 5–13.
9. George Whetstone, *The right excellent and famous historye, of Promos and Cassandra deuided into two commicall discourses* (London: by [John Charlewood for] Richarde Ihones, 1578), A2*r* 5–16.
10. Whetstone, *Promos and Cassandra*, A3*v* 2–11.
11. See J. K. Moore, *Primary Materials Relating to Copy and Print in English Books of the Sixteenth and Seventeenth Centuries* (Oxford Bibliographical Society, 1992).

12. Question marks indicate that the editorial pledge occurs in the earliest edition, or in the earliest extant edition, and that there is therefore no way of assessing their significance in practical, textual terms.
13. Sonia Massai, *Shakespeare and the Rise of the Editor* (Cambridge University Press, 2007), 102. Although STC 22280 is usually referred to as the *first* quarto edition of *1 Henry IV*, there is another earlier quarto edition, which was also printed by Peter Short for Andrew Wise in 1598 (STC 22279a), and which is known as Q0 from the only extant fragment (quire C) now in the holdings of the Folger Shakespeare Library in Washington DC. For further details, see, for example, David Scott Kastan (ed.), *King Henry IV, Part 1*, The Arden Shakespeare (London: Thomson Learning, 2002), 108–9. Kastan's edition includes a facsimile of the fragment in Appendix 5 (357–65).
14. '*Stabs him*' is added to Edward's line, 'Take that, thou likenesse of this railer here' in the printer's copy (Q2r 17). See also K4v 27 and O1v 7.
15. *2 Henry VI* adds '*Edward*' to the original entrance direction in the first quarto at H3v 11–12, 'Alarmes, and then flourish, and enter the Duke of *Yorke* and *Richard*'; similarly *3 Henry VI* adds '*Gloster*' to 'Enter King Edward, Queene Elizabeth, and a Nurse with the young prince and Clarence, and Hastings, and others' (O1, E7r 13–15).
16. 'Vnckle of *Winchester* I pray you reade on.', followed by the prefix '*Cardinal*.' in the next line at A3r 2–3 in the first quarto becomes 'My Lord of Yorke, I pray do you reade on.', followed by the prefix '*Yorke*.' at A3r 1–2 in Pavier's edition.
17. Examples of early modern proof-sheets can be found in Percy Simpson, *Proof-Reading by English Authors of the Sixteenth and Seventeenth Centuries* (Oxford Bibliographical Society, 1928); Percy Simpson, *Proof-Reading in the Sixteenth, Seventeenth and Eighteenth Centuries* (London: Oxford University Press, 1935); and Moore, *Primary Materials*.
18. Charles Read Baskerville, 'A Prompt Copy of *A Looking Glass for London and England*', *Modern Philology*, 30 (1932–3), 29–51; Leslie Thomson, 'A Quarto "Marked for Performance": Evidence of What?', *Medieval and Renaissance Drama in England*, 8 (1996), 176–210.
19. The head-title is corrected from 'IOHN DRVMS' to 'IACKE DRVMS' (D2r 1).
20. Gail Kern Paster (ed.), *Thomas Middleton, Michaelmas Term*, The Revels Plays (Manchester University Press, 2000), 1. Corrections at A4v 14–15, B1v 16, B3v 6–7, C4r 31, F4v 13, and 13r 26–7 in the second edition may indeed be compositorial.
21. Thomas Middleton, *Michaelmas terme* (London: by T[homas] H[arper] for R. Meighen, 1630), E1v 23–6.
22. See, for example, B7r 1, C6r 33, D2v 29, and D5r 24. More challenging, but still within the scope of a solicitous compositor, are four corrections at B1v 31–4, F4r 28–30, G5r 31, and G6r 28–31.
23. Thomas Goffe, *Three excellent tragoedies. Viz. The raging Turk, or, Bajazet the Second. The courageous Turk, or, Amurath the First. And The tragoedie of Orestes* (London: for G. Bedell and T. Collins, 1656), F6r 22.
24. Goffe, *Three excellent tragedies*, G2v 7–8.

25. Compare B2r 14–15, E2r 8–9, E4v 23–4, L1v 31, N3v 30 in the printer's copy with A4r 24–5, C1r 27, C4r 19, F3r 10, G6r 9 in the second edition.
26. See, for example, A4v 7–8 and B2r 13–14.
27. In the first edition, for example, Bajazet gives the province of Amasia to his son Mahomates, who gratefully accepts it; he then gives him the province of Manesia, which he, once again, accepts. This sequence of events in the first edition leaves Achomates, Mahomates's brother, empty-handed for no apparent reason. The second edition rectifies this anomaly by replacing the name 'Mahomates' twice in the dialogue and once as a speech prefix with the name Achomates. Similarly suggestive of an intimate familiarity with the fictive world of the play is another correction towards the end. The compositor who set the text of the first edition may be responsible for a mistake which lends support to my methodological assumption that the consistency of plot and characterisation would only be self-evident to somebody who was reading, as opposed to somebody who was setting, the play. Having just set type for the following entry direction at M4v 31, '*Enter Cherseogles, Isaacke, Mesithes, Mustapha*', the compositor of the first edition may have altered the next two lines, '*Cherse*. See where they stand / *Isaacke Achomates* and *Selymus*?' (M4v 32–3). Only a careful reader of the play would have known that Cherseogles, who is in disguise, has led Isaack, Mesithes and Mustapha to believe that they can lay ambush on their common enemies, Achomates and Cherseogles, and not on Selymus, who is their leader. The corrector of the second edition rectified what must have seemed like an anomaly to the compositor of the first, by replacing '*Selymus*' with '*Cherseogles*' (G2v 23), which, being the correct reading, is likely to have been in the manuscript from which the first edition was set.
28. Italic type is used and the half-lines in questions are realigned to the right margin on at least three occasions in the second edition at C4r 26, C8r 14, and G2v 20. The second edition also adds three exit directions (C4v 8, E1v 21, E3v 30), although it drops one at the end of 4.4 (E2v 17).
29. See, for example, E1v 34, where the repositioning of the exit direction correctly suggests that it is Isaack who leaves the stage, and not Bajazet, as the original position of this direction in the first edition at I1r 35 erroneously suggests.
30. The original directions, '*Opens the Letters*' (I3r 37), '*Reades second*' (I3v 4), and '*Reads*' (I3v 9), become fuller and more regular in the second edition, where they read '*Opens the Letters; Reads the first*' (E4r 8), '*Reades the second*' (E4r 13), and '*Reades the third*' (E4r 19).
31. See, for example, D2v 32 and I4v 12.
32. See, for example, F2r 10.
33. John Marston, *Parasitaster, or The favvne* (London: Printed by T[homas] P[urfoot] for W. C[otton], 1606), A2v 25–7.
34. 'and mount with them whome fortune heaues, nay driues: A stoy- / call sower vertue seldome thriues. Oppose such fortune, and then / bursts with those are pitied' at C1v 2–4 in the first quarto becomes 'And mount with them whom fortune heaues, nay driues; / A stoycall sower vertue seldome thriues. / Oppose such fortune, and then burst with those are pitied, / The hill of Chaunce is

pau'd with poore mens bones, / And bulkes of luckless soules, ouer whose eyes, / Their charriot wheeles must ruthless grate, that rise.' at C1*v* 1–6 in the second quarto. The second quarto also rewrites and expands three further sections of the dialogue at F3*r* 22–9, G3*r* 31–2, and 14*v* 4 and describes Gonzago, the Duke of Urbino, as 'a weake Lord of a / selfe admiring wisedome' in the list of dramatis personae at A3*v* 5–6.

35. Unnecessary single-word additions occur at C1*v* 11, D3*r* 17, F1*r* 4, F3*v* 17, G1*v* 23.
36. The unusual practice of setting at least part of the second edition of this play from type that had been left standing in Thomas Purfoot's printing house suggests that the first and second editions were printed one shortly after the other, or that the printing of these two editions may even have overlapped. Whatever prompted the printer Thomas Purfoot or the publisher William Cotton to pursue this peculiar course of action, one can assume that the manuscript from which the first edition was set was still readily available; see Fredson Bowers, *Principles of Bibliographical Description* (Princeton University Press, 1949); David A. Blostein (ed.), *Parasitaster. Or, The Fawn*, The Revels Plays (Manchester University Press, 1978). Examples of single-word additions which improve the metrical regularity of the verse can be found at D2*v* 38 and E4*v* 27; single-word additions which compensate for obvious omissions in the first edition are also added at B3*v* 30, C1*v* 9, C3*v* 5, E2*r* 10, G2*v* 36, G3*v* 7, G4*r* 16, H2*v* 4, I2*v* 11, I2*v* 20, and 14*v* 16.
37. D1*r* 12, D1*r* 20, D1*r* 35–6, and D1*r* 36–9.
38. See, for example, D3*v* 32, D4*v* 29, E1*v* 1, E4*v* 26, F3*r* 34, F4*v* 24, G3*r* 16, H2*v* 8, H2*v* 29, I2*r* 24, I3*r* 37 and 14*r* 29, I2*v* 6, I2*v* 14, and I3*r* 37.
39. One new speech prefix is added at G4*r* 25, and two are regularised at I2*v* 6 and I2*v* 12, but the same prefix is left unaltered at I2*v* 7. Similarly the second edition omits to correct two prefixes at B4*v* 4 and E4*v* 5 and to add a missing prefix at B4*v* 5. Last but not least, a new mistake creeps in when a correct prefix in the first edition is replaced by a wrong one in the second at G2*v* 38. Two exit directions are added at E1*v* 28 and H2*v* 26 and two descriptive ones, '*Dulcinel & Tiberio / conferre priuatly*' and '*Tibereo reads / the imbroder skarfs*', at B2*v* 24–5 and F1*v* 25–7, but one direction of the first edition '*Enter Dondolo*' at C3*v* 36 is botched in the second, where it reads '*Exit Dondolo*'.
40. A factual correction occurs at E2*v* 11, where Dulcimel points out that she is too young to be expected to marry the old Duke of Ferrara, by stressing that she is only thirteen in the first edition and only fifteen in the second. Her age had been mentioned once before in both editions at B3*r* 37–8, but only a careful reader, or, in this case, Marston himself, is likely to have noticed and redressed this inaccuracy.
41. Blostein (ed.), *Parasitaster*, 187.
42. See, for example, A4*v* 27, B2*r* 34, B3*v* 40, B4*v* 13, C1*v* 19, C3*v* 18, C4*v* 14, D2*v* 30, F1*r* 11–12, F1*r* 39, F3*v* 20, F3*v* 25, F4*r* 1, F4*v* 9, F4*r* 10, F4*r* 30, G3*r* 19, G3*v* 10, G4*v* 7, H1*r* 16, H1*r* 18, H1*r* 37, H2*r* 5, H2*r* 7 and 19, H3*r* 21, H3*r* 22, H3*r* 23, H3*v* 39, H4*v* 6, H4*v* 25, H4*v* 26, I3*r* 22, I3*v* 11–12.

43. Heywood's involvement is confirmed by the gratuitousness of the majority of changes introduced in this edition – 'the earths vaste wombe' (B1*v* 25) in the first edition becomes 'cold' (B1*v* 24) in the second; 'much profites' (B2*r* 31) become 'great' (B2*r* 31); the 'stormy tempests, that disturbe the sea' in the first edition (C1*r* 8) disturb the 'Maine' in the second (C1*r* 8); '*Canwicke-streete*' (D4*v* 15) is changed into '*Gracious-streete*' (D4*v* 14).
44. 'Lis: to him selfe / For all this laughter / I lyke not this' (H4*v*, left margin, opposite lines 32–5); 'Lis: to the King / S^r, as you loue goodness / or your selfe, let me / haue halfe an hours free / & priuat discourse with / you, before you goe to Bed. Kin: I will.' (I1*r*, right margin, opposite lines 6–11).
45. Percy Simpson, 'King Charles the First as Dramatic Critic', *The Bodleian Quarterly Record*, 8 (1935), 261.
46. References to the recovery or preservation of authorial intentions become more frequent in editorial pledges starting from the second half of the seventeenth century (see, for example, Humphrey Moseley's address to the reader in his 1659 edition of *The Last Remains of Sr John Suckling*), but authorial intentions and non-authorial correction of copy continue to coexist and they are not regarded as mutually exclusive (in 1679, for example, Henry Herringman advertised non-authorial annotation of copy for the plays included in the second Folio edition of Beaumont and Fletcher's *Comedies and Tragedies*, while simultaneously describing this edition as 'incorrupt and genuine' (A1*v* 4–5)).
47. Nicholas Brooke (ed.), *Bussy D'Ambois, George Chapman*, The Revels Plays (Manchester University Press, 1964), lxi.
48. *Ibid.*, lxii.
49. *Ibid.*, lxvii.
50. *Ibid.*, lxvii.
51. *Ibid.*, lxx–lxxi.
52. Henry Herringman, 'The Book-sellers to the Reader', in Francis Beaumont and John Fletcher, *Fifty comedies and tragedies written by Francis Beaumont and John Fletcher, Gentlemen* (London: by J. Macock, for John Martyn, Henry Herringman, Richard Marriot, 1679), A1 5–16.
53. Pavier's edition of *The Yorkshire Tragedy* (1619), for example, changes the following directions as they appear in the printer's copy, 'spurns her; Teares his haire; Striues with her for the child; Throwes her down; W. wakes catches up the youngest; ouer comes him' (Q1, B1*r* 8–9; C2*r* 20; C3*r* 11–12; C3*r* 15; C3*r* 19–20; C3*v* 19), to 'He spurns her; He teares his haire; he striues with her for the childe; He throwes her downe; His wife awakes, and catches up the youngest; Husband ouercomes him' (Q2, A4*r* 8; C1*r* 20; C2*r* 11; C2*r* 16; C2*r* 20; C2*v* 22). Similarly Pavier's edition of *The Merchant of Venice* (1619) changes 'opens the letter; play Musique' (Q1, F2*v* 27; I2*v* 20) to 'He opens the Letter; Musicke playes' (Q2, F2*v* 33; I4*v* 7). This peculiar type of intervention can also be found in Pavier's edition of *A Looking Glass for London and England* (1602), where the following directions 'Embrace him; Embrace his necke; Kisse.; Kisse him.; Faints. Point; Embrace' (Q2 G1*r* 10, G1*r* 14, G1*r* 16, G1*r* 20, G1*r* 26, G1*v* 2) are changed to 'She imbraceth him; She embraceth his

necke; She kisseth him; She kisseth him againe.; She faints, and points; She embraceth' (Q3 F3*v* 10, F3*v* 14, F3*v* 16, F3*v* 20, F3*v* 26, F4*r* 2).
54. See, for example, Wise's second quarto edition of *Richard II* (1598), Pavier's edition of *A Looking Glass for London and England* (1602), or Jaggard's edition of *A Woman Killed with Kindness* (1617).

6 STATUS ANXIETY AND ENGLISH RENAISSANCE TRANSLATION

1. See H. S. Bennett, *English Books and Readers 1558–1603* (Cambridge University Press, 1965), xvi.
2. F. O. Matthiessen, *Translation: An Elizabethan Art* (Cambridge, Mass.: Harvard University Press, 1931), 1; Warren Boutcher, 'The Renaissance', in Peter France (ed.), *The Oxford Guide to Literature in English Translation* (Oxford University Press, 2000), 46.
3. Francis Meres, *Palladis Tamia. Wits treasury* (London: Cuthbert Burbie, 1598), 285–6.
4. John Florio, *Firste fruites* (London: Thomas Woodcock, 1578), 50.
5. William Camden, *Remaines . . . concerning Britaine* (London: Simon Waterson, 1605), D3*r*.
6. Gérard Genette, *Paratexts: Thresholds of Interpretation*, trans. Jane E. Lewin (Cambridge University Press, 1997), 405.
7. Francis Kinaston, *Amorum Troili et Criseidæ Libri duo priores Anglico-Latini* (Oxford: John Lichfield, 1635), A3*v*; see also Lawrence V. Ryan, 'Chaucer's Criseyde in Neo-Latin Dress', *English Literary Renaissance*, 17 (1987), 288–302.
8. Genette, *Paratexts*, 5.
9. See Louise Wilson, 121–5 below.
10. Genette, *Paratexts*, 207–8.
11. John Harington, 'A preface, or rather a briefe apologie of poetrie and of the author and translator of this poem' in *Orlando Furioso in English heroical verse* (London: Richard Field, 1591), iii*v*.
12. Harington, *Orlando Furioso*, vii*r*.
13. Philemon Holland, *The naturall historie of C. Plinius Secundus* (London: Adam Islip, 1601), (x) 3*v*, and see Bennett, *English Books and Readers 1558–1603*, 94–103, for further examples of translators' apologies.
14. George Chapman, *The Iliads of Homer* (London: Nathaniel Butter, 1611), A1*r*.
15. George Chapman, *Achilles shield* (London: John Windet, 1598), A2*v*–A3*v*.
16. See Jennifer Richards, *Rhetoric and Courtliness in Early Modern Literature* (Cambridge University Press, 2003), 64.
17. Thomas Hoby, *The courtyer of Count Baldesar Castilio* (London: William Seres, 1561), Aiiii*r*.
18. *Ibid.*, Aiiii*v*.
19. *Ibid.*, Bi*r*.
20. Massimiliano Morini, *Tudor Translation in Theory and Practice* (Aldershot: Ashgate, 2006), 21.

21. On Cheke and Hoby, see also Cathy Shrank, *Writing the Nation in Reformation England* (Oxford University Press, 2004), who points out that Hoby's translation was actually far from purist, 189–92, at 190.
22. Bartholomew Clerke, *Baltharis Castionis Comitis De Curiali siue Aulico* (London: Henry Binneman, 1577).
23. See Peter Burke, *The Fortunes of the 'Courtier': The European Reception of Castiglione's 'Cortegiano'* (Cambridge: Polity Press, 1995), 65.
24. John Florio, *The essayes or morall, politike and militarie discourses of Lo: Michaell de Montaigne*, 3 vols. (London: Edward Blount, 1603).
25. 'Fondling' means 'doting' here, but it is also an obsolete version of 'foundling' and the double meaning is clearly intended.
26. Florio, *Montaigne*, A2v.
27. John Florio, *A worlde of wordes* (London: Edward Blount, 1598), A3v. 'Brain-babe' is not recorded in the *OED* and predates the earliest comparable formation, 'brain-brats' (1630). 'Brainchild' is not recorded until 1921. In the poem by 'Il Candido' that follows, the term 'Anacephalaiosis' (not recorded in the *OED* until 1650) is used in a similar sense and also puns on Queen Anne who was the dedicatee of the second edition of the *Worlde of wordes* (1611).
28. *Ibid.*, A4v.
29. *Ibid.*, A5r.
30. On Florio's Petrarchan 'grotesque', see Christopher Johnson, 'Florio's Conversion of Montaigne, Sidney and Six Patronesses', *Cahiers Elisabéthains*, 64 (2003), 9–18.
31. Florio, *Montaigne*, A2v–A3r. The reference to the collared male deer echoes Petrarch's sonnet CXC, 'Una candida cerva ...' and possibly also Wyatt's version of the poem.
32. Florio, *Worlde of wordes*, A5r.
33. Florio, *Montaigne*, A5r.
34. Frances A. Yates, *John Florio: The Life of an Italian in Shakespeare's England* (Cambridge University Press, 1934), 226.
35. Hoby, *Courtyer*, [appendix].
36. Florio, *Montaigne*, A5r.
37. Brian Twine (1597) quoted in James McConica, 'Elizabethan Oxford: The Collegiate Society', in *The History of the University of Oxford*, ed. James McConica, vol. III (Oxford: Clarendon Press, 1986), 724.
38. British Library, Add. MSS 15,214, 6. I have slightly expanded the version of this in Yates, *John Florio*, 47.
39. John Florio, *Queen Anna's new world of words* (London: Edward Blount and William Barret, 1611), [frontispiece].
40. On Florio as a language teacher, see Michael Wyatt, *The Italian Encounter with Tudor England* (Cambridge University Press, 2005), 157–202.
41. See Warren Boutcher, 'A French Dexterity, & an Italian Confidence: New Documents on John Florio, Learned Strangers and Protestant Humanist Study of Modern Languages in Renaissance England from c. 1547 to c. 1625', *Reformation*, 2 (1997), 39–109: 49.

42. Meres, *Palladis Tamia*, 249.
43. Florio, *Montaigne*, A6v.
44. Daniel refers to Florio as his 'brother' in the commendatory poem for his translation of Montaigne and in the 1611 *Worlde of wordes*. On Florio's teaching of Italian and French to Daniel, and on the relationship between modern language learning and poetic composition, see Jason Lawrence, *'Who the Devil taught thee so much Italian?': Italian Language Learning and Literary Imitation in Early Modern England* (Manchester University Press, 2005), 62–117.
45. Mark Bauerlein, 'A Thanking Task', *Times Literary Supplement*, 9 November 2001, 17; another example is Henry Alford, 'I Thank You', *The New York Times*, 15 January 2006, for which I thank Peter Lindenbaum.
46. See Yates, *John Florio*, 225.
47. John Donne, *The Courtier's Library*, ed. Evelyn Mary Simpson (London: Nonesuch Press, 1930), 46–7.
48. See John Hale, *The Civilisation of Europe in the Renaissance* (London: Harper Collins, 1993), 284; George Steiner, *After Babel: Aspects of Language and Translation*, 3rd edn (Oxford University Press, 1998), 261; Raphael Lyne, *Ovid's Changing Worlds: English 'Metamorphoses', 1567–1632* (Oxford University Press, 2001), 10.
49. Samuel Daniel, 'To my deere friend M. Iohn Florio, concerning his translation of Montaigne', in Florio, *Montaigne*, B1r–v.
50. Samuel Daniel, *A panegyrike congratvlatory . . . with a defence of ryme* (London: Edward Blount, 1603), 11r.
51. George Chapman, *Achilles shield*, B2r. Bennett, *English Books and Readers 1558–1603* (Cambridge University Press, 1965), xvi.

7 PLAYFUL PARATEXTS: THE FRONT MATTER OF ANTHONY MUNDAY'S IBERIAN ROMANCE TRANSLATIONS

1. This is the date of the earliest extant copy of *Amadís de Gaula*. For more on the origins and early Spanish printing of the romance, see Helen D. Moore (ed.), *Amadis de Gaule: By Anthony Munday* (Aldershot: Ashgate, 2004), x; and Henry Thomas, *Spanish and Portuguese Romances of Chivalry: The Revival of the Romance of Chivalry in the Spanish Peninsula and its Extension and Influences Abroad* (Cambridge University Press, 1920), 42–64.
2. This is discussed in Alex Davis, *Chivalry and Romance in the English Renaissance* (Cambridge: D. S. Brewer, 2003), 7–16. See also, Goran V. Stanivukovic, 'English Renaissance Romances as Conduct Books for Young Men', in Naomi Conn Liebler (ed.), *Early Modern Prose Fiction: The Cultural Politics of Reading* (New York: Routledge, 2007), 60–78.
3. Brian C. Lockey, *Law and Empire in English Renaissance Literature* (Cambridge University Press, 2006), 20–1; and Joshua Phillips, 'Chronicles of Wasted Time: Anthony Munday, Tudor Romance, and Literary Labor', *English Literary History*, 73 (2006), 781–803: 789.

4. See, for example, Steve Mentz, *Romance for Sale in Early Modern England: The Rise of Prose Fiction* (Aldershot: Ashgate, 2006); Michael Saenger, *The Commodification of Textual Engagements in the English Renaissance* (Aldershot: Ashgate, 2006); and Paul J. Voss, 'Romance for Sale: Advertising and Patronage in Late Elizabethan England', *Sixteenth Century Journal*, 29 (1998), 733–56.
5. Celeste Turner Wright, '"Lazarus Pyott" and Other Inventions of Anthony Munday', *Philological Quarterly*, 42 (1963), 532–41: 532.
6. Donna B. Hamilton, *Anthony Munday and the Catholics, 1560–1633* (Aldershot: Ashgate, 2005), 73. Gerald R. Hayes, 'Anthony Munday's Romances of Chivalry', *The Library*, 4th series, 6 (1925–6), 57–81, gives a useful bibliographical overview of the publication of the romances.
7. Anthony Munday (trans.), *Palmerin d'Oliva* (London: John Charlewood, 1588), *ii*v.
8. Munday, *Palmerin d'Oliva*, *iii*r. See Tracey Hill, *Anthony Munday and Civic Culture: Theatre, History and Power in Early Modern London 1580–1633* (Manchester University Press, 2004), 45–6; and Phillips, 'Chronicles of Wasted Time', 792–3.
9. Gérard Genette, *Paratexts: Thresholds of Interpretation*, trans. Jane E. Lewin (Cambridge University Press, 1997), 263.
10. For a full discussion of this, see Marc Fumaroli, 'Jacques Amyot and the Clerical Polemic Against the Chivalric Novel', *Renaissance Quarterly*, 38 (1985), 22–40: 34.
11. Marian Rothstein, *Reading in the Renaissance: 'Amadis de Gaule' and the Lessons of Memory* (Newark: University of Delaware Press, 1999), 23. Rothstein's translation.
12. Anthony Munday (trans.), *Palmerin of England*, Part 3 (London: James Roberts, 1602), A3r.
13. The title-page of the only surviving copy, held in the British Library, is missing.
14. Anthony Munday (trans.) *The ancient, famous and honourable history of Amadis de Gaule*, Book 2 (London: Nicholas Okes, 1618–19), A2r.
15. Anthony Munday (trans.), *Palmerin of England*, Parts 1–2 (London: Thomas Creede, 1596), A3r.
16. For details, see Hayes, 'Anthony Munday's Romances of Chivalry'.
17. Hill, *Anthony Munday and Civic Culture*, 72.
18. The Earl of Oxford was not supplanted entirely from the position of dedicatee; Munday continued to dedicate certain translations to him and, after his death, to his son Henry de Vere, the new Earl of Oxford.
19. Anthony Munday, *The first [-second] part, of the . . . historie of the famous and fortunate prince, Palmerin of England* (London: Thomas Creede, 1609), A3r–v. Although the front matter to the first book of *Palmerin of England* in 1596 is no longer extant, we can suppose that it is the same as this text, since Munday's prefatory matter to the other volumes is reproduced from the original in many subsequent editions.
20. Anthony Munday (trans.), *Palmerin d'Oliva*, Part 1 (London: T. C. and B. A. for Richard Higgenbotham, 1616), A3r.

21. Anthony Munday (trans.), *The second part of . . . Palmerin of England* (London: Thomas Creede, 1596), A3r.
22. Antonii Panormitae [Antonio Beccardelli], *De dictis et factis Alphonsi regis Aragonum libri quatuor* [sic] (Basel, 1538). The text is cited as a source for Amyot's epistle by Bernard Weinberg (ed.), *Critical Prefaces of the French Renaissance* (Evanston: Northwestern University Press, 1950), 173.
23. Matthieu Coignet, *Politique discourses upon trueth and lying*, trans. Sir Edward Hoby (London: [John Windet for] Rafe Newberie, 1586), 70.
24. Sir Thomas North, 'Amiot to the Readers', *The lives of the noble Grecians and Romanes* (London: Thomas Vautroullier and John Wight, 1579), *vv.
25. *Ibid.*, *vv.
26. *Ibid.*, *iiir.
27. Marc Eccles, 'Anthony Munday', in Josephine W. Bennett, Oscar Cargill, and Vernon Hall, Jr. (eds.), *Studies in the English Renaissance Drama* (New York University Press, 1959), 95–105: 97.
28. Hill, *Anthony Munday and Civic Culture*, especially 19–37, usefully details Munday's network of associates in the printing trade.
29. Celeste Turner Wright, 'Young Anthony Munday Again', *Studies in Philology*, 56 (1959), 150–68.
30. For a discussion of Munday's pseudonymous translation of Silvayn's *The Orator*, see Neil Rhodes, *Shakespeare and the Origins of English* (Oxford University Press, 2004), 102–17.
31. Turner Wright, '"Lazarus Pyott"', 532–41. For a summary of the history of the debate on the identification of Lazarus Pyott as Anthony Munday, see 532.
32. Turner Wright, '"Lazarus Pyott"', 535.
33. Hamilton, *Anthony Munday and the Catholics*, 78.
34. John Jowett, 'Henry Chettle: "Your old Compositor"', *Text*, 15 (2003), 141–61: 150.
35. Anthony Munday (trans.), *The second booke of Primaleon of Greece* (London: John Danter for Cuthbert Burby, 1596), A3r. For more on the importance of Chettle's working relationship with the printer, John Danter, see John Jowett, 'Johannes Factotum: Henry Chettle and *Greene's Groatsworth of Wit*', *Papers of the Bibliographical Society of America*, 87 (1993), 453–86: 466–75, and Jowett, 'Henry Chettle: "Your old Compositor"', 143–6.
36. Munday, *Primaleon*, A4v.
37. Jowett, 'Henry Chettle: "Your old Compositor"', 158.
38. I am grateful to Neil Rhodes for drawing my attention to the punning French meaning of 'Pyott/piot' as 'magpie'.
39. Jowett 'Johannes Factotum: Henry Chettle and *Greene's Groatsworth of Wit*', 475. This is also the conclusion of the recent editor of *Greene's Groatsworth of Wit*: Robert Greene, *Greene's Groatsworth of Wit, Bought with a Million of Repentance (1592)*, ed. D. Allen Carroll (Binghamton: Medieval and Renaissance Texts & Studies, 1994). Steve Mentz considers instead that 'we don't know who wrote it' (Steve Mentz, 'Forming Greene: Theorizing the Early Modern Author in the *Groatsworth of Wit*', in Kirk Melnikoff and

Edward Gieskes (eds.), *Writing Robert Greene: Essays on England's First Notorious Professional Writer* (Aldershot: Ashgate, 2008), 114–31: 117).
40. Anthony Munday (trans.) *Gerileon of England* [Part 2] (London: Thomas Scarlet [?] for Cuthbert Burby, 1592), A4v.
41. Henry Chettle, *Kind-harts dreame* (London: John Danter and John Wolfe for William Wright, 1593), A4r.
42. Joseph Loewenstein, *The Author's Due: Printing and the Prehistory of Copyright* (University of Chicago Press, 2002), 40.
43. Hill, *Anthony Munday and Civic Culture*, 70.

8 'SIGNIFYING, BUT NOT SOUNDING': GENDER AND PARATEXT IN THE COMPLAINT GENRE

1. From Richard Mulcaster, *The first part of the elementarie* (London: Thomas Vautroullier, 1582).
2. Gérard Genette, *Paratexts: Thresholds of Interpretation*, trans. Jane E. Lewin (Cambridge University Press, 1997), 2.
3. See Juliet Fleming, 'The Ladies' Man and the Age of Elizabeth', in James Grantham Turner (ed.), *Sexuality and Gender in Early Modern Europe: Institutions, Texts, Images* (Cambridge University Press, 1993), 158–81.
4. See Alastair Fowler, *Renaissance Realism: Narrative Images in Literature and Art* (Oxford University Press, 2003). On Ovid, and the *Heroides* in particular, see Jonathan Bate, *Shakespeare and Ovid* (Oxford: Clarendon Press, 1993); Warren Boutcher, '"Who Taught Thee Rhetoricke to Deceive a Maid?": Christopher Marlowe's Hero and Leander, Juan Boscán's 'Leandro, and Renaissance Vernacular Humanism', *Comparative Literature*, 52 (2000), 11–52; Philip Hardie, *Ovid's Poetics of Illusion* (Cambridge University Press, 2002); Patricia B. Phillippy, '"Loytering in Love": Ovid's Heroides, Hospitality, and Humanist Education in the Taming of the Shrew', *Criticism*, 40 (1998), 27–53.
5. J. L. Austin, *How to Do Things with Words*, 2nd edn (Oxford: Clarendon Press, 1975); James Loxley, *Performativity* (London: Routledge, 2007).
6. Catherine M. S. Alexander and Jonathan Hope, *Shakespeare and Language* (Cambridge University Press, 2004), 12.
7. Cathy Shrank, '"These Fewe Scribbled Rules": Representing Scribal Intimacy in Early Modern Print', *Huntington Library Quarterly*, 67 (2004), 295–314: 296.
8. The notion that women's speech is freer from corruption goes back to Cicero, *De Oratore*, Book 3, xii., 45–6.
9. Genette, *Paratexts*, 34.
10. See Linda S. Kauffman, *Discourses of Desire: Gender, Genre, and Epistolary Fictions* (Ithaca: Cornell University Press, 1986). On complaint, see John Kerrigan (ed.), *Motives of Woe: Shakespeare and 'Female Complaint': A Critical Anthology* (Oxford: Clarendon Press, 1991); Howard Jacobson, *Ovid's Heroides* (Princeton University Press, 1974).
11. See Robert Southwell, *Saint Peters complaint, with other poemes* (London: Imprinted by Iohn Wolfe, 1595).

12. Alastair Fowler, 'The Formation of Genres in the Renaissance and After', *New Literary History*, 34 (2003), 185–200.
13. Other titles that specifically evoke Ovid are translations; see George Turberville, *The heroycall epistles of … Publius Ouidius Naso, in English vers* ([London: Henrie Denham], 1567); Wye Saltonstall, *Ovids heroicall epistles* (London: R[ichard]: B[adger]: for M. Sparke, 1637).
14. Fowler, 'Formation', 193–4; for *A Lover's Complaint*, see Katherine Rowe, '*A Lover's Complaint*', in Patrick Cheney (ed.), *The Cambridge Companion to Shakespeare's Poetry* (Cambridge University Press, 2007), 144–60.
15. See Danielle Clarke, '"Formd into Words by Your Divided Lips": Women, Rhetoric and the Ovidian Tradition', in Danielle Clarke and Elizabeth Clarke (eds.), *This Double Voice: Gendered Writing in Early Modern England* (Basingstoke: Macmillan, 2000), 61–87.
16. Drayton's *Idea* inverts this practice, being appended to *Endimion and Phoebe*, and subsequently being placed *after* the *Epistles*.
17. See Wendy Wall, *The Imprint of Gender: Authorship and Publication in the English Renaissance* (Ithaca: Cornell University Press, 1993), 250–60.
18. For bifurcated readerships, see Jonathan Crewe, *Hidden Designs: The Critical Profession and Renaissance Literature* (New York: Methuen, 1986); Caroline Lucas, *Writing for Women: The Example of Woman as Reader in Elizabethan Romance* (Milton Keynes: Open University Press, 1989).
19. This is an example of, in Fleming's terms, 'the book as mould into which words are poured in order to give expression to *its structure as a device for reading*' (this volume, 57), emphasis added.
20. For an interesting account of the relationship between textual space and interpretation, see Coleman Hutchison, 'Breaking the Book Known as Q', *Proceedings of the Modern Language Association*, 121 (2006), 33–66.
21. On attribution, see Danielle Clarke, '"in Sort as She It Sung": Spenser's Doleful Lay and the Construction of Female Authorship', *Criticism*, 42 (2000), 451–68.
22. One of the few recent essays on Drayton is Andrew Hadfield, 'Michael Drayton's Brilliant Career', *Proceedings of the British Academy*, 125 (2003), 119–47.
23. See Fleming, this volume, on James Roberts's use of flowers, 56, 58–62. The 1595 edition of *Delia* was printed by Roberts, who also printed most editions of Drayton's *Heroicall epistles*.
24. It is the figure of Rosamund who takes pole position in Drayton's *Englands heroicall epistles* in 1597, echoing the moral pre-eminence signalled by placing Penelope at the beginning of the *Heroides*; Rosamund is also allied to the female patron with the highest social standing, Lucy, Countess of Bedford.
25. See Hadfield, 'Michael Drayton's Brilliant Career', 130–2.
26. See Evelyn B. Tribble, *Margins and Marginality: The Printed Page in Early Modern England* (Charlottesville: University Press of Virginia, 1993), ch. 2.
27. Later editions modify this balanced structure: Henry Howard to Geraldine (1598, STC 7194) has no reply; the generally female to male/male to female pattern is inverted in the epistles between Edward, the Black Prince and Alice, Countess of Salisbury (1599, STC 7195).

28. Michael Drayton, *Englands heroicall epistles* (London: I[ames] R[oberts] for N. Ling, 1597), 12v.
29. George Puttenham, *The Arte of English Poesie* (London: Richard Field, 1589), L1r.
30. There is a case to be argued as to whether punctuation marks are textual or not. In the early modern period, as most scholars agree, punctuation was in a process of transition from a system designed to assist with oratorical delivery to one which marked logical and grammatical distinctions. See Walter J. Ong, 'Historical Backgrounds of Elizabethan and Jacobean Punctuation Theory', *Proceedings of the Modern Language Association*, 59 (1944), 349–60; M. B. Parkes, *Pause and Effect: An Introduction to the History of Punctuation in the West* (Aldershot: Scolar, 1992); Mindele Anne Treip, *Milton's Punctuation and Changing English Usage, 1582–1676* (London: Methuen, 1970).
31. See Clarke, 'Spenser's Doleful Lay'.
32. Samuel Daniel, *Delia. Contayning certayne sonnets: vvith the complaint of Rosamond* (London: J. C. for Simon Waterson, 1592), M4r.
33. Thomas Lodge, *Phillis: honoured vvith pastorall sonnets, elegies, and amorous delights VVhere-vnto is annexed, the tragicall complaynt of Elstred* (London: [James Roberts] for Iohn Busbie, 1593), L4r.
34. Parkes notes that in the 1570s the *diple* was used 'alongside passages containing direct speech' (*Pause and Effect*, 59); however, he also notes that there was little consistency of practice 'into the seventeenth century' (*ibid.*). I have not found this usage in any of the complaints I discuss here.
35. See George Gascoigne, *The steele glas A satyre co[m]piled by George Gascoigne Esquire. Togither with The complainte of Phylomene* ([London]: [Henrie Binneman] for Richard Smith, [1576], Mv, M2v, and N4r, and John Weever, *Faunus and Melliflora or, The original of our English satyres* (London: Valentine Simmes, 1600), Cv.
36. Parkes, *Pause and Effect*, 54–5.
37. Ben Jonson, *Works*, ed. C. H. Herford and Percy and Evelyn Simpson (Oxford: Clarendon Press, 1947), VIII, 551; Richard Mulcaster, *The first part of the elementarie* (London: Thomas Vautroullier, 1582).
38. Parkes, *Pause and Effect*, 59.
39. Mulcaster, *First part*, 148.
40. Simon Daines, *Orthoepia Anglicana: Or, the first principall part of the English grammar* (London: Robert Young and Richard Badger, 1640), 72.
41. Weever, *Faunus and Melliflora*, E4r
42. Jonson, *Works*, VIII, 551.

9 UNANNOTATING SPENSER

1. Neil Rhodes and Jonathan Sawday (eds.), *The Renaissance Computer: Knowledge Technology in the First Age of Print* (London: Routledge, 2000); Bradin Cormack and Carla Mazzio, *Book Use, Book Theory: 1500–1700* (University of Chicago Library, 2005).

2. Walter Ong, *Orality and Literacy: The Technologizing of the Word* (London: Methuen, 1982).
3. Peter Stallybrass, 'Books and Scrolls: Navigating the Bible', in Jennifer Andersen and Elizabeth Sauer (eds.), *Books and Readers in Early Modern England* (Philadelphia: University of Pennsylvania Press, 2002), 42–79.
4. S. K. Heninger, Jr., 'The Typographical Layout of Spenser's *Shepheardes Calender*', in Karl Josef Höltgen, Peter M. Daly, and Wolfgang Lottes (eds.), *Word and Visual Imagination* (Nürnberg: Erlangen, 1988), 33–71. For recent commentary on the interaction of Spenser's text and E. K.'s paratexts, see Richard A. McCabe, '"Little booke: thy selfe present": The Politics of Presentation in *The Shepheardes Calender*', in Howard Erskine-Hill and Richard A. McCabe (eds.), *Presenting Poetry: Composition, Publication, Reception* (Cambridge University Press, 1995), 15–40; and 'Annotating Anonymity, or Putting a Gloss on *The Shepheardes Calender*', in Joe Bray, Miriam Handley, and Anne C. Henry (eds.), *Ma(r)king the Text: The Presentation of Meaning on the Literary Page* (Aldershot: Ashgate, 2000), 35–54.
5. Sir John Harington (trans.), *Orlando Furioso* (London: Richard Field, 1591), 2M2r, 2M6v, 2N5v, 203v.
6. *Ibid.*, A1r.
7. Randall McLeod (writing as Random Cloud), 'from Tranceformations in the Text of Orlando Furioso', *Library Chronicle of the University of Texas at Austin*, 20 (1990), 60–85.
8. *Oh read ouer D. Iohn Bridges* (Fawsley: Robert Waldegrave, 1588), B1r.
9. Edmund Spenser, *The Faerie Queene*, ed. A. C. Hamilton (London: Longman, 2001). For this editor's reflections upon the history and philosophy of annotation, see A. C. Hamilton, 'On Annotating Spenser's *Faerie Queene*: A New Approach to the Poem', in R. C. Frushell and B. J. Vondersmith (eds.), *Contemporary Thought on Edmund Spenser* (Carbondale: University of Illinois Press, 1975), 41–60; and 'The Philosophy of the Footnote', in A. H. de Quehen (ed.), *Editing Poetry from Spenser to Dryden* (New York: Garland, 1981), 127–63.
10. Jonathan Gibson, 'Significant Space in Manuscript Letters', *The Seventeenth Century*, 12 (1997), 1–9.
11. Francis R. Johnson, *A Critical Bibliography of the Works of Edmund Spenser Printed Before 1700* (Baltimore: Johns Hopkins University Press, 1933), 15. For further commentary, see Andrew Zurcher, 'Getting it Back to Front in 1590: Spenser's Dedications, Nashe's Insinuations and Ralegh's Equivocations', *Studies in the Literary Imagination*, 38 (2005), 173–98: 175–6.
12. 'Front matter' was usually printed last but placed first in early modern books; the back and the front of the codex are of course cognate, but in an age when many books were sold unbound the final leaves of a book may have been viewed as particularly prone to fall away.
13. A. C. Hamilton (ed.), *The Spenser Encyclopedia* (University of Toronto Press, 2000). For a fuller analysis, see Wayne Erickson, 'Spenser's Letter to Ralegh and the Literary Politics of *The Faerie Queene*'s 1590 Publication', *Spenser Studies*, 10 (1992), 139–74.

14. 'The Authors Intention' is how the running headline refers to the 'Letter' in the Jacobean folio editions.
15. Jean R. Brink, 'Materialist History of the Publication of Spenser's *Faerie Queene*', *Review of English Studies*, n.s. 54 (2003), 1–26, dismisses the narrative about Burghley and suggests that some more mundane mistake in the printing house gave rise to this textual situation. In the wake of this influential article, the new orthodoxy seems to be that 2Q was printed as a replacement not for 2P6–7 but for 2P6–8. Spenser 'intended' a series of fifteen poems rather than a series of ten (as originally printed) or of seventeen (which results if 2Q is inserted in place of 2P6–7). This paves the way for the treatment of the 2Q series as a coherent sonnet sequence, in (for example) Wayne Erickson, 'The Poet's Power and the Rhetoric of Humility in Spenser's Dedicatory Sonnets', *Studies in the Literary Imagination*, 38 (2005), 91–118. Yet the absence of a 'FINIS' and an errata list on 2Q, as well as the strange omission of the two sonnets on 2P8r, remains troubling; there is clearly more bibliographical work to be done on this question.
16. Edmund Spenser, *The Faerie Queene* (London: William Ponsonby, 1596), A5v.
17. Paul J. Voss, '*The Faerie Queene* 1590–1596: The Case of Saint George', *Ben Jonson Journal*, 3 (1996), 61–73. See also Mark Bland, 'The Appearance of the Text in Early Modern England', *TEXT*, 11 (1998), 91–154: 112, n. 69.
18. Thynne's folio edition of Chaucer's *Workes* first appeared in 1532. There are some other scattered exceptions to the rule; William Baldwin's *A memorial of suche princes, as . . . haue been unfortunate* (London: J. Wayland, 1554) appeared in folio, and was designed to accompany a folio translation of Boccaccio's *De casibus illustrium virorum*, but subsequent editions of what became *A myrroure for magistrates* were in quarto. Skelton's *Magnyfycence* (London: J. Rastell, 1530?) was a folio. And in the 1480s and 1490s the works of Lydgate (real and suppositious) were often folios.
19. Simon Cauchi, 'The "setting foorth" of Harington's Ariosto' (unpublished master's thesis, Victoria University of Wellington, 1981), 17–18.
20. David Scott Kastan, *Shakespeare and the Book* (Cambridge University Press, 2001), 30–49.
21. See, for example, John Rolland, *Ane treatise callit the court of Venus* (Edinburgh: Johne Ros, 1575); Thomas Blenerhasset, *A reuelation of the true Minerua* (London: Thomas Woodcocke, 1582); Richard Lloyd, *A briefe discourse . . . of those puissant princes, called the nine worthies* (London: R. Warde, 1584).
22. On the patronage politics of the *Orlando*, see my *Sir John Harington and the Book as Gift* (Oxford University Press, 2001), 25–55.
23. Heninger, 'Typographical Layout'.
24. Evelyn B. Tribble, *Margins and Marginality: The Printed Page in Early Modern England* (Charlottesville: University Press of Virginia, 1993), ch. 2; Wendy Wall, *The Imprint of Gender: Authorship and Publication in the English Renaissance* (Ithaca: Cornell University Press, 1993), 233–43.
25. Stephen Orgel, 'Margins of Truth', in Andrew Murphy (ed.), *The Renaissance Text: Theory, Editing, Textuality* (Manchester University Press, 2000), 91–107.

26. *Ibid.*, 103–4.
27. *Ibid.*, 104.
28. Graham Hough (ed.), *The First Commentary on the Faerie Queene* (n.p.: privately published, 1964). See further Bart van Es, 'The Life of John Dixon, *The Faerie Queene*'s First Annotator', *Notes and Queries*, 246 (2001), 259–61.
29. Hough, *First Commentary*, 3.
30. *Ibid.*, 13. Compare the historical annotations noted in Cambridge University Library Sel. 5. 102 (a copy of the 1596 *Faerie Queene*, Books 4–6), discussed in Anon., 'MS Notes to Spenser's "Faerie Queene"', *Notes and Queries*, 202 (1957), 509–15; and those to Book 5 in Queen's University of Belfast, Percy 638, discussed in John Manning, 'Notes and Marginalia in Bishop Percy's Copy of Spenser's *Works* (1611)', *Notes and Queries*, 229 (1984), 225–7.
31. Bodleian Library, F 2 62 Linc. Hoby's reading is discussed in Alastair Fowler, 'Oxford and London Marginalia to "The Faerie Queene"', *Notes and Queries*, 206 (1961), 416–19. Fowler curiously states that Thomas Posthumus was 'no close kin with the Thomas Hoby who translated *The Courtier*' (417, n. 9); he was in fact his son, born after his father's death. See also Neil Rhodes, 111–12, in this volume.
32. *Ibid.*, N2r–N3r.
33. A comparable variety of purposes is evident in Jonson's annotations in a copy of the 1611 Spenser folio; Jonson marks similes, summarises the narrative, exposes the allegory and adds names in the margins when characters first appear. See James A. Riddell and Stanley Stewart, *Jonson's Spenser: Evidence and Historical Criticism* (Pittsburgh: Duquesne University Press, 1995), 73–131.
34. See for example British Library G.11537, a 1596 edition with marginal crosses marking epic similes and a flattened '2' marking sententiae; British Library, 686.g.21, another 1596 edition in which epic similes are marked with marginal flowers up to Book 11 Canto 11; and Oxford, Wadham College A39.2, a 1617 folio in which epic similes are noted for the first few cantos.
35. John Kerrigan, 'The Reader as Editor', in James Raven, Helen Small, and Naomi Tadmor (eds.), *The Practice and Representation of Reading in England* (Cambridge University Press, 1996), 102–24: 105.
36. For the 'communications circuit', see Robert Darnton, 'What is the History of Books?', in *The Kiss of Lamourette: Reflections in Cultural History* (London: Faber, 1990), 107–35: 112. One of the few articles to attempt to think about authorial and readerly paratexts together is Brian Richardson, 'Inscribed Meanings: Authorial Self-Fashioning and Reader's Annotations in Sixteenth-Century Italian Printed Books', in Ian Frederick Moulton (ed.), *Reading and Literacy in the Middle Ages and Renaissance* (Turnhout: Brepols, 2004), 85–104. For an exploration of how readerly demands might work to shape subsequent printed editions of a text, see Peter Lindenbaum, 'Sidney's *Arcadia* as Cultural Monument and Proto-Novel', in Cedric C. Brown and Arthur F. Marotti (eds.), *Texts and Cultural Change in Early Modern England* (Basingstoke: Macmillan, 1997), 80–94.

37. Anthony Grafton and Lisa Jardine, '"Studied for action": How Gabriel Harvey Read His Livy', *Past and Present*, 129 (1990), 30–78; William H. Sherman, *John Dee: The Politics of Reading and Writing in the English Renaissance* (Amherst: University of Massachusetts Press, 1995).
38. Huntington Library, call no. 17938. The poem follows after the signature of Nicholas Hare, presumably the Inns-of-Court poet of that name (1582–1622), for whom see John Carey, 'The Poems of Nicholas Hare', *Review of English Studies*, 11/44 (1960), 365–83. The attraction of the identification in the context of my present argument is that Hare wrote one poem on how different the world would be 'if each mans fault weare in his forehead writt' (*ibid.*, p. 374). Hare adds a number of derisive annotations to the *Decades*, including a string of sarcastic comments on the list of 'Fautes escaped in the pryntynge' (ff. 5A6r–v).
39. The book is in the library of Holkham Hall, Norfolk; for a reproduction see Jason Scott-Warren, *Early Modern English Literature* (Cambridge: Polity, 2005), 133. On shaming, see James Grantham Turner, *Libertines and Radicals in Early Modern London: Sexuality, Politics and Literary Culture, 1630–1685* (Cambridge University Press, 2002), 24–37.
40. Gérard Genette, *Paratexts: Thresholds of Interpretation*, trans. Jane E. Lewin (Cambridge University Press, 1997), 1–2.

10 READING THE HOME: THE CASE OF *THE ENGLISH HOUSEWIFE*

1. Sandra Sherman, '"The Whole Art and Mystery of Cooking": What Cookbooks Taught Readers in the Eighteenth Century', *Eighteenth-Century Life*, 28 (2004), 118.
2. Gervase Markham, *The English hus-wife*, in *Country contentments* (London: Iohn Beal for R. Jackson, 1615), title-page. Editions of *The English Housewife* appeared in 1615 (in *Country contentments*), 1623 (under the umbrella title *Country contentments*), 1631 (perhaps in two editions this year), 1649, 1653, 1660, 1664, 1683 (two separate editions), and 1695. Some later editions appeared under the title *Way to get wealth*.
3. For just two of the many different scholarly works that explore this divide, see Peter Stallybrass, 'Books and Scrolls: Navigating the Bible', in Jennifer Andersen and Elizabeth Sauer (eds.), *Books and Readers in Early Modern England: Material Studies* (Philadelphia: University of Pennsylvania Press, 2002), 42–79; and James J. O'Donnell, *Avatars of the Word: From Papyrus to Cyberspace* (Cambridge, Mass.: Harvard University Press, 1998).
4. The earliest cookery books in England might be said to be *This is the boke of cokery* (London: Rycharde Pynson, 1500) and *Here begynneth the boke of keruynge* (London: Wynkyn de Worde, 1508). Each of these offered a print version of a medieval manuscript, one centrally concerned with the presentation of meals by servants rather than individual recipes.
5. John Partridge, *Treasurie of commodious conceites & hidden secrets* (London: Richarde Iones, 1573), c6v. On Partridge's book as related to the 'book of

secrets', see Allison Kavey, *Book of Secrets: Natural Philosophy in England, 1550–1600* (Urbana and Chicago: University of Illinois Press, 2007), 95–125.

6. Robert Burton, *Anatomy of melancholy* (London: Henry Cripps, 1638), 33, 261, 283, 597.
7. On Prynne's index entry, see Bradin Cormack and Carla Mazzio, *Book Use, Book Theory, 1500–1700* (University of Chicago Library, 2005), 65. This exhibition catalogue offers a compelling overview of ways in which early modern texts encourage and theorise modes of reading. For their discussion of tables and indices, see especially 1–22, 65–6. On reading practices, see also Roger Chartier (ed.), *The Culture of Print: Power and the Uses of Print in Early Modern Europe*, trans. Lydia G. Cochrane (Cambridge University Press, 1989); the Folger exhibition catalogue, Sabrina Alcorn Baron, with Elizabeth Walsh and Susan Scola (eds.), *The Reader Revealed* (Seattle: Washington Press, 2001); and Heidi Brayman Hackel, *Reading Material in Early Modern England: Print, Gender, and Literacy* (Cambridge University Press, 2005).
8. See Robert Appelbaum, *Aguecheek's Beef, Belch's Hiccup and Other Gastronomic Interjections: Literature, Culture, and Food among the Early Moderns* (University of Chicago Press, 2006), esp. 86; Ken Albala, *Eating Right in the Renaissance* (Berkeley: University of California Press, 2001) and Gilly Lehmann, *The British Housewife: Cookery Books, Cooking and Society in Eighteenth-Century Britain* (Totnes, Devon: Blackawton, 2003). On the history of cookery books in England, see also Lynette Hunter, '"Sweet Secrets" from Occasional Receipt to Specialised Books: The Growth of a Genre', in C. Anne Wilson (ed.), *'Banquetting Stuffe': The Fare and Social Background of the Tudor and Stuart Banquet* (Edinburgh University Press, 1988), 9–36.
9. John Murrell's opening table for *A newe book of cookery* (London: Iohn Browne, 1615) does provide loose sets of groupings such as jellies, pastries, and puddings.
10. One exception is Hugh Plat's *Delights for ladies* (London: Peter Short, 1602), a dainty text that also included an exhaustive alphabetic table of contents. Complete with a prefatory poem imitating Horace, Plat's text could never be considered to be typical.
11. Elizabeth Grey, Countess of Kent, *A choice manual of rare and select secrets in physick and chirurgery ... published by W. I. Gent.* (London: by G[artrude] D[awson], sold William Shears, 1653). This text was published with *A true gentlewoman's delight*, which offered recipes for preserves, candies, and conserves. The latter text opens with an introductory table listing the receipts simply in the order in which they appear (with page numbers).
12. Hannah Woolley, *The queenlike closet* (London: R. Lowndes, 1670). This text addresses 'all Ladies, Gentlewomen, and to others of the Female Sex who do delight in, or be desirous of good Accomplishments'.
13. Hannah Glasse, *The art of cookery, made plain and easy; ... To which are added, one hundred and fifty new and useful receipts, and a copious index. By a lady* (London: Alexander Donaldson, 1774).
14. Markham, *English Housewife* (1615), A2v.
15. Roger Jackson, front matter to Markham, *English Housewife* (1615), Q1v.

16. Markham, *English Housewife* (1623), A2r.
17. Markham, *English Housewife* (1631), marginal note, 5. Burket, legend has it, cured the young Queen Elizabeth of smallpox; Bomelius was a physician associated with magic. Markham attributes his work to these popular authorities in the same paragraph in which he disavows his own authorship ('farre bee it from me, to attribute this goodnesse unto mine owne knowledge'), warns housewives not to attempt difficult curatives, and reaffirms that his elite knowledge is verified by 'ordinary experience'. Markham's strategies for authorisation remain complicated. For information about these doctors, see Michael Best's indispensable commentary in his modern edition of *The English Housewife* (Kingston: McGill-Queen's University Press, 1986).
18. *OED*, 'digest', v. 2.
19. Jackson's prefatory nervousness about a man knowing women's work is an incarnation of a problem saturating domestic advice books. In *Staging Domesticity* I address the quandary that the first English estate manual writer, John Fitzherbert, experienced when he turned to the domain of housewifery. Having staked the worth of his book on the fact that he refused to accept inherited maxims without testing them by his own hands, he found himself unable to explain how he had knowledge of tasks that, by his own definition, only women could do. This problem is repeatedly engaged in estate manuals. See Wendy Wall, *Staging Domesticity: Household Work and English Identity in Early Modern Drama* (Cambridge University Press, 2002), 29–36.
20. In some ways neither Jackson nor Markham quite tell the truth about the origins of Markham's domestic advice; for it is clear that Markham did not simply draw his information from a noblewoman's manuscript or his own experience. He also repeated advice from printed foreign texts that he elsewhere declared inappropriate for English citizens (e.g., Richard Surflet's *Country farme*) and from cookery books advocating leisure (e.g., Hugh Plat's *Delights for ladies*). An 'honorable personage' might have coincidentally used the same recipes, but it seems more likely that Markham was not chiefly relying on private writing.
21. *Here begynneth a newe mater, ye whiche sheweth and treateth of ye vertues [and] propertes of herbes, the whiche is called an herbal* (London, 1526). Because the book was printed by Richard Banckes, it is standardly called *Banckes Herbal*.
22. See, for instance, *The 'Liber de Diversis Medicinis'* in the Thornton Manuscript (MS Lincoln Cathedral A.5.2), ed. Margaret Sinclair Ogden (London: Oxford University Press for the Early English Text Society, 1938).
23. *OED*, 'table', n. 10. 'An arrangement of numbers, words, or items of any kind, in a definite and compact form, so as to exhibit some set of facts or relations in a distinct and comprehensive way, for convenience of study, reference, or calculation. Now chiefly applied to an arrangement in columns and lines occupying a single page or sheet, as the multiplication table, tables of weights and measures, a table of logarithms, astronomical tables, insurance tables, time-tables, etc. But formerly sometimes merely: An orderly arrangement of particulars. A concise and orderly list of contents, or an index'. On the early modern book's spatial arrangements, see Neil Rhodes and Jonathan

Sawday, 'Paperworlds: Imagining the Renaissance Computer', in Neil Rhodes and Jonathan Sawday (eds.), *The Renaissance Computer: Knowledge Technology in the First Age of Print* (New York: Routledge, 2000), 1–17.

24. On the works of Peter Ramus (or Petrus Ramus), see Walter Ong, *Ramus: Method, and the Decay of Dialogue: From the Art of Discourse to the Art of Reason* (Cambridge, Mass.: Harvard University Press, 1958).

25. William Sherman, *Used Books: Marking Readers in Renaissance England* (Philadelphia: University of Pennsylvania Press, 2008), 25–52. Sherman's interest is in the reader's drawn annotations as a personalised appropriation of knowledge.

26. For example, the 1676 edition of *The English Housewife* uses intersecting lines to demarcate chapters in the table; the 1683 edition employs blank lines to separate recipes within the text.

27. Markham, *English Housewife* (1623), 12r.

28. Ibid., 12v.

29. Ibid., Q1r.

30. On cookery books and food in the early modern period, see Appelbaum, *Aguecheek's Beef*; Ken Albala, *Eating Right in the Renaissance* (Berkeley: University of California Press, 2002). On mnemonic clusters in recipe books, see Robert Appelbaum, 'Rhetoric and Epistemology in Early Printed Recipe Collections', *Journal for Early Modern Cultural Studies*, 3 (2003), 1–35.

31. Sherman, '"The Whole Art and Mystery of Cooking"', 118.

32. The Latin *habitus*, means condition (of the body); character, quality: style of dress, attire, disposition, state of feeling; habit, viz. *Oxford Latin Dictionary*, 2nd edn, s.v. 'habitus'. This concept has been given a more particular meaning by Pierre Bourdieu who sees 'habitus' as referring to socially acquired, embodied systems of dispositions and/or predispositions. See Pierre Bourdieu, *Distinction: A Social Critique of the Judgment of Taste*, trans. Richard Nice (Cambridge, Mass.: Harvard University Press, 1984).

33. Markham, *English Housewife* (1623), Aav, Gg3r.

34. In *Shakespeare's Domestic Economies: Gender and Property in Early Modern England* (Philadelphia: University of Pennsylvania Press, 2002), Natasha Korda argues, by contrast, that *The English Housewife* contributes to the ideological redefinition of the household as it moves towards a consumption that it devalues.

35. We have scant evidence about who owned these texts, but we do know that Lady Elinor Fettiplace owned an estate manual much like Markham's. There is also evidence of female signatures in various editions of Markham's works now housed in the Folger Library.

36. See Appelbaum, *Aguecheek's Beef*, on how profusion as a value gave way to subtlety in both the practice of food preparation and the layout of cookbooks: 'What may be thought of as a change in the relations between food and words took hold: increasingly, the food practices were submitted to the discipline of the word, especially the printed word, and the ramifications of what one ate and drank and how one ate and drank multiplied exponentially. That

scientific, agricultural, and demographic revolutions were in the making only compounded the complexity of the intervention of the discourse on consumption, juxtaposing new models and modes of physicality against the old. Not as only a subject of discipline but also as an object of wishes did food and food practices change' (14).

37. Numerous historians have taken up issues pertinent to domestic life in this period. For a sample, see Susan Amussen, *An Ordered Society: Gender and Class in Early Modern England* (New York: Columbia University Press, 1988); Ian W. Archer, *The Pursuit of Stability: Social Relations in Elizabethan London* (Cambridge University Press, 1991); and Mark Girouard, *Life in the English Country House: A Social and Architectural History* (New Haven: Yale University Press, 1978).

38. Alice Clark, *The Working Life of Women in the Seventeenth Century* (New York: E. P. Dutton & Co., 1919); Susan Cahn, *Industry of Devotion: The Transformation of Women's Work in England, 1500–1650* (New York: Columbia University Press, 1987); Amy Louise Erickson, 'Introduction' to Clark, *The Working Life of Women in the Seventeenth Century* (New York: Routledge, 1992). Korda reads Markham's *English Housewife* as steering the reader towards a mystified ideology of consumption. I argue instead that Markham replaces the authority gained by production with a compensatory intellectual schema in which the *organisation* of goods and knowledges is rationalised.

39. Lena Cowen Orlin, *Private Matters and Public Culture in Post-Reformation England* (Ithaca: Cornell University Press, 1994).

40. William Shakespeare, *The Merry Wives of Windsor*, ed. H. J. Oliver (London: Routledge, 1993), 4.2.53–7. I discuss the overall representation of domesticity in *Merry Wives*, especially the yoking of domesticity, popular culture, and fairylore in *Staging Domesticity*, 112–26.

41. Thomas Dekker, *The Shoemaker's Holiday*, ed. Anthony Parr (London: A. C. Black, 1990), 18.194–200.

42. Rather than evidencing a clear progress narrative about print's increasingly Ramus-like order, domestic guides of all sorts (almanacs, recipe books, estate manuals) show the uneven way that book features could be deployed in different discourses. Different types of books relied upon tables at different times, depending on the particularities and prestige of the discourse and social conceptions about the content. For example, recipe books published between 1570 and 1630 largely did not promote a vision of domestic ideology that rested on efficiency.

11 PICTURES, PLACES, AND SPACES: SIDNEY, WROTH, WILTON HOUSE, AND THE *SONGE DE POLIPHILE*

1. 'Meme' was coined by Richard Dawkins in *The Selfish Gene* (Oxford University Press, 1976). For her purposes, Helen Cooper further defines the meme as 'an idea that behaves like a gene in its ability to replicate faithfully and abundantly,

but also on occasion to adapt, mutate, and therefore survive in different forms and cultures' (*The English Romance in Time: Transforming Motifs from Geoffrey of Monmouth to the Death of Shakespeare* (Oxford University Press, 2004)), 3.
2. Cooper, *The English Romance*, 8.
3. Philip Sidney (1594–1620) was the subject of Ben Jonson's 'Epigram CXIV'.
4. Even before Jonson wrote 'To Penshurst' (before Prince Henry, probably alluded to in line 77, died in November 1612), Sir John Harington had lamented that the Sidney Psalms 'shall owtlast Wilton walls, meethinke it is pitty they are unpublyshed, but lye still inclosed within those walls lyke prisoners, though many have made great suyt for theyr liberty'. As Gavin Alexander and others have pointed out, Harington was in turn alluding to Samuel Daniel's praise of Mary Sidney Herbert and her psalm translations in his 1594 edition of *Delia*: 'By this, (Great Lady,) thou must then be knowne, / VVhen *Wilton* lyes low leuell'd with the ground', *Delia and Rosamond augmented. Cleopatra* (London, 1594), H6v. Sir John Harington, *Nugae Antiquae* 2.6, quoted by Gavin Alexander, *Writing After Sidney: The Literary Response to Sir Philip Sidney 1596–1640* (Oxford University Press, 2006), 132.
5. Marion Wynne-Davies, '"For *Worth*, Not Weakness, Makes in Use but One": Literary Dialogues in an English Renaissance Family', in Danielle Clarke and Elizabeth Clarke (eds.), *This Double Voice: Gendered Writing in Early Modern England* (London: Macmillan, 2000), 164–85: 164, 166–7.
6. Don E. Wayne, *Penshurst: The Semiotics of Place and the Poetics of History* (London: Methuen, 1984).
7. Gary F. Waller, *The Sidney Family Romance: Mary Wroth, William Herbert and the Early Modern Construction of Gender* (Detroit: Wayne State University Press, 1993), 136.
8. Sheila T. Cavanagh, *Cherished Torment: The Emotional Geography of Lady Mary Wroth's* Urania (Pittsburgh: Duquesne University Press, 2001), 53.
9. Virginia Woolf, 'The Countess of Pembroke's Arcadia', in *Collected Essays*, vol. 1 (London: The Hogarth Press, 1966), 19, 26 (first published in *The Common Reader II* (1932)).
10. See, for example, 387–9, 392–3.
11. Woolf, 'The Countess of Pembroke's Arcadia', 26.
12. Richard Macksey, 'Foreword', in Gérard Genette, *Paratexts: Thresholds of Interpretation*, trans. Jane E. Lewin (Cambridge University Press, 1997), xvii.
13. Macksey, 'Foreword', xx.
14. The potential here for a playful proliferation of prefixes, and the temptation to explore the nuances of peri-, epi-, and meta- should probably be resisted.
15. Quotations are taken from Maurice Evans (ed.), *The Countess of Pembroke's Arcadia* (London: Penguin, 1977). For a detailed account of the manuscripts of Sidney's works, see H. R. Woudhuysen, *Sir Philip Sidney and the Circulation of Manuscripts 1558–1640* (Oxford: Clarendon Press, 1996), as well as Alexander, *Writing After Sidney*.
16. Quotations are taken from Josephine A. Roberts (ed.), *The First Part of the Countess of Montgomery's Urania* (Binghamton, NY: Medieval and Renaissance

Texts and Studies, 1995), and Josephine A. Roberts, Suzanne Gossett, and Janel Mueller (eds.), *The Second Part of the Countess of Montgomery's Urania* (Tempe, Ariz.: Renaissance English Text Society, 1999): henceforth *Urania*.
17. It was certainly regarded as such by many of its early readers, most notably Lord Denny, Baron Waltham, who attacked the *Urania* and its author in a poem entitled 'To Pamphilia from the Father-in-Law of Seralius' for what he had interpreted as an allusion to a contemporary scandal.
18. A modernised French edition appeared in 1994: Francesco Colonna, *Le Songe de Poliphile*, ed. Gilles Polizzi (Paris: Imprimerie Nationale, 1994). Quotations are taken from this edition; translations into English are my own.
19. Francesco Colonna, *Hypnerotomachia Poliphili*, trans. Joscelyn Godwin (London: Thames and Hudson, 1999).
20. Philip Sidney, *The Major Works*, ed. Katherine Duncan-Jones (Oxford University Press, 1989), *Astrophil and Stella* 1.5–7.
21. *Ibid.*, 11.5–7. See my discussion of this sonnet in Chapter 1 of *England's Helicon: Fountains in Early Modern Literature and Culture* (Oxford University Press, 2007).
22. Adonis's tomb, from which the fountain has been made. I am translating only from the *Songe de Poliphile* as the slight differences between the Italian and French texts are not of substantive importance here. For more explicit comparison of the French and Italian texts with the *Arcadia*, see my 'Sidney's Zelmane and the *Songe de Poliphile*', *Sidney Journal*, 21 (2003), 67–75.
23. Polizzi (ed.), *Songe de Poliphile*, 336.
24. Evans (ed.), *The Countess of Pembroke's Arcadia*, 73–4.
25. From 'The Critic as Host', in Harold Bloom, Paul De Man, Jacques Derrida, Geoffrey H. Hartman, and J. Hillis Miller (eds.), *Deconstruction and Criticism* (New York: Seabury Press, 1979), 219, quoted in Genette, *Paratexts*, 1, n. 2. See also the 'Introduction' to this volume, 221, n.13.
26. The detail of the reflecting pool also recalls Greek romance. See Achilles Tatius, *Leucippe and Clitophon*, trans. Tim Whitmarsh (Oxford University Press, 2001), 16. See also the discussion of the substitution of Aeneas for Cupid and Sidney's reworking of Colonna's fountain in Lees-Jeffries, *England's Helicon*, 85–99.
27. This is close to the description in the *Hypnerotomachia*; the few exceptions are noted below.
28. Polizzi (ed.), *Songe de Poliphile*, 333–4.
29. Polizzi (ed.), *Songe de Poliphile* (1994), 312.
30. I.e. 'shoot'.
31. Mary Wroth, *Pamphilia to Amphilanthus* 1, in Wroth, *The Countesse of Mountgomeries Urania* (London: for Ioh[n] Marriott and Iohn Grismand, 1621), Aaaa1.
32. 'Sweet kiss, thy sweets I fain would sweetly endite, / Which even of sweetness sweetest sweetener art: / Pleasing'st consort, where each sense holds a part; / Which, coupling doves, guides Venus' chariot right'. From *Astrophil and Stella*, in Duncan-Jones (ed.), *Sir Philip Sidney*, 79.1–4. There is an interesting

discrepancy here: the *Songe*'s illustration clearly shows swans pulling the chariot, while the text gives 'colombes'; the *Hypnerotomachia* illustrates doves, while the text has swans.
33. *4: Her Triumph*: 'See the chariot at hand here of Love / Wherein my lady rideth! / Each that draws, is a swan, or a dove, / And well the car Love guideth', in *Ben Jonson: The Complete Poems*, ed. George Parfitt (Harmondsworth: Penguin, 1996), 129, 1–4. At least the last stanza of this had been written by 1616, when it appeared in *The Devil is an Ass*. Jonson also owned a copy of the *Hypnerotomachia*, the 1545 Venetian edition, although I have suggested elsewhere that he may not have acquired it until the 1620s. His copy is now in the British Library. See *England's Helicon*, ch. 1, 43–4.
34. Genette, *Paratexts*, 406.
35. *Ibid*.: 'a plain "literary person"' translates 'du simple "littéraire"', perhaps without conveying its full force of self-deprecation.
36. See Germaine Warkentin, 'The Library of the Sidney Family', *Sidney Newsletter and Journal*, 15 (1997), 3–13, and 'Jonson's Penshurst Reveal'd? A Penshurst Inventory of 1623', *Sidney Journal*, 20 (2002), 1–25.
37. I cannot discover its current location; it was sold again at Sotheby's in 1961.
38. Roberts *et al.* (eds.), *Urania*, 2.171.
39. See Isaac de Caus, *Wilton Garden* (London: for Thomas Rowlett, 1645) and *Wilton Garden: New and Rare Inventions of Water-Works* (New York: Garland, 1982).
40. John Taylor, *A Discovery by Sea, from London to Salisbury* (London: by Edward Allde for John Taylor, 1623), C2v–C3.
41. *Ibid*.
42. Roberts (ed.), *Urania* 1.423–4.
43. Genette, *Paratexts*, 20–2. The *Hypnerotomachia*, the *Songe de Poliphile*, the *Arcadia*, and the *Urania* all originally appeared as folios.
44. Genette, *Paratexts*, 8.
45. *The Countess of Pembroke's Arcadia* contains a bridging passage written by Sir William Alexander; the prolific and ubiquitous Gervase Markham (?1568–1637) published two prose continuations, in 1607 and 1613.
46. Henri Lefebvre, *The Production of Space*, trans. Donald Nicholson-Smith (Oxford: Blackwell, 1991), 164.
47. Genette, *Paratexts*, 2.

AFTERWORD

1. Gérard Genette, *Paratexts: Thresholds of Interpretation*, trans. Jane E. Lewin (Cambridge University Press, 1997), 5, 3.
2. Richard Maurice Bucke (ed.), *Notes and Fragments: Left by Walt Whitman* (Folcroft, Pa.: Folcroft Library Editions, 1972), v.
3. John Milton, *Paradise lost: a poem in twelve books* (London: Printed by Miles Flesher for Richard Bently and Jacob Tonsson, 1688) and *Paradise Lost*, ed. David Scott Kastan (Indianapolis: Hacket, 2005). The illustration was designed by John Baptist Medina and engraved by Michael Burghers.

4. *The Byble in Englyshe* [the Great Bible] (London: Edward Whytchurche, 1540).
5. John Milton, *Paradise lost. A poem in twelve books* (London: S. Simmons, 1674), 257–8, Book X, lines 211–23.
6. *The Holy Byble* [Bishops' Bible] (London: R. Jugge, 1574).
7. *The Book of Common Prayer* (London: Bonham Norton and John Bill, 1625).
8. T. W., *A Right Godly and Learned Exposition, Vpon the Whole Booke of Psalmes wherein is set forth the true diuision, sence, and doctrine contained in euery Psalme: for the great furtheraunce and necessarie instruction of euery Christian reader. Newly and faithfully set forth by a godly minister and preacher of the word of God* (London: Printed [by Thomas Dawson] for T. Man and W. Brome, 1586), B1r.
9. *The Holie Bible faithfully translated into English, out of the authentical Latin* (Douai: Laurence Kellam, [1609–10]), vol. II, C2r.
10. *The Souldiers Pocket Bible: containing the most (if not all) those places contained in holy Scripture, which doe shew the qualifications of his inner man, that is a fit souldier to fight the Lords battels, both before he fight, in the fight, and after the fight; which Scriptures are reduced to severall heads, and fitly applyed to the souldiers severall occasions, and so may supply the want of the whole Bible, which a souldier cannot conveniently carry about him: and may bee also usefull for any Christian to meditate upon, now in this miserable time of warre* (London: G. C., 1643).
11. *Hamlet*, ed. Harold Jenkins, The Arden Shakespeare (London and New York: Methuen, 1982); *Hamlet*, ed. Ann Thompson and Neil Taylor, The Arden Shakespeare, third series (London: Thomson Learning, 2006), two vols.; *The Tragicall Historie of Hamlet Prince of Denmarke. By William Shake-speare. As it hath beene diuerse times acted by his Highnesse seruants in the Cittie of London: as also in the Vniuersities of Cambridge and Oxford and elsewhere* (London: N[icholas]. L[ing]. and John Trundell, 1603); *The Tragicall Historie of Hamlet, Prince of Denmarke. By William Shakespeare. Newly imprinted and enlarged to almost as much againe as it was, according to the true and perfect Coppie* (London: Printed by James Roberts for Nicholas Ling, 1604–5).
12. British Library Add. MS 44848, f. 167v; Harvard Eng 628, p. 385; Derbyshire Record Office, D 258/67/6b, f. 3v.
13. British Library Add. MS 18044, f. 153; Rosenbach MS 239/16, p. 6; Sir Henry Wotton, *Reliquiae Wottonianae* (London: Printed by T. Roycroft for R. Marriott, F. Tyton, T. Collins and J. Ford, 1672), 396; British Library Stowe MS 141, f. 74v; Folger MS v.b.303, p. 229; Oxford, Bodleian Library, MS Tanner 299, f. 28v; Folger MS v.a.345, 31; British Library Add. MS 10309, f. 141.
14. London, Public Record Office, SP. 14/103/51v; British Library Harley MS 7056, f. 50v; British Library Add. MS 40838, f. 30v; Pforzheimer Library MS 112, f. 54; St John's College, Cambridge, MS s. 32, f. 34v; Oxford, Bodleian Library, MS Eng. hist. c. 272, p. 50; Folger MS v.a.103, f. 29v; Cambridge University Library, MS Add. 7196, f. 20 reverse.
15. Orlando Gibbons, *The first set of madrigals and motets* (London: Printed by Thomas Snodham, the assigne of W. Barley, 1612), A2r.

16. Michael Rudick (ed.), *The Poems of Sir Walter Ralegh: A Historical Edition* (Tempe, Ariz.: Arizona Center for Medieval and Renaissance Studies, 1999), lii–liv and no. 29A, 69.
17. *Judicious and Select Essayes and Observations* (London, 1650), A4. Quoted in Anna Beer, 'Textual Politics: The Execution of Sir Walter Ralegh', *Modern Philology*, 94 (1996), 36.
18. British Library Harley MS 7332, f. 215.
19. *OED*, 'Manuscript', Def. A.

Select bibliography

Allen, Graham, *Intertextuality* (London: Routledge, 2000)
Andersen, Jennifer and Sauer, Elizabeth (eds.), *Books and Readers in Early Modern England* (Philadelphia: University of Pennsylvania Press, 2002)
Baron, Sabrina Alcorn, Lindquist, Eric N., and Shevlin, Eleanor F. (eds.), *Agent of Change: Print Culture Studies After Elizabeth L. Eisenstein* (Amherst: University of Massachusetts Press, 2007)
Baron, Sabrina Alcorn, with Walsh, Elizabeth and Scola, Susan (eds.), *The Reader Revealed* (Seattle: Washington Press, 2001)
Bland, Mark, 'The Appearance of the Text in Early Modern England', *TEXT*, 11 (1998), 91–154
Blayney, Peter W. M., 'The Publication of Playbooks', in John D. Cox and David Scott Kastan (eds.), *A New History of Early English Drama* (New York: Columbia University Press, 1997), 383–422
Bray, Joe, Handley, Miriam, and Henry, Anne C., *Ma(r)king the Text: The Presentation of Meaning on the Literary Page* (Aldershot: Ashgate, 2000)
Capp, Bernard, *The World of John Taylor the Water-Poet* (Oxford: Clarendon Press, 1994)
Cave, Terence (ed.), *Thomas More's* Utopia *in Early Modern Europe: Paratexts and Contexts* (Manchester University Press, 2008)
Chartier, Roger (ed.), *The Culture of Print: Power and the Uses of Print in Early Modern Europe*, trans. Lydia G. Cochrane (Princeton University Press, 1989)
Clarke, Danielle and Clarke, Elizabeth (eds.), *This Double Voice: Gendered Writing in Early Modern England* (Basingstoke: Macmillan, 2000)
Corbett, Margery and Lightbowm, Ronald, *The Comely Frontispiece: The Emblematic Title-Page in England, 1550–1660* (London: Routledge, 1979)
Cormack, Bradin and Mazzio, Carla, *Book Use, Book Theory: 1500–1700* (University of Chicago Library, 2005)
de Grazia, Margreta and Stallybrass, Peter, 'The Materiality of the Shakespearean Text', *Shakespeare Quarterly*, 14 (1993), 255–83
Derrida, Jacques, *The Truth in Painting*, trans. Geoff Bennington and Ian McLeod (Chicago University Press, 1987)
Dobranski, Stephen B., *Readers and Authorship in Early Modern England* (Cambridge University Press, 2005)

Eisenstein, Elizabeth, *The Printing Revolution in Early Modern Europe* (Cambridge University Press, 1993)
Fleming, Juliet, *Graffiti and the Writing Arts of Early Modern England* (Philadelphia: University of Pennsylvania Press, 2001)
  'How to Look at a Printed Flower', *Word & Image*, 22 (2006), 165–87
  'How Not to Look at a Printed Flower', *The Journal of Medieval and Early Modern Studies*, 38 (2008), 345–70
Gaskell, Philip, *A New Introduction to Bibliography* (Oxford: Clarendon Press, 1972)
Genette, Gérard, *Paratexts: Thresholds of Interpretation*, trans. Jane E. Lewin (Cambridge University Press, 1997)
Grafton, Anthony, *The Footnote: A Curious History* (Cambridge, Mass.: Harvard University Press, 1999)
Greetham, D. C., *Textual Scholarship: An Introduction* (New York: Garland, 1994)
Hackel, Heidi Brayman, *Reading Material in Early Modern England* (Cambridge University Press, 2005)
Halasz, Alexandra, *The Marketplace of Print: Pamphlets and the Public Sphere in Early Modern England* (Cambridge University Press, 1997)
Hamilton, A. C., 'The Philosophy of the Footnote', in A. H. de Quehen (ed.), *Editing Poetry from Spenser to Dryden* (New York: Garland, 1981), 127–63
Hutchison, Coleman, 'Breaking the Book Known as Q', *Proceedings of the Modern Language Association*, 122 (2006), 33–66
Johns, Adrian, *The Nature of the Book: Print and Knowledge in the Making* (University of Chicago Press, 1998)
Kalas, Rayna, *Frame, Glass, Verse: The Technology of Poetic Invention in the English Renaissance* (Ithaca: Cornell University Press, 2007)
Kastan, David Scott, *Shakespeare and the Book* (Cambridge University Press, 2001)
King, John (ed.), *Tudor Books and Readers: Materiality and the Construction of Meaning* (Cambridge University Press, 2010)
Lees-Jeffries, Hester, *England's Helicon: Fountains in Early Modern Literature and Culture* (Oxford University Press, 2007)
Lesser, Zachary, *Renaissance Drama and the Politics of Publication* (Cambridge University Press, 2004)
Liebler, Naomi Conn (ed.), *Early Modern Prose Fiction: The Cultural Politics of Reading* (New York: Routledge, 2007)
Loewenstein, Joseph, *The Author's Due: Printing and the Prehistory of Copyright* (University of Chicago Press, 2002)
M Leod, Randall (ed.), *Crisis in Editing: Texts of the English Renaissance* (New York: AMS Press, 1994)
Maclean, Marie, 'Pretexts and Paratexts: The Art of the Peripheral', *New Literary History*, 22 (1991), 273–80
Maguire, Laurie and Berger, Thomas L. (eds.), *Textual Formations and Reformations* (Newark: University of Delaware Press, 1999)
Marotti, Arthur F., *Manuscript, Print, and the English Renaissance Lyric* (Ithaca: Cornell University Press, 1995)

Massai, Sonia, *Shakespeare and the Rise of the Editor* (Cambridge University Press, 2007)
McGann, Jerome, *The Textual Condition* (Princeton University Press, 1991)
Mentz, Steve, *Romance for Sale in Early Modern England: The Rise of Prose Fiction* (Aldershot: Ashgate, 2006)
Murphy, Andrew (ed.), *The Renaissance Text: Theory, Editing, Textuality* (Manchester University Press, 2000)
O'Donnell, James J., *Avatars of the Word: From Papyrus to Cyberspace* (Cambridge, Mass.: Harvard University Press, 1998)
Ong, Walter J., *Orality and Literacy: The Technologizing of the Word* (London: Methuen, 1982)
Parkes, M. B., *Pause and Effect: An Introduction to the History of Punctuation in the West* (Aldershot: Scolar Press, 1992)
Peters, Julie Stone, *The Theatre of the Book, 1480–1880: Print, Text, and Performance in Europe* (Oxford University Press, 2000)
Raven, James, Small, Helen, and Tadmor, Naomi (eds.), *The Practice and Representation of Reading in England* (Cambridge University Press, 1996)
Raymond, Joad, *Pamphlets and Pamphleteering in Early Modern Britain* (Cambridge University Press, 2003)
Rhodes, Neil, *Shakespeare and the Origins of English* (Oxford University Press, 2004)
Rhodes, Neil and Sawday, Jonathan (eds.), *The Renaissance Computer: Knowledge Technology in the First Age of Print* (London: Routledge, 2000)
Saenger, Michael, *The Commodification of Textual Engagements in the English Renaissance* (Aldershot: Ashgate, 2006)
Sharpe, Kevin and Zwicker, Steven (eds.), *Reading, Society and Politics in Early Modern England* (Cambridge University Press, 2003)
Sherman, William H., *Used Books: Marking Readers in Renaissance England* (Philadelphia: University of Pennsylvania Press, 2007)
Shevlin, Eleanor, '"To Reconcile Book and Title, and Make 'em kin to one another": The Evolution of the Title's Contractual Function', *Book History*, 2 (1999), 42–78
Shrank, Cathy, '"These Fewe Scribbled Wordes": Representing Scribal Intimacy in Early Modern Print', *Huntington Library Quarterly*, 67 (2004), 295–314
Slights, William, *Managing Readers: Printed Marginalia in English Renaissance Books* (Ann Arbor: University of Michigan Press, 2001)
Smith, Margaret, *The Title-Page: Its Early Development, 1460–1510* (Delaware: Oak Knoll Press, 2000)
Tribble, Evelyn, *Margins and Marginality: The Printed Page in Early Modern England* (Charlottesville: University of Virginia Press, 1993)
Wall, Wendy, *The Imprint of Gender: Authorship and Publication in the English Renaissance* (Ithaca: Cornell University Press, 1993)
Woudhuysen, H. R., *Sir Philip Sidney and the Circulation of Manuscripts 1558–1640* (Oxford: Clarendon Press, 1996)

Yates, Julian, *Error, Misuse, Failure: Object Lessons from the English Renaissance* (Minneapolis and London: University of Minnesota Press, 2003)

Zurcher, Andrew, 'Getting it Back to Front in 1590: Spenser's Dedications, Nashe's Insinuations and Ralegh's Equivocations', *Studies in the Literary Imagination*, 38 (2005), 173–98

Index

à Wood, Louis, 37
Actes and Monuments (Foxe), 44–6, 213
Adams, Thomas, 21
addresses, 6, 9, 66, 112, 118, 172, 210. See also dedications; pledges
advertising and marketing, 35, 59, 85, 122
　editorial pledges, 91, 99, 103
　running titles, 38, 40
Æthiopica (Heliodorus), 123
Affectionate Shepherd (Barnfield), 56
Ainsworth, John, 30
Alchemist, The (Jonson), 25
Allde, Edward, 58, 125
Allde, John, 129
Allen, Cardinal William, 66
Amadis de Gaule, 123, 130, 193
Amoretti and Epithalamion (Spenser), 54, 55, 56, 60, 62–3
Amours (Ronsard), 153
Amyot, Jacques, 109, 123–4, 128–9, 131
Anatomy of Melancholy (Burton), 170
annotations and corrections (readers'), 9, 32, 66, 71, 75, 99, 103, 158–60, 163–4
Apologie pour le sermon de fidelite (James VI and I), 22, 23
Arcadia (Sannazaro), 153
Arcadia (Sidney), 157, 186, 187, 188, 189, 197, 201, 202
Ariosto, Ludovico, 13, 53, 107, 110, 154, 157, 160
Arte of English Poesie (Puttenham), 53
Astrophel (Spenser), 139, 143
Astrophel and Stella (Sidney), 196
authors, 6, 29, 141, 161. See also dedications; individual authors by name; translations
　and printers' flowers, 53–4
　and running titles, 34, 36–47
　correction of dramatic texts, 92–3, 101–2, 103, 104–5, 213
　influence of domestic space, 13–14, 185–6, 187, 203

text endings, 69, 73, 75, 76–7, 79, 81–5, 87–8
authorship (ascription of), 14, 210–18

Bacon, Francis, 163
Barker, Christopher, 28
Barnes, Emmanuel and Barnabe, 116
Barnfield, Richard, 53–4, 55, 56, 58, 60, 139, 145
Barthlet, John, 41
Beale, John, 217
Beaumont, Francis, 103, 105
Beccadelli, Antonio, 127
Bedford, Lucy Russell, Countess of, 112, 113, 114
Bill, John, 21
bindings, 4, 9, 66, 85
Blainchard, William, 28
Blount, Edward, 210
Bond, Henry, 31
Book Made by John Frith while he was Prisoner in the Tower (Frith), 43–4
booksellers, 8, 160, 213
　correction of dramatic texts, 105–6
　identity and imprints, 23, 29
　marks and signs, 25–9
borders and frames, 4, 11, 53–4, 58–9, 60–3, 143, 171. See also printers' flowers
Bostock, Robert, 28
Bradley, Martha, 171
Brathwaite, Richard, 214, 217, 218
Breton, Nicholas, 53
Briefe Discourse against the Outwarde Apparell and Ministering Garments of the Popishe Churche (Crowley), 41
Brome, Andrew, 85
Bruno, Giodano, 115
Buck, Thomas, 26
Bucke, Richard Maurice, 205
Burby, Cuthbert, 130, 131
Burkitt, William, 39
Burton, Henry, 8, 9
Burton, Robert, 170

268

Index 269

Busbie, John, 56
Bussy D'Ambois (Chapman), 94, 103–4

Calvin, John, 40
Camden, William, 108
Cameron, John, 36
Campion, Edmund, 41
Canterbury Tales (Chaucer), 68, 69
Capel, Arthur, 112
Carew, Thomas, 100
Cast ouer the water (Tayor), 32
Castiglione, Baldassare, 111, 112, 159
Cawood, Gabriel, 56
Caxton, William, 69, 71, 75, 81, 157
Cecil, William (Lord Burghley), 28, 41, 156
Celebration of Charis (Jonson), 196
certaine relation of the hog-faced gentlewoman called Mistris Tannakin Skinker..., 39
Chapman, George, 94, 103–4, 107, 110, 157
chapter and section headings, 43–4, 45, 46, 47, 76, 103–4. *See also* running titles
Charles I, King, 28, 103
Charles IX, of France, 123
Charlewood, John, 55, 56, 60, 129, 130
Chartreuse, 35
Chaucer, Geoffrey, 67, 68, 69, 75, 76, 79–81, 108, 109, 157
Cheke, Sir John, 111–12, 115, 116
Chettle, Henry, 130–1
Choice Manual, or Rare and Select Secrets (Grey), 171
Chronicle of St. Albans, 71
Chrysostom, John, 111
Cicero, 212
Clerke, Bartholomew, 112
Coignet, Matthieu, 128
Cokain, Sir Aston, 92
Coke, Edward, 163
Coles, Peter, 28
Colin Clouts come home againe (Spenser), 136, 139, 146
Colonna, Francesco, 188, 191, 193, 197
colophons, 17, 20, 28, 69–70, 71
Comparison betwixt a Whore and a Booke (Taylor), 85
complaint genre, 13, 134–50
Complaint of Elstred (Lodge), 136, 145, 148
Complaint of Rosamond (Daniel), 136, 139, 141, 146
compositors, 3, 53, 55, 61, 62, 63, 100, 102, 156, 206–8. *See also* printers
Confutation of the Romish Testament (Fulke), 21
Constable, Henry, 56, 58, 60, 62
contents pages, 66, 168, 171, 174–6, 178, 181, 213, 219
Conway, John, 50, 56

Coote, Edmund, 5
Cornu-copiae, Pasquils Nightcap (Fennor), 18
Corolla varia (Hawkins), 26
Countess of Pembroke's Arcadia (Sidney), 185, 186, 188
Courtier (Castiglione), 159
Courtier (Castiglione and trans.), 111, 112, 115
Courtier's Library (Donne), 118
Cowley, Abraham, 87, 92, 105
Creede, Thomas, 126
Crowley, Robert, 40, 41, 71
Culpeper, Nicholas, 39
Cynthia (Barnfield), 55, 58, 60, 145

d'Albin de Valsergues, Jean, 40
Daines, Simon, 149
Dallington, Robert, 188
Daniel, Samuel, 54, 55, 57, 58, 62, 112, 117, 119, 120, 136, 139–42, 146, 157
Danter, John, 20, 53, 56, 130
Daphnis and Chloe (Longus), 123
Davenant, William, 92, 105
David's Sling against great Goliath (Hutchins), 61
Davies, John, 87
Day, John, 24
Day, Thomas, 41
Decades of the Newe Worlde (Matire d'Anghiera and trans.), 163
decorative letters, 206–10
dedications, 66, 111, 147, 148, 168, 172, 210, 215
 in Florio's translations, 112, 115, 116, 118
 in Munday's translations, 122, 125–8, 131–2
 in Spenser's *Faerie Queene*, 155, 158, 160
Defence of Poesie (Sidney), 191
Defence of Ryme (Daniel), 119
Dekker, Thomas, 18, 30, 183
Delia (Daniel), 54, 55, 58, 60, 62, 139–41, 146
Delia and Rosamond augmented Cleopatra (Daniel), 136, 141, 146
Deliberat Answere Made to a Rash Offer, which a Popish Antichristian Catholique... (Crowley), 40
Denham, Henry, 48, 59
Diamond of Devotion (Fleming), 61
Diana (Constable), 56, 58, 60, 62
Diella (Lince), 58
Differing Worships (Taylor), 76
Diodati, Theodore, 117
Diodorus, 124
Discourse Concerning Publick Oaths... (Gauden), 37
Discourse Concerning the Idolatory Practised in the Church of Rome (Sergeant), 38
Dixon, John, 158, 159
Dodd, Thomas, 215

domestic space *See* dedications
domestic space, influence of, 185–6, 187, 198–203
Donne, John, 29, 118, 215
dramatic texts, 91–106
Drayton, Michael, 56, 59, 135, 136, 139, 141, 142–3, 147–8
Dyer, Sir Edward, 116

Earle, John, 7
East, Thomas, 122
Eastward ho (Chapman, Jonson and Marston), 18
Eclogues (Virgil and trans.), 153
Eden, Richard, 163
Education of a Christian Prince (Erasmus), 126
Elizabeth I, of England, 4, 38, 87, 107, 112, 128, 154, 155, 157, 160
end matter, 65–7, 75, 79, 146
  'Amen', 68–9
  authors, 69–70, 73, 75, 76–7, 79, 81–5, 87–8
  colophons, 17, 20, 28, 69–70, 71
  envoi, 75–6
  epitaphs and mourning pages, 83
  errata notices, 9, 10, 37, 75, 156
  explicits, 68–9
  'Finis' and 'The End', 68, 75
  printers, 69, 71, 75, 81
Endimion and Phoebe (Drayton), 136
Englands Heroicall Epistles (Drayton), 135, 136, 139, 142, 143, 147–8
English Housewife (Markham), 13, 165–7, 171–82, 183–4, 219
envoi, 75–6
Epistle of the Reverend Father in God Hieronimus Osorius Bishop of Arcoburge in Portugal (Shacklock), 38
epistles. *See* dedications
epitaphs, 81–3
Erasmus, Desiderius, 126
errata notices, 5, 10, 37, 75, 156
Errour non-Plust, or Dr Stillingfleet Shown To Be the Man of No Principles (Sergeant), 37
Espejo de príncipes y caballeros (Ortúñez de Calahorra), 122
Essayes of a Prentise, in the Divine Art of Poesie (James VI and I), 76–7, 81
Evelyn, John, 40
Even such is time (Ralegh), 214–15, 216, 217, 218
Examination of Those Plausible Appearances which Seeme Most to Commend the Romish Church... (Cameron), 36
Execution of Justice in England for Maintenance of Publique and Christian Peace..., 41
explicits, 68–9

Faerie Queene (Spenser), 13, 87, 145, 154–60, 210
Fairfax, Sir Thomas, 157
Faunus and Melliflora (Weever), 136, 150
Fawn, The (Marston), 100, 101–2
Fennor, William, 18, 32
Fertel, Martin, 52
Fidessa (Griffin), 59
Field, Richard, 23, 53, 55, 154
Finnegans Wake (Joyce), 87
First Set of Madrigals (Gibbons), 215, 218
Firste Fruites (Florio), 108, 115
Fisher, Samuel, 37
Fleming, Abraham, 61, 153
Fletcher, Giles, 56
Fletcher, John, 103, 105
Florio, John, 12, 107, 108, 112–20, 210–11
Forest, François, 123
Four Prentices of London (Heywood), 103
Foure Letters and Certaine Sonnets (Harvey), 42
Foxe, John, 44–6, 47, 213
François I, of France, 123
Free Conference Touching the Present State of England Both at Home and Abroad, 43
Frith, John, 32, 43–4
Fryer John Frauncis of Nigeon in Fraunce (Crowley), 40
Fulke, William, 21

Galien of France (Munday trans.), 122
Garnier, Robert, 54
Gascoigne, George, 87, 136, 139
Gauden, Dr John, 37
gender (identification in text), 12, 133–4, 136, 150
  punctuation and typography, 148–50
  use of names, 135–6
  use of titles and space, 135, 137–48
geography of London, 23–5
Gerileon of England (de Maisonneufve and trans.), 131
Gibbons, Orlando, 215, 218
Glasse, Hannah, 171
Goddard, William, 29
Godwin, Francis, 31
Goffe, Thomas, 100
Golding, Arthur, 107
Great Britaine, all in blacke (Taylor), 83
Greene, Robert, 131
Greene's Funeralls (Danter), 53
Greene's Groatsworth of Wit, 131
Grey, Elizabeth, 171
Grief of Ioye (Gascoigne), 87
Griffin, Bartholomew, 59
Gwinne, Matthew, 117, 118

Index

Haestens, Henrik van, 39
Hall, Arthur, 157
Hamlet (Shakespeare), 94, 214
Harding, Thomas, 215
Harington, Sir John, 13, 53, 55, 107, 110, 154, 157, 159, 160
Harrington, Lady Anne, 112
Harvey, Gabriel, 42, 112, 156, 158, 164
Hastings, Lord (Henry), 111, 116
Hawes, Stephen, 75
Hawkins, William, 26
Hayes, Robert, 46
Hekatompathia (Watson), 56
Heliodorus, 123
Henri III, of France, 123
Henry IV (Shakespeare), 94, 99
Henry VI (Shakespeare), 99
Herbal (Turner), 4, 9
Herberay, Nicolas, 123, 124
Heroides (Ovid), 134, 135, 142
Herringman, Henry, 105
Heywood, Thomas, 102, 136
Histoire éthiopique d'Heliodore (Amyot trans.), 124
Histrio-mastix (Prynne), 170
Hoby, Edward, 111–12, 115, 116, 128, 159
Hoby, Thomas Posthumus, 159
Hoccleve, Thomas, 75
Holland, Philemon, 110
Homer, 107, 110, 111, 157
House of Fame (Chaucer), 79
Hutchins, Edward, 61
Hypnerotomachia Poliphili (Colonna), 187, 188, 189, 191, 198, 201

Iberian romances
    contemporary criticism, 121, 123, 124
    paratext in Munday's translations, 121–2, 124–9, 130–2
Ideas Mirrour (Drayton), 56
Il Primaléon de Grèce (de Vernassal trans.), 124
Iliad (Homer and trans.), 110
illustrations
    influence of, 200, 202
    illustrations and imagery, 205–6
    decorative letters, 206–10
    influence of, 187, 189, 191–8
imprints, 10. *See also* title-pages
    and London, 23–7
    as narrative of possession, 29
    fictitious, 17–18, 21–3, 29–33
    geographical information from, 23–5
    identity of collaborators, 23, 29
    narrative of possession, 21
    signifying verisimilitude, 20, 22

indices, 85, 87, 170, 171, 219
Instauratio Magno (Bacon), 163
Instruction aux princes pour garder la foy promise (Coignet), 128
intertextual and transtextual references, 12, 42, 79, 85, 113
    in imprints, 32
    in Munday's translations, 122, 129, 130–2
Islip, Adam, 130

Jack Drum's Entertainment (Marston), 100
Jackson, Roger, 172
Jaggard, Isaac, 106
Jaggard, William, 129
James VI and I, of England and Scotland, 21, 22, 23, 77, 81, 208
Johnson, Samuel, 91
Jones, Richard, 92, 93
Jones, William, 20, 27
Jonson, Ben, 18, 25, 73, 150, 157, 158, 185, 186, 193, 196
Joyce, James, 87
Joye, George, 44

Ker, George, 43
Kinaston, Sir Francis, 109
Kind-Heart's Dream (Chettle), 131

Langland, William, 71
Leake, William, 125
Legat, John, 56
Leicester, Robert Dudley, Earl of, 127, 185
Lenton, Francis, 7
Les Amours pastorals de Daphnis et de Chloé (Amyot trans.), 123
Les Œvres morales et mêlées (Amyot trans.), 123
Les Vies de homes illustres grecs ou romains (Amyot trans.), 128
Les Vies des homes illustres grecs ou romains (Amyot trans.), 123
Licia (Fletcher), 56
Lince, Richard, 58
Ling, Nicholas, 56, 139
Lisle, Lawrence, 31
Lives (Plutarch and trans.), 123, 128, 129
Lodge, Thomas, 56, 136, 139, 145, 146, 148
Loeb editions, 108, 109
London, 18, 22
    geography and imprints, 25
    trade signs and marks, 25–8
London Dispensatory (Culpeper), 39
London prodigall, 18
Looking Glass for London and England, 99
Lover's Complaint (Shakespeare), 136, 139, 148
Lownes, Humfrey, 58, 59

Lownes, Matthew, 60
Lydgate, John, 75

Maid's Tragedy (Beaumont and Fletcher), 103
Maisonneufve, Etienne de, 131
Majestie of King James (Drayton), 59
Malory, Thomas, 69
manicules, 176–80
manuscripts, 55, 56, 218
  dramatic texts, 91–3, 103
  endings, 68, 69, 85
Manutius, Aldus, 69, 188
Markham, Gervase, 13, 58, 60, 62, 165–7, 171–82, 183–4, 219
Marot, Clement, 153
Marprelate, Martin, 22, 29, 31, 44–5, 154
Marston, John, 18, 59, 99, 100, 101–2
Martire d'Anghiera, Pietro, 163
Masque of Queens (Jonson), 193
Mastif vvhelp and other ruff-island-like currs (Goddard), 29
Matts, Edmond, 59
Mechanick Exercises (Moxori), 50
Mede, Joseph, 37
Meighen, Richard, 99
Meres, Francis, 107
Merry Wives of Windsor (Shakespeare), 99, 182
Metamorphosis of Pygmalion's Image (Marston), 59
Michaelmas Term (Middleton), 100
Middleton, Thomas, 100
Milbourn, Robert, 26
Milton, John, 117, 206, 213
Mirrour of princely deedes and knighthood (Tyler), 122
Montaigne, Michel de, 210–11
Montaigne, Michel de (and trans.), 107, 116, 117–20
Montgomery, Philip Herbert, Earl of, 125
Moral practice of the Jesuits (Evelyn), 40
Moralia (Plutarch and trans.), 123
Moray, John, 83
Mores, Edward Rowe, 52, 53
Morte Darthur (Malory), 69
Most honourable tragedy of Sir Richard Grinvile (Markham), 60
Moulin, Louis de, 37
mourning pages, 83
Moxori, Joseph, 50
Mulcaster, Richard, 149
Munday, Anthony, 12, 121–3, 124, 125, 126–8, 129–32
Munday, Christopher, 129
Muret, Marc-Antoine de, 153
Murrel, John, 171
Muses Mourning (Taylor), 83

Nashe, Thomas, 17, 20, 23, 27, 31, 42, 131
New boke of gauging (Bond), 31
Newbery, Ralph, 128
Newe Book of Cookery (Murrel), 171
Newman, Thomas, 60
Newton, Sir Theodore, 172
North, Thomas, 107, 109, 110, 128–9, 131–2
Norton, Bonham, 21
Norton, John, 22
Notable Discourse Plainlye and Truly Discussing who be the Right Ministers of the Catholique Churche (d'Albin de Valsergue), 40
Notes and Fragments (Bucke), 205
Noue, François de la, 123
November Boughs (Whitman), 204
Nuncius Inanimatus (Godwin), 31

Oenone to Paris (Heywood), 136
Ogden, Hester, 21
Oh read over D. Iohn Bridges for it is worthy worke (Marprelate), 22, 44
Old, Old, Very Old Man (Taylor), 85
Olney, Henry, 58
Orator, The (Silvayn), 130
Orchestra (Davies), 87
Orlando Furioso (Ariosto and trans.), 53, 55, 154, 157, 159
Orler, Jan, 39
Ortúñez de Calahorra, Diego, 122
Orwin, Widow, 56, 60
Osorius, 38
Our Ancient Testimony Renewed Concerning our Lord and Saviour Jesus Christ . . ., 42
Ovid, 134, 135, 136, 142, 147
Owles Almanacke (Dekker), 30
Oxford, Edward de vere, Earl of, 122, 126

Palladine of England (Munday trans.), 122
Palladis Tamia (Meres), 107
Palmerin d'Oliva (Munday trans.), 122, 127
Palmerin of England (Munday trans.), 125, 126, 127
Panzer, Katherine, 34
Paradise Lost (Milton), 206
Partridge, John, 167–8, 170
Patronus bonae fidei (de Moulin), 37
Pavier, Thomas, 94, 99, 106
Payne, John, 38
Pedegrewe of Heretiques wherein is Truely and Plainely Set Out (Barthlet), 41
Pembroke, Mary Sidney Herbert, Countess of, 54, 60, 145, 185, 188, 198
Pembroke, William Herbert, 3rd Earl of, 188, 198, 201
Pennyless pilgrimage (Taylor), 27

Peoples Zeal Provok't to an Holy Emulation (Burkitt), 39
Perkins, William, 39
Phillis (Lodge), 56, 145, 146
Piccolomini, Enea Silvio (later Pope Pius II), 127
Piers Plowman (Langland), 71
playbooks. *See* dramatic texts
pledges, 11, 91
   authors' corrections, 92–3, 100–2, 103–4, 213
   booksellers' corrections, 105–6
   printers' corrections, 100, 102
Pliny, 110
Plutarch, 107, 109, 110, 123, 124, 128, 132
Poem of Poems, or Sions Muse (Markham), 58
Poem on the Late Civil War (Cowley), 87
Poesie of floured praiers (Conway), 49–50, 56
Politicke and Militarie Discourses of the Lord de la Noue (La Noue and trans.), 123
Politique discourses upon trueth and lying (Hoby), 128
Ponsonby, William, 56, 60, 145, 154
Pope's pittiful lamentation . . . (Chettle), 130
Practise how to finde ease, rest, repose, content, and happines (Thomas X), 22
printers, 8, 9, 34, 212. *See also* booksellers
   compositors, 3, 53, 55, 61, 62, 63, 100, 156
   correction of dramatic texts, 99, 100, 102, 106
   decorative letters, 206–10
   endings, 69–71, 75, 81
   imprints and signs, 23–4, 29–31, 71
   printers' flowers, 11, 25, 48–50, 55–8, 71, 171
      authors' influence, 53–5
      borders and frames, 60
      conformity and conventions, 50, 52–3, 58–62
      division of space, 3, 50, 52, 55–6, 134, 139, 143, 145–6, 147, 205
      identity of printer, 58 60, 63
Printers' Grammar (Smith), 50
Promos and Cassandra (Whetstone), 92
Prynne, William, 170
publishers. *See* booksellers
Purchas, Samuel, 37, 46
Purchas his Pilgrimes (Purchas), 37, 46, 47
Puttenham, George, 53, 58, 143
Pynson, Richard, 69, 71

Queenlike Closet or Rich Cabinet (Woolley), 171

Raffald, Elizabeth, 171
Raging Turk (Goffe), 100, 101
Ralegh, Sir Walter, 155, 214–18
readers/purchasers
   annotations and corrections, 9, 32, 66, 71, 75, 99, 158–64
   running titles, 35, 37, 38, 40

recipe books, 167–71; See also *English Housewife* (Markham)
religious publications, 68, 205–6, 213
   decorative letters, 206–10
   issue of authorship, 211–12
   use of running titles, 35, 37–9, 40–2, 43–6
Remains After Death (Brathwaite), 214, 217
Returne of the Renowned Caualiero (Nashe), 31
Rishton, Edward, 40
Roberts, James, 56, 59, 60, 62, 125, 129, 139
Rodríguez de Montalvo, Garci, 121
Romeo and Juliet (Shakespeare), 94
Ronsard, Pierre de, 153
Rouge, 35
Royall exchange: to suche worshipfull citezins/ marchants/gentlemen . . . (Payne), 38
running titles, 3, 10, 34–6, 42, 205
   and marketing, 38, 40
   and religious texts, 37–9, 40–2, 43–6
   and xenophobic views, 42–3, 47
   differentiation of voice, 138–9, 145, 146
   page headlines, 44–6

Sannazaro, Jacopo, 153
Schollers Purgatory (Wither), 38
Second booke of Primaleon of Greece (Munday trans.), 130
Seres, William, 28
Sergeant, John, 38
Shacklock, Richard, 38, 39
Shakespeare, William, 91, 94–100, 115, 136, 139, 146, 148, 157, 182, 204, 213, 215
Shepheardes Calender (Spenser), 75, 115, 142, 153, 154, 158
Shoemaker's Holiday (Dekker), 183
Short, Peter, 62, 63
Shute, W., 39
Sidney, Philip, 13, 60, 87, 110, 139, 145, 157, 185, 186, 187, 188, 189, 191, 193, 196, 197, 201, 202–3
Sidney, Robert, 185
Silvayn, Alexander, 130
Simmes, Valentine, 59, 210
Singleton, Hugh, 153
skeleton frames, 50, 60–2
Skelton, John, 75
Smith, Henry, 34
Smith, John, 50, 61, 63
Smith, R., 56, 58
Songe de Poliphile, 13, 187, 188, 189–98, 199, 201–2
sonnets (not included), 219

Sonnets (Shakespeare), 146
Souper of the Lorde (Tyndale), 43
Spanish Colonie, or Briefe Chronicle of the Acts and Gestes of the Spaniardes in the West Indies . . ., 42
Speght, Thomas, 108
Spenser, Edmund, 13, 54, 55, 60, 75, 87, 136, 139, 146, 154, 160, 210
Spiegel, Jacobus, 127
Stafford, Simon, 94
stationers. *See* booksellers; printers
Stillingfleet, Edward, 37–8
Stone, Ben, 215
Stow, John, 24
Strange Newes, of the Intercepting Certaine Letters (Nashe), 42
Strife of Love in a Dreame (Dallington), 188
Strode, William, 215
Subversio[n] of Moris False Foundacion (Joye), 44
Survey of London (Stow), 24, 27

Taylor, John, 3, 17, 27, 32–3, 67, 76, 85, 198–200
Taylor's Revenge (Taylor), 17
Taylors Motto (Taylor), 85
Terrors of the Night (Nashe), 17, 20, 23, 27
Théagène et Chariclée (Heliodore and trans.), 124
Thomason, George, 32
Thynne, William, 81
title-pages, 7, 8, 25, 30, 66, 185, 210. *See also* imprints; pledges
  complaint genre, 136, 141
  Faerie Queene (Spenser), 155, 157, 210
  relation to running titles, 38–9, 41–2, 43
Tottell, Richard, 28
trade signs, 25–9
Tragedie of Antonie (Garnier and trans.), 54, 60, 62
Tragedie of Sir Richard Grinvile (Markham), 58, 60, 62
translations, 107
  apologies and defence, 110–12, 114–16, 117
  author identity and ascription, 210–12
  inferiority of English language, 108, 110–11
  parallel texts, 109
Traubel, Horace, 204
Treasure of pore men, 28
Treasurie of Commodious Conceites & hidden Secrets (Partridge), 167–8, 170
Triumphs of Nassau (Orler and Haesten), 39

Troilus and Criseyde (Chaucer), 75, 108
True, sincere and modest defence of English Catholics (Allen), 66
True Gaine: More in Worth Then All the Goods in the World (Perkins), 39
Trundle, John, 27
Trying out of the truth (Ainsworth), 30
Turberville, George, 142
Turner, William, 4, 9
Two Merry Milke-maids, 99
Tyler, Margaret, 122
Tyndale, William, 43
Tyron, Antoine, 123

Urania (Wroth), 186, 187, 188, 189, 191–5, 197, 198, 201, 202
Utopia (More), 5

Vernassal, François de, 124
Virgil, 135, 153, 157

Wallis, John, 36
Walsingham, Sir Francis, 28
Waterson, Simon, 58, 139
Waterstone, Simon, 55, 58
Watson, Thomas, 56, 107
Webster, John, 125
Weever, John, 136, 139, 150
Whetstone, George, 92
Whitman, Walt, 204–5
Windet, John, 128
Wise, Andrew, 94, 99, 106
Wither, George, 38
Wolfe, John, 24, 56, 112, 123, 130, 154, 156
Wonderfull Straunge Sightes Seene in the Element, over the Citie of London (Day), 41
Woolley, Hannah, 171
Worde, Wynkyn de, 71
Worlde of Wordes (Florio), 113, 114, 115
Wotton, Sir Edward, 114
Wroth, Mary, 13, 185, 186, 187, 188, 191–8, 200, 201, 202–3

Yates, Frances, 118
Young, Francis and Susan, 126–7

Zeperia, 56